Journey Toward the Caring Classroom

Using Adventure to Create Community in the Classroom & Beyond

Laurie S. Frank

Published by:

Wood 'N' Barnes Publishing & Distribution
2717 NW 50th
Oklahoma City, OK 73112
(405) 942-6812

Cover Design by Blue Design
Copyediting, Interior Design & Layout by Ramona Cunningham
Illustrations by Delores Kroutil of Art House

Printed in the United States of America
Oklahoma City, Oklahoma
ISBN # 1-885473-60-5

To order copies of this book, please call:
Jean Barnes Books/Creative Solutions
405-946-0621 • 800-678-0621
www.creativesolutionscatalog.com

Acknowledgments

Life really is an adventurous journey. We truly do not know what is going to happen next. As such, I believe it is part of the human condition to make things up as we go along. We add to our own sense of the world by interacting with others and the environment. Nothing, really, is new. Each of us simply takes the golden oldies and puts new music to them. The themes stay the same, the words change a bit, and the dancing moves evolve as time goes by.

It is with this understanding that I acknowledge those who have influenced this work. Many are mentioned below in the original acknowledgment. This book is an expansion of *The Caring Classroom*, which was published by Project Adventure. The people at Project Adventure continue to be an inspiration to me and to the field of Adventure Education.

In the time since the original book came out in 2001, some events have occurred to push my thinking in the area of community building:

> Janet Dyment took a workshop from me and suggested I read *Inviting School Success* by Purkey and Novak. If every educator read this book, we could transform education.

> It has been an honor and a gift to work and play with the staff and students at Mendota Elementary School. Sandy Gunderson is a principal who embodies the power of having a clear vision. They have proven that whole-school reform is possible.

> D.D. Sturdevant and I have spent hours pondering the philosophy and theories around community building. These discussions have clarified my views, and it is a joy to watch her put these ideas into action.

> I have spent the past two years facilitating a continuous improvement process for program standards with youth workers in Chicago under the auspices of the Chicago Department of Human Services. The commitment and heart these frontline workers share is inspirational. Maybe we can change the world.

> Collaborative leadership has become more a part of my life through the Wisconsin Leadership Institute. Through them, I have had the pleasure of working with Jack Christ and Carol Carlin in the creation of a high school curriculum on the subject. As this process unfolds, it becomes clearer to me that everyone really can be a leader. Exploring the concepts of leadership and, more importantly, seeing young people as resources is the stuff of empowerment and growth.

> I must give credit to the *No Child Left Behind* act. I truly believe it is a mistake. It is causing educators to forego creativity in the name of arbitrary test scores. It invites shifting the focus from the learner to ledger, where people become graphs and numbers. It has, however, caused many educators to reassess their purpose. What is education all about? How does teaching style affect learning? What does relationship and engagement have to do with learning? Now we must take these thoughts and put them into action to turn schools into caring, safe, learning environments.

Finally, a hearty "thank you" to Mony Cunningham and David Wood of Wood 'N' Barnes Publishing. This whole process has seemed easy due to their expertise, sensitivity, and enthusiasm.

Laurie Frank
July, 2004

From the Original Acknowledgments in *The Caring Classroom*

Bert Zipperer is my partner, best friend, and biggest encourager. It all begins and ends with him. There is no way this project would have reached fruition without his willingness to hear my ideas, frustrations, and periodic whining. Anyone who knows Bert knows that he handled this 3-year project with grace and good humor.

The process leading to this book began almost two decades ago when I was working for the Madison Metropolitan School District in Wisconsin as a special education teacher. Sandy Gunderson offered me an opportunity to go to Project Adventure as part of a grant because she "knew" I'd like it. Was I that transparent? She couldn't have been more correct. I returned from the workshop with renewed spirit, as if I had come home. Pete Albert had been developing the idea of Stress/Challenge for a few years already, and Dee Tull was an administrator willing to take a chance by putting resources into it. Pete and Tom Solyst took me under their wings and taught me the "ropes" about ropes courses. In the early years, before the full-time position was created, I benefited from the unyielding support of my co-teachers: Sara Bringman, Wenda Mincberg, and Lynne Behrendt; and Marian Wright, the best educational assistant in the universe, whose organizational skills saved my life on more than one occasion.

I can pinpoint the moment when a huge light bulb went on for me (it felt more like a spotlight). I was working with a class of 3rd-graders who had been struggling. This day they made a breakthrough and really seemed to understand what "trust" was all about. These students (and the others who came before them) made me see that it's not the activities but the *process* that makes the difference, and I started to create the model that is highlighted in this book. I can't thank the teachers enough – especially those who invited me in when Stress/Challenge was a very new concept. These teachers and students are the real pioneers.

The Stress/Challenge program would not continue to exist without help from Diana Kabat, who took over when I went on leave, and it continues to thrive under the leadership of Carla Hacker and Jim Dunn. Thanks to all the teachers, administrators, social workers, counselors, secretaries, nurses, custodians, educational assistants, and parents who have given of their own time to receive training and work with students on the ropes course. How many school systems can boast of that type of commitment?

The book all but wrote itself. I took two weeks in the north woods – first in the loving care of Ruth Gudinas and Dorothy Davids. They gave me space, food, encouragement, and understanding as I paced around in their bunk room and talked to my computer. The heart of the book was written there. The next week was spent at Camp Manito-wish YMCA sequestered in a cabin with a huge supply of firewood and no telephone. The soul of the book was born there ....

Finally, I must acknowledge four dear friends who probably are unaware of their contribution to this project. Sylvia Dresser, Chris Lupton, Gloree Certoma Rohnke, and Nancy Constable have spent hours chatting with me about adventure and experiential education. Many of my thoughts were clarified through those discussions.

And, of course, it all begins and ends with Bert.

Laurie Frank
February 2001

I don't believe we need to change the state of education in this country. Let me put it another way: I don't believe we should look at "changing" the way our youth are educated. We are not going to be able to change education like we change the sheets – we can't remove the one and replace it with another. Think about change. Think about something you changed, or tried to change in your life. You didn't just remove what you wanted to change and replace it with something else. If we continue to look at the picture of education today and just keep saying it needs to change, nothing is going to happen. We need a different perspective.

I would like to see us look at "adding to" our way of educating. But you say, "How can we add anything; we're already overwhelmed as it is?" Consider this: If we add something that will encourage the growth and well-being of our youth so they can better cope with the challenges of their lives, wouldn't that be worthwhile? I believe that if we add something good, in balance, that which we no longer need will fade away. This is what I would call "evolution." Education in our country needs to evolve.

I propose that a little more "affective" education be added to our way of thinking and educating. We truly have a pretty good handle on the academic part, but what about the personal part – the affect? We need to spend more time on the subject of relationships with the world at large. When a young person finishes school, he or she will spend more time in relationships with others than using all the academic subjects combined – think about that. Are we preparing our youth for life?

In *Journey Toward the Caring Classroom*, Laurie shares with us some incredible ideas from educators throughout history and today. John Dewey, Howard Gardner, William Glasser, Alfie Kohn, Jeanne Gibbs – all tell us that we need to get to know our students, get to know our children. If we get to know our students, we can help educate them toward their desires, their dreams, their needs – not only for the test they have to take tomorrow, but for the relationships they are in every moment of the day.

This book, I can say with commitment, is filled with exciting and adventurous ideas and activities to bring affective education to our youth today. Grounded in the theory of experiential education and practiced through adventure-based programming, Laurie gently guides educators toward building caring communities – caring classrooms. These activity experiences, besides being fun and engaging to our youth, help students get to know themselves and those around them. They learn about cooperation, trust, problem solving, and taking appropriate risks. With such a supportive community, students are better able to "step up to the challenge" – and that challenge is their life and how they believe they can live it.

Your efforts and commitment to the youth of our country will continue to make all the difference in the world.

Chris Cavert
Educator and Author

"Community"... is a place in which students feel cared about and are encouraged to care about each other. They experience a sense of being valued and respected; the children matter to one another and to the teacher. They have come to think in the plural: they feel connected to each other; they are part of an "us." — Alfie Kohn

Content

☞ Introduction

I'm a late boomer ... or is it "bloomer"? Actually, it's both. I was born at the end of the big boom, which means I am firmly planted on the cusp between being a baby boomer and a Generation Xer. I came of age during the era of Twinkies™ and Slinkies™, TV and radioactivity, Viet Nam and the American Dream. Rugged independence was the name of the game, which included competing and being number one. We all knew this to be true because we learned it in school and from television every day. We teethed on clichés like, "It's a dog-eat-dog world," and "It's a war zone out there." The casualties? Generosity, affiliation, kindness, community ....

Community has gone from the realm of lifestyle and philosophy to the domain of buzzword. Today we struggle to reinvent feelings of connection, sharing, interdependence – in essence, what we had for centuries. Is it really gone? Have we lost our capacities for empathy, respect, kindness, tolerance, and even compassion?

Or are we all just late bloomers?

Although powerful, my lessons in competition never really took hold. I wore the unhealthy mindset of "get ahead at all costs" halfheartedly, wondering if there was another way – yet not knowing there was another way. Don't get me wrong; I struggle every day with our society's teachings about competition. They are ingrained, and I must make a conscious effort to recognize the signs and step back from potentially unhealthy situations. Sometimes, I am in the middle of them before I see the symptoms. Other times, I can only see it from the vantage point of hindsight.

I carried these lessons with me into the teaching profession. I was certified to teach students with emotional disabilities. My first year was spent "controlling" the students. If there was a problem, I was there in light speed, directing traffic, telling kids what to do and how to do it. By the end of the year, the students left the way they had come: no wiser about dealing with their feelings or treating themselves and others with respect. I had done it all for them, achieving the goal of a quiet room, which looked good from the outside (I had "won"), but accomplished very little for those who mattered most.

As a trained behaviorist, I thought I knew how everyone should act, and I became the ultimate enforcer. Every night I shuffled home with a headache caused by taking on the responsibility of every student's behavior. By the end of the year, I reached the startling conclusion that it was no fun playing the role of a goddess.

Year two saw a dramatic shift. I began to draw on my experience as a camp counselor. We played more, interacted more, shared more. Older students tutored the younger students, and younger ones tutored the older. We laughed and even made noise.

We also argued more. When conflicts arose, I did not rush to judgment, but assumed there was a reason for it. We talked it through, came up with solutions, and moved on. By midyear, we had a family feel to the room. We stuck up for each other, cheered each other up, and became friends. My headaches went away ... and our *journey toward the caring classroom* was underway.

 # Why Community Building?

The assembly-line approach to school, work, and life in general is a Titanic on the sea of a changing social order. Collaboration is the wave that we are riding in this new century. We live in an information-rich world that is shrinking, almost on a daily basis. As our smaller communities give way to a global society, the number (and kind) of people with whom we come into contact increases. In order to make sense of an increasingly complex society, people specialize, thus causing greater interdependence among us all.

Collaboration is an act of co-creation.[1] It is not a top-down approach, nor is it a jigsaw puzzle scenario, where everyone does his or her own piece independent of the rest. Collaborative group members must approach a task as equals, willing to take risks that will cause all to sink or swim together. In the world of Cooperative Learning, this is known as "positive interdependence." This collective stake in an outcome implies a group that thrives on respect, trust, and common goals.

Traditionally, our role as educators has been to impart knowledge to our students. This has meant a passive education, with children sitting at desks while a teacher pours facts into heads which are attached to bodies that can't wait to get out of there. Today, however, programs such as Expeditionary Learning, Project Adventure, TRIBES, and service learning are making their mark. Their common themes involve community, integrated/thematic instruction, reflection, authentic learning, and empowerment. They are based on the foundation that people are whole beings connected to a larger environment and to each other. The benevolent dictator approach to teaching is giving way to participatory democracy. A sense of community is replacing isolationism. Cooperative learning is eroding the notion that we need competition in order to motivate our students.

In order to accomplish this ideal, we must begin with the idea of classroom as community. A community is any group having common interests, where there is joint participation or common ownership. Creating community is not so cut and dried, however. It is necessary to begin with an environment that values each member, creating a safe place where members can disagree without being torn apart. In *The Different Drum: Community Making and Peace*, M. Scott Peck describes a community in this way:

> In genuine community there are no sides. It is not always easy but by the time they reach community the members have learned how to give up cliques and factions. They have learned how to listen to each other and how not to reject each other. Sometimes consensus in community is reached with miraculous rapidity. But at other times it is arrived at only after lengthy struggle. Just because it is a safe place does not mean community is a place without conflict. It is, however, a place where conflict can be resolved without physical or emotional bloodshed and with wisdom as well as grace. A community is a group that can fight gracefully.[2]

In this scenario, the teacher is an equal member of the community, whose role changes from information provider to facilitator.

Considering that most teachers have grown up in traditional classrooms, and learned traditional teaching techniques from traditional professors in traditional universities, the very idea of relinquishing some control to our students is an exercise in risk taking. The question we must all ask ourselves, however, is this: "How can we expect students to learn how to act responsibly if they are not given the opportunity to have responsibility?" In order to learn how to live in a democratic society, it is necessary to experience democracy. Experiencing true community in the classroom may just breed true community in our society.

We would be laughed out of the teaching profession if we suggested that instead of teaching literacy every day in school, we would substitute with one "reading day." This special day would involve learning reading skills and practicing them for just that one day. After that, we would ignore reading unless a problem arose with it. Then the student would be punished for not handling reading very well.

We do this all the time, however, with skills like cooperation and conflict resolution. We talk about how to cooperate; we drop the students into cooperative learning groups. Then we wonder why they don't cooperate. Many times, conflict resolution is given even less attention. When students "misbehave," "act up," or become "disruptive," they are summarily sent from the room to the "great punisher" known as the principal. This type of disciplinary approach provokes the question, "What are the students learning?" Are we preparing them for life in prison, or life with families, work, and community?

Imagine, instead, a classroom where students and teachers are partners in learning. Students are not simply engaged in the learning process, but excited about it. This is a classroom where it is safe to make mistakes, and learn from those mistakes. In this classroom, learning is not seen as smooth and simple. It is regarded as messy, sometimes loud, and often the result of a struggle. Grappling with concepts, theories, algorithms, writer's block, and the fear of giving a speech are ways in which students push the edge of their comfort zones toward knowledge and understanding. In this place, learning is considered an act of risk taking, and the community of learners supports each individual who takes the necessary risks to learn.

> *"Community"... is a place in which students feel cared about and are encouraged to care about each other. They experience a sense of being valued and respected; the children matter to one another and to the teacher. They have come to think in the plural: they feel connected to each other; they are part of an "us."* — Alfie Kohn[3]

Schools are a perfect place to learn collaboration and conflict-resolution skills. They are places that offer constant opportunities to interact. This book provides one process-oriented approach that gives students a chance to learn and practice these life skills.

In order to undertake this journey, we must outfit ourselves with the proper tools. Chapter One of this book, Foundations, provides a compass to get our bearings – beginning with a foundational perspective of adventure and experiential education with some of the thinkers who have informed the field. We start with John Dewey and his prescient musings about reconciling the polarized views of concentration on content versus focus on the child; then we move all the way to Howard Gardner's thoughts on multiple intelligences, and William Glasser's Choice Theory. Along the way we consider Kurt Hahn with the advent of Outward Bound, which led to Project Adventure's Integrated Adventure Model. Structure and rationale are provided with the experiential learning cycle–central to all forms of experiential education, Susan Kovalik's theories on brain-compatible learning, and the Search Institute's 40 Developmental Assets, while emotional intelligence and Alfie Kohn's case for building classroom communities give us purpose. Jeanne Gibb's process-oriented approach to actually creating that community and Purkey & Novak's invitation to school success offer ways to put these ideas into action. All of these foundations are but the tip of the iceberg, yet without this basic understanding of where we have come from, it is difficult to know where we are now or where we should be heading.

> "A boy in one of my classes hadn't said a word all year. Billy was extremely overweight and had a bad complexion. Some of the other kids teased him. This all changed, however, after playing Italian Golf. It turned out that he was the best thrower and catcher. He was the major asset. This surprised me as much as anyone, and I was sure to play it up. Ever since that day, Billy has joined the group. He has even dared to get into mischief along with the others. This was the best affirmation I had as a teacher." – MARGIE, TEACHER, GRADE 7

Chapter Two, Creating the Conditions for Community, discusses how group development and sequencing can help us connect our compass with the "big-picture" map of community building. If we have an understanding of what motivates individuals in groups, we can better prepare a course of action and develop an appropriate sequence of events.

Next, Chapter Three, Mapping the Journey, describes the issues, skills, and activities pertinent to any given phase in the process. This community-building map provides the bridge between theory and practice to guide us on our way.

Chapters Four through Seven, Cooperation, Trust, Problem Solving and Challenge, are the "provisions" for the journey. More than 130 activities can be found in the "backpack" that will sustain our energy and enthusiasm for the work and play ahead.

Chapter Eight, Facilitating the Process, provides underlying theory, suggestions, and ideas about how to navigate through the journey.

The final section addresses how to start a program of your own. It acts as a springboard for developing an action plan to use in your individual situation. The journey itself is up to you.

Any teacher or youth worker can pick up this book and begin implementing a community-building process. Each journey begins with one step. Simply using these activities in your classroom signals a change in the status quo for teachers and students alike. With experience, the activities become part of a larger process that creates a foundation of safety, security, and trust. This foundation supports the collaboration that propels learning to new heights.

Every journey requires preparation, a little planning, and a bit of expertise. More than anything else, it needs commitment, especially to get through the rough spots. With commitment, a difficulty becomes just one more bump in the trail; struggles are seen as learning opportunities rather than barriers. As you begin your excursion, remember that it will be shared by countless others who will join you in your *journey toward the caring classroom.*

---

[1] Schrage, M. (1995). *No More Teams!* New York, NY: Doubleday (p. 5)
[2] Schoel, J. and M. Stratton, eds. (1990). *Gold Nuggets: Readings for Experiential Education.* Hamilton, MA: Project Adventure, Inc. (p. 26)
[3] Kohn, A. (1996). *Beyond Discipline: From Compliance to Community.* Alexandria, VA: Association for Supervision and Curriculum Development. (p. 101)

1 Foundations

A casual observer watching a group engaged in an activity of Moon Ball sees only a game involving hitting a beach ball. While it is true that the participants are having fun, it is much more than a game. If the observer sticks around long enough, she might see the group discuss why certain people are "hogging" the ball while others never get to touch it. The "ball hoggers" respond that the others don't seem to want the ball, because all they do is stand back waiting for the ball to come to them. This discussion might turn into a larger metaphor for how the students can be more interdependent when working together on class projects – with those who tend to jump into the work choosing to share the load, and those who tend to sit back becoming more assertive about getting involved.

This Moon Ball scenario is just one brief example of deceptive appearances. There is much more to this type of education than playing games. The broad field of Experiential Education, and the specific field of Adventure Education, are informed by a plethora of thinkers. Some like Dewey, Hahn, Glasser, and Kolb offer philosophical and theoretical bases; others like Gardner, Goleman, and Kovalik share ideas that support the use of experiential and adventure techniques in schools today. Kohn, Gibbs, the SEARCH Institute, and Project Adventure give us insights about why creating a classroom community is needed and how to go about it. The combined wisdom of these philosophers, researchers, and theorists offers a solid foundation on which to place Experiential and Adventure Education today. The following is a very short introduction to some of the theories informing the many fields of Experiential Education. The bibliography contains more comprehensive resources on these topics.

John Dewey: Experience and Education

The way out of scholastic systems that made the past an end in itself is to make acquaintance with the past as a means of understanding the present. Until this problem is worked out, the present clash of educational ideas and practices will continue. — John Dewey[1]

At the turn of the 20th century, John Dewey was contemplating the role of the child in education. He compared the two opposing thoughts of the time as "... marked by opposition between the idea that education is development from within and that it is formation from without ...."[2]

Today we continue to argue about the merits of curriculum-based instruction over a child-centered approach. The current back-to-basics movement calls for standards and an emphasis on test scores, while proponents of effective education call for the teaching of pro-social skills. One of the most visible cases of polarization in educational philosophy today is the phonics versus whole language debate.

Dewey disputed the all-or-nothing approach by calling on both sides to take a slightly different view:

Abandon the notion of subject-matter as something fixed and ready-made in itself, outside the child's experience; cease thinking of the child's experience as also something hard and fast; see it as something fluent, embryonic, vital; and we realize that the child and the curriculum are simply two limits which define a single process .... It is continuous reconstruction, moving from the child's present experience out into that represented by the organized bodies of truth that we call studies.[3]

Dewey was no fan of the "assign-study-recite" technique. He considered education to be a "conscious, purposive, informed activity." He advocated a process-oriented approach that taught students how to solve problems since "the method of solution ... is determined by the problem to be solved. As problems change, modes of solution must also change."[4]

Dewey maintained that education consists of a continuity of developing experiences, in which students interact with their environment and gain insight and understanding from those experiences. Experiences are connected, as opposed to interacting with subject matter in isolation. In this way, students can apply present learning to future experiences. In Dewey's view, education must be inherently useful:

> What avail is it to win prescribed amounts of information about geography and history, to win the ability to read and write, if in the process the individual loses his own soul: loses his appreciation of things worth while, of the values to which these things are relative; if he loses desire to apply what he has learned and, above all, loses the ability to extract meaning from his future experiences as they occur?[5]

Almost a century has passed since John Dewey started to ponder the meaning and practice of education, yet his words still ring true today. His writings helped launch a new way of viewing the educative process. Indeed, he helped show that education is a process. Since then, people have taken Dewey's ideas and have continued to forge ahead into an era where Experiential Education meets the needs of a global and information-rich society.

Kurt Hahn: Outward Bound

> I regard it as the foremost task of education to insure the survival of these qualities: • an enterprising curiosity, • an undefeatable spirit, • tenacity in pursuit, • readiness for sensible self-denial, • and, above all, compassion. — Kurt Hahn[6]

A contemporary of Dewey, Kurt Hahn is widely known as the guiding spirit behind the Outward Bound movement. Founded as a way to help sailors survive in difficult times during World War II, it is just one of Hahn's forays into progressive education. His first endeavor was the Salem School in Germany. Salem, which means "peace," was a place where students could learn habits that would protect them against what Hahn saw as the deteriorating values of modern life.[7] This was accomplished by allowing students to experience both success and failure, thus giving them the tools to overcome adversity. Thomas James, in his biography of Kurt Hahn, describes Hahn's experiential approach:

> As an educator, he would always be devising ways to turn his classrooms out of doors, putting students into motion and forcing his teachers to come to grips with the healing powers of direct experience. [8]

One of Hahn's influences came from the Nazi movement in Germany. As headmaster of the Salem School, he saw the Nazis twist the progressive teaching methods of the day into destructive and effective tools with which to indoctrinate the Hitler Youth. He recognized the fine line between "compassionate service [and] destructive egotism."[9] After landing in a Nazi jail, he was exiled from his homeland to Britain, where Outward Bound was born in 1934.

Hahn was also profoundly influenced by Plato, as evidenced in the Outward Bound philosophy that personal goals must be compatible with those of the larger community. James described Hahn's focus on compassion as being placed "above all other values of Outward Bound because it among all emotions is capable of reconciling individual strength with collective need."[10] Service to the community is stressed in Hahn's philosophy. He truly sought to incorporate the human spirit into education.

This spirit lives on today in the many Outward Bound schools around the world. Although Outward Bound was not his only endeavor, it is the one most widely recognized around the globe. In fact, it has become the parent and grandparent of many other experiential programs. Project Adventure is a child of Outward Bound, as is Expeditionary Learning.

Kurt Hahn had a profound effect upon the Experiential and Adventure Education movements. With his proven methods that teach to the whole person, and his unwavering belief that individuals are members of a larger community, he "believed that education should cultivate a passion for life and that this can be accomplished only through experience, a shared sense of moment in the journey toward an exciting goal."[11]

Project Adventure: The Adventure-Integrated Model

The original idea for Project Adventure came from Jerry Pieh, who grew up in the Minnesota Outward Bound School that his father directed. Jerry dreamed of bringing the benefits of Outward Bound to a much larger audience. In 1971, as principal of Hamilton-Wenham High School in Hamilton, Massachusetts, Jerry received funding for a grant that proposed to change the school climate and motivate students to achieve through an integrated interdisciplinary program design entitled Project Adventure. After 3 years of very creative development and implementation, the grant program received an outstanding evaluation from the Department of Education. The department credited the program with improving the self-concept of participants, positively effecting the internal locus of control, and improving school climate for learning.

Now, more than 35 years later, the methods and techniques that began in that program at Hamilton-Wenham have evolved and spread to many thousands of programs all over the U.S. and abroad. Project Adventure has helped pioneer a whole field of facilities-based adventure, bringing the team and leadership results of Outward Bound to the masses through an approach of integrated programming at institutions of education, recreation, therapy, and professional development.

Project Adventure has developed three foundational concepts that have affected the field and my work tremendously – Challenge by Choice, Full Value Contract, and Goal Setting.

Challenge By Choice: Karl Rohnke and the physical educators he was working closely with in the first decade of Project Adventure coined this phrase. The concept they developed was to have students decide on their own, without teacher or peer pressure, to take on a challenge such as deciding to step off a Zip Wire platform into space 40 feet above the ground (on belay, of course). This method of deepening learning through the leverage of choice, so different from Karl's Outward Bound instructor experience, was calculated to provide more actual learning because the student was in control of the learning. As explained later in this book, this concept has taken on more meaning as it has spread over the field worldwide. It is a concept now that, when used with skill, can empower a learner to choose the level of challenge that makes for optimum learning.

Full Value Contract: This concept was first published in *Islands of Healing* (1988) by Schoel, Prouty, and Radcliffe. This approach to group process of norm development uses the safety of the group, both physical and emotional, as the reason for the contract. The group develops a series of commitments that has the effect of agreeing to find positive value in the efforts of group members. This positive value is expressed in encouragement, goal setting, group dialog, a spirit of forgiveness, and confrontation. The concept makes it possible to develop norms and trust more quickly and effectively in the experiential process.

Goal Setting: Goal setting is a traditional learning method advocated by many. Kurt Lewin, in 1944, first laid out the importance of goal setting for experiencing psychological success and effectively developing a group. Schoel, et al., in *Islands of Healing* make a very practical case that goal setting, both individual and group, should be a key fundamental of an effective group development process for the experiential practitioner. And Mary Henton, in *Adventure in the Classroom* (1996), shows how the classroom teacher can effectively integrate both individual and group goal setting into the classroom experiential process.

These three fundamentals, when used with the widespread activities base of Experiential Education today (initiatives, games, challenge course, and project-based activities), have allowed Project Adventure to pioneer the way in the development of an Adventure Education model. That model, now widely adopted by many types of institutions and organizations, has fostered a whole field of facilities-based Adventure Education. It is possible for any school to bring the benefits of adventure to the classroom.

David Kolb: Experiential Learning Cycle

Both Dewey and Hahn were proponents of learning by doing, which is the basis of Experiential Education. The experience itself, though, is not enough. Without taking the time to reflect upon the experience in order to gain insight, and transfer the insight into the rest of one's life, it is learning in isolation. Hahn stressed the need to reflect upon one's experience in order to gain meaning. Dewey stressed the need to connect experiences in order to have an impact upon future learning.

David Kolb articulated this very process in his Experiential Learning Cycle in the mid 1980's.* This model is the cornerstone of experiential education, whether used in a classroom academic model, in Adventure Education, during Service Learning, in Outdoor Education, or in any of the myriad incarnations of Experiential Education.

Kolb's four-phase cycle (figure 1.1) depicts experiences as a related series of educational opportunities rather than isolated activities. When people have experiences, they take the next step of reflecting on what has occurred. This reflection time ensures that people can formulate meaning from these experiences. Generalizing is a time to make connections and look for patterns. Finally, applying the information affords people the opportunity to incorporate the

Experiential Learning Cycle

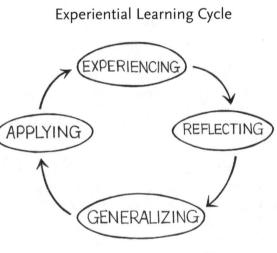

Figure 1.1

learning into their lives or into the next experience. Although two-dimensional in this diagram, the Experiential Learning Cycle is a dynamic and fluid model. It has been described as a spiral, in which people move to higher planes of thinking and understanding.

Kolb and others have also taken the Experiential Learning Cycle into the realm of learning styles. Each phase of the cycle plays to different strengths. Some people naturally reflect upon their experiences; others prefer to make connections through research. Some create and test models, while still others seek out experiences so they can learn through trial and error. The beauty of the cycle is that it meets a variety of needs, while tapping into learning methods that have been around since the dawn of time. As Aldous Huxley so deftly stated, "Experience is not what happens to you; it is what you do with what happens to you."[12]

---

* The Experiential Learning Cycle will be discussed in greater depth in Chapter 8. It is mentioned here because it is a basic foundation of Experiential Education.

Howard Gardner: Multiple Intelligences

... the purpose of school should be to develop intelligences and to help people reach vocational and avocational goals that are appropriate to their particular spectrum of intelligences. People who are helped to do so, I believe, feel more engaged and competent, and therefore more inclined to serve the society in a constructive way. — Howard Gardner [13]

There is a popular story about the animals of the forest starting a school for their offspring. In order to provide a well-rounded education, they design a program for all the animals that includes running, jumping, swimming, and flying. The school administrators decide that running and jumping are the more important skills because they take place in the areas that make up most of the surrounding habitat.

After the first year, the school counselor sits down with the rabbit to review her grades. He informs her that she is getting excellent grades and should keep up the good work. Later, he calls the turtle into his office. The turtle, it appears, is failing miserably. Although he excels at swimming, he has made absolutely no progress in running and jumping, the core curriculum. Because of this sorry record, the turtle must drop swimming in order to concentrate on the "more important" skills.

At graduation time, the rabbit gives the valedictorian speech, while the turtle has dropped out of school.

This story illustrates a narrow notion of intelligence that has been in vogue since the time of Alfred Binet in the early 1900's. This view is based on the need to quantify intelligence through measuring devices such as the Scholastic Aptitude Test, which is designed to predict future success in school. These tests require the takers to read and write and solve mathematical problems.

Gardner proposes a "... pluralistic view of mind, recognizing many different and discrete facets of cognition, acknowledging that people have different cognitive strengths and contrasting cognitive styles."[14] He posits that intelligence is "the ability to solve problems, or to fashion products, that are valued in one or more cultural or community settings."[15] His model includes nine types of intelligence: linguistic, logical-mathematical, spatial, musical, bodily-kinesthetic, interpersonal, intrapersonal, naturalistic, and existential.

With the acceptance of this paradigm shift comes a responsibility to change the ways in which students are taught. In Gardener's view, students are seen as whole people rather than just cognitive beings. Students must be given a variety of avenues in which to learn, and other areas of content need to be brought into the curriculum.

The activity focus of Adventure Education, along with the processing techniques used to help students draw meaning from their experiences, brings to the forefront areas of intelligence that have historically been ignored. We ask children to reflect upon their experiences (intrapersonal intelligence), to consider the perspectives of others (interpersonal intelligence), and to move around during games and activities (bodily-kinesthetic intelligence). Many times, we venture out into the natural world for a ropes course experience or other outdoor pursuit (naturalistic intelligence). Through group problem-solving initiatives and school projects, students use a variety of Gardner's intelligences to arrive at mutual academic and behavioral goals.

That people do not all learn in the same way is widely accepted. Gardner's theory of multiple intelligences gives us a framework, and Experiential Education offers a vehicle in which to educate a variety of people.

Susan Kovalik: Brain Research and Integrated Thematic Instruction

"How far have we come?" The painful but truthful answer is that we have not changed at all in over a hundred years. The curricular, instructional, and structural features of the American

School (high school and elementary) are still virtually identical to the Prussian model brought back from Europe by Horace Mann in 1840, whose instructional traditions stemmed from cadet corps training of a highly regimented military tradition and whose curricular modeling goes back to the catechism of the medieval church (one right answer from a single source, single point of view). — Susan Kovalik [16]

Susan Kovalik's Integrated Thematic Instruction (ITI) Model has its foundations in brain research; it offers both a biological and sociological rationale for using experiential techniques in the classroom. Kovalik believes that bringing our educational system up to date depends on changing curriculum to be compatible with how the brain works. She identifies eight brain-compatible elements: absence of threat, meaningful content, choices, adequate time, enriched environment, collaboration, immediate feedback, and mastery (application). [17] By focusing on these elements, students are preparing for life in the real world, as opposed to preparing for the next exam.

Kovalik states that every successful learning experience should contain three or more of these eight components. [18] She also notes that the classroom teacher has much control over these elements and that schools must create an environment that is physically and emotionally safe for all. In Kovalik's words, "The environment – school wide as well as in the classroom – must eliminate all real and perceived threat between teacher and students and among students. Next, the teacher must engineer and nurture trust and trustworthiness." [19]

Unless this basic safety need is met, people cannot learn; their brains won't let them. Information comes through a "gatekeeper" known as the limbic system. If the environment is perceived to be safe, then the limbic system "upshifts" to the cerebral cortex, which is where academic learning occurs. "Consequently, the first step toward brain-compatibility in the classroom is creating an environment with an absence of threat and curriculum that is truly engaging to students." [20]

The ITI model also stresses five lifelong behavior guidelines that are uniquely suited to creating a classroom community: Trustworthiness, Truthfulness, Active Listening, No Put-Downs, and Personal Best. [21] Each of these guidelines is an integral part of any well-functioning community. To strive toward these ideals can only propel learning to new heights as the students and teacher alike gain a deeper respect for each other and themselves.

Daniel Goleman: Emotional Intelligence

Educators, long disturbed by schoolchildren's lagging scores in math and reading, are realizing there is a different and more alarming deficiency: emotional illiteracy. And while laudable efforts are being made to raise academic standards, this new and troubling deficiency is not being addressed in the standard school curriculum. — Daniel Goleman [22]

Perhaps there is no greater reason to create community in the classroom than because it enhances the emotional literacy of students. Emotional illiteracy manifests itself in depression, aggression, eating disorders, dropping out of school, addiction to drugs or alcohol, and high pregnancy rates. Young people need more than information. Children need the emotional skills to deal with difficult issues in their lives. These skills include "self-awareness; identifying, expressing, and managing feelings; impulse control and delaying gratification; and handling stress and anxiety." [23]

Goleman discusses how emotional learning is developed through habit: "... as experiences are repeated over and over, the brain reflects them as strengthened pathways, neural habits to apply in times of duress, frustration, hurt." [24] A classroom community is a place where students can experience and practice emotional skills that will benefit them throughout their lifetimes.

The methods of community building through Adventure Education are perfectly suited to helping students become emotionally literate. Based on Dewey's philosophy whereby students interact with and gain insight from their environment, adventure activities provide a forum where students can discuss incidents that arise. Instead of sitting around talking about the abstract possibility that someone might call another person a name, adventure activities engage learners in real situations. When someone actually calls someone a name during an activity, the class stops to discuss what has happened and how it might be handled. From these experiences, children learn – *and practice* – methods for handling their emotions. In this way, emotions become another content area:

> *This new departure in bringing emotional literacy into schools makes emotions and social life themselves topics, rather than treating these most compelling facets of a child's day as irrelevant intrusions or, when they lead to eruptions, relegating them to occasional disciplinary trips to the guidance counselor or the principal's office.* — Daniel Goleman[25]

William Glasser: Choice Theory

> *It is my contention that unless we stop talking in generalities and begin to talk about some specific changes in the structure of our teaching and in the role of the teacher in that new structure, and give these changes a fair trial, we will not make a dent in the growing number of unmotivated students who are essentially forced to attend school.* — William Glasser[26]

Who and what define a classroom environment? The beginning of a school year is generally filled with optimism and high hopes. Although some students may come with a "reputation," most students are given a chance to prove themselves with no strings attached. By the third month of school, however, many teachers are complaining about one or a few students who are "ruining" their class. Every day is a struggle because these few students are constantly vying for attention, questioning the teacher's motives, refusing to work, or playing around. It is a test of a teacher's patience to try to teach students who just don't seem to want to learn.

William Glasser asserts that up to half of all students experience school as unsatisfying because the structure can stifle five universal human needs: survival, belonging, power, freedom, and fun.[27] Depending upon how these needs are being met, people may seek to satisfy one or more that are lacking. Glasser talks about how these needs are like being thirsty – we don't have a choice about it and we must satisfy the need eventually. Therefore, if we are able to find water soon, then the thirst need goes away for the time being, and we can focus on other, more pressing, needs. Glasser would say that it is not possible to teach someone who doesn't want to learn. His Choice Theory suggests that "What goes on in the outside world never "makes" us do anything. All of our behavior, simple to complex, is our best attempt to control ourselves to satisfy our needs."[28]

It follows, then, that a person who feels controlled and has few opportunities to make choices may feel a need for freedom and chafe at rules that are imposed at school. Someone who is ignored is more likely to challenge the authority figures at school than someone who has their power needs met. Someone who does not feel a sense of belonging anywhere in his or her life may seek it in ways that are less socially acceptable than we would like. And, of course, bored or hungry students make poor learners.

A conventional approach in our schools focuses on controlling the student so that she or he will learn (or at the very least, allow others to learn). This method can undermine a young person's need for power. Additionally, a daily dose of learning in isolation by reading, listening, and taking tests can be wholly unsatisfying in light of the human needs for fun and belonging.

Giving more young people a reason to want to come to school requires a "depth that is necessary for more of them to make the vital relationship between knowledge and power."[29] This can be accomplished through cooperative learning methods that Glasser labels "The Learning Team Model." In this model, the teacher shares power by having students work together on long-term projects with others. As students work toward a common goal, they are asked to prove they have learned the material and are given choices about how to do that.

Creating a classroom community is vital to the cooperative learning process. Students must be able to share their strengths as equals and be able to expose weaknesses without threat of teasing. A give-and-take relationship can be developed through the intentional formation of a community in the classroom.

At the end of 12+ years of schooling, it is hoped that young people are independent, responsible, and ready to take on what life has to offer. Glasser advocates that it starts with the sharing of power and engagement in a learning process that is need-satisfying. He states that "the more they [teachers] act as facilitators, resource people and coaches, the more they will find that the students in learning-teams take much more responsibility than now for their own education."[30] And, as a bonus, it will be more satisfying for the teacher, too.

Alfie Kohn: On Compliance and Community

> This ... is neither a recipe nor a different technique for getting mindless compliance. It requires that we transform the classroom, give up some power, and reconsider the way we define and think about misbehavior. — Alfie Kohn[31]

What is wrong with our children? Why don't they just behave?! Alfie Kohn, in his direct manner, confronts us with the notion that it is we the adults who must answer this question, not the students. He questions our motives by pointing out that classroom behavior management is designed to control students, sometimes through threats and coercion. When students do not live up to our expectations of "appropriate" behavior, we blame them, and then focus on what they can do to change (read: "conform") to meet the required rules and regulations. Kohn asks educators to consider "the possibility that it may be the teacher's request, rather than the child's unwillingness to comply with it, that needs to be addressed."[32]

In many ways, Kohn harkens back to Dewey's questions about purpose. Are we teaching children to mindlessly obey authority, or are we preparing them to live in a pluralistic society? Our teaching techniques have a direct effect on the outcome. The environment that we create in the classroom and school as a whole – how we teach our children – should be a model of what is expected of adults in our society. In other words, if we truly are a participatory democracy, we must teach our children how to live in a democracy by *being* one.

Kohn discusses the need to take on a community approach that goes beyond teacher-student interaction and asks us to consider the broader question of how everyone gets along together. It is a change from the notion of "doing to" students to "working with" them.[33] To do so means changing our attitudes about and toward children. Rather than viewing them as empty receptacles needing to be filled, we must see them as partners in the educational process. If we create a classroom community, we can then learn what it means to be members of a community. If we want students to act responsibly, we must *give* them responsibility. This microcosm of "the real world" is at the core of experiential education: to learn by doing and to gain insight from the experience.

Search Institute: 40 Developmental Assets

> Children who have high levels of developmental assets achieve more and are involved in fewer high-risk behaviors. Simply put, children who feel better about school do better in school.[34]

In a workshop, Alfie Kohn led the group through a simple exercise that you can try with any group of educators: Think about the children or youth with whom you work today. Then think about them 20 years from now. What skills, attributes, and qualities do you want them to have? Before reading on, make a list yourself. Invariably there will be words such as: respect, health, commitment, discernment, honesty, and compassion. The next question to ask is, what are we doing today to help our young people achieve this vision? Sometimes it is difficult to come up with an answer because educators become focused on the nuts and bolts of teaching and on the concrete outcomes that are expected of students so that they are cleared to graduate. It is difficult to help students succeed academically and take care of their social and emotional needs, too – especially since these needs can be so abstract and varied. Where does one start?

The Search Institute has an answer. Founded as a research organization, they started by asking youth questions with the resulting book, *What are Youth Thinking*, published in 1961. Their commitment to youth development and subsequent surveys led them to create the 40 Developmental Assets in 1995-96 and launch their Healthy Communities, Healthy Youth initiative. These assets are "building blocks of healthy development that help young people grow up healthy, caring, and responsible."[35]

The assets are concrete and specific. They include 20 external assets (e.g. caring school climate, service to others, and positive peer influence) under the headings of Support, Empowerment, Boundaries & Expectations, and Constructive Use of Time. There are also 20 internal assets (e.g. school engagement, planning and decision making, and positive view of personal future) categorized under the headings of Commitment to Learning, Positive Values, Social Competencies, and Positive Identity.[*]

The more assets a young person has, the less likely he or she is to become involved with alcohol, drugs, sexual activity and violence; and the more likely to succeed in school, value diversity, maintain good health, and delay gratification.[36] The assets provide a blueprint to help young people because everyone is an asset builder. Helping a student gain even one asset can help a young person grow into a healthy adult.

Helping each individual youth develop assets can be a daunting task. It is not necessary to focus on every individual every day, however. Classroom communities are inherently asset-building. Starkman, et al., share that "an asset-rich environment is one in which students and, indeed, school adults feel safe and secure."[37] By creating a safe place where students can build positive relationships, conflicts are experienced and resolved and community members feel supported and valued. Students can feel empowered, learn social competencies, experience positive values, and ultimately develop a commitment to learning. The vision can, indeed, be realized.

Jeanne Gibbs: The TRIBES Process

Although massive funds for school improvement, restructuring, and reform have flowed through school districts for more than 20 years, the traditional pattern of interaction between teachers and students has changed very little. — Jeanne Gibbs[38]

Jeanne Gibbs and her cohorts are pioneers in the area of rethinking how we teach children. They point us away from a traditional teacher-centered milieu to one that values interdependence and collaboration. The teacher, in this scenario, becomes a partner in the process of learning.

Creating community, though, takes more than an attitudinal shift. It takes perseverance, empathy, and commitment. It must be intentional. If a teacher is outfitted with a variety of tools and techniques, it makes the process that much more robust in a world where students have many stresses and preoccupa-

---

[*] Search Institute (1997). 40 Developmental Assets. For a complete listing of the assets and more information, visit the Search Institute Web site. See Bibliography.

tions outside of school. In *TRIBES: A New Way of Learning and Being Together*, Jeanne Gibbs offers both a well-articulated rationale and a blueprint for focusing on the *process* of classroom community building.

Although we may all want a recipe for making our classrooms safe and caring communities, Gibbs reminds us that the process takes time – and it requires making the classroom *student-centered*: "Gradually, as cooperative learning tasks and much of the classroom management are transferred to students themselves, the teacher has time to encourage initiative, give feedback, facilitate student communication, suggest resources, help and praise students."[39] In short, the teacher is no longer the focus of power in the classroom, but is part of a collaborative effort for all to learn.

TRIBES is loaded with tools for teachers to begin and maintain the community-building process. Gibbs talks of the stages of group development (discussed in detail in Chapter Two). She also shares practical strategies such as convening community circles, creating community agreements, offering appreciations, and the teaching of collaborative skills. Her model has paved the way for educators to rethink their paradigm of what it means to learn in a school setting, and it helps us focus on helping *all* students learn in a safe and challenging environment.

Many schools are now combining a TRIBES approach with an adventure approach to community building. The adventure approach, as listed below, was developed and spread widely by Project Adventure. Mary Henton, in *Adventure in the Classroom* (1995), addressed most of the elements in the Creating Community through Adventure graphic listed below. The two processes are similar in philosophy; together they provide strategies to meet the needs of a variety of students (see figure 1.2).

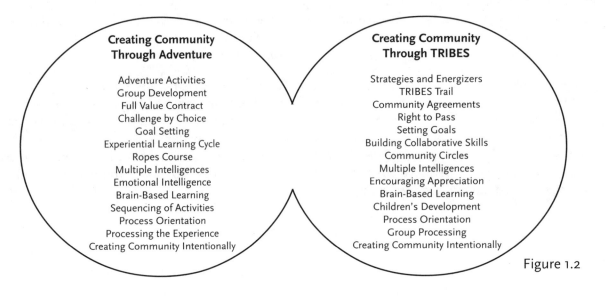

Creating Community Through Adventure

Adventure Activities
Group Development
Full Value Contract
Challenge by Choice
Goal Setting
Experiential Learning Cycle
Ropes Course
Multiple Intelligences
Emotional Intelligence
Brain-Based Learning
Sequencing of Activities
Process Orientation
Processing the Experience
Creating Community Intentionally

Creating Community Through TRIBES

Strategies and Energizers
TRIBES Trail
Community Agreements
Right to Pass
Setting Goals
Building Collaborative Skills
Community Circles
Multiple Intelligences
Encouraging Appreciation
Brain-Based Learning
Children's Development
Process Orientation
Group Processing
Creating Community Intentionally

Figure 1.2

Purkey and Novak: Invitational Education

People and environments are never neutral; they are either summoning or shunning the development of human potential. — Purkey and Novak[40]

If there is one overarching theme to creating classroom community, it can be summed up in the axiom: "I teach people, not subjects." As many of the thinkers cited in this chapter point out, there is a ubiquitous mood in our educational system that is uninviting. It begins with the reality that school is mandatory, and is perpetuated by the political pressures for high-stakes accountability which puts everyone on edge. Compound that with methodologies that do not meet the changing needs of the school population, and it is a wonder that some students can even get in the door.

Fortunately, as pervasive as this scenario may be, it is not all-inclusive. There are many schools (and countless classrooms) where the door is wide open and a welcome mat greets all who enter. William Watson Purkey and John Novak share a theory of practice called Invitational Education which encompasses "a democratically oriented, perceptually based, self-concept approach to teaching and learning."[41]

Invitational Education is based upon how people perceive themselves. The perceptual tradition explains that people's actions stem from how they view the world at that moment in time. In this way every action, even if it appears unreasonable from the outside, makes sense to the person who is initiating the behavior. As in Glasser's Choice Theory, every behavior has a reason for occurring.

Perceptions of oneself are learned and impact self-concept: "By experiencing the world through inviting and disinviting interactions with others, as well as through interactions with oneself, the developing person organizes a theory of personal existence."[42] The message, according to Invitational Education for teachers, is that everything done with, for, by, and to students has an impact, either positively or negatively. If education is to be truly inviting, then it must be intentionally so, with the underlying belief that students are able, valuable, and responsible. Invitational teaching requires the practitioner to examine her or his own perceptions and develop an outlook, or "stance," that includes the development of trust, respect, optimism, and intentionality.[43] In other words, to create a school environment, one must align one's beliefs, feelings, and perceptions so that it comes from within. An external orientation of trying some techniques to make others feel welcome falls flat because it is not authentic.

Invitational education takes the entire school environment into account – from the schedule to the signs on the walls. Everything and everyone matters. Purkey and Novak present a 12-step model for transformation to an inviting school. Any school or individual can start the process, and they offer lists of ideas for people to be more intentionally inviting.

Creating community is an intentional act. It does not magically happen unless the conditions are right. To create the conditions for a community to grow and flourish takes forethought and a deep-down belief that it is the right thing to do. Purkey and Novak remind us of our real mission as educators: "Of all the things that count, nothing is as important as the people in the process .... Teaching is a way of being with people."

Summary

This chapter presents a collection of theories, philosophies and models that create a foundation for understanding how experiential and adventure methodologies can be used to create a classroom community – and, ultimately, help all students learn. John Dewey delved into why experiential learning is good learning, while Kurt Hahn showed that progressive education works. David Kolb, then, took the next step by showing how the process works through the Experiential Learning Cycle.

Howard Gardner, Daniel Goleman, and Susan Kovalik all present compelling evidence that a classroom must look at the whole person, rather than solely focusing on the cognitive being. Multiple intelligences, emotional intelligence, and brain-based learning are essential components of a total classroom experience. Addressing the myriad of student needs can be accomplished through creating a safe environment in which to learn, teaching of applicable skills, and offering choices to students.

Alfie Kohn, William Glasser, and the Search Institute's 40 Assets are presented as rationales for creating community in the classroom. Jeanne Gibb's TRIBES and Project Adventure's integrated adventure approach extend that into how these visions can actually be accomplished.

As with any paradigm shift, it is necessary to recognize one's underlying assumptions in order to put the new ideas into action. Purkey and Novak remind us that students must be invited into the process. If we are to make our classrooms inclusive and safe, we must acknowledge the "assumption that interdependence and connection to others is key to human development, learning, and the accomplishment of task."[44] Without accepting this assumption, the methods described in this book are, at best, an interesting exercise. At worst, the tools to create community become new tools of control.

---

[1] Dewey, John (1938). *Experience and Education.* New York, NY: Touchstone. (p. 78)

[2] Dewey (p. 17)

[3] Dewey, *John Dewey on Education*, 1902, (p. 343)

[4] Archambault, Reginald D., editor (1964). *John Dewey on Education: Selected Writings.* New York, NY: Random House. (p. xxiv)

[5] Dewey, John (1938). *Experience and Education.* New York, NY: Touchstone. (p. 49)

[6] Schoel, Jim and Michael Stratton (1990). *Gold Nuggets: Readings for Experiential Education.* Hamilton, MA: Project Adventure, Inc. (p. 128)

[7] Warren, Karen, Mitchell Sakofs, and Jasper S. Hunt, Jr., eds. (1995). *The Theory of Experiential Education.* Dubuque, IA: Kendall Hunt Publishing. (p. 35)

[8] —Warren, et al. (p. 37)

[9] Cousins, Emily and Melissa Rodgers, eds. (1995). *Fieldwork: An Expeditionary Learning Outward Bound Reader.* Dubuque, IA: Kendall Hunt Publishing. James, (p. 68)

[10] Cousins and Rodgers (p. 60)

[11] Cousins and Rodgers (p. 63)

[12] Henton, Mary (1996). *Adventure in the Classroom.* Dubuque, IA: Kendall Hunt Publishing. (p. 39)

[13] Gardner, Howard (1993). *Multiple Intelligences: The Theory in Practice.* New York, NY: BasicBooks. (p. 9)

[14] Henton (p. 6)

[15] Henton (p. 7)

[16] Kovalic, Susan (1997). *ITI: The Model, Integrated Thematic Instruction.* Kent, WA: Books for Educators. (p. vii)

[17] Kovalic (p. xxiii)

[18] Kovalic (p. xxiii)

[19] Kovalic (p. xxiii)

[20] Kovalic (p. 19)

[21] Kovalic (p. 25)

[22] Goleman, Daniel (1995). *Emotional Intelligence: Why It Can Matter More Than IQ.* New York, NY: Bantam Books. (p. 231)

[23] Goleman (p. 259)

[24] Goleman (p. 263)

[25] Goleman (p. 263)

[26] Glasser, W. (1988). *Choice Theory in the Classroom.* New York: NY: HarperCollins Publishers, Inc. (p. 6)

[27] Glasser (p. 25)

[28] Glasser (p. 19)

[29] Glasser (p. 78)

[30] Glasser (p. 90)

[31] Kohn, Alfie (1996). *Beyond Discipline: From Compliance to Community.* Alexandria, VA: Association for Supervision and Curriculum Development. (p. 13)

[32] Kohn (p. 13)

[33] Kohn (p.104)

[34] Starkman, N., Scales, P., and Roberts, C. (1999). *Great Places to Learn: How Asset Building Schools Help Students Succeed.* Minneapolis, MN: Search Institute. (p. 2)

[35] Search Institute (1997). *What is Healthy Communities, Healthy Youth?* Minneapolis, MN: Search Institute (p. 2)

[36] Search Institute (1997). (p. 4)

[37] Starkman, et al. (p. 129)

[38] Gibbs, Jeanne (1995). *TRIBES: A New Way of Learning and Being Together.* Sausalito, CA: CenterSource Systems, LLC (p. 17)

[39] Gibbs (pp. 57-58)

[40] Purkey, W.N. and Novak, J.M. (1996). *Inviting School Success: A Self-Concept Approach to Teaching, Learning, and Democratic Practice.* Belmont, CA: Wadsworth Publishing Company. (p. 3)

[41] Purkey and Novak (pp.7-8)

[42] Purkey and Novak (pp. 26-27)

[43] Purkey and Novak (pp. 39-54)

[44] Gibbs (p. 82)

2 Creating the Conditions for Community

A few years ago my partner, Bert, and I traveled halfway across the United States by train. It was a 52-hour trip in a car with about 100 other people who represented various slices of life. We shared the space with people of all socioeconomic classes, races, and cultural backgrounds. We traveled with children, elders, parents, and singles.

At first, we all stayed put, happily reading or looking out the window. Worried that we might disturb others, we rarely raised our voices above a whisper. All of this changed during the trip. By the end of the journey, all the children in the car had become everyone's children. We laughed and shared with the people around us, learning names and even a few life stories. None of us, of course, had taken a shower during the 2-plus days, and most of us enjoyed only a few scattered hours of sleep. We said our good-byes as if we were waving to old friends. Somewhere along the tracks a community had formed.

The opposite was true during my college and high-school years. I joined a new high school during my junior year. By the end of the year, I knew a handful of people and considered fewer of them friends. Although my grades were good and I participated in sports, it was an isolated existence in which I focused on listening to the teachers and getting my assignments in on time.

College offered even fewer opportunities to make connections. How is it possible to spend a full semester with dozens of people and not know the name of anyone in the class? Many of us were successful at avoiding eye contact with anyone else for the entire semester. Communities were established in the dorm rooms, not in the classrooms.

If we believe that learning is enhanced by creating a safe and valuing environment which allows the brain to make connections at a higher cognitive level (highlighted by brain research), it is rational to conclude that some of us learn *in spite of* the conditions in many classrooms across this country. The rest of us are relegated to other situations that rely on labeling: *at-risk, special education,* or *dropout.* Creating a classroom community can be the most important tool at a teacher's fingertips. Once a class of individuals comes together to work toward common goals, with everyone valued and respected, the business of learning can take place fully, without reservation.

It is difficult for me to say what made the difference between the train car and the classroom. Certainly the conditions for creating community existed on those western tracks, while those conditions were absent among the rows of desks. It is also my heartfelt belief that, as teachers, we can create the necessary conditions for community in our classrooms if we pay attention to the process. Community building takes work. It is predicated on trust, risk taking, and open communication. It is a process that needs constant attention.

The following chapters contain the necessary tools and resources to begin a journey together toward an ideal: a world that values collaboration, cooperation, and interdependence. It is a journey undertaken away from the mean-spiritedness that is eating away at the core of our collective being. It is our *journey toward the caring classroom.*

Group Development*

Most classrooms are granted a "honeymoon" period, in which students are quiet, even polite, and arguments are either nonexistent or minimal. Depending on the personalities and backgrounds of the students, the honeymoon period can last for weeks, hours, or minutes. It is a sure bet, however, that the honeymoon will come to an end, and the teacher's classroom management style will be tested. Sometimes every strategy seems futile, with the students locked in eternal conflict with the teacher and each other. At other times, the atmosphere is magic, with students learning to resolve their conflicts and soar. At still other times, the teacher attempts to avoid conflict by clamping down an ironclad list of rules and punishments.

These observations are not random; they are based on a process that is as consistent as gravity itself: the process of group development. Every group of individuals goes through this process. Some get stuck at certain phases, while others work through the issues and progress to the next phase. A knowledge of group development will help you work with the process, thus enhancing the opportunity to create the conditions for community in the classroom.

Picture a person with whom you have developed a close relationship over a period of time – a partner or a good friend. Remember back to the time when you first met. Hold the memories of those first days and weeks. This was a time when your friend could do no wrong. If something was said or done that did not sit well, you simply ignored it, or felt it did not really matter. This was your new dear friend, after all.

As your relationship progressed, there came a point when those same little things suddenly mattered. Some friction began to develop. The issues were probably not overtly stated; the things that were actually said and done were symptoms of larger issues centering around values, space, power, and control. If these themes were not worked through, they did not go away. And if the issues were not dealt with at all, the relationship probably cooled and you grew apart.

If, on the other hand, you worked through the conflict, norms for the relationship began to develop. You learned about your partner's boundaries, and your partner learned yours. This precipitated a time of closeness and affection because you had struggled together, and the relationship had great focus.

After awhile, new conflicts arose. The symptoms may have been different, but the issues were actually the same. It seemed as if you were meeting this person for the first time. In reality, though, you were dealing with the same issues at a deeper level. You worked through them again, and your relationship regained focus – until the next time, as the spiral continues.

Groups of people gathered for a common purpose go through a similar cycle. It is the dynamic nature of relationships that comes into play whenever people get together. It is a force that has been documented over and over again, and it is a force to be reckoned with.

This group developmental process is all around us. It is there whether we choose to see it or not. Sometimes conflicts are worked through and we move on; at other times we are stymied, and the group process stagnates or the group disbands. Look around at your family, in your church and social groups. The process is there. Look at gangs and political systems. The process is there. It respects no bounds of values, political persuasion, or morality.

To recognize this developmental cycle of a group makes it an ally, a companion that can make group work a little less a matter of guesswork. It is common to hear accomplished facilitators say, "Trust the process." They are referring to this group cycle. Especially during times of conflict, when it is necessary to face it rather than run from it, that phrase pops up. Sometimes it feels like a banner in a gale, but it is

---

* See pp. 76-84, *TRIBES: A New Way of Learning and Being Together*, by Jeanne Gibbs for a concise description of the stages of group development.

well worth the effort. If a group of people work through the conflict, calmer times are ahead – when individuals understand the group norms because they have had a part in establishing them, and a time when the nature of the group comes into focus. It is a marvelous dynamic to watch in action.

The literature on stage theory of group development is long and includes treatises comparing the differing models. The terms used vary, but they all describe the same process.

The Life Cycle of a Group

In this view of group development, a group is seen as an organic entity – one that goes through the life stages as any living being. This view uses human growth and development as a metaphor for group development.

Forming: Birth and Infancy*

People come together for a variety of reasons. They may or may not have a choice to be involved in the group. School is a place where both types of groups are present, since individuals have little choice about who their classmates are, but they gather in social groups of their own choosing during unstructured time. Whether by choice or not, groups are formed for a reason, and the feelings of the individuals joining the groups are similar.

When classes come together for the first time, there is a general feeling of anxiety. Individuals worry about whether or not they will be accepted, if they will like the other students in the class, and if the other students will like them. People are generally polite and unwilling to take risks because they are not clear about what behavior is acceptable in this particular class. This is the "honeymoon" period.

The main issue at this time is one of inclusion. How can we make the environment a safe place where everyone is included? Since norms are not yet established, the students depend on the teacher for leadership. If it is not provided, they will seek other avenues that offer guidance and leadership. Therefore, it is incumbent upon the teacher to provide experiences that help the students get to know each other, allow them to offer their hopes and expectations for the class, and establish ground rules that protect the individuals from physical or emotional attacks.

Storming**: Adolescence

Once students know each other better, have developed a foundation of trust, and feel it is safe to take some risks, inevitably conflict will arise. As people interact on a more complex level, differences in style, opinion, and perspective become evident. Just as in a two-person relationship, the problems that occur are symptoms indicating larger issues of values, space, power, and control. When a class identity has not yet been established, students might alternately turn *toward* the teacher for guidance or turn *on* the teacher for taking too much control of the class. Individuals struggle with issues of leadership and decision making. **The main concern at this stage is one of influence.**

When signs of conflict arise, the teacher needs to watch her own influence on the class. When students begin to ask for (and sometimes demand) more responsibility, it is essential to give it to them. They are indicating readiness. This does not mean that they are left to their own devices. The role of the teacher simply changes from *leader* to *guide*. Time and space must be set aside for students to discuss their issues of conflict. Both scheduled and spontaneous group meetings can be helpful tools for students to either prevent or work through conflicts.

---

* Forming, Storming, Norming, Performing, and Adjourning are stages of group development first identified by Bruce Tuckman and Mary Anne Jensen.

** Denise Mitten, professor and former director of Woodswoman, prefers the term "sorting" to "storming" as it changes the negative connotation, thus honoring the positive nature of this stage in the process.

Storming (or Sorting) is a natural part of human interaction, but that does not mean it is easy to deal with. Yet, although difficult, it is usually a time to celebrate. Conflicts are indications that the group process is moving along. Teachers must recognize that conflicts are not a direct result of their teaching techniques but part of a larger process. That realization allows teachers to be most effective; they can provide time for students to discuss the conflicts as they arise and choose activities that meet the needs of each class as they practice the developing norms.

Norming: Young Adulthood

As students work through issues around leadership, decision making, and group goals, they develop norms for the class. For example, many times during class tasks, one person takes over leadership by doing all of the talking. This can spark complaints from other students about being bossed around or excluded from the activity. Upon discussion, the person in question discloses that since no one stepped up, he was filling a leadership gap, not meaning to be bossy, but making an effort to get the task accomplished. After awhile, the class agrees to apply some structure to class planning time, whereby everyone is asked for their opinion before the class decides on a course of action. They agree to try this scheme for the next task.

At this point, the class has turned the corner from dependence upon the teacher to a growing independence as a cohesive unit. Norms are being developed that are unique to this class. The role of the teacher is now one of process observer and questioner. It is a relationship that is similar to mentoring, where the students have the combined skills to accomplish many tasks but are still at a point where they are establishing the structure to really strike out on their own.

Denise Mitten, who has decades of facilitation expertise, warns of an uninvited group "member" that may appear at this stage of a group's development. She calls it "Norm" or "Norma." Denise tells about being part of a group that began meeting to plan an expedition. After awhile, they got into the habit of celebrating these meetings with a particular type of cookie. After finishing a difficult task, they would break out the cookies to share. During the actual trek, however, they reached their goal only to find that no one had brought the cookies. There was a tangible feeling of disappointment that their ritual would be broken at so momentous a time. Finally, someone admitted that she did not even like that kind of cookie. In fact, it turned out that nobody did. "Norma" had joined the expedition;[1] a norm had been created without thought. Everyone assumed that everyone else felt the same way about the cookies, and the result was a tradition without real meaning.

Every group's identity is unique. It is formed by individuals working together toward common goals, struggling through conflicts, and developing norms. Vigilance must be exercised, however, lest the individuals in the class be superseded by a group-think mentality. In a classroom, uninvited norms can appear as competition for the best grades or in the form of scapegoating one particular student or group. In adventure activities, risk taking can be healthy, or the wielding of peer pressure can cause students to take risks without thinking – for example, doing trust activities when an individual may not be ready to put on an eye covering for a trust walk.

Norms are created whether we think about them or not. Teachers need to help students create norms that are socially enhancing and healthy. The philosophy of Challenge by Choice (discussed in detail later) must always be in place to preserve the rights of individuals, and group members should always question why a particular norm is in place.

Performing: Middle Age

Once students have practiced ways of working together and have arrived at a mutual understanding of what it means to be part of the class, a remarkable event takes place. The class, sometimes suddenly, begins to act as a cohesive unit. Collaboration is now possible, and people care about each other more deeply than before. People behave less superficially and are willing to take greater risks without fear of reprisal. Individuals are seen as having unique talents, not just as being part of a class. Each student has had a hand in creating this class. It is not often possible to put a finger on when this happens; it almost seems like magic.

The teacher can now sit back and watch. There is a feeling of needing to be somewhere but having nowhere to go as the students take steps on their own. There is also a sense of wonder and awe at how efficient and capable a group of individuals can be. They are truly interdependent and able to take care of needs that arise. When conflicts come up, people understand what is expected because they have been there before. Individuals step up to facilitate the discussion, the students make a decision, and they move on. It is a thing of beauty.

The role of the teacher now is to act as a consultant for the class. Are there safety considerations that are not being discussed? What outside influences need to be brought in? What does the class need in order to accomplish its mission? By asking relevant questions, offering advice when solicited, and helping the students make necessary connections outside their class, the teacher helps them stay focused on their mission.

Transforming: Elderhood and Death

After a group of individuals reaches a level of cohesion and experience, a couple of avenues await. First, it is possible for them to recycle through the phases again. The longer a class stays together, the more times they may recycle through the process. Each time, the students' collective experience and wisdom come into play, allowing the individuals to continue in the spiral at a deeper level of understanding and insight. It is a process that, theoretically, could last forever.

Reality, though, has another agenda. Sooner or later, groups disband, either because their allotted time is up, the task is complete, or physical age takes its toll. Groups die, and people grieve for what has been. Their group experience may be duplicated in the future, but it will never be the same as the experience with this particular group of people.

The teacher's role takes on a temporary level of importance at a time of class transformation. It is important to provide students with space and opportunity to "close" this chapter of their lives. If possible, the class should be given an opportunity to decide on its future. Depending on circumstances, they may choose to reconvene for another task, or they may attempt to plan a reunion. It is also necessary to offer time for individuals to celebrate, share memories, and say their good-byes and thank yous.

Stages of Group Development: A Comparison

The following chart (figure 2.1) delineates the similarities among the three schools of thought discussed thus far with regard to their influences on Adventure Education (The TRIBES process was highlighted in Chapter One).

TRIBES (Gibbs)	Life Cycle Metaphor	Tuckman and Jensen
Inclusion	Birth and Infancy	Forming
Influence	Adolescence	Storming
Influence/Community	Young Adulthood	Norming
Community	Middle Age	Performing
Spiral of Renewal	Elderhood and Death	Transforming (Adjourning)

Figure 2.1

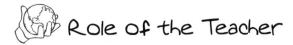 # Role of the Teacher

Throughout the life cycle of the class, the teacher must pay close attention to his or her role in the process, especially since it keeps changing. At the beginning, it is necessary to take a strong leadership position in order to help the students come together in a safe environment. Then, as the students are ready to take on more leadership responsibility, the teacher must back off and become a guide. Guides offer activities, teach necessary skills, and continue to act as safety monitors. Next, during the norming stage, the guide's role changes to one of mentor – asking questions and mediating discussions. As the students become more interdependent, the mentor role then changes to one of consultant. Finally, the teacher must temporarily reassert himself or herself as a leader in order to facilitate the process of closure as a class's life comes to an end.

The Group Cycle in Action

The artistry with group facilitation, of course, is to assess the class's needs and to take on the role that will best suit those needs. Since every group is made up of different individuals, every class is different. Moreover, it is possible to get stuck at any given stage of the cycle. If people do not feel safe or included, they will invariably stay at the forming stage, unwilling to take risks or confront the issues that will allow them to grow as a group. Many times a class stagnates at the storming stage because of unspoken issues and hidden agendas that people are unwilling to discuss. Sometimes it takes an enormous amount of patience to wait for these issues to surface. Sometimes they never do, and the class stays put.

It is also possible to regress to earlier stages. When new members join or old members leave, the class as a whole is different. The teacher can arrange activities to help students get reacquainted and discussion time to clarify community standards and norms. As a rule, every time a class meets, a mini reforming time can be offered to help people transition into class.

How a class progresses, however, has as much to do with external pressures as internal group chemistry. If students come together by choice, for example, attitudes about wanting to work together are different than for those who are brought together because of some external requirement in which they had no voice. The amount of time a class is together is also highly influential when working through group process. The standard 45-minute time period in a high school is not as conducive to developing group dynamics as a 90-minute block schedule, for example.

Exploring: Always in the big woods when you leave familiar ground and step off alone into a new place there will be, along with the feelings of curiosity and excitement, a little nagging of dread. It is the ancient fear of the Unknown, and it is your first bond with the wilderness you are going into. What you are doing is exploring. You are undertaking the first experience, not of the place, but of yourself in that place. It is an experience of our essential loneliness; for nobody can discover the world for anybody else. It is only after we have discovered it for ourselves that it becomes a common ground and a common bond, and we cease to be alone. –WENDELL BERRY, *THE ONE-INCH JOURNEY*[2]

Since each class is dealing with a surplus of internal and external variables, predicting the pace at which a given class will move through the process is difficult. Some classes leap, while others take baby steps. Some classes take two steps forward and one back, while still others take one step forward and two back. This unpredictability makes for an exciting adventure for students and teacher alike.

Although rarely smooth and orderly, the group process *can* move forward. Recognizing the forces that drive groups offers a compass to the teacher for navigating the journey of community building. As in any journey, it may not be possible to know where we will end up, but accept that we will know more about who we are when we have traveled the road together.

Sequencing and Flow

At a conference, Tom Smith, who has been an adventure/experiential educator longer than I've been alive, made the following statement: "We must remember that sequencing is the most important thing we do. Then we must remember that there is no sequence." After shaking my head to make sure I heard him correctly and then reflecting upon that statement for a few years, it has occurred to me that he was making the distinction between sequencing activities for a class and the flow of the activities when they are used by a class.

There is general agreement in the field of adventure education that activities can be sequenced to help facilitate the development of group cohesion. In general, activities are selected to help a group of students progress through four main areas, as shown in figure 2.2 below.

	Group Formation	Group Challenge	Group Support	Group Achievement
Focus	Cooperation, Trust Building	Problem Solving	Challenge (Individual ropes course elements and projects)	Challenge (Outdoor pursuits, Urban experiences, small-group projects)
Tuckman's Phase of Group Development	Forming	Storming/Norming	Norming/Performing	Performing

Figure 2.2: Sequence and Group Development*

A useful approach would be to start out with a sequence of acquaintance activities with a low level of threat, then progress through activities that require more commitment and trust from students. Finally, students will be asked to support – and be supported by – others as they attempt individual challenges.

One must take into consideration a variety of external and internal group influences when choosing an activity. In the classic book, *Islands of Healing*, Schoel, Prouty, and Radcliffe describe a model for choosing the "right" activity for a group at any given time. They call it the GRABBS Modality checklist (see figure 2.3).

Although cumbersome at first, the GRABBS Modality Checklist becomes internalized with practice. After awhile, it is no longer necessary to think consciously about group development or to remind yourself to check for affect of the students. With time, one can learn to scan the group and "GRABB" an activity within seconds. Certainly mistakes will be made (bringing the opportunity to learn from those mistakes), but it is all part of learning through experience.

The *science* of sequencing begins with the knowledge of a hypothetically correct sequence and a list of activities drawn up by the teacher. It is impossible, however, to stick to that list; the needs of the class will affect it. Karl Rohnke and Steve Butler describe sequencing in their book, *Quicksilver*, as:

> ... being *in the right place at the right time*. The same principle applies when leading adventure activities .... If you happen to know the appropriate activity for a given

---

* Adapted from Christian Bisson, unpublished dissertation, 1997 (p. 94). Please see Chapter Three for a detailed description of each level.

situation, you're halfway to a successful experience; the other half is recognizing that it fits the needs of the group and the situation. [3]

The interaction between the planned sequence of activities and the class is the "flow." You might have the perfect sequence mapped out, but if it does not meet the needs of the students, it is useless. This is where knowledge of the stages of group development comes in handy. If the class is sorting through an issue of leadership, for example, you'll need to choose an activity that gives them the opportunity to practice leadership skills. If students are dozing after a heavy lunch, choose an energizer to get the blood pumping. If people are tired of playing "silly" games (a sign that they are ready to move on), jump over the 17 other games that were planned and move into more serious activities. This is the *art* of sequencing.

With experience, the teacher develops a personal instinct about sequencing and the flow of activities. Every adventure educator can share stories about the activities that flopped because each was the wrong activity at the wrong time. Luckily, we can also share the magical moments that came from choosing the right activity at the right time. Karl and Steve remind us that "there are no right and wrong ways to sequence a program. You need to develop your own sequencing instincts." [4] Having the big picture of group development along with the GRABBS Modality checklist in mind, and connecting it to real experience, makes for a powerful combination when trying to meet the needs of your class.

Goals:	How does the activity relate to the group and individual goals that have been set?
Readiness:	This regards levels of instruction (skills) and safety capabilities. Is the group ready to do the activity? Will they endanger themselves and others? Do they have the ability to attempt or complete? What do you have to do to change the event to compensate for lack of readiness?
Affect:	What is the feeling of the group? What kinds of sensations are they having? What is the level of empathy or caring in the group?
Behavior:	How is the group acting? Are they resistive? Disruptive? Agreeable? Are they more self-involved, or group-involved? Are there any interactions that are affecting the group, both positive and negative? How cooperative are they?
Body:	What kind of physical shape are they in? How tired are they? Do they substance abuse? Are they on medication? How do they see their own bodies?
Stage:	Which developmental stage [phase] is the group at? Groups will go through levels of functioning, and a schema to describe these levels will provide you with another means of assessment (e.g., forming, storming/sorting, norming, performing, transforming).

Figure 2.3: GRABBS Modality Checklist[5]

Summary

Community does not just happen; conditions must be right for it to occur. Community is also not magic, although it might seem like it at times. Understanding the nature of group development helps a teacher offer experiences that can help a group of students along in their journey. Sequencing activities to conform with the stages of group development requires both knowledge of a hypothetically correct sequence (the *science* of sequencing) and the willingness to alter that sequence (the *art* of sequencing) in order to meet immediate needs and establish a "flow." The science comes with education, while the art is gained through experience.

[1] Association for Experiential Education International Conference, Lake Tahoe, 1997
[2] Schoel, J. and Stratton, M. (1990). *Gold Nuggets: Readings for Experiential Education.* Hamilton, MA: Project Adventure, Inc. (p. 76)
[3] Rohnke, Karl and Steve Butler. *Quicksilver.* (p. 41)
[4] Rohnke and Butler, (p. 42)
[5] Schoel, et al. *Islands of Healing,* (p. 80)

3 Mapping the Journey

Once outfitted with an understanding of the developmental stages of a group and an awareness of sequencing, it is time to study our map. The community-building sequence on page 27 (figure 3.1) loosely follows the group development cycle discussed earlier by highlighting some of the key issues that group members deal with at each phase of development. If these issues are addressed, students can have their needs met at any given stage of the process.

This chapter contains a detailed description of a community-building sequence which can help teachers choose appropriate activities.

A Community-Building Sequence

Choosing the right activity to meet students' needs is one important teacher skill. Another is to know when to stand back while the students work out a conflict, and when to step in to facilitate a discussion – to reflect and process as a group. The Community-Building Sequence model (figure 3.1) helps provide a structure with which to make decisions about sequencing and processing.

We begin with creating a safe environment within the class. Remember that people are coming with anxiety about what to expect and how they will fit in. Creating a place where people feel included is imperative. Therefore, learning or reinforcing **Cooperation** skills produces an atmosphere where people can work together rather than compete against each other. Put-downs are firmly discouraged, while encouragement is consistently reinforced. Hidden agendas are teased out so that they can be dealt with in the open. Ice Breaker/Acquaintance activities are used to bring students together and help them meet each other.

This is a barrier-breaking time, when people can actually see each other as human beings rather than as objects. A classic example of this is the "us" and "them" mentality of cliques. Often people do not have the opportunity to meet each other as equals because the "in" and "out" lines are so strongly drawn. Students involved in community-building groups report that they were able to meet people they never could meet before. It is common to hear "I learned you can't judge a book by its cover" from students who have participated in a community-building process.

If students feel included, can work together, and encourage rather than humiliate each other, they are ready to deal with **Trust** issues. These include the all-important question: Is it okay to make a mistake? Group members delve into the concepts of risk taking and what it means to be trustworthy. Specific activities to explore trust are chosen and processed.

Cooperation and Trust are the *group formation* parts of the process. They provide the foundation for the next step, **Problem Solving**. This is a time for members to take on some *group challenges* together. They wrestle with how to make decisions, take leadership, and resolve conflicts. This is frequently a time when group goals and individual goals clash. Issues of influence are prevalent during this time, and conflict is evident. There is a switch in focus from participating in activities to taking ownership in solving problems. Communication between people becomes more complex, thus giving rise to concerns about power and control. Processing the experience becomes paramount while engaged in this part of the journey.

After group members have struggled through conflict, solved problems together, and met group goals, there is generally a sense of group cohesion. Norms are established, and students are ready to take some individual challenges *with the support of their group*. There is a true community feel to the group now. It is safe to be together, but it is also safe to strike out on one's own, knowing that these people will be there for support. Whether the **Challenge** is 30 feet up on a high ropes course, standing up in front of a group to give a speech, or planning a service project, the issues are similar. People need to be able to state their needs and ask for help when necessary. They set individual goals and offer mutual support. They experience success and failure. No matter what happens, the community is there to offer support and feedback. To challenge oneself by taking risks is the stuff of growth, and community support is a safety net that allows people to step up to the challenge.

A Community-Building Model

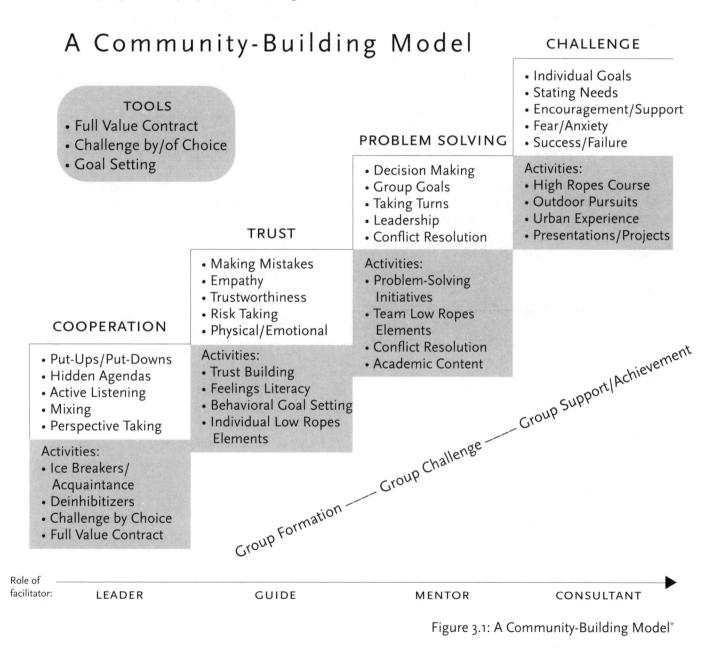

Figure 3.1: A Community-Building Model*

* Group Formation, Group Challenge, Group Support, and Group Achievement are from p. 32 of "A Dissertation of Varying the Sequence of Categories of Adventure Activities on the Development of Group Cohesion," an unpublished dissertation by Christian Bisson, 1997.

☞ Community-Building Tools: Creating a Safe Environment

Throughout the journey, certain tools can be used to help a group come together, and then to take care of group needs along the way. When initiating a community-building process, it is necessary to establish certain ground rules. The ultimate goal is to create an environment where everyone feels physically and emotionally safe. Once a safe atmosphere is achieved, participants are more willing to take risks, such as making mistakes and trying new ideas. The act of risk taking encourages emotional growth and aids in building confidence.

Three main tools are helpful in the community-building process: Full Value Contract, Challenge by Choice, and Goal Setting. (All of these concepts have been developed by Project Adventure; see Appendices for further information).

Full Value Contract

Every class consists of individuals who have arrived at that point in time in a unique way; no two people have the exact same history. A person's frame of reference dictates how she or he views the world. One person may feel that teasing someone about his hair is humorous, while another views it as cruel. A Full Value Contract is a starting point for any group. It affords group members an opportunity to establish ground rules to which everyone can agree. It can be as simple as a verbal "Play hard, play safe, play fair, have fun," a concept originally developed by the New Games Foundation in the 1970's, or as complicated as a written document that everyone signs.

A Full Value Contract should contain an agreement that everyone is committed to the physical and emotional safety of all group members. There should also be a mechanism for discussing problems as they arise. (For example, if a participant throws an object at someone during an activity, or calls someone a name, the members should feel that they have the right to stop the activity to call attention to the breach of safety.) In the beginning, the teacher may need to model this behavior, acting as a safety expert until students are more willing to confront the issues themselves.

Another feature of a Full Value Contract is a willingness to work toward group goals and help others achieve personal goals. In the beginning of a group's life, when the safety parameters are still being set, some students may feel it is necessary to sabotage the group process in order to meet some personal needs. This is known as a hidden agenda. If, as part of the Full Value Contract, participants agree to work toward group goals, they can be asked to bring hidden agendas out into the open. Many times, a group can help satisfy an individual's agenda while meeting group goals. If the individual's agenda runs counter to the group goals, he or she can be asked either to delay the individual need or to choose to participate in another way. This is known as Challenge by Choice.

Challenge by Choice

The Full Value Contract addresses the group needs; Challenge by Choice meets individual needs. In order to feel safe in a community, a person must have control over what she or he will and will not do. At some times it is appropriate to say no, even in the face of acute peer pressure. This is especially necessary when participants are asked to take risks.

The concept of Challenge by Choice allows each person to be in control of her or his level of participation. This means that a person may *choose* how much personal information to share with the group. It means that someone may choose to be totally involved – physically and emotionally – in an activity, or may choose to sit back and watch. It does **not** mean that someone may sit and read the newspaper while the group goes about its business. No matter what level of participation an individual chooses, he or she is still part of the group, even if it means being an observer.

Challenge by Choice in action may look like this: During a jump rope activity called Turnstile, a participant says he does not want to jump. At first, the students give him some encouragement, and the teacher asks, "Is there anything we can do to help you to jump?" When he says, "No, I just don't want to jump," he is offered the rope to act as a rope turner.

In group situations, rarely is everyone asked to do the same thing – there are many roles to take. When planning a project, for example, someone might need to make phone contacts, while someone else chooses marketing. Still others create artwork, work on logistics, or do the note taking. If we practice the art of Challenge by Choice in the beginning stages of community building, group members will benefit later when asked to engage in real-life projects.

Challenge by Choice is sometimes difficult to conceptualize in a school setting where students are required to get their work done, be present, and complete a given curriculum. It is helpful to remember that Challenge by Choice is not an "on/off switch," that allows students to make either/or decisions about participating. Rather, students are given choices *within* the school structure. Challenge by Choice, then, does not ask, "Will you do this?" Instead it asks, "*How* will you do this?" In keeping with the idea of multiple intelligences, students can make choices about how a certain concept will be learned – helping to decide how to best meet their own learning styles. Again, during community-building activities, Challenge by Choice can range from observing to total involvement. We must remember that there are many ways to be engaged in an activity or lesson.

Depending upon the age and maturity level of the students, they need varying degrees of guidance when considering choices, especially if they have very little experience in making informed choices. A common concern for teachers is a scenario in which a student chooses (read: *refuses*) to participate at all, and a whole group of other students follow that lead. This is a perfect moment to teach about choices and how individual choices affect others. If necessary, you can stop the action for a discussion about choices – what causes people to make the choices they do, internal and external factors and pressures, how individual and group goals sometimes clash, and what can be done to support people's choices while continuing the group process.

As we struggle with the notion of Challenge by Choice in a school setting, other issues arise. As teachers, we must ask ourselves, "Are students *really* being given a choice?" In our zeal to make sure everyone is included, do we push and prod students into positions where they virtually have no choice? Carla Hacker, an elementary school teacher and adventure educator, believes that when students are unable, for physical or emotional reasons, to participate in an activity as it is presented, they should be consulted about *how* they want to participate. She has labeled this concept "inclusion by choice." If, for example, the class is involved in a running activity, and a student is on crutches, just handing him a "busy" chore (like cheering everyone on) can be at best pointless, and at worst demeaning. *Ask* students how they want to be included, *respect* their choices, and they will be empowered to make real choices later on. Being included at all costs is not always the best choice.

Another factor to consider is the need to modify and adapt activities to meet differing levels of physical and cognitive abilities. At the beginning of a group's journey, the teacher's role is to consider the needs of the class, then to choose appropriate activities and modify them accordingly. As the class becomes more cohesive and accepting, that responsibility can be shared among all community members as issues of inclusivity arise.

Goal Setting
Another tool at the disposal of a community-building group is the art of goal setting. One of the most difficult, never-ending tasks a group must undertake is reconciling individual versus group goals. A Full Value Contract and Challenge by Choice can help in dealing with these issues, but students must practice

the conscious act of goal setting in order to create a direction for the class as well as for themselves. Goal setting offers students the opportunity to define who they are and where they are headed.

Group goals can be the most difficult, as everyone may have a different idea about what the group should and could be doing. One strategy is to help students first practice with small goals. For example, when working on a timed initiative (such as Don't Touch Me, in which students switch places with partners while being timed), ask participants to agree on a goal for that particular activity. The goal might be to meet a set time or to reach a faster time. The goal might be to find as many different ways to do the switching as they can, or it could be to forget about the time and just have some fun.

Once a class has established a way to make decisions about small goals, it graduates to larger goals – such as, "What do you want to accomplish in this activity?" Finally, students can be encouraged to set goals for larger class projects or school functions. Ideally, they will set goals that have real impact on their lives in their class and at school.

Individual goals can be behavioral or task-oriented. Each individual can choose a specific behavioral goal that he or she wishes to work toward. One person may wish to speak up more in class; another might want to be less overbearing or "bossy." The key is for each person to really *want* to work on the goal in order to effect positive personal change. Once a goal is made public, students can support each other in achieving their goals.

A task-oriented goal helps an individual work toward getting a job done. During the Turnstile activity mentioned earlier, someone may state, "I want to jump through three times without stopping the rope." As simple a goal as that may seem, it is an important practice for later, more complex, tasks. During a class project, for example, once a group goal has been established and tasks have been divided among students, an individual may set a timetable for getting his or her part done.

Summary

This community-building process includes a sequence that loosely follows the life cycle of a group. The steps include Cooperation, Trust, Problem Solving, and Challenge. Every step builds on the next to address issues and needs of the students. The teacher's role changes as the students form a more cohesive group and become more adept at handling issues that arise.

Communities cannot form in a vacuum, so it is important to have a variety of tools that help create a safe environment. These are used throughout the community-building process to cultivate a safe and respectful work environment. A Full Value Contract is used to help establish norms for the community. While this contract takes care of group needs, Challenge by Choice allows individuals to have control over *how* they will participate in activities. Goal setting helps to set the stage, then provides a structure within which to deal with conflicts and decision making. Later, students use goal setting to create action plans that incorporate both behavioral and academic goals.

4 Cooperation

Put-Ups/Put-Downs • Hidden Agendas • Active Listening • Mixing • Perspective Taking

ACTIVITIES

Ice Breakers/Acquaintance
Deinhibitizers
Challenge by Choice
Full Value Contract

Setting the Stage

Take yourself back to a time when you were about to join a group. Maybe it was a sports team, a workshop, a party, a committee, or even a community meeting called to deal with a conflict or problem in the neighborhood. Chances are that you tried to find a friend to accompany you so you wouldn't feel so out of place. Dredge up those feelings of anxiety. To one degree or another, they were no doubt there.

These feelings surrounding inclusion always exist in newly forming (or reforming) groups. There are ways to help people ease into this awkward situation, whether the group's life span is one hour or 20 years. Obviously, the longer a group is together, the deeper its level of community building. However, even a short-lived group can make people feel included just by allowing them all to introduce themselves.

In a classroom situation, where students stay together for a whole semester or a year, this process can go much further. Students arrive anxious and excited. They are dependent upon the teacher for leadership, and they have hopes and expectations for the class. This is a good time to begin setting the stage by informing the class about the journey they will be embarking on together. The classroom is a safe place where everyone is valued and everyone is included. Share your vision by showing them the map for the journey; it's no secret.

Move into a short, initial Full Value Contract by asking group members what they can do to make this a safe place, both physically and emotionally. At first, this will be rather superficial, but it is used only as a starting point. Later in the process, the students will develop a more comprehensive Full Value Contract. Make sure that your agenda is incorporated into the contract and that issues around name calling and put-downs are included.

Mention Challenge by Choice to the students. Let them know they have a choice about the level to which they participate. Tell them this level runs a continuum from simply watching a given activity all the way to being 100 percent involved – physically, emotionally, cognitively, spiritually .... It is not an "on/off switch" that allows people to leave the class to read a book, talk with friends, or do other work. They are still members of the class and can offer insights just from watching the class in action. Some teachers even provide a list for observers who are choosing to watch an activity so that they can help monitor a class's progress.

At first, you as the teacher will be the main safety expert. As you do activities, watch for instances of physical or emotional tension between group members. Stop the activity to discuss safety issues that arise, if necessary. Do not ignore these issues. They will not go away, and by ignoring them you are sending a powerful signal to the group that safety is unimportant. This discussion need not be a diatribe on safety. It may only take a moment to point out that what just happened was an example of a put-down, which is an emotional safety issue. Reminders such as these help students identify what is acceptable and what is not when engaged in conscious community building. As time goes by, students will begin to identify put-downs without any prompting.

Following are some issues that can arise during the beginning stages of the life of a group. They must be addressed if students are to feel safe and included. These issues can be either formally introduced or simply acknowledged; it all depends on the age, maturity level, and experience of the individuals in the group. A group of at-risk second graders will need to focus on these issues; they might even need to learn them as skills to practice. A group of high-school seniors, on the other hand, may need only the opportunity to introduce themselves through a few Icebreaker activities before they are ready to move on.

Have fun! Although this community-building process sounds like a serious undertaking, it is not as heavy as it seems. There are times to be serious and times to be silly. Life frequently involves this type of balancing act. Create a structure to ensure that safety is taken seriously, and then go out and have some fun. Meeting people should be enjoyable. Give students time to chat, tell stories, and laugh. The Ice Breaker and Deinhibitizer activities are designed for people to do just that.

Cooperation Issues and Skills

Put-Ups Instead of Put-Downs

Teasing is a form of passive violence – passive violence is the root of physical violence. —Gandhi*

People love to tease each other. Watch siblings or good friends poke fun at each other's appearance or behavior. Sometimes, one's most embarrassing moments are brought up for public view by a close friend or partner. Sarcastic humor is a common form of teasing between friends. Sarcasm, though, can destroy group cohesion. Even if two people who know each other well use it as a form of affection, others may not appreciate this type of humor. They may be unwilling to risk getting to know people who use sarcastic humor for fear of being put down. The result can be a group that cannot progress past the forming stage.

The issue of put-ups and put-downs is probably the most basic for any group to grapple with. A put-down can be a sign of affection between close friends, or it can be a weapon to wield judgment and evoke pain. Since how teasing is interpreted is situational, it is vital to address it when coming together as a community. Sometimes it is necessary to determine what a put-down or a put-up even is. At other times agreeing that students will refrain from using sarcasm to cause pain is enough.

Imagine that a student uses a derogatory term for a homosexual or uses a racial slur. Maybe one student flashes a nonverbal sign to another student that starts a war of words. What do you do? How you, as the teacher, handle these situations speaks volumes to your students. If a community is to develop, it is vital that these episodes are dealt with. Ignoring put-downs implies that they are okay. A variety of interventions are available; the choices you make depend on the situation that unfolds. Here are a few suggestions:

- Engage in a series of activities and discussions to help students appreciate diversity. Allow students to learn about their own commonalities and differences. Then branch out into the world at large. If students can appreciate people as human beings, rather than as labels, it is a step in the direction of preventing future bouts of name calling.

---

*Thanks to Dan Creely, adventure educator at Northeastern Illinois University, for this contribution. Dan also highlights the idea of put-ups and put-downs in this way: "This could be the most critical part of the program. If people know they will not be made fun of, they will try!"

- Stop everything and talk. This can be a short session to check out what's going on, or it can turn into a longer philosophical discussion about how name calling can be hurtful. Even young children can participate in this kind of talk. No matter how long the discussion, it sends the message that this is a serious matter.

- If it is a minor incident and the class is engaged in another activity, make a note on the board as a reminder to talk about it at a later time – either privately with the parties involved or with the class as a whole.

- Create a "Peace Place"* where students can go to de-escalate their anger and talk about the incident – perhaps with a peer or with you as a mediator.[1]

- If it is a major incident, address it in a class meeting when people are not in the heat of the moment. Make sure there is time to discuss what happened and how the situation might be rectified. Talk about how to prevent incidents such as these in the future.

As a teacher, you need to be alert for put-ups and put-downs. It may not be possible to know how students will deal with this issue until they have had some experience together. After an activity or two, you will know whether you need to bring it up for discussion, or whether it will take care of itself.

Hidden Agendas

Hidden agendas frequently surface as sabotage of the group process. They can manifest themselves as acting out behaviors or an unwillingness to participate. You might see students purposefully putting others down, sitting out, or refusing to "play by the rules." A classic school example has to do with the faculty

An organization called PlayBoard has an initiative called Games Not Names. Based in Northern Ireland, this group offers "Do's and do not's of dealing with sectarianism." *Sectarianism* is defined as the act of being devoted to a sect, "especially a narrow-minded or strongly prejudiced member of a sect." (*The World Book Dictionary*, 1970). Their advice is helpful when dealing with any kind of put-down:

DO: Think in advance about strategies that could be used to cope with sectarian behavior.

DO: Probe the children's understanding of what they have said/done.

DO: Promote equality in all aspects of the play scheme.

DO: Provide a supportive atmosphere where children are encouraged to ask questions and discuss their feelings.

DO: Act as a mediator, helping the children to clarify their feelings, fears, and concerns.

DO: Promote the understanding that all people have the right to have their opinions respected, and help the children to empathize with others: "How would you feel if ...?"

DO: Use games promoting good feelings, cooperation, and communication.

DO: Help to develop nonviolent conflict resolution skills.

DO NOT: Give children inconsistent messages – always deal with sectarian behavior.

DO NOT: Stop sectarian behavior without explaining why it is unacceptable. Further exploration of the incident may also be necessary.

DO NOT: Forget that children are influenced by the behavior which is accepted in the play scheme.

DO NOT: Be afraid to let children discuss issues among themselves – they learn a lot from each other and from the process itself.

DO NOT: Allow any discriminatory practice, language, or behavior to go unchallenged. This should cover race, culture, disability, and color as well as religion (and sexual orientation).

and administration. Many staff meetings look something like this: An administrator stands in the front of the room talking about her or his agenda, while many teachers sit in the back of the room with their arms crossed. Later, in the parking lot, those same teachers complain about the meeting and the administrator.

---

* See *Adventures in Peacemaking*, by Kreidler and Furlong, p. 8.

These acts of resistance are usually symptoms of underlying needs, such as power, belonging, or freedom. The need for power may look like attention-seeking behavior or refusal to participate. If someone feels excluded because s/he did not get a turn (belonging/power), s/he may be seen sulking or trying to ruin the game for others. And if participants perceive that they are being forced to do something against their will, they may exercise their freedom to "check out" from the group.

People hide their agendas because they feel they cannot get their needs met any other way. They may have little experience with getting needs met, so they believe it is important to get them met covertly. It is important to remember that they are doing this for a reason – not to be mean, naughty, or cruel. Hidden agendas can be teased out if it is safe to do so, meaning that students will not run the danger of later being mocked, punished, or rejected.

Given that this is learned behavior that has been incorporated into each person's perception of him/herself, it will take time to change. The first step is in bringing it out into the open. For example, if, during an activity, a student is rejected or excluded in some way, she might pull out of the group, exercising her right to Challenge by Choice. Bringing the agenda out into the open can be a delicate matter. If the student is hurt and unwilling to discuss it, you, as the teacher, can broach the subject with the class by saying something like, "If that had happened to me, I would feel hurt." Later, the excluded student may be willing to discuss it.

Even being forced to participate in a community-building process can be cause for a hidden agenda. Think about it: If students feel forced to play "silly games," it is likely that they will play by different rules or in some other way upset the process. Students are rarely given an opportunity to have a say in their own education. If they have not chosen to be in your class, sit down with them to discuss the community-building process. Fill them in on the underlying rationale and share the sequence. Ask for input about how they might put the process into action.

The beauty of experiential activities is that they offer opportunities to deal with real situations in a low-threat environment. Rather than sitting around abstractly talking about a situation that *might* occur, activities provide situations that actually *do* occur. For example, during an activity called Neighbors, in which students must find a new spot according to questions asked by a person in the middle of the circle, many students "pretend" that they do not see the empty spaces. Although it may appear that these students are sabotaging the game, thus making it boring for those rushing to the empty spots (and then waiting), the reality is that they wish to have a turn in the middle. Since they are used to sneaking around to get what they want (their individual needs/goals), their hidden agendas cause a group goal (having fun) to fall by the wayside.

By using this "teachable moment" as a topic of discussion to compare the feelings and thoughts of all parties, the hidden agenda can be exposed. The students can then brainstorm ways to create a win-win situation in which all people can have their needs met, thus making the game fun and allowing all to have a chance in the middle. This is a simple yet important lesson about stating needs, as well as an exercise in conflict resolution.

Set a group goal, such as going to a high ropes course when the group is ready or working together on a community service project. The important part about planning is that the students are partners in the planning. It is not that they go to the ropes course if they are "good" enough; it is brainstorming options and having the students create a shared vision. This may take some time, but it is part of "walking the talk." "Facilitating" a community-building sequence as a dictator defeats the whole purpose.

Active Listening

Listening is a basic skill that allows people in a community to share ideas and insights. Without the sharing of ideas, the community cannot operate. Without the sharing of insights, it is impossible for students to learn from each other. Active listening is a skill that can be taught and practiced at this early stage of group work. It involves people looking at the speaker and sending cues showing a speaker that he or she is being heard.

I have witnessed both children and adults sending out a message to the rest of their group, and it appears that everyone is wearing earplugs. There is no acknowledgment that the speaker even exists, much less has said anything. As a teacher, you can model active listening by looking at the speaker, nodding or making sounds that show you are hearing their message. Follow up with questions or a summary of what the person has said, and thank the speaker for sharing her or his thoughts.

Modeling is one way to show that active listening is important. However, some groups may need to learn active listening skills before being asked to use them. Many activities and subsequent processing sessions can be used to teach active listening.

Active listening is a useful life skill that can be taught, but must be practiced as well. Here are three strategies to help students learn to use this skill:

Modeling: You must use the skill in your class.

Direct Instruction: Teach the skill through the use of activities such as One-to-One Interview. Go through the steps:

  a) Look at the person who is speaking, think about what the speaker is saying,

  b) show you are listening by nodding your head,

  c) ask questions if you don't understand, and

  d) repeat/summarize what the speaker has said.

Practice: Encourage your students to use the skill whenever possible. Offer immediate feedback to students about their active listening skills.

Mixing

Put a bunch of people in a room together, and they will gravitate to groups where they feel most comfortable. They might hang out with people from their neighborhood or people of the same gender, color, age, or clique. But in a community where everyone is working toward common goals, it is important to be able to work with anybody from the community. It is not necessary to be best friends – just be able to work with anyone else in the class on any given task. In the professional world, this is called collegiality.

With some classes, this is no issue whatsoever. In other classes, it is the major focus of the Cooperation step of the community-building process. Sometimes one person is ostracized by everyone else. This person may be a special education student or have a history of being scapegoated. You can choose activities to focus on mixing and discuss what it feels like to be left out of an activity when everyone else is involved. Again, these issues are often delicate, especially if one person is being left out. Many times, however, the larger concepts of inclusion and mixing can be explored without putting anyone on the spot.

Exclusion can be a severe and vengeful form of put-down. Since most people wish to be part of the group and activities, being left out can be most painful. This scapegoating scenario can be dealt with by using approaches that are used with put-downs. These situations often become traditions, occurring over many years when the same person (or family) is treated as an outcast. Breaking the tradition can be difficult because the culture must change. A healthy community accepts all who wish to be a part, so it is imperative that any scapegoating be addressed promptly. Create and practice the norm of including everyone in the community.

Perspective Taking

Alfie Kohn discusses the importance of perspective taking in the community-building process:

> *A community rests on the knowledge of, and connections among, the individuals who are part of it. This knowledge, in turn, is deepened by helping students imagine how things ap-*

pear from other people's points of view. What psychologists call "perspective taking" plays a critical role in helping children become generous, caring people ... and activities designed to promote an understanding of how others think and feel ... have the added advantage of creating the basis for community.[2]

Perspective taking is the precursor of empathy. If individuals can share their perspectives and hear others' perspectives, they are gaining the foundation to be able to actually imagine what it is like to walk in another person's shoes. This can be accomplished by offering activities that require group members to share about themselves – their families, feelings, cultures, opinions, and values. Perspective taking results in individuals who can then be respected for who they are and an atmosphere where differing views are accepted.

Perspective taking can also offer a chance to enrich social studies. Ask everyone in the class to bring in a special custom or story from their own family. Allow time for each person to present the custom or story to the class. Have students work in groups to brainstorm how these customs might have originated. Do some research, if possible. Compare the different cultures and perspectives represented by your class. (Dan Creely calls this Cultural Circle)

Cooperation Activities

Role of the Teacher

When a class is just beginning, the teacher takes an active leadership role. There is usually a fair amount of confusion, along with anxiety, as students try to make sense of their environment. The teacher sets the tone, and people welcome the leadership. Anyone walking by the classroom would see the teacher directing the activities. The students would be focused on the rules of each activity, asking many questions to make sure they understand what they are "supposed to do." At this point, the teacher is seen as the expert.

The activities in this chapter are designed to give students a chance to learn names, share about themselves, and learn about others. These Ice Breaker/Acquaintance activities and Deinhibitizers are light and do not require people to take large risks. People have opportunities to laugh and play.

Processing, described in Chapter Eight, is kept short and focused. Unless there is a safety issue, many activities can be strung together before a formal processing session occurs. Questions at this stage center around hopes and expectations, safety, and how students think the class, as a whole, is doing with the issues.

Play with Purpose: Depending on the goal, an activity can be used for myriad purposes. Sometimes it is enough to play and see where it goes. Many times, however, an activity can be used as a connection or springboard for academic concepts, life skills development, or reinforcement of skills/issues the class has been working on. With this in mind, the activities in this book contain an "Extensions" section with suggestions for how each activity can be used for a particular purpose.

A word of caution/disclaimer: Be prepared for students to think, do, and say things that are different than you expect. Just because you have decided on the purpose of an activity does not mean the students will react the way you want them to. As a matter of fact, they generally don't. Be open and go with it. Be careful about leading them where you want to go, rather than moving forward from where they are. It may be necessary to set your prepared reflection questions aside so they can process what is actually happening rather than what you hoped would happen. Learning will occur if you stay "in the moment" and see where you travel together.

An illustration of this phenomenon occurred with a group of 5th-graders. We were focusing on the idea of perspective taking by doing an activity in which small groups each got a sheet of questions to answer about themselves. The directions were to add up points based on queries like, "A point for each brother and sister you have." I frontloaded the activity by asking them what they knew about each other and talking about how people have similarities and differences. The stage was set, of course, for a huge competition. This was not my intent, but it sure happened.

I had a decision to make – do I push my agenda and ask my questions about perspective taking, or do we process the put-downs, tears, and hurt feelings engendered by the competition? This was an easy decision, and realistically, I had no choice because they were already talking about it. People shared what they were feeling about the activity and why they thought it had occurred. We talked about competition in general and how it affects their lives. Some shared that they loved competition, while others admitted that they didn't like it at all, and it was even scary to them at times. One student noticed that the directions were to add up points and that everyone would have had lots more points had they cooperated and added them up for the whole class rather than competing and hoarding their own points. Finally, we brainstormed ways to collaborate rather than compete in class. In the end, we ended up having a powerful lesson in perspective taking about competition.

Ice Breakers/Acquaintance Activities

These activities give students an opportunity to meet each other and loosen up a bit. They are low-threat activities that do not require people to take large risks. They should be light, allowing for some introductory self-disclosure; processing is kept to a minimum.

Life skills and character education have received much attention as a way to deliberately concentrate on skills and qualities that help people succeed in life. These include: cooperation, courage, integrity, organization, effort, empathy, problem solving, and patience, to name a few. The use of activity is a powerful way to open the doors to discussion around life skills. These discussions can be followed with literature, journaling, projects, surveys, and other tools to help students reflect and connect the concept with action, thus integrating and incorporating the quality into their lives.

Some excellent resources for life skills and character development are *Tools for Citizenship and Life* by Sue Pearson, and the companion book for parents, *Character Begins at Home*. These books grew out of the Kovalik ITI model. They define a total of 18 life skills and five lifelong guidelines, presenting specific descriptions and ideas for teachers and parents to use with children. They also offer ideas of children's literature that highlight each of the life skills.

For older students, Barbara Lewis helps young people examine their character traits through the use of stories, surveys, and ideas in *What Do You Stand For?*

 I. Memory Circle

Focus: Learning names
Materials: Many soft throwable objects such as fleece balls, wadded-up pieces of paper, Nerf™ balls
Level: Grades K and higher

SUGGESTED PROCEDURE
1. Clear the desks or tables away and have students stand in a circle. Tell them that this is an activity designed to help people learn names.

2. Provide an object to pass around the group. Each person who receives the object says her or his name and gives some personal information – such as number of siblings, something that has happened this week, or something else that group members don't know.

3. When the object returns to you, go over throwing etiquette: Make sure that the receiver knows the object is coming! This can be accomplished by calling the receiver's name and making eye contact before throwing the item. Model this by calling a group member's name and tossing the item to her or him.

4. The person who receives the ball then continues by calling someone else's name and throwing the item to him, and so on. Anyone can receive the object more than once.

5. After this has gone on for a while, start throwing an additional object, then another, and another. Pretty soon all the items are being thrown, and the energy and laughter levels have risen exponentially.

6. Continue for a while. Then stop the action and see if there is anyone who would like to name everyone in the group.

Sample Processing Questions for Memory Circle
- Why might it be important to make an effort to learn the names of people in the class?
- What does it mean to include others? Why might it be important to be inclusive?
- How might we make an effort to include everybody in the class?
- How can each of us make an effort to learn names of others outside of this class?
- How did we keep each other safe (or not), even when it got chaotic?
- How can we be aware of other ways to stay safe in class?

Connections for Memory Circle
Life Skill Links: caring, communication, cooperation, curiosity, friendship, organization, relationships, safety
Academic Applications: • Use characters from a book the class is reading or the vocabulary words from social studies. • Use the sounds of the alphabet or musical notes. • Assign each person a part of a cell as their "name." • Give each student a sight word to put on their shirts so people must read it before throwing the item.
Variations/Modifications: • *For younger students:* Use fewer items and items that are easier to catch, like stuffed animals. Start with one and see how it goes. Stop the action, then ask the students if they would like to try two items. Ask for strategies to make it work so that people can stay safe. If that goes well, try three items, etc. • *For older students:* After they have gotten the idea with soft items, go outside and bring out a raw egg or water balloon. Tell them that the egg or water balloon represents a first impression – how can they treat the first impression so that it remains intact?
Extensions: • Once in a while, stop the class and see if someone would like to try to name everyone.

Facilitation Notes
The element of surprise is effective here. After students get lulled into a sense of ease by having only one item going around, then begin introducing the additional items with increasing frequency. Chaos is bound to reign, which is why the objects must be soft. Wadded-up pieces of paper are not only cost effective, but they work well in a room full of equipment. Intersperse the paper with a few fun toys (such as rubber chickens) to add another element of fun. **CAUTION: Tennis balls and other objects with hard surfaces can be hazardous. Do not use them.**
If the students already know each other, try this same activity by having them call out a word or phrase that tells something else about themselves, like a favorite story or movie character.

Adaptations for Students with Disabilities[1]: Memory Circle

Cognitive Disabilities	• Adjective Memory Circle may be beneficial to help with memory problems – using an adjective with each name (such as, "Little Laurie"), and a motion (e.g., squatting down to show "little") instead of throwing an object.

Orthopedic Impairment	• Individuals with orthopedic difficulties may have trouble throwing and catching the balls. • Use the variation of adjective memory circle, but without the movements. • Roll the ball or bounce it. • Use a beach ball.
Hearing Impairment	• Have an interpreter available if necessary. • The person throwing the ball needs to gain eye contact with these individuals before throwing the ball.
Visual Impairment	• This is a difficult activity for individuals with a visual impairment. • Students could have "catching partners." Each partner could catch the ball and hand it to the visual impaired student. • Use the Adjective Memory Circle as an option. • There are balls available that beep to facilitate object location.

MPS*

2 Name Tag

Focus: Hearing and sharing names
Materials: Stopwatch
Level: Grades K and higher

Suggested Procedure

1. Have students stand or sit in a circle so that everyone can see everyone else. Tell them this community-building process begins with easy, nonthreatening activities and is designed to get increasingly difficult. With that in mind, everyone must remember their own first name.
2. Tell the person to your right (or left) that you will say your name, then he will say his, the person next to him will say hers, and so on, until everyone has said his or her name in order. This will be timed. Try it, then announce the time.
3. Do it again, moving in the same direction. Announce the time. Then do the activity in the other direction a couple of times.
4. Now tell the group that, as promised, the task will get more difficult. It will now go both directions. When you say your name, the people on each side of you say their names, then on down each half of the circle. It will cross in the middle somewhere and everyone will see which side finishes first.
5. Try this dual method a few times, each time holding up your hand for the side that finishes first.

Sample Processing Questions for Name Tag

• Who won? Why?
• Was this a competitive activity?
• Was it possible to learn names this way? Why or why not?
• Were you rooting for one side to make it back first? Why or why not?
• How did the people caught in the middle feel? Were your classmates supportive of your difficult situation?

---

* Thanks to Dave Braby and the Milwaukee Public Schools for use of their *Accessible Curriculum Supplement* for their adventure program. They have provided the adaptations for many of the activities, which are noted with an "MPS" below the adaptation. Kathy Hellenbrand, a Physical Education Teacher with adaptive P. E. expertise, helped me adapt the rest of the activities.

Connections for Name Tag

Life Skill Links: communication, cooperation, effort, empathy, patience, perseverance

Academic Applications: • *For young children:* Use as a way to hear the order of numbers, vowels, or the whole alphabet. Assign a letter or number to each student, then time it as they each say their numbers in order. It's also a great way to practice counting backwards, or skip counting.

Variations/Modifications: • *For younger students:* Have an item to pass. When the students receive the items, they say their names. • *For older students:* Instead of saying their own names, the students must say the names of the persons on their left, their own names, then the persons on their right.

Facilitation Notes

This is an activity that does not necessarily need to be processed. It is enough to hear the names and enjoy the activity. At times, however, the people caught in the middle are the objects of some teasing if they have trouble with passing the names along. This can be a teachable moment to address putting others down versus supporting each other. For added challenge and fun, try having people say their names backwards (i.e., "Carol" would be "lorac," "Jim" would me "mij" and "Bob" would be "bob").

Adaptations for Students with Disabilities: Name Tag

Cognitive Disabilities	• Try this first as an untimed activity.
Orthopedic Impairment	No major modifications necessary.
Hearing Impairment	• Include a motion to go with each name. Students can either say their name and do their motion together, or they can just do the motion. • Use sign-language names for everyone to include when they speak their names.
Visual Impairment	No major modifications necessary.

3. Paired Activities

Focus: Learning about others, mixing with others in the group
Materials: None
Level: Grades K and higher

Suggested Procedure

1. Clear the desks or tables away and have students stand in a circle. Ask people to find partners. (Have them do this quickly; they will switch partners later.)
2. Have the partners look at each other and, according to an attribute (e.g., whoever has shorter hair, more jewelry on, the most blue on ...), separate themselves. The person with the shorter hair stands on the inside of the circle, facing the longer-haired partner. There are now two circles – one inside the other – with the inside circle facing the outer one.
3. Give the pairs an activity to do. (See Activities A through G listed on the following pages.)
4. After the activity, have partners discuss something about themselves. Possible discussion topics are: your family, your favorite place in the world, your favorite food, a hope or goal in your life, something you hope to learn someday, how you got your name (if you know), etc.
5. After the activity and discussion, have *one* of the circles rotate to the right or left by one or two people. Each person will then have a new partner, and a new activity and discussion topic can be done.

Activity A Last Detail

Everyone looks at his or her partner. On a signal, everyone turns around and changes three things about their clothing (e.g., turning collars, switching shoes, taking out earrings, untucking shirts). When each pair is ready, they turn around and try to guess the three things that were switched by their partner.

Connections for Last Detail

Academic Applications: • Do this with paper puzzles for body parts, parts of a cell, the periodic table, formulas, words, or anything that has parts of a whole. Give each pair a complete model and have them move three parts around. Their partners are to guess which parts were moved.

Variations/Modifications: Do this as a whole class when you have a few spare minutes. Over time, give each person an opportunity to be the one to leave the room and change some things for all to guess.

Adaptations for Students with Disabilities: Last Detail

Cognitive Disabilities	• Have students change fewer than three things. • Do this as a large group activity, with one person changing things and everyone guessing.
Orthopedic Impairment	• Some students may need assistance.
Hearing Impairment	No major modifications necessary.
Visual Impairment	• This may not be an appropriate activity for the visually impaired.

Pairing Strategies: Depending on the age and maturity level of your class, you can use a variety of techniques to select pairs for a given activity. Here are a few suggestions:

• Ask everyone to find a partner.

• Tell the students to find someone who has the same/different size thumb (or eye color). (Thanks to Pete Albert.)

• Tell students to find someone who was born in a different season or month.

• Have people think about their birthday and whether they were born on an odd or even day. Find a partner whose birthday is also even or odd.

• Have students add the days of the month of their birthdays together. If it's odd/even, then they are partners.

• Ask people to self-identify as a spoon or a fork. The spoons hold their hands clasped over their heads, while the forks hold their hands up over their heads pointed toward the ceiling or sky. When you say "spork," they find someone to partner with who is the opposite utensil. (Thanks to Mark Roark.)

• Have the group do a lineup. Fold the line in half; the person everyone faces is his/her partner.

• Keep a can of tongue depressors with the name of every student on a depressor. Choose two depressors at a time; they are partners.

• Keep a deck of cards with pairs that number the size of your class. Each person gets one card; students match up their cards with partners.

• Use index cards for this one. Cut each card in half creatively – so that only those two halves match. Each person gets one and finds the matching half.

• Have different well-known songs written on scraps of paper. Make sure there are two of each song. Throw the papers into a hat. Everyone picks one and hums that tune until they find their humming partner.

Sometimes it is important to split up friends, while at other times it may be nice to allow people who know each other well to work together. It is probably beneficial to mix it up so that students can have an opportunity to experience a variety of scenarios.

Activity B ✋ Tie Your Shoe

Each pair should have at least one person with tied shoes or the ability to borrow a laced shoe from someone else. The shoe(s) are untied, and the task is to re-tie the shoe(s). The problem is that each person in the pair can use only one hand!

Adaptations for Students with Disabilities: Tie Your Shoe

Cognitive Disabilities	• Do this activity only if students know how to tie their shoes already. • Instead of tying shoes, students can take shoes off and put them back on together, using only one hand each. • Have students put on a sock instead of a shoe.
Orthopedic Impairment	• Activity may not be appropriate if students have little fine-motor coordination. • Put shoes on tray and allow the use of three out of four hands to tie the shoe.
Hearing Impairment	No major modifications necessary.
Visual Impairment	No major modifications necessary.

Activity C ✋ Me Switch

Teach the students three different motions. It doesn't really matter what they are, but here are some examples: Both hands above eyes, both arms crossed over the chest, or one hand touching the other elbow in an "L" shape. Then have each pair designate a person who is "the counter." This person counts to three, at which point both people simultaneously go into one of the motions. "The counter" wants the other person to do the same motion. If the partner does, she or he is now "the counter," and does the counting. If the partner doesn't do the same motion, the original partner remains as "the counter" and counts again.

Adaptations for Students with Disabilities: Me Switch

Cognitive Disabilities	• Use two motions instead of three.
Orthopedic Impairment	• Create motions that all the people in a group can do.
Hearing Impairment	No major modifications necessary.
Visual Impairment	• Use sounds or tactile motions (e.g., clap, snap, stomp).

Activity D ✋ Macro Rock/Paper/Scissors

(Thanks to Dick Jensen and others at Toki Middle School.)

Make sure everyone knows the rules to Rock/Paper/Scissors (Rock = a closed fist; Paper = open hand; and Scissors = fingers in a V, like a peace sign). On a signal, the partners do one of the three motions to see who wins. The winning combinations are: Rock beats scissors, because it crushes the scissors; Scissors beats paper, because it cuts the paper; Paper beats rock, because it covers the rock. It is also possible to tie. For the macro version, substitute these motions: Rock = crouching down with hands over head; Paper = standing with arms at sides; Scissors = standing with arms over head in a V. Have partners stand back-to-back. Each person must take a step forward to avoid hitting the other. They count to three while jumping up and down, spinning around and going into one of the motions. The same winning combinations apply.

Connections for Macro Rock/Paper/Scissors

Academic Applications: Using the variation below, give students a theme from which to choose what to do together. For example, it has to relate to a book the class is reading, to giving and answering math equations, or to acting out certain people that are being studied in history.

Variations/Modifications: Winners get to choose one thing for the pair to do together. They can do 10 jumping jacks, hop on one foot, sing a song, recite a poem, do a high five, etc. If using this variation, emphasize a few things: a) Whatever the partner who wins chooses to do, their partner must agree to do it — otherwise something else must be chosen; b) Keep it safe; c) They must remain in the room.

Adaptations for Students with Disabilities: Macro Rock/Paper/Scissors

Cognitive Disabilities	• Create two motions instead of three. For each round, call out which one "wins" so that it is a surprise (e.g., Monsters and Ghosts).
Orthopedic Impairment	• Do regular rock/paper/scissors, or make up three motions that all can do. Agree as a group which motions win over the others.
Hearing Impairment	• Stand front to front instead of back to back.
Visual Impairment	• Stand front to front instead of back to back. • Say the name of the motion they choose aloud.

Activity E High Fives

Have partners create three new high fives. Tell people to be creative and that it's okay to borrow ideas by looking around at others. Once done, ask each pair to choose their favorite to share with the group.

Connections for High Fives

Variations/Modifications: Create a class high five that is used when something good happens or when students have struggled to get a task done, gotten through some frustrating times, etc.

Adaptations for Students with Disabilities: High Fives

Cognitive Disabilities	• Make up one new high five instead of three. • Students can show a high five they have done or seen before. • Students take turns showing a new high five and having everyone else try it.
Orthopedic Impairment	No major modifications necessary.
Hearing Impairment	No major modifications necessary.
Visual Impairment	No major modifications necessary.

Activity F One-to-One Interview

Each person gets a minute or so to tell his or her life story to a partner. Afterward, partners take turns introducing each other to the group and telling what they can remember about their partner's "autobiography."

Connections for One-to-One Interview

Academic Applications: • After researching someone known for their given field, or someone famous (i.e., scientist, political or historical figure, sports personality, etc.), students tell their partners some things about their chosen figures. Their partners, then, "introduce" these persons to the class.

Variations/Modifications: Decide on a few questions that partners can share the answers to.

Adaptations for Students with Disabilities: One-to-One Interviews

Cognitive Disabilities	• Brainstorm two or three questions that everyone can ask their partner. • Have questions made up in advance for students to use.
Orthopedic Impairment	No major modifications necessary.
Hearing Impairment	• Make sure students have an interpreter if necessary.
Visual Impairment	No major modifications necessary.

Activity G 🙏 Celebration (Thanks to Jim Dunn for this activity.)

Partners create some way to celebrate – high fives, a dance, a cheer, or some other expression. Throughout the day, when someone yells "celebrate," students must find their partners and celebrate together.

Adaptations for Students with Disabilities: Celebration

Cognitive Disabilities	• Model different ways to celebrate and allow them to choose the ones they want to do. • Have a large group celebration rather than partner celebrations.
Orthopedic Impairment	No major modifications necessary.
Hearing Impairment	• Make sure students have an interpreter if necessary.
Visual Impairment	No major modifications necessary.

Sample Processing Questions for Paired Activities
- How was it to work with so many different people?
- Why might it be important to be able to work with everyone in this class?
- Is it easy or hard for you to approach someone new?
- Did you learn anything about anyone in this class?
- Which was easier for you – to do the activity with your partner or to share information with them?

Connections for Paired Activities
Life Skill Links: caring, choice and accountability, cooperation, courage, curiosity, effort, empathy, flexibility, imagination, initiative, positive attitude, relationships, respect
Academic Applications: • Before working in pairs for a class assignment, task, or project, do one of these activities to help students feel connected with their partners.
Variations/Modifications: Do these activities in small groups rather than as pairs.

Facilitation Notes
As you can see, these activities have no deep underlying meaning. They are just fun things to do with another person and are rather nonthreatening. Some groups need to hear that there is no point to the actual activity, but that there is a purpose to the exercise as a whole.

Depending on the group, it may be necessary to help students find initial partners, especially if you are aware of triads or students who are regularly excluded. Once you have done Celebration, initial partners for other activities can be assigned by having students find their Celebration partners.

Another consideration is preparing students for working with partners they may or may not care for. Acknowledge that working with all others is difficult, and it is a skill to be developed. Talk with the students about the concept of collegiality. As teachers, for example, it is important to be able to serve on committees with other teachers, even if we are not social friends. Give the students a phrase, such as, "Thanks for working with me," to say to whomever they are paired with, whether they are best friends or not. Practice this as a way to show politeness and respect to others. Then ask them to do the same when working together on tasks in class.

4. Group Bingo

Focus: Mixing with others in the group, learning about others, perspective taking
Materials: Pre-made group bingo cards (see sample on next page for design ideas)
Level: Grades 3 and higher

Suggested Procedure
1. Each person gets a group bingo card (see sample on next page).
2. The task for students is to get as many different signatures on their cards as possible in the amount of time allotted.

Sample Processing Questions for Group Bingo
- Did you learn anything about others in the class? What?
- Does anyone have a personal story to tell about any of the items on the card?
- What other things do you want to know about other people in the class?

Connections for Group Bingo
Life Skill Links: caring, communication, cooperation, relationships
Academic Applications: • Use as a warm up for studying the writing of biography and autobiography. Ask students what types of things they think are important to have in a biography. What types of things would they want to include in an autobiography? • Create a group bingo card with statements that call for opinions about health and fitness issues or current events, for example. Have students find others who agree or disagree with their own opinions on these items.
Variations/Modifications: • *For younger students:* Have fewer spaces and use pictures to go with words.
• Rather than using the pre-made bingo card, the class can make up its own. Have the class split into small groups and come up with three to five things they want to know about others in the class. Then they can make up cards that include the small groups' questions.

Facilitation Notes
Taking some time after the Group Bingo activity to let students compare notes about class members is important. Have them find out how many left-handers you have in the room or how many people have broken a bone. Encourage individuals to share stories so that everyone can learn more about each other. Share some stories of your own.

Adaptations for Students with Disabilities: Group Bingo

Cognitive Disabilities	• Create a simpler card with fewer options. • Do this in pairs, putting those who need help reading with better readers. • Do this in small groups. Students can see how many of the squares they can fill in with their group members.
Orthopedic Impairment	• Have ink stamps/daubers or allow students to X off each square instead of getting them signed.

Hearing Impairment	• Have interpreters available, if necessary.
Visual Impairment	• Have students do the activity in pairs.

BINGO

Someone who was born in the same season as you.	Someone who has a different color of eyes than you.	Someone who has been west of the Mississippi.	Someone who is left-handed.	Someone who likes cats.
Someone who has a different number of brothers and sisters than you.	Someone who has been (or wants to go) bungee jumping.	Someone who has been out of the United States.	Someone who can speak more than one language.	Someone who has a pet other than a cat or dog.
Someone who has twins in the family.	Someone who enjoys reading.	Free Space	Someone who plays a team sport.	Someone who likes dogs.
Someone who was born on a holiday.	Someone who can play an instrument.	Someone who thinks 6:00 a.m. is too early to get up.	Someone who has broken a bone.	Someone who has eaten venison.
Someone who has been cross-country skiing.	Someone who has gotten stitches.	Someone who knows who Maya Angelou is.	Someone who belongs to a club.	Someone who likes to fish.

5. Categories and Lineups

Focus: Mixing with others, learning more about each other, appreciating diversity, perspective taking
Materials: None
Level: Grades K and higher

Suggested Procedure

1. Clear away an area so that people can move around with ease.
2. Ask the class to line up according to:
   - Alphabetical order by first name
   - Alphabetical order by last name
   - Alphabetical order by mother's first name
   - Birthday
   - Shoe size
   - Height (shortest to tallest)
   - Hair color (darkest to lightest)
   - Skin color (darkest to lightest)
   - Thumb size (shortest to longest)
3. Have the class get into groups according to a certain category:
   - Season in which they were born
   - Favorite ice cream
   - Favorite day of the week
   - Shirt color
   - Eye color
   - Types of pets at home
   - Plans for after high school
   - Number of siblings (count half and stepbrothers/sisters)
   - Holidays you might celebrate in winter (Hanukkah, Christmas, Kwaanza, Ramadan, none ...)
   - Number of generations born in this country (i.e., are they the first generation, second?)
4. For each set of groups, have students take the time to notice the diversity in the room. Make and take comments about what people observe. Maybe there are a lot of chocolate ice cream lovers in the room, or everyone seems to like the same day of the week. Why is that?

Sample Processing Questions for Categories and Lineups

- What do we seem to have in common in this class?
- What are some of our differences?
- How do you like the idea of this kind of diversity?
- What are some of the other things that make each one of us unique?

Connections for Categories and Lineups

Life Skill Links: caring, curiosity, relationships, respect

Academic Applications: • Use to teach or reinforce chronologies or time lines. As an introductory piece, do some lineups, and then reflect about how some things go in sequential order. As a review, assign each student a piece of a time line and ask them to get into order. Check to see if it is correct. • Use categories to help students understand how things can be sorted and labeled. Sorting themselves can help them make the connection and generalize to other things.

Variations/Modifications: • *For younger students:* Use attributes that are visible, such as length of hair or skin color. • Try doing these silently.

Facilitation Notes

This activity can be repeated throughout the year. Each time, the categories and lineups can be used to explore diversity issues on a deeper level. Have students create their own categories and lineups. Then use one as a warm up for class.

Sometimes a student may not know the answer to a question, such as a mother's first name or what generation he or she is in this country. Make sure that students know that Challenge by Choice is in effect – they can choose to observe, use another family member's name, or join any group they wish. The object is not to be legally correct about such things, but to learn more about others.

Adaptations for Students with Disabilities: Categories and Lineups

Cognitive Disabilities	• Students sort themselves into groups by physical attributes, such as shirt color. • Do not time the activity.
Orthopedic Impairment	No major modifications necessary.
Hearing Impairment	• Write the category or lineup question on the board.
Visual Impairment	• Do not do a silent lineup – allow everyone to communicate verbally.

6. Differences and Commonalities

Focus: Perspective taking, mixing with others, appreciating diversity
Materials: None
Level: Grades 2 and higher

Suggested Procedure

1. Following the format of the Categories and Lineups activity, ask the students to get into groups according to certain criteria (e.g., number of brothers and sisters).
2. If any of the groups have more than four or five people in them, have them split into smaller groups.
3. Each time groups are formed, give them 30–60 seconds to come up with as many things as possible that they all have in common that they **cannot see**.
4. Do the same with differences – have them identify at least one person in the group who is different from the others in some way that is not overtly apparent.
5. Have each group report at least one finding each time the category changes.

Sample Processing Questions for Differences and Commonalities

• How easy or difficult was it for your group to find things in common?
• When you were the only one who was different, how did that feel?
• What can you learn about yourself when comparing yourself to others? What can you learn about others?
• Was it easier or harder to discover differences as opposed to commonalities? Why?
• Have you ever been in a situation where it seemed that you had nothing in common with those around you? Does anyone have a situation like that to share?
• When meeting new people, how can you find out more about them?

Connections for Differences and Commonalities

Life Skill Links: caring, cooperation, curiosity, relationships, respect
Academic Applications: • Use the same setup to get students into groups through the use of category criteria. Give students a theme or question related to an area of study for them to brainstorm around. Have each group share one or two items from their brainstorming session before moving on to the next one.
Variations/Modifications: • *For younger students:* Give them paper to write down what they have come up with for commonalities and differences. *For very young children:* Bring in older elementary students to act as scribes for each group.

Facilitation Notes

Keep this activity moving fairly quickly so that students can experience how easy or difficult it is to discover commonalities or differences. With some groups, it might also be necessary to ask that the commonalities and differences be kept G-rated.

Adaptations for Students with Disabilities: Differences and Commonalities

Cognitive Disabilities	• Allow students to use commonalities and differences they can see. • Do this activity in pairs.
Orthopedic Impairment	No major modifications necessary.
Hearing Impairment	• Write the category question on the board. • Have interpreters available, if necessary.
Visual Impairment	• Do not do a silent category – allow everyone to communicate verbally.

7. Interactive Video (Adapted from Captian Video, *New Games for the Whole Family*, p. 42)

Focus: Active listening, hidden agendas, perspective taking
Materials: None
Level: Grades 4 and higher

Suggested Procedure

1. Ask students to stand in a circle with everyone facing away from the middle.
2. One person stands in the middle and taps another on the shoulder. When the "tapped" person turns around, the person in the middle does a simple visual routine (e.g., hands on hips, tapping toe, with a cheerleading jump at the end).
3. Person #2 taps the next person in the circle and repeats the routine.
4. Person #3 continues by tapping the next person in the circle, etc.
5. When the routine goes all the way around the circle, the first person (the originator of the routine) and the last person face each other. They count to three and do their respective routines (the first person does his or her original routine, the last person does what he or she saw).
6. Once someone has done the routine, she or he may watch the progression around the circle but may not comment on it (other than to laugh when appropriate).

Sample Processing Questions for Interactive Video

- Did the activity change as it was repeated? What do you think was the cause of the change(s)?
- Do you believe everything you see or hear?
- Have you ever been in a situation where someone has reported they saw another person mishandling your property? Or that they heard something about someone else? How do you usually react?
- How do you know it's the whole story? What can you do to make sure you are not overreacting?
- How can our own perspectives or abilities cause us to change a message?
- Did you find this fun or humorous to watch? If you laughed, was it in a way to put someone down, or was it respectful? How do you know? How would they know?

Connections for Interactive Video

Life Skill Links: communication, respect, sense of humor
Academic Applications: • Do this at the beginning of a unit or lesson on communication.
Variations/Modifications: • *For younger students:* Do this as a large group by sending a few students out of the room. Decide on one simple routine as a large group, then call each student in one by one. Show the first student the routine, then call in the next student. The first student shows the routine to the second student. In this way, the whole class can see the routine change. Make sure to prepare the students to expect the change, so that those in front of the class do not feel as if they have failed or done something wrong.
Extensions: • Every so often, surprise your students by sending conflicting verbal and nonverbal signals (e.g., sit very quietly and somberly tell them that you would like to plan something really fun with them).
• Brainstorm what nonactive listening is. Post this alongside the Attentive/Active listening guidelines.

Periodically ask individuals, small groups, or the whole class to check in on how they think they are doing with these skills. • Ask your students to notice how people are doing with active listening outside of class. Have them report their findings (without using names).

Facilitation Notes

As you can see, this is a visual form of the game Telephone (or Operator). Generally, the routines change by becoming simpler, as it is impossible to keep track of all the details that one is witnessing. There is usually much laughing as the audience sees the changes taking place.

In some cases, especially in the elementary grades, students do not wait for the tapped person to turn around before beginning the routine. Obviously, this person will not have the benefit of seeing the full routine and will be at a severe disadvantage. This is a good teachable moment to focus on how one must be tuned in to the person they are trying to communicate with.

Adaptations for Students with Disabilities: Interactive Video

Cognitive Disabilities	• Make the motions simple – one or two in a row. • Try doing the game Telephone/Operator first (i.e., pass along a short phrase).
Orthopedic Impairment	• Make sure the motions can be done by all in the class (e.g., sitting instead of standing, using only upper body). • This activity could be performed by an assistant, or with the help of an assistant.
Hearing Impairment	No major modifications necessary.
Visual Impairment	• This is not an appropriate activity for students with a visual impairment. Try the game Telephone/Operator instead.

8. King/Queen Frog

Focus: Active listening
Materials: None
Level: Grades 3 and higher

Suggested Procedure

1. Have students sit in a circle.
2. Start by showing the motions of a King or Queen Frog (that is you), and have everyone practice it. The King/Queen frog motion consists of placing one hand in front of you, palm up, and slapping it with the other hand, followed by an upward motion (a jumping motion).
3. The person next to you indicates another animal using motions only. For example, he may represent a skunk by holding his nose. The next person might signify a bird by flapping her arms. This continues until everyone has created a unique motion, and everyone has practiced each one.
4. The game is now ready to begin. You start by showing the King/Queen Frog motion, and then another one (say, the skunk – hold your nose). You have just passed it to the person who is the skunk.
5. Skunk now does his own motion, holding his nose; then he flaps his arms, thus passing it to the bird. This continues until someone makes a mistake by taking too long, forgetting a motion, or doing a motion wrong, for example.
6. That person then becomes the King/Queen Frog and takes your chair. Everyone else moves over one chair until the empty chair is filled. This often means that only part of the group moves, while the others stay put.
7. The catch is that the animal motion stays with the chair; it does not move with the person. So, those who have just moved have to learn the new motion.

Sample Processing Questions for King/Queen Frog

- Did you ever feel put "on the spot?" When?
- How much concentration did it take to stay focused on the activity? What strategies did you use?
- Are there things that we all did that helped us stay focused or distracted us during this game?
- Was this activity communication? How do you know?
- What other forms of nonverbal communication are there? Can you demonstrate some?
- How can you tell how someone might be feeling by his or her body language?

Connections for King/Queen Frog

Life Skill Links: communication, imagination, patience

Academic Applications: • Use as a way to introduce the concept of nonverbal communication or body language. • Use vocabulary words or concepts from your classes for the students to create visual representations.

Variations/Modifications: • Have someone who knows sign language teach the symbols for the various chosen animals.

Extensions: • Create a rubric as a class for focus. Define what it means to be unfocused and make this "0." Then define a little focused and make this "1." Finally, define very focused and make this "2." Have each student rate him/herself at the end of each morning and afternoon for a week. • Discuss strategies to help make the room a place where focus is supported and valued (e.g., some people like to have soft music playing during work time).

Facilitation Notes

Once this activity gets started, it is possible to hear a pin drop. Great concentration is required, and students really get drawn into this quiet game. Although it is possible to do this in large groups, it is best done with groups of about 10–15. If you have a large class, teach it in a large group, and practice for a while. Then have the class split into smaller groups to play.

Generally, making a mistake is of little consequence in this activity because the person just takes a different spot in the circle. If it appears that it may be a problem (e.g., where someone is chided for making the mistake or appears to be making the mistake on purpose), then it may be necessary to have a short discussion about put-downs or hidden agendas.

This is a good activity to pull out when the class needs to calm down after a loud and rambunctious project.

Adaptations for Students with Disabilities: King/Queen Frog

Cognitive Disabilities	• Do this in small groups. • Have the motion stay with the person when everyone moves.
Orthopedic Impairment	• Make sure that all motions can be done by all students in the class. • Allow a longer time to complete motions.
Hearing Impairment	No major modifications necessary.
Visual Impairment	• Use sounds instead of motions. • Do this in smaller groups.

9. Welcome Circle (Thanks to Candace Peterson for this activity.)

Focus: Perspective taking, valuing diversity, using put-ups

Materials: None

Level: Grades K and higher

Suggested Procedure

1. Gather in a circle.
2. Teach the students a welcome greeting to perform while saying "Welcome":
   - Pat your thighs twice
   - Clap twice
   - Snap twice
   - Thumbs up
3. Tell them that you will call out different things. If it is true for them, they are to take a step or two into the middle of the circle.
4. Everyone else then does the welcome greeting.
5. As an example, call out: "Everyone who is a student at this school (all the students will take a step in and you will do the welcome greeting for them).
6. Call out a variety of things. Examples are:

Everyone who:

is a girl	celebrates Ramadan
is a boy	does not celebrate holidays
has a brother, sister	has a birthday this month
has a pet	lives in an apartment
does not have a middle name	lives in a house
is right-handed	lives on a farm
is left-handed	likes math
likes to play soccer	likes reading
likes to sing	likes art
celebrates Kwaanza	likes sports
celebrates Hanukah	has moved this year
celebrates Christmas	

Sample Processing Questions for Welcome Circle

- Did you find that you had anything in common with anyone else in this room? What?
- Were you surprised at how many times you stepped into the circle?
- How did we welcome each other, and how did it feel?
- What can we do to make everyone feel welcome in this class?

Connections for Welcome Circle

Life Skill Links: caring, cooperation, curiosity, relationships, respect

Extensions: • Create a list of questions to ask throughout the week, and do this activity for a short time each day. • Create a plan for how to include a new student during the year. What can you do to make the new student feel welcome?

Facilitation Notes

Choose your questions carefully for this activity. Make sure that everyone gets to go into the circle a few times. Order the questions so that many people are stepping in together toward the beginning. By the end you may have some questions that allow only a few to step in.

Adaptations for Students with Disabilities: Welcome Circle

Cognitive Disabilities	No major modifications necessary.
Orthopedic Impairment	• Choose a welcome signal that everyone can do. • Make sure there is enough time for students to move in and out of the circle.
Hearing Impairment	• Have interpreters available, if necessary.
Visual Impairment	No major modifications necessary.

10. The Big Question (Thanks to Sarah Shatz for this activity.)

Focus: Perspective taking, active listening
Materials: Scratch paper and pencils
Level: Grades 4 and higher

Suggested Procedure

1. Hand out a piece of scratch paper to each student.
2. Ask the students to write a question that anyone in the room can answer. Some examples are:
   - What is your favorite book or movie?
   - What is an activity that you like to do?
   - What food do you not like?
3. Wait until students are done writing their questions on their pieces of scratch paper.
4. Ask for a student volunteer to show how this will work. Go up to him or her and ask the question you wrote on your paper. He or she answers it, then asks you a question.
5. After you answer the student's questions, **trade papers**. You will now find someone new to ask your new question, while the student you were with will find someone new to ask your old question.
6. Each time you talk to a new person, you trade questions.
7. Everyone will do this at once. Encourage students to talk to at least five different people.

Sample Processing Questions for The Big Question
- What were you able to learn about people in this class?
- Were you surprised by some of the questions or answers? Why?
- What strategies did you use to hear people when everyone was talking at once?
- Did you find that you approached people or waited for people to come to you? Is this your usual style? Why do you think you have this style?

Connections: The Big Question
Life Skill Links: caring, communication, cooperation, curiosity, respect
Academic Applications: • Have students write questions about something they are studying. Each person then tries to answer the posed question. Afterward, read each question and discuss.
Variations/Modifications: *For younger students:* If reading or writing is an issue, have students think of a question they will ask everyone. They can then ask the same question to a variety of people.

Facilitation Notes
This activity is a quick energizer, usually taking no more than 5–10 minutes. Encourage students to be creative, but make sure the questions are not too narrow. Depending upon the needs of your class you can either participate or wander around listening to the action and helping those who need it.

Adaptations for Students with Disabilities: The Big Question

Cognitive Disabilities	• Brainstorm questions that can be asked, and students can choose one to use.
Orthopedic Impairment	• Have someone write the question, if necessary.
Hearing Impairment	• Have interpreters available, if necessary.
Visual Impairment	• Have someone write the questions and answers, if necessary.

Deinhibitizer Activities

After students have relaxed a bit, learned each other's names, and shared a little about themselves, Deinhibitizer activities can be introduced. These activities require a little more risk taking than Ice Breakers. People may be asked to hold hands for an activity, they might be put on the spot by being in the middle of the class for a game, or the activity may call for people to act silly. Deinhibitizers are meant to get people laughing and relaxed. Ice Breakers begin to loosen people up, and Deinhibitizers continue the process.

These activities also allow a group to begin exploring trust issues. Since many of these activities are silly, ask the students where they would be willing to play the games. Then discuss why they might choose to play here, but not in public. Since this class of individuals has been together for a while, they will probably be willing to risk acting silly because they are no longer with strangers. This is a good distinction when moving into trust issues.

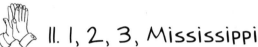 II. 1, 2, 3, Mississippi

Focus: Being put on the spot, name reminder
Materials: None
Level: Grades 3 and higher

Suggested Procedure

1. The group stands in a circle, with you in the middle.
2. Ask students to make sure they know the names of the people to their immediate right and left.
3. Notify them that this game is intended to put people on the spot. Then point to someone and say "right." That person is to say the name of the person on her right.
4. Next point to someone and say "left." He is to say the name of the person on his left.
5. After some practice, tell the class that you are now going to interject a distraction while they are trying to think. It is the phrase "1, 2, 3, Mississippi." Whoever is being pointed to must say the correct name before you get to the end of the phrase. If not, that person takes your place in the middle.
6. Practice this a few times before putting anyone in the hot seat.
7. For more of a challenge, add "2-left" or "2-right." Whoever is being pointed to must say the correct name of the person two away from him or her in the correct direction.
8. You can also say "you" or "me." If "you" is stated, then whoever is being pointed to must say his or her own name. If "me" is stated, then whoever is being pointed to must say the pointer's name.

Sample Processing Questions for 1, 2, 3, Mississippi

- How did it feel to be put on the spot?
- Did it seem as if people were able to laugh at themselves, or was it too risky? Why do you think this is?
- Why do you think it was so difficult to focus when someone was yelling "1, 2, 3, Mississippi" at you?
- Are there other situations when it is difficult to focus at school? Does anyone want to share one?

Connections for 1, 2, 3, Mississippi

Life Skill Links: communication, effort, patience, perseverance, respect, self-discipline, sense of humor
Academic Applications: • Do this activity in preparation for a test to introduce focus strategies.

Facilitation Notes

Depending on the age of your class, use the basic version or add more challenges. It is also possible to start with the basic version and make it harder as you progress through the year. If students know each other's names already, try having people assume a persona from your studies or a favorite book character.

The class should be prepared to be put on the spot and ready to laugh at themselves and with others. This is generally not a problem unless there is some active antagonism in the class. If so, this activity should be avoided for the time being. If you have a large class, try having more than one person in the middle at a time.

Adaptations for Students with Disabilities: 1, 2, 3, Mississippi

Cognitive Disabilities	• Use only "you" and "me." • Point first to the person who is calling the name, then at the person you want named. • Count to 5 or 10 instead of the "1, 2, 3 Mississippi." • You stay in the middle throughout this activity.
Orthopedic Impairment	• Allow students more time to call each name.
Hearing Impairment	• Teach everyone the sign for "right" and "left" so all can use it. • Count by putting up fingers. • Allow for signing of names.
Visual Impairment	• Give people time to learn who is next to them whenever anyone moves.

12. ¿Como Estás?

Focus: Acting silly, name reminder
Materials: None
Level: Grades 3 and higher

Suggested Procedure

1. This can be an active game, so it is best done outside or in a large room such as a gym or all-purpose room. It can be done in the classroom if people move slowly – walking instead of running.
2. Have the class stand in a circle. Two people stand outside the circle.
3. The two people outside are "it." They decide on a way to "locomote" (e.g., walk, skip, gallop) and use this locomotion as they go around the circle together.
4. They choose two people standing next to each other and tap them on the shoulder. The two new people turn around to face the ones who are "it."
5. Each person from one pair shakes hands with someone from the other pair. Simultaneously, each person says "¿Como estás?" Then, simultaneously, each one answers, "Me llamo (name)." They do this three times.
6. They then shake hands with the other person in the opposite pair and repeat the niceties three times.
7. Now each pair, using the original locomotion, takes off in opposite directions around the circle. (The empty spot left by the second pair should stay open.)
8. When the pairs meet on the other side, they go through the whole "¿Como estás?" routine again, after which they continue on their separate ways around the circle.
9. The pair that gets back to the empty spot first stays. The other team is "it." They decide on a new form of locomotion, and the whole thing starts over.

Sample Processing Questions for ¿Como Estás?

• Were there winners and losers in this game? Why or why not?
• How did you feel playing this game?
• What if we did this in a public place? Would you have played? Why or why not?
• Did you find it difficult to wait your turn? How about those that went toward the beginning – was it difficult to be patient knowing you would not get another turn?
• If we had run out of time for everyone to go, what are some ways to deal with that situation?
• Sometimes when things seem unfair, it is difficult to remain patient. What are different ways to react to that situation? How can being patient help us find a fair solution?
• What are some times when you have to be very patient? (My example is when my mother used to take me to fabric stores. I was bored, but found ways to entertain myself without bothering other people.)

Connections for ¿Como Estás?

Life Skill Links: communication, cooperation, patience, relationships, safety, sense of humor

Academic Applications: • Do this using songs they have sung in music or reciting haikus they have written.

Variations/Modifications: • *For younger students:* Try this first as individuals, and without the different locomotion styles. Once they have the idea, add a new variable before adding the second one.

Extensions: • Create fair ways for deciding who gets their turn next. Then use these strategies during class whenever something calls for taking turns (e.g., alphabetical order forward or backward, birthdays). • Encourage students to mix it up when taking turns. For example, those who usually go first stand back and allow others to go first for a change, and those who hang back take the initiative to try something first.

Facilitation Notes

As with most Ice Breakers and Deinhibitizers, it is not usually necessary to spend a great deal of time processing. If there are issues that arise – like someone putting another down, or people not wanting to stand next to someone (mixing issue) – then it may be necessary to spend some time talking about what happened during the activity. For the most part, though, the point is to have fun and create an atmosphere where people can feel comfortable with each other – to "connect."

Caution: One safety note with this activity: If a pair decides to "locomote" backwards, other group members must watch out for their safety by warning them when they are approaching the other pair (who are also going backwards) when they meet around the other side of the circle.

Adaptations for Students with Disabilities: ¿Como Estás?

Cognitive Disabilities	• Have students say "¿Como estás?" and their names only once each time. • Instead of "¿Como estás?" say "How do you do?" or "Hello."
Orthopedic Impairment	• This may not be appropriate for students who have an orthopedic impairment. • Use only walking for this activity. • Ask the class to choose a type of locomotion that allows everyone to participate.
Hearing Impairment	• Students can shake hands only. • Teach and do a short patty-cake rhythm instead of "¿Como estás?"
Visual Impairment	• Have students walk only.

 13. Morphing

Focus: Acting silly, mixing
Materials: Stopwatch (optional)
Level: Grades K and higher

Suggested Procedure

1. Clear a small area in the room. Have everyone stand in a circle.
2. Make sure everyone knows the game Rock/Paper/Scissors, and agree on the rules for that game.
3. Show everyone the following motions: egg (squatting down), chicken (hands under armpits squawking like a chicken), dinosaur (arms up, making roaring noises), superhero (flying through the air), know-it-all smarty-pants (arms crossed, looking smug)
4. The object is to get as high up the chain as possible in a given amount of time (go for two minutes or so).
5. Everyone begins as an egg. Everyone then finds another egg and does Rock/Paper/Scissors until a winner is established. Whoever wins gets to move up the chain to chicken. He or she must then find another chicken with whom to do Rock/Paper/Scissors.

6. The winner moves up to the next step (dinosaur), while the loser goes down a step (back to egg).
7. This continues for the allotted time. When someone makes it up to know-it-all smarty-pants, that person then stands outside of the circle, arms crossed, looking smug.
8. In other words, if you win, you're out.

Sample Processing Questions for Morphing
- How do you feel about where you ended up in the sequence?
- Did you think this game was fun? Why or why not?
- How did you like acting like a chicken/dinosaur with everyone else?

Connections for Morphing
Life Skill Links: choice and accountability, communication, flexibility, sense of humor
Academic Applications: • This can be used as a fun way to introduce, review, or remember any sequence. Decide on what the sequence is and then make up motions to go with each piece of the sequence. • Use this activity to show the process of evolution.
Variations/Modifications: You can add a choice and risk-taking element to this activity by giving those who make it to know-it-all smarty-pants the opportunity to take the "ultimate risk." If they choose, they can Rock/Paper/Scissors with another know-it-all smarty-pants. Whoever wins stays at that level. The person who loses, however, starts over as an egg. It can be interesting to discuss why some people chose to take that risk while others were comfortable where they were.

Facilitation Notes
This game can be played with any group larger than eight. It has been played with hundreds. People love it because it is funny, and an element of challenge is injected by having to beat the clock. I like to joke with people that wherever they end up, they must walk that way for the rest of the day ....

Also try making up your own motions. We have done the history of candy (i.e., licorice, taffy, lollipop, chewing gum, chocolate bar). Or, have the students make up the sequence and motions.

Adaptations for Students with Disabilities: Morphing

Cognitive Disabilities	• Use fewer stages in the chain. • Teach Rock/Paper/Scissors first and play it for a while before attempting to add this variation.
Orthopedic Impairment	• Create motions that all students can do.
Hearing Impairment	No major modifications necessary.
Visual Impairment	• Do this in pairs; each partner takes a turn doing the Rock/Paper/Scissors.

14. Screaming Toes

Focus: Acting silly, mixing
Materials: None
Level: Grades 2 and higher

Suggested Procedure
1. Clear away a space and have the class stand in a circle.
2. Tell everyone to look down at someone else's shoes. When you say "look up," they should look that person in the face.

3. If that person is looking at someone else, nothing happens.
4. If that person is looking directly back – making eye contact – then both parties act surprised by letting out a little scream or yell.
5. Those who make eye contact then meet in the middle for a high-five and switch places in the circle.

Sample Processing Questions for Screaming Toes
- How did you like screaming in this activity?
- Did you try to avoid eye contact or to get eye contact? Why?
- What made this game fun/not fun for you?

Connections for Screaming Toes
Life Skill Links: choice and accountability, communication, patience, sense of humor
Academic Applications: • When someone makes eye contact, they must call out something that has to do with an area of study. *For young students:* It could be a word that starts with a letter of the alphabet they are working on. *For older students:* It could be a theorem from geometry, for example.
Variations/Modifications: • Instead of using a scream, practice and try belly laughs. If the group is in the mood this variation can be quite humorous, and laughter is contagious. • If you have a large class, teach the activity as written above, then try the following variations. 1) Have each person identify a partner across the circle (they should know that they are each other's partner). When you say look down, they can then either look at the shoes of their partner, **or at the shoes of the person to their own left or right.** The choices are narrowed down to three, and more action will take place. Even after they change places with someone, they should keep their same partner. 2) Have the class make two or three smaller circles. They can look at anyone in their circle. If eye contact is made, they both scream, and then join a different circle.

Facilitation Notes
Sometimes it is necessary to practice screaming with the entire group before asking them to scream solo. Try that a few times, but first make sure the class next door isn't taping something or trying to have quiet reading time ....

Adaptations for Students with Disabilities: Screaming Toes

Cognitive Disabilities	• Explain directions slowly with a demonstration if necessary.
Orthopedic Impairment	No major modifications necessary.
Hearing Impairment	No major modifications necessary.
Visual Impairment	• This is not a good activity for students with a visual impairment.

MPS

15. Get the Point
Focus: Unselfconscious touch
Materials: None
Level: Grades 1 and higher

Suggested Procedure
1. Clear a space and have the class stand in a circle.
2. Ask everyone to put out their right hand, palm up.
3. Go around the circle to make sure people are using their right hand.
4. Then have everyone put the pointer finger of their left hand in the palm of the person to their left.

5. When you say "go," people should try to catch the neighbor's finger in their palm, but not let their own finger get caught.
6. Try this a few times, then switch hands.

Sample Processing Questions for Get the Point
- Was it difficult to touch (or be touched by) someone else in this activity? Why or why not?
- What kinds of touching can be threatening?
- If you do not want to be touched in this class during an activity, how should you (and we) respond to that?
- What guidelines could we make about touching to make sure it is a safe/acceptable thing for everyone?

Connections for Get the Point
Life Skill Links: caring, choice and accountability, cooperation, respect, safety
Variations/Modifications: This activity can also be done in pairs or small groups. • The "go" signal can be a special word. Try choosing one that has meaning to the class, or use one that has many similar sounding words, such as "Pickle." That way if you tell a story about "Pete the Pickle," you can talk about how fickle he is, and how he likes to be tickled ....

Facilitation Notes
This is a short activity that can be used as an energizer or if you only have a few minutes left in class. Try mixing up the "go" signal to keep people a little off balance. For example, say "go" a couple of times, then say, "On your mark, get set ...." People will jump in before you say "go." Or try "On your mark, go!"

This is a good activity to use if you are concerned about touching issues. It allows people to touch each other in a very nonthreatening way, which then allows you to talk about it.

Adaptations for Students with Disabilities: Get the Point

Cognitive Disabilities	• Students can try this with partners first, using only one hand to begin with, then two hands. Then try the whole class together.
Orthopedic Impairment	• This activity may not be appropriate for students with orthopedic impairment.
Hearing Impairment	• Use a visual signal or a drumbeat to signal "go."
Visual Impairment	No major modifications necessary.

16. Speed Rabbit

Focus: Acting silly, being put on the spot, mixing
Materials: None
Level: Grades K and higher

Suggested Procedure
1. Clear a space and stand in a circle. You take the middle.
2. Teach a variety of motions to be made by three people as described below.
3. Point to someone and say "elephant": The person you point to makes the trunk by clasping her hands together, arms held straight, pointed to the ground, while people on either side make ears (one hand up near the middle person's head, the other hand near his or her hip).
4. Point to someone and say "moose": That person puts both hands up by her eyes, and sticks her elbows out in front of her (this is the nose of the moose), the people on either side turn their backs to her and put their arms in the air (antlers).

5. Point to someone and say, "flight attendant": That person mimes putting on an oxygen mask, while the people on either side smile and point to the "exits."
6. Once these have been established and practiced, the game can begin. Tell students that you will point to someone, say "elephant" or "moose" or "flight attendant," and count to 10 as fast as you can. If they make the motion before you get to 10, continue. If not, the person you pointed to takes your place in the middle.
7. After doing this for a while, add more. Here are some suggestions:

> Cow: Middle – hold hands out with thumbs down. Sides – pull on thumbs.
> Roller Coaster: Middle – put hands on face/cheeks and pull back to simulate G force. Sides – put hands in air and scream.
> Rabbit: Middle – hands on head to make ears. Sides – stomp a foot like Thumper.
> Palm Tree: Middle – arms over head and swaying. Sides – do hula dance.
> Ostrich: Sides – hold hands with each other to make a circle. Middle – put head in circle to simulate putting head in sand.
> Jell-O: Sides – hold hands with each other around middle person (this is the bowl). Middle – jiggle.
> Try making up your own.

Sample Processing Questions for Speed Rabbit
- What is the point to this game?
- Did you have fun playing it? Why or why not?
- How did you feel about being put in the middle? Did you feel put on the spot, or were you looking forward to it? Why?

Connections for Speed Rabbit
Life Skill Links: choice and accountability, cooperation, effort, flexibility, imagination, patience, purpose, sense of humor
Academic Applications: • Use as a fun way to review subject matter. Make up motions to go with anything you might be studying – types of clouds or weather systems, for example.
Variations/Modifications: • *For younger students:* Start with motions that one person can do alone. Some examples are: Frog – crouch down. Bunny – hands on head for ears while stomping one foot. Tree – arms up and swaying in the breeze. • *Adventures in Peacemaking* has a nice variation to explore feelings. It is presented on page 129 of this book as the activity Feelings Speed Rabbit.
Extensions: • Make a group commitment to try to see the humor in situations and try to laugh as much as possible during each day.

Facilitation Notes
This is a classic Deinhibitizer activity. As with most of these games, there is not much of a point in and of itself. They are designed to be silly and fun if people are ready to let their guard down a bit. This game has helped many classes finally break down and laugh. Other classes see some students exercise their choice to observe because they are not ready to be quite this silly yet. Whatever happens, you will have more information about your class by doing this activity. By the way, unless you are working with young children, I recommend that you do not do this on the first day.

If the team doesn't do the motion in time, you can create an interesting dynamic by having the person who is pointed to go in the middle. Basically, even if the person in the middle does his or her job, they can still be held accountable for what happens with the rest of the team. This issue can be good to discuss the idea of interdependence during cooperative learning when group grades are given.

Adaptations for Students with Disabilities: Speed Rabbit

Cognitive Disabilities	• Create motions that require one person or pairs only.
	• Only do two different motions at first. Add more later.
	• Don't count at first.
	• You stay in the middle.
Orthopedic Impairment	• Make sure all students can do the motions – ask for help from the students about how to modify them.
Hearing Impairment	• Use your fingers to count.
	• Stay with the student in the middle to help say the name of the animal or thing.
Visual Impairment	• Teach motions verbally, and allow practice time for the motions.
	• Stay with student in the middle to help with pointing.
	• Have people say the name of the person they are pointing to, and make sure each student knows who is on either side of him or her.
	• Agree on a physical touch (i.e., a tap on the shoulder) for the people who are being called on to do the motion.

17. Elbow Tag

Focus: Unselfconscious touch, acting silly, hidden agendas, mixing
Materials: None
Level: Grades 4 and higher

Suggested Procedure

1. This activity should be done in a large room or outside. People will be running.
2. Have the class get into pairs.
3. Students should be standing in a large circle, or scattered about, and interlock elbows with their partners. They do not move unless tagged.
4. One pair is chosen to unlock elbows. One person in the pair is the "chaser," while the other is the "flee-er." They run around.
5. This is a typical tag game. If the "chaser" tags the "flee-er," they switch roles.
6. If the "flee-er" doesn't want to be caught, then she or he can lock elbows with someone.
7. Since three is a crowd, the person on the end of the trio must now unlock his or her elbow and become the new "flee-er." For example, if the "flee-er" (A) locks elbows with B, who is attached to C, then C is now the new "flee-er."
8. This continues until time is up or people fall down from exhaustion.

Sample Processing Questions for Elbow Tag
• Would you rather be the "flee-er" or the "chaser"? Why?
• Did it matter who you were partnered with? Why or why not? How did you feel about changing partners?
• Why is it important to be able to work with everyone in the class? When is it appropriate to expect mixing, and when might it be unrealistic?

Connections for Elbow Tag
Life Skill Links: choice and accountability, effort, empathy, loyalty, patience, problem solving, purpose, relationships, respect, safety, self-discipline
Academic Applications: Using the "graduate school" variation described below is a great way to teach the difference between offense and defense because the "chaser" (offense) suddenly becomes the "flee-er" (de-

fense). • If you are studying civil rights or the civil rights movement, help make connections between hidden agendas, inclusion, and what they are studying about voting rights and racial equality. • If you are studying about Native Americans, notice how reservations were established. Help make the connection between how native people were moved from one place to another and excluded from their homelands onto reservations. Discuss hidden agendas and inclusion/exclusion.

Variations/Modifications: • For groups in which touching may be a concern, give the "chaser" a soft item to use for tagging. • During an event called the "Metaphorical Potluck," where groups created metaphors to go with activities, our group of educators came up with one called "Hook, Don't Look" to get at issues of exclusion and cliques. The play is the same as in Elbow Tag except that only people wearing red can be hooked onto. If no one is wearing red, choose another color, but not a common one. The result is that some people get to play all the time, while others never get a chance to play. This can make for some interesting processing and a connection to what may be happening in the classroom. • Have the "flee-er" spontaneously choose a form of movement (e.g., skipping, crab walking, hopping, twisting). The "chaser" must copy that movement when chasing. The next person who is chased can change the movement. This adds a new dimension to the game. • Another variation is what I call the "graduate school" level. When the "flee-er" links up to an established pair, the person released is now the **chaser** (the tagger). This variation causes quite a bit of confusion, which can be fun if the students are ready for it.

Extensions: Create some standards about choosing sides for teams during recess so that everyone feels that they are fair, and so that people are included rather than excluded.

Facilitation Notes

Once people understand how this game works, it is a favorite of all ages. It is helpful to show this in slow motion at first. Later there will inevitably be some confusion, e.g., when someone thinks that a partner has been linked to and takes off. Suddenly there will be three people running around instead of two. The students will figure it out eventually, and it is good practice for later problem solving. Watching their strategies during the confusion can give you some insight into the decision-making style of this particular group of students.

A few issues tend to come up during Elbow Tag. One is when someone gets stuck being the "chaser" for a long time and is obviously getting tired. One strategy to deal with this situation is for the "chaser" to hook on to someone else, thus making a new "chaser." Another issue is when someone is enjoying being chased, and doesn't hook on to anyone, but keeps on running around. This scenario offers an opportunity to talk about hidden agendas, since the rest of the class is getting fidgety, frustrated, or bored by standing around and watching the action instead of being a part of it.

Another issue that can arise in some groups is the issue of being paired with others. This is a great activity in which to have people choose their own partners because they will be mixed up anyway by the end of the game. It is also obvious when students will only latch onto their friends, or if girls hook onto girls, and boys to boys (a classic issue in grades 4 and 5). This is not necessarily a bad thing, but offers an opportunity to talk about mixing and why it is important to be able to work with everyone in the class. It can also be a time for the students to relate how difficult it is to mix, and how it might be unreasonable to expect them to do it all of the time (a valid point that I have discussed with many groups).

Adaptations for Students with Disabilities: Elbow Tag

Cognitive Disabilities	• Reiterate rules. Practice game before beginning, talk about it and then go on.
Orthopedic Impairment	• This activity may not be appropriate for orthopedically impaired students. • In the case of a person who is non-ambulatory, the partner can put a hand on the wheelchair handle or tray instead of hooking elbows.
Hearing Impairment	No major modifications are necessary.

Visual Impairment	• Make the play area smaller. • Make a defined area on the floor by using a rope, mat, etc., so students can feel the boundary when moving around. • Walk rather than run.

MPS

> When working on **inclusion** in class, it is important to "frontload" the topic – especially for upper-elementary through middle-school students. Discuss the concept of how being able to work with everyone is a sign of a healthy community. Remind them that we are not asking people to be best friends, but only to work together on specified tasks. Ask students to give examples of how one's reaction to a new partner might be a put-down and how one can react in a way that is welcoming. Then have them practice.

18. Little Bert (Adapted from Little Ernie, *New Games for the Whole Family*, p. 61)

Focus: Acting silly, active listening
Materials: Little Bert story (see below)
Level: Grades 3 and higher

Suggested Procedure
1. Clear a space in the room and have chairs (one for each student) in the middle. Chairs should be in two rows, back to back. You can also do this outside by sitting or standing in two lines, back to back.
2. From a hat, each person picks a persona from the story. Depending on the number of students in your class, each character will probably have more than one person playing the part.
3. Students should sit randomly in the chairs.
4. Read the Little Bert story. Each time a character's name is said, those representing the character stand up, run clockwise around the chairs, and sit back down in their chairs.
5. If "everyone," or "the whole family" is said, everyone stands up, runs around their chairs and sits back down.

Little Bert

This is a story about Little Bert. He lived with Victoria, his younger sister, and his mom, dad and grandma. They lived in an apartment in the city with a cat named C'mere and a parrot named Geraldine. One day, Little Bert and Victoria wanted to ride their bikes to the park. Mom and Dad thought it was too dangerous, but Grandma told them that the kids had to have some freedom. C'mere just sat watching Geraldine. Geraldine was nervous.

Finally Mom and Dad relented, so Little Bert and Victoria put on their helmets, and away they rode. About an hour later, Victoria came running in the house yelling that Little Bert was nowhere to be found. So everyone but Bert went running to the park. Even C'mere and Geraldine got into the action.

Grandma called, "Little Bert, where are you?" Victoria looked in all their secret hiding places, and Mom and Dad just walked around being worried. Geraldine flew up into a tree and spied Little Bert across the street in the ice cream shop. Geraldine flew down to Grandma and tried to land in her hair as a signal. Grandma just got angry. Finally, Geraldine called, "C'mere, C'mere, I found him!" Understanding the universal animal language, C'mere got Victoria's attention and led her to the store.

Little Bert and Victoria came running across the street, and the whole family was united once again. Mom and Dad took everyone out for ice cream.

Little Bert: Low-Impact Version

1. Stand in a circle.
2. Split your large group into seven small groups.
3. Ask each group to come up with a sound-motion combination that they can do even if they are on the other side of the room from each other (e.g., something that doesn't require a group effort or touching like high five).
4. As each group shares their sound-motion combination, assign them a role from the story (choices are: Little Bert, Victoria, Mom, Dad, Grandma, C'mere the Cat, and Geraldine the Bird).
5. Next have the group mix up and reform their circle.
6. Read the Little Bert story. Each time a character's name is called, those representing that character should take a step in and do their sound-motion combination.
7. If "everyone" or "whole family" is said, everyone takes a step in and does their sound-motion combination.

Sample Processing Questions for Little Bert

- Were you happy with the character you portrayed? Why or why not?
- Were you hoping that your character had a large part or a small one? Why?
- What did you do to listen for your character's name? What strategies did you use?
- What are the strategies for active listening? Which ones did you use?
- Was there any entertainment value for you with this activity? What made it entertaining or not entertaining?
- Are there some things you do just for fun? What?
- Things become not fun very quickly when people get hurt or feel unsafe. How did we keep things safe for everyone so that everyone could enjoy the activity?

Connections: Little Bert

Life Skill Links: choice and accountability, communication, cooperation, patience, responsibility, safety, sense of humor

Academic Applications: • Have people write their own "Little Bert" story and try it with the class. • Use it as a way to recognize parts of speech – people can be assigned to be a "verb," "noun," "adjective," or "adverb." Every time that part of speech is said, those assigned stand up and sit down again.

Extensions: • Brainstorm ways to help make the room less distracting and noisy so that people can focus and listen better. Post them and remind students about these strategies when necessary.

Facilitation Notes

This is a fun activity that gets people moving around and acting spontaneously. It is a good activity to do in conjunction with activity 19, Night at the Improv.

Rather than using the random method of choosing characters, try having people choose their character. This may mean that you have more of one than another, but it can offer some fun discussion about why people chose the characters they did. Sometimes everyone wants to be the title character because it seemingly is the most glamorous. If this occurs, then the idea of sharing responsibility can be discussed, because not all parts of a task are glamorous but must still be done.

Adaptations for Students with Disabilities: Little Bert

Cognitive Disabilities	• Students stand up and sit down again when their character's name is called.
Orthopedic Impairment	• Use the low-impact version of this activity.
Hearing Impairment	• May not be appropriate for students who have a hearing impairment. • Have an interpreter sign the story as you go.
Visual Impairment	• Students stand up and sit down again when their character's name is called.

19. Night at the Improv

(Thanks to Michael Popowits of Michael T. Popowits & Associates for these ideas.)

Focus: Spontaneity, being put on the spot, active listening
Materials: None
Level: Grades 5 and higher

Suggested Procedure

1. **Phase I:** Clear a space and have people get into pairs.
2. Create a sentence by having partners alternate words. The trick is to listen to what your partner is saying, rather than jump to conclusions about what you think he or she will say. For example – You: "Once," Partner: "there," You: "was," Partner: "a," You: "yellow," Partner: "jacket," You: "that," Partner: "flew," You: "up," Partner: "under," You: "your," Partner: "shirt," You: "period."
3. Have partners practice for a while.
4. **Phase II:** Now have the group form a circle.
5. Create sentences with the whole group by having each person contribute a word around the circle.
6. **Phase III:** Designate a stage area.
7. Create a whole story as described below. Have someone contribute a sentence that is the beginning of a story. Examples might include: "Once upon a time there was a little goblin," or "Call me Ishmael," or "The whole thing was a big mess." This person stands on the stage area facing everyone, stage right.
8. Then have someone contribute the ending sentence of the story. Examples might include "And they lived miserably ever after" or "They rode off into the sunset," or "The whole thing was a big mess." This person stands on the other end of the stage area, stage left. Have the two people on the stage say their parts of the story in order.
9. Have someone give the middle of the story. This could be, "We thought the truth was out there," or "He fell asleep for a long time," or "The whole thing was a big mess." This person stands between the beginning and end people. In turn, they should say their lines of the whole story, as is.
10. Now have people begin putting themselves into the story with their own lines, one or two people at a time. Then, repeat the story as it stands.
11. Finally, the whole class should be lined up in the stage area. The entire story should be recited with emotion.

Sample Processing Questions for Night at the Improv

- At the beginning of this activity, how did you like being put on the spot to come up with a word or phrase so quickly?
- During the story, did you wait until the story unfolded or did you jump in right away? Why did you use that particular strategy?
- Was this difficult or easy for you? Why do you think so?
- Were there times when someone put in a word or sentence that was surprising? How did you/we react?
- How did you listen carefully in order for the sentence or story to make sense?

Connections for Night at the Improv

Life Skill Links: choice and accountability, communication, cooperation, imagination, patience
Academic Applications: • Have students try this before writing on their own. • Focus on point of view by giving the students a person who is telling the story.
Extensions: • Try doing 1-minute speeches as the next step in the improv sequence. This is where students are asked to give a 1-minute speech about anything they want. Give one yourself as a model.

Facilitation Notes

If the students are ready to be spontaneous, this can be a wonderfully fun activity. Even if they aren't feeling very spontaneous at the beginning, try doing this periodically throughout the year. It provides good listening practice, and the creativity level rises each time it is attempted.

During the story, some people stand back for a while to reflect on the story, while others jump in right away. This can open the door to a discussion about people who are more action-oriented versus people who prefer to reflect before taking action. There may be someone who just can't seem to think of what to add to the story. Mention to him or her that there is always a need for "the end" or a punctuation mark here or there.

Some classes might need to be reminded to keep it G-rated. Also, remind students to use names of people that no one knows. It can get rather messy if the story is about someone in the class or someone that everyone knows.

Adaptations for Students with Disabilities: Night at the Improv

Cognitive Disabilities	• Do this in small groups. Have students write down each word.
Orthopedic Impairment	No major modifications necessary.
Hearing Impairment	• Write down the words and sentences.
Visual Impairment	No major modifications necessary.

20. Red/Yellow/Green

Focus: Mixing, hidden agendas, active listening
Materials: None
Level: Grades K–3

Suggested Procedure
1. Clear a space and have everyone get a partner.
2. Teach the following signals: When you say "red," partners hold hands and put their hands up in the air (like a bridge). When you say "yellow," they continue to hold this bridge position, but also jump up and down together. When you say "green," everyone finds a new partner.
3. Practice the signals before beginning the game in earnest. Once everyone understands the rules, call the signals at a brisk pace so that students do not have time to be too choosy about their partners.

Sample Processing Questions for Red/Yellow/Green
- Did you or anyone else choose not to be a partner with someone? Without using names, what happened?
- How do you think it feels to want to be someone's partner when they don't want to be yours?
- What can we do in here to include people?
- Are there times when it is okay to choose not to play or work with someone? Give an example.
- Whose responsibility was it in this game to make sure that everyone was included? How did we do with that?
- Whose responsibility was it in this game to make sure everyone got a turn? How did we do with that?
- Why do you think it is important to take responsibility for making things fair?

Connections: Red/Yellow/Green
Life Skill Links: caring, choice and accountability, cooperation, empathy, relationships, respect, responsibility
Academic Applications: • *For younger students:* Use other colors, shapes, letters, or numbers that you might be learning instead of red/yellow/green.
Extensions: • Decide to implement Vivian Gussin Paley's concept of *You Can't Say You Can't Play* • Come up with other things in the classroom that are shared responsibilities (e.g., keeping the room organized, safety). Discuss how everyone in the class can share the responsibility to make these things happen.
• Identify ways that people share responsibilities in the school, at home, and in the community.

Facilitation Notes

This activity is superbly suited for the younger crowd, but even older students enjoy playing it after they have been together for a while and feel comfortable.

Keep an eye out for students who find themselves facing someone, but then turn away when they realize who that person is. Notice the reactions when this happens because it is important to process with the class.

Adaptations for Students with Disabilities: Red/Yellow/Green

Cognitive Disabilities	• Try using two colors at first.
Orthopedic Impairment	• Rather than jumping, come up with a different motion that everyone can do.
Hearing Impairment	• Hold colored paper along with the signals.
Visual Impairment	• This activity can get rowdy, so if students are uncomfortable being in the middle of that much activity, have an area earmarked for visually impaired students so that other students know where they are.

21. People to People

Focus: Mixing, hidden agendas, active listening, unselfconscious touch, choices
Materials: None
Level: Grades K and higher

Suggested Procedure

1. Clear an area and have everyone stand next to their partner in a circle.
2. You do not have a partner, and you are the caller. If you have an odd number of people, you can have a partner and be the caller.
3. Call out "people to people," and have them repeat it back.
4. Then call out two body parts (e.g., hand to hand, elbow to knee).
5. The partners touch these body parts together.
6. Call out two more body parts. They touch those two parts together.
7. When you call out "people to people" a second time, they are to find a new partner.

Sample Processing Questions for People to People

- Did it matter who you were partners with?
- Was this game fun for you? Why or why not?
- Did you feel like you could work/play with anyone else in the class – that you would welcome them and they would welcome you? Why or why not?
- If someone didn't want to touch, but used the extension (see Facilitation Notes), did you honor their choice?
- What are ways for people to connect so they have an opportunity to become friends?

Connections for People to People

Life Skill Links: caring, choice and accountability, cooperation, empathy, relationships, respect, safety
Academic Applications: • *For younger students:* This is a great way to review body parts. • *For older students:* Use this during a science unit on the human body. Instead of using the common name, use the names of muscle groups, bones, or joints (e.g., it isn't a kneecap; it's as patella).
Variations/Modifications: • *For younger students:* Allow students to stay with the same partner during the whole activity • After the students get the hang of the basic "people to people," graduate to the "twister" version. Now, people must keep all body parts stuck together until the second "people to people" is called.

Extensions: • Challenge students to choose to approach one new classmate during the week and ask him or her to work or play together. Process how it went during the next class. • Discuss or do a T-chart on what it means to be friendly. What does friendliness look, sound, and feel like?

Facilitation Notes

For Challenge by Choice, teach an extension: thumb and pinky out, while curling in the rest of the fingers. That way they can touch pinkies if they are uncomfortable with touching. This is important, especially when someone decides to call out "lips to lips."

Like all of these get-a-partner activities, watch for instances when people are rejecting or excluding others. Bring it up as something that happens among human beings, but something that needs to be addressed for the community to be healthy. If this issue is not addressed, the group will get stuck at the forming or inclusion stage of development.

Try doing this activity to a rhythm while snapping your fingers and tapping your toes.

Adaptations for Students with Disabilities: People to People

Cognitive Disabilities	• Have students stay with the same partner, rather than changing partners. • Partners can help students identify body parts. • Point to the body parts that you are calling.
Orthopedic Impairment	• Only call out body parts that can be reached while in a wheelchair.
Hearing Impairment	• Have an interpreter available, if necessary. • Point to the body parts that you are calling. • Have an agreed-upon hand signal for "people to people."
Visual Impairment	• This activity can get rowdy, so if students are uncomfortable being in the middle of that much activity, have an area earmarked for visually impaired students so that other students know where they are.

22 Martian/Politician/Tiger/Salmon

(Thanks to Sarah Shatz for this activity.)
Focus: Inclusion/exclusion, mixing, cliques
Materials: None
Level: Grades 2 and higher

Suggested Procedure

1. Clear a space in the room and stand in a circle.
2. Teach the class motions and sounds for each of the following (or make up your own).
   Martian – fingers on head like antennae, and make a "doodle, doodle, doo" noise.
   Tiger – hands out like claws, and growl.
   Politician – reach out to shake hands and say "hello there."
   Salmon – arms close to sides and jump from side to side (like swimming upstream), and say "whoosh, whoosh."
3. The object of this game is to try to do the same thing as others and then join up with them.
4. Everyone starts alone, finding one other person.
5. Without saying what each is doing, the pair counts to three and each does one of the four things.
6. If the two do different things, then nothing happens, and they go on to find someone else to try again.

7. If they do the same thing, they link elbows. They are now a team.
8. The pairs then decide on one thing to do, find another person or pair, and do their thing. If it is the same as the other person or pair, they join up.
9. In this way, small groups will begin to form. This continues until there are two large groups, with each group deciding what to do and trying to end up as one large group.
10. In the process, as groups form, some people will continue to be alone. Notice what those in groups do to try to include the ones who are alone (if anything).

Sample Processing Questions for Martian/Politician/Tiger/Salmon
- How did it feel to match up with others and be included?
- For those who were alone for a long time, how did it feel to not match up?
- Did anyone do anything to try to include those who were alone? If so, what? If not, what could they have done?
- Being excluded can be hurtful. When are there times in here when people are excluded?

Connections for Martian/Politician/Tiger/Salmon
Life Skill Links: caring, cooperation, relationships, respect
Variations/Modifications: • *For younger students:* Use fewer motions. Have the students make them up.
Extensions: • Create a code of conduct for dealing with exclusion for the classroom. When is it okay not to invite someone in (e.g., when an activity or project is in midstream and having someone join would be disruptive)? When is it not okay to exclude someone? • *For older students:* Read excerpts from the book, *It's Not OK to Say You Can't Play* by Vivian Paley. As young people who may be looking after younger children, they may be in a situation to use these ideas and also incorporate them into their own lives.

Facilitation Notes
If you are working directly on issues of inclusion and mixing, note that this activity sometimes causes a few people to be left alone. Suggest that they think about how to include people if this happens.

Sometimes when two or three larger groups are left, a dynamic occurs in which one or more groups will consciously try not to match up with the others. This can result in a great discussion about conformity and individuality.

This activity can be quite loud, so make sure it won't be disruptive to another classroom.

Adaptations for Students with Disabilities: Martian/Politician/Tiger/Salmon

Cognitive Disabilities	• Use two or three motions.
Orthopedic Impairment	• Create motions that everyone can do.
Hearing Impairment	• Have an interpreter available, if necessary. • Ask people to use fingers when counting. • Use ASL signs or other hand signs for the motions.
Visual Impairment	• Make sure to use sounds along with motions.

23. Mixing Game (Thanks to Kathy Hellenbrand for this activity.)
Focus: Put-ups/put-downs, mixing, perspective taking
Materials: None
Level: Grades K–2

Suggested Procedure

1. Tell the students that you are going to call out a word. One that has like-sounding rhymes is fun – like "dog" or "boot."
2. When you call out the word, they are to find a partner and hold their hands in the air.
3. Meanwhile, you are going to count to three out loud. Those who have a partner by the time you get to three stay where they are for the next round.
4. Those who did not get a partner in time get to join you to count for the next round.
5. If there is an odd number, one group of three is okay – but only one. If there is more than one group of three, they all join you for the next round.
6. Call out "dog" and count very slowly to three so that everyone has time to get a partner. This is the practice round.
7. Call out "dog" again and count a little faster. Those who do not have partners join you. You call out "dog" and they all count together.
8. Continue until there are just a few pairs left. Then start all over.
9. This time call out words that sound like "dog" – "fog", "hog." They can't move until they hear "dog."
10. Speed it up so that it becomes harder to choose partners and students have to go to whomever is closest.

Sample Processing Questions for Mixing Game

- Did you have a strategy for getting partners?
- What happened if you thought about it too much?
- Did you pay attention to whom you were trying to partner with, or did it not matter?
- How did it feel not to have a partner?
- What can we do to include people when we are working/playing?

Connections for Mixing Game

Life Skill Links: caring, choice and accountability, cooperation, relationships, respect

Extensions: • When you want students to work in pairs during class, do this activity for a few rounds to get people paired up with someone they may not usually choose to work with. • Practice being welcoming to a partner or small group members. Decide on a phrase and action when working in groups (such as, "I'm glad we're working together" with a high five) for students to say when they get a partner or into small groups. After finishing a task, have students thank their partners. This may seem superficial, but it is a way to practice respect and how to be polite. Eventually it will become second nature.

Facilitation Notes

This activity is a great way to get students to start thinking about mixing with each other. Start out slowly so students feel successful. When people do not get partners, make sure it is not presented as a punishment, but as a part of the game. Say things like, "All right, you get to come and count with me!" rather than, "Oh, you're too slow and have to come out of the game." Processing, then, is focused on what choices they made, as opposed to how you used your power to pull them out of the game. This is a subtle distinction, but one that makes a big difference.

Adaptations for Students with Disabilities: Mixing Game

Cognitive Disabilities	No major modifications necessary.
Orthopedic Impairment	• Make sure people have time to get partners.
Hearing Impairment	• Use a visual signal to indicate "go."
Visual Impairment	• This activity can get rowdy, so if students are uncomfortable being in the middle of that much activity, have an area earmarked for visually impaired students so that other students know where they are.

24. Group Cheers

Focus: Active listening, put-ups/put-downs, mixing
Materials: None
Level: Grades 5 and higher

Suggested Procedure

1. Ask your class to divide up into groups according to the season in which they were born. You will probably have groups of different sizes.
2. Give the groups 5 minutes to create a cheer about their birth season for the rest of the class.
3. Before the groups present their cheers, discuss how to be an audience. Make sure to remind students that when there is a performance, it is common practice to applaud at the end.
4. Have each group present their cheer.

Sample Processing Questions for Group Cheers

- How did you have to use your attentive listening skills when planning your cheer?
- What kind of give and take was necessary to make quick decisions about what your cheer would be?
- Did you feel embarrassed to do this in front of the class? Why or why not?
- How were you responsible to your group during this activity?
- How was working with people when you didn't really have a choice about which group you would be in?

Connections for Group Cheers

Life Skill Links: choice and accountability, communication, cooperation, flexibility, imagination, leadership, relationships, respect, responsibility
Academic Applications: • Students can do a cheer for just about anything. How about, "Algebra, algebra it's the best! X's and Y's and all the rest!" Encourage them to use the vocabulary and concepts they are learning.
Extensions: • Create a short class cheer that can be used when energy is low or there is something to celebrate.

Facilitation Notes

My experience is that people really enjoy cheering about things. It is a way to honor uniqueness and ideas, and it also brings people together. The amount of creativity is endless. Have fun with this one.

Adaptations for Students with Disabilities: Group Cheers

Cognitive Disabilities	No major modifications necessary.
Orthopedic Impairment	No major modifications necessary.
Hearing Impairment	• Write cheer on board. • Have an interpreter available, if necessary.
Visual Impairment	No major modifications necessary.

Challenge By Choice Activities

It is one thing to talk about Challenge by Choice; it is another to experience it. A main goal for any group is for its members to be as independent as possible, with people getting their needs met because they are able to ask for what they need. In the beginning, when norms are not yet established, many people are willing to subjugate their own needs in order to fit into the group. Challenge by Choice cannot be over-emphasized in these cases. An atmosphere where choice is honored is empowering; it allows students to take the first steps away from dependence.

These activities are Ice Breakers and Deinhibitizers that lend themselves to a beginning exploration of Challenge by Choice. They are not the only possible activities. Moreover, when an issue of choice is brought up during any activity, a teachable moment exists.

 ## 25. Neighbors

Focus: Challenge by Choice, being put on the spot, hidden agendas, perspective taking
Materials: Place markers for everyone (poly dots, scrap paper, pieces of cloth, etc.)
Level: Grades K and higher

Suggested Procedure

1. Clear a space and have students stand in a circle. You take the middle.
2. Each person stands on a place marker.
3. The person in the middle (you at this point) asks a question that is true for him or her (e.g., "Is there anyone here who has a brother?" because I have a brother. I cannot ask, "Is there anyone here who has been to Alaska?" because I have not been to Alaska.)
4. Once the question is asked, anyone who can answer "yes" to the question steps forward into the middle of the circle. Then, each of these people should move to find any empty place that is not their own.
5. The person in the middle also finds an empty place – thus leaving someone without a spot, which makes this new person take the middle to ask the next question.
6. Some rules you may wish to interject after the game gets going: 1) No one can move to the place next to him or her; everyone must skip at least one place marker. 2) To add another dynamic you can allow anyone who says "no" to the question to fill an empty spot next to him or her if available.

Sample Processing Questions for Neighbors

- Would it have been possible not to move even if you could answer "yes" to the question? How would we know? Would it matter?
- Is it dishonest to hold information back? Why or why not?
- What kind of choices did you make? For example, how did you interpret number of brothers and sisters (if this was asked)? Did you include half or stepsiblings? Is one interpretation right and another wrong?
- What happened when someone was challenged about their interpretation? How did they/the group handle that?
- How should we handle the choices that people make, even if we don't agree with them? When is it necessary to intervene or challenge a choice that someone is making?

Connections: Neighbors

Life Skill Links: choice and accountability, curiosity, effort, forgiveness, honesty, justice, patience, relationships, respect, responsibility, truthfulness
Variations/Modifications: • *For younger students:* At first, you may need to stay in the middle. Also, practice moving around safely and doing this with "walking feet" before starting. • Do this activity in pairs. Each marker is occupied by two people who stay together for the whole activity. Two people are in the middle and must decide on something that is true for both of them. In order to move to a new place

marker, the question must be true for both people in a pair. They run together to a different marker. Give the pairs a minute to come up with three things that they have in common so that they are ready with a question when they get into the middle. (Thanks to Jim Dunn for this variation).

Extensions: • Create a system or agreement for the classroom about the right to pass. If someone doesn't want to share and others are pressuring her or him, or if someone is being challenged by being called a cheater or liar – How should we deal with that situation in here? It may be a simple agreement to take 5 minutes of discussion time, or to ask the parties to step into the hallway with a mediator. Try it and evaluate if it works or not. This strategy can be helpful when power struggles and loud disagreements arise.

Facilitation Notes

This activity provides a nonthreatening way to bring up the issue of choice. Sometimes there are disagreements of interpretation about questions. Is one wrong and the other right? Or are they just different? This can lead to a larger discussion about choices and when to question the choices that a peer or friend is making, especially if it seems to cause harm. Challenge by Choice is also "fuzzy" because people genuinely want others to succeed. Success, in itself, is open to many different interpretations. The only way to come to a mutual understanding about these issues is to discuss the varying points of view.

Caution: A safety concern with this activity occurs when people don't want to be in the middle and become aggressive about finding a spot. Caution students that no tackling or body checking is allowed in this activity. Also, remind students to keep it G-rated.

Adaptations for Students with Disabilities: Neighbors

Cognitive Disabilities	• Reiterate rules and provide several examples. • Create some generic prompt cards that say: "I wonder if any of my neighbors ..." (have shoes on, like pizza, watch TV, etc.). • Smaller groups may work better.
Orthopedic Impairment	• Have another participant assist in pushing the wheelchair if necessary. • Do not use the rule that people cannot go to the spot next to him or her.
Hearing Impairment	• Use another participant or interpreter to indicate the students' questions and inform them of others' statements. •Have students make up cards ahead of time with their questions.
Visual Impairment	• Have another participant act as a guide to assist the person with a visual impairment to a place marker. • Do this activity in pairs.
Notes	• Play the entire game with all the participants working as partners.

MPS

26. Everybody's It

Focus: Challenge by Choice
Materials: None
Level: Grades K and higher

Suggested Procedure

1. This is an outside or gym activity. Create boundaries of which everyone is aware.
2. The only rule for this game is that *everybody* is "it."
3. Once the game starts, if a person gets tagged, he or she must squat down.

4. If two people tag each other, they both squat down.
5. When a few people are left, count down from 10 and start again. This goes quickly.
6. Try playing this a few times before talking about it. Then play it again after your discussion.

Sample Processing Questions for Everybody's It
- Did you find yourself backing away from others or going after people? Did you do both?
- What were some ways (strategies) that you used to dodge the taggers? When did you use these strategies, and how effective were they?
- What were ways that you helped keep other people safe?
- Did it take more effort to keep others safe? Why or why not?
- Are there times in your life (school, home, teams, organizations) when you go after something?
- Are there times in your life (school, home, teams, organizations) when you sit back and wait?
- What are some choices you have made in your life (even today)?
- Did anyone choose to be tagged quickly so they didn't have to keep playing? Is that an acceptable choice? Why or why not?

Connections for Everybody's It
Life Skill Links: caring, choice and accountability, effort, empathy, initiative, integrity, safety
Academic Applications: • Use this activity as a way to connect with choices when exploring these ideas in health class.
Variations/Modifications: • *For younger students:* Divide the class either into groups of 4–5 or split the class in half (depending upon what your class is ready for) with each group being in a separate playing area. (Thanks to D.D. Sturdevant for this variation) • Play Hospital Tag: The same rules apply except that each person gets tagged three times before squatting down. Each time a person is tagged, he or she puts a hand over that spot. **A cautionary statement should be made that tagging with the feet is not acceptable, as it can cause someone to be kicked.**
Extensions: • At the end of the day, ask students to rate from 1–5 (one being lowest, five highest) what kind of effort they put into the activities for that day. Add them up and get an average. Keep track of the average to look for patterns. Ask why they rated themselves that way. • Brainstorm ways to appreciate and celebrate individual and group effort. • Check in with other teachers about the effort they see your students making. Maybe choose a few students each day to focus on so that every student is covered throughout the week. Have a one-to-one chat with these students to get their opinion on the type of effort they are making. • Have a form for students to fill out about their effort and choices in each class throughout the day. Return to it and reassess periodically. Have them set goals to maximize effort.

Facilitation Notes
This activity offers an opportunity to talk about other choices during the year because the activity itself is the picture of choices – sometimes running after something, sometimes backing away.

This activity can also stimulate some heated discussion about competition and integrity – was someone really tagged or not? Periodically, a student will not squat down because he or she is so focused on "winning" that a tag is only a tag if someone else sees it. This makes for good food for thought and discussion.

Adaptations for Students with Disabilities: Everybody's It

Cognitive Disabilities	• For safety reasons, you may want participants to move out of the defined area after they are tagged.
Orthopedic Impairment	• For safety reasons, you may want participants to move out of the defined area after they are tagged. • Don't have students squat down, but freeze instead.

Adaptations for Students with Disabilities: Everybody's It (cont.)

Hearing Impairment	No major modifications necessary.
Visual Impairment	• Play the game with auditory feedback (bells, clapping, talking). Boundaries should be physically marked (rope, mats, etc.). • For safety reasons, you may want participants to move out of the defined area after they are tagged. • Walk rather than run.

MPS

27. Growth Circles

Focus: Challenge by Choice, perspective taking
Materials: Ropes or tape on the floor – three concentric circles (see figure 4.1)
Level: Grades 5 and higher

Growth circles[3] look like this:

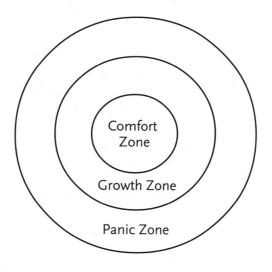

Figure 4.1

Suggested Procedure

1. Outline the growth circles on the floor and discuss the meaning of growth circles (see facilitation notes).
2. Ask questions like the following, and have people put themselves into the circles they feel are most appropriate. How do you feel about ...
    - spiders?
    - speaking in front of a large group?
    - singing solo in front of a large group?
    - singing in a choir?
    - bungee jumping?
    - telling a family member that you love him or her?
    - heights?
    - confronting a friend about something they did or said?
    - snakes?
    - taking a math test?
    - introducing yourself to someone new?
    - taking a driver's test?
3. After each question is asked and people have moved into position, give the students a chance to comment on why they put themselves in their particular spots. Is there a story to share? Who is sharing a point of view?
4. After a few of your questions, allow the students to ask any questions they have for the class.

Sample Processing Questions for Growth Circles
- Were you surprised by where you ended up compared with others?
- How can we support the choices each of us makes?
- How can we encourage you to step into your growth zone without putting too much pressure on you? What kind of encouragement is useful to you?
- What can we do to respectfully tell people when the encouragement they are giving is too much?
- How did your experiences influence the choices you made? What is your personal wisdom?

Connections for Growth Circles
Life Skill Links: caring, choice and accountability, communication, courage, curiosity, effort, empathy, perseverance, positive attitude, respect, responsibility, safety, wisdom

Academic Applications: • Take examples of people from history, biographies, or stories in which people have stretched their comfort zones and spent much time in their growth zones. Take other examples of people who did not take risks, and those who pushed too far and went into their panic zones. Discuss and write about the implications of each person's choice. • This is a good activity to do before a big standardized test or a final because it gives people a chance to acknowledge the anxiety that is present and talk about ways – both individually and collectively – they can cope with the stress. Choosing a way to celebrate the completion of the test, for example, can help to validate that it is a difficult task and that each student is not alone in his or her anxiety.

Extensions: • Have students write in a journal about something they would like to try in school this week/month/quarter/semester/year that would be a stretch for them. See if anyone would like to share with the whole class (offer the right to pass). Then check in with them individually and help them to attain their goal. • When students choose to pass, honor their decision. If you think they are capable of doing something they are choosing not to do, check in with the students individually and encourage them to step out of their comfort zone without exerting too much pressure on the them. • Discuss when it is important to allow others to make choices and when it might be necessary to step in when someone is making a harmful choice. What are safe choices, and what are harmful ones? When might it be helpful to provide encouragement, and when does that cross the line to pressure?

Facilitation Notes
When considering the idea of Challenge by Choice, it is helpful to talk about the idea of challenge as well as choice. The Growth Circles activity allows this. When we are in our comfort zones, each of us is in a place that is safe and secure. By choosing to step out of our comfort zones to the growth zone, we are open to new ideas and experiences. We are, in essence, breaking new ground. Although not always comfortable, this is a place for optimum learning.

What we try to avoid is going beyond the growth zone into the panic zone. The panic zone is a place where learning cannot take place because the threat is too great.

Competence is built by moving between the comfort zone and the growth zone. Take, for example, the task of learning how to ride a bike. Most youngsters do not simply hop on a two-wheel bike and take off. This would be too difficult and anxiety-producing. Ideally, they start with the support of training wheels. The challenge remains without the risk of undue harm. Eventually, the training wheels become easy (moving the rider into the comfort zone). The training wheels come off, but the rider is not left alone yet. Generally, an adult or older sibling tags along, holding onto the back of the bike for stability. Now back in the growth zone, the rider has more control of the bike than having training wheels, but with less support. Eventually, this, too, becomes easy (comfort zone), and the helping person lets go. The rider is now on his or her own and back in the growth zone.

Challenge by Choice affords the opportunity for students (and teachers) to make the decisions that are right for them. It is a delicate balancing act for each individual – how to take advantage of challenging opportunities without going over the edge. This activity helps the class to explore these issues. Through discussion, boundaries can begin to be established about how much to encourage people to push themselves and how to support the choices each person makes.

Adaptations for Students with Disabilities: Growth Circles

Cognitive Disabilities	• Focus on one area at a time (comfort zone first, then growth zone, then panic zone) so students can more easily distinguish their feelings.
Orthopedic Impairment	• Make sure there is enough room for wheelchairs in each zone.
Hearing Impairment	• Have an interpreter available, if necessary.
Visual Impairment	• Have a partner help the student to the area of his or her choice. • Make sure the boundaries are well-defined.

28. Song Tag (Thanks to Nancy Constable for this activity.)

Focus: Challenge by Choice, being put on the spot, acting silly, perspective taking
Materials: None
Level: Grades 4 and higher

Suggested Procedure
1. Clear an area and have students stand in a circle. You stand in the middle.
2. Tell the class that you will start singing a song.
3. When someone thinks of a song that connects with your song in any way, that person steps in and starts singing his or her song.
4. You will then take that person's place in the circle.
5. This continues for a while. People choose to step in the middle and sing; in fact, some people will take more than one turn, but not everyone is expected to take a turn.

Sample Processing Questions for Song Tag
• Why did you choose either to step in the middle and sing, or to stay back and observe?
• Was it possible to participate in the activity without taking a turn in the middle? How?
• Were you singing along with anyone in the middle? Is that participating? Why or why not?
• What does Challenge by Choice mean to you?

Connections for Song Tag
Life Skill Links: caring, choice and accountability, empathy, respect
Academic Applications: • After doing the activity, see if students can remember all the songs that were sung, and then try to identify the genre of music for each song.
Variations/Modifications: • Do this with books and movie titles/themes, or try it as Dance Tag.
Extensions: • In small groups, ask students to define what Challenge by Choice means to them. Have them share it with the class and discuss. • Before doing a class or small group project, have students discuss how people can participate in different ways. For example, if they are doing a project that involves a variety of tasks (writing, drawing, charting, researching, etc.), how can they split up the tasks to get the whole project done?

Facilitation Notes
This activity can be highly threatening for some people. Others can't wait to get in the middle and sing. It is a good way to explore the issue of choice because all participants feel involved in the activity even if they are observers. It is also possible to branch off into a discussion of individual strengths. Some love to sing, others to dance, read, participate in athletics, communicate, and so on.

At the beginning, be prepared to take multiple turns in the middle yourself. It may take some time before many people will risk a turn in the middle.

Adaptations for Students with Disabilities: Song Tag

Cognitive Disabilities	• Brainstorm a list of songs in advance on a given topic. Practice them all first, then try the activity.
Orthopedic Impairment	No major modifications necessary.
Hearing Impairment	• This activity may not be appropriate for people with hearing impairments. • Try this activity with dance moves.
Visual Impairment	• Have well-defined boundaries. • Do this sitting, and have people stand up when they wish.

 # 29. Group Interview

Focus: Challenge by Choice, being put on the spot, active listening, perspective taking
Materials: None
Level: Grades 4 and higher

Suggested Procedure

1. Sit in a circle.
2. Brainstorm a list of questions that people are curious about to ask students in the class.
3. Ask for a volunteer who will be interviewed by the whole group.
4. The idea is for this person to be questioned by the others and answer the questions as honestly as possible.
5. If the person being interviewed doesn't want to answer a question, she or he can pass.
6. Allow yourself to be interviewed as well.

Sample Processing Questions for Group Interview

- How did it feel to be the center of attention?
- Did it seem like you really had a choice about answering the questions? Why or why not?
- How did your classmates treat you when you were being interviewed?

Connections for Group Interview

Life Skill Links: choice and accountability, communication, courage, curiosity, honesty, patience, respect
Academic Applications: • Have students research someone from history and be interviewed as that person. • Teach interviewing techniques and have students practice with this activity. They can then interview others in the school or in the community.
Variations/Modifications: • Do this in small groups so that more people get a turn. Have each small group report on what they have learned about the person who was interviewed.
Extensions: • Have adults from the school (principal, custodian, social worker, nurse, secretary, other teachers, etc.) come into class for an interview. Have students brainstorm questions and practice their active listening skills during the interview.

Facilitation Notes

Group interview is an activity that can be revisited throughout the school year so that everyone who wants to be interviewed can do so. It is a great activity to do when 10 minutes of time are left at the end of a class. Be prepared with your own questions to help the process get going.

Generally, students are respectful of the difficult position the interviewee is in and will ask respectful questions. With practice, the questions become deeper and more thoughtful.

If it is early in the year and a student who has a history of being teased is being interviewed, you may need to be alert to questions with hidden put-downs. If this occurs, it needs to be talked about so students understand that a community is a place that is both physically and emotionally safe.

Adaptations for Students with Disabilities: Group Interview

Cognitive Disabilities	• Brainstorm a list of questions first.
Orthopedic Impairment	No major modifications necessary.
Hearing Impairment	• Have an interpreter available if necessary. • Write questions on the board.
Visual Impairment	No major modifications necessary.

 # 30. 1001 Questions

Focus: Taking turns, active listening, perspective taking
Materials: Item to pass or talking stick
Level: Grades K–3

Suggested Procedure

1. Sit in a circle.
2. Have a list of short-answer questions ready. Here are some:
    - How old are you?
    - What is one of your favorite colors?
    - Where were you born?
    - How many brothers and sisters do you have?
    - Do you have a pet? If so, what kind?
    - What is something you want to learn to do?
    - Where is a place you have traveled?
    - Do you know the first name of an adult who lives with you?
    - What is a kind of food you could eat every day?
    - What is your middle name (if you have one)?
3. Tell the class that you will ask the first question and then you will pass the talking stick around. Whoever has the stick can either answer the question, or say "pass." They then pass the stick on to the person next to them.
4. Before you start, review active listening skills.

Sample Processing Questions for 1001 Questions

- Did you feel like you were all active listeners? How could you tell?
- Is it easy or difficult for you to choose to pass? What makes it easy or difficult?
- How easy or hard was it to wait your turn?
- Were we respectful of those talking after we had our turn?

Connections for 1001 Questions

Life Skill Links: choice and accountability, communication, cooperation, curiosity, patience, respect, self-discipline
Academic Applications: • Have students write their own questions for use with this activity.

Variations/Modifications: • Ask other people to join the class for this activity — maybe some older students, parents, or other adults in the school.

Extensions: • Have students create their own talking sticks. Use a different one each time you have a community circle.

Facilitation Notes

The first time you do this, you might use a couple of questions. This is also an activity you can do every day or every week when you open up your community circle — one question per day. As the year progresses, the questions can get more involved. Also, have students create their own questions, and draw one out of the hat each day.

Adaptations for Students with Disabilities: 1001 Questions

Cognitive Disabilities	No major modifications necessary.
Orthopedic Impairment	No major modifications necessary.
Hearing Impairment	• Have an interpreter available if necessary. • Write questions on the board.
Visual Impairment	No major modifications necessary.

 ## 31. Laughing Matters (Adapted from "Mookie," *Adventures in Peacemaking*, p. 123)

Focus: Being put on the spot, dealing with teasing and conflict
Materials: None
Level: Grades K–5

Suggested Procedure

1. Begin with a discussion about what it feels like to be teased.
2. Introduce a nonsensical word like "fiddlesticks."
3. Practice saying the word in different ways. How would an opera singer say it, a baby, a goat, a dog, a rapper, a monster, or a ghost?
4. Have the class line up in two lines, facing each other.
5. Tell the students that the object is to have someone walk between the two lines without smiling or laughing.
6. Rules are: The walker must keep his or her eyes open. The people in the lines must stay out of the walker's way (give them space to walk) and may not touch the walker in any way. The only word that may be spoken is the nonsensical word that was introduced. The people in the lines, though, may say the word any way they want, and make any kinds of faces they would like.
7. Give everyone the right to pass by starting at one end and asking if that person would like to try it. She or he can either say "yes" and do it or say "pass," at which point you will move to the next person.
8. Once through the whole line, go back to give the people who passed an opportunity to try it. They still have the right to pass.

Sample Processing Questions for Laughing Matters

• Was this hard for you? How? What strategies did you use to try not to smile?
• How did it feel to be the ones saying "fiddlesticks?"
• How did it feel to walk down the line?
• Was it easy or hard for you to decide to take a turn? Are you glad you had the choice?

Connections for Laughing Matters

Life Skill Links: caring, choice and accountability, empathy, patience, peacefulness, positive attitude, problem solving, relationships, respect, resourcefulness, safety, self-discipline

Extensions: • Ignoring is one way to deal with teasing. When is it not appropriate to ignore it? Brainstorm other ways to deal with teasing. • Discuss why some people chose to do this while others did not. Go around and ask each person an activity they might choose (or have chosen in the past) not to participate in. What caused them to make that choice? • Create a chart of school activities in which students do and do not have a choice. For example, you might list recess as not being a choice, but what they do at recess as a choice. Or you might have times when students must work in groups, but they have a choice about whom they work with.

Facilitation Notes

It is common for adults to tell children to ignore teasing, but youngsters are seldom given concrete strategies to do this very difficult thing. This activity is a way to do that because the strategies used to ignore someone who is trying to make them laugh are similar to the ones used when someone is trying to make them upset. Any strategies they choose to use are acceptable. Common ones are: looking away or focusing on something else, thinking about other things, and getting through it quickly (walking away).

It is imperative that students really feel like they have a choice to do or not do this activity. Walking a gauntlet can be intimidating, even if it is about laughing.

Adaptations for Students with Disabilities: Laughing Matters

Cognitive Disabilities	• This activity may not be appropriate for students with cognitive disabilities.
Orthopedic Impairment	• Make sure there is space in and between the lines for a wheelchair.
Hearing Impairment	• Have an interpreter available if necessary.
Visual Impairment	• Have students in the lines use "bumpers up" – hands up in front of them, palms facing out – to help the participant know where the lines are.

Full Value Contract Activities

As with Challenge by Choice, Full Value Contract (FVC) is better experienced than talked about. There are many ways, and times, to introduce FVC. Some facilitators like to begin their community building with a FVC, while others prefer to wait until the group has some history together. I like to begin with one that lays a foundation for the beginning of group norms around safety and respect. Later, when students are more willing to share their thoughts with people who are no longer strangers, we develop a more extensive FVC that is put in place for the life of the community.

No matter your preference as a facilitator, it is important to have a FVC in place before a group heads into trust issues. In this way, students

It is difficult to reach consensus in large groups. **Strategies for Dealing with Full Value Contracts (FVC)** with large classes:

• Have students do a FVC in groups of four to six. Then share their process and discussion with the whole class. Generally, there is an overlap of ideas. Tape all ideas together into a large scroll or mural. The contract can be referred to over time, and certain ideals will become more pertinent to the class than others.

• Brainstorm 10 to 15 ideals. Each week focus on one and add it to the FVC, which is hanging in the room.

• Create a group history mural/scroll using butcher paper. Every so often ask the students what they have learned about their community, and have them depict it on the scroll. This group history becomes the FVC for the class.

have established ownership for their class by helping to set the ground rules. Make sure you also commit to the FVC.

Once a FVC is established, it is seen as a working document to which everyone has made a commitment. The qualities that are agreed upon provide a structure for the operation of this particular class. During processing sessions, the FVC can be referred to when discussing how group members are interacting. If one or more of the qualities are disregarded, it can be discussed. The qualities that are written are ideals – something to work toward. Every time one is ignored, it is an opportunity to learn. One pitfall of a FVC is that it is sometimes used to punish someone if he or she does not live up to the community standards. Remember that it is a guide. If the same quality is consistently violated, then it must be discussed.

• Using sticky notes, have each student write what is important to her or him in this community. Post the notes; over time give people a chance to explain their messages.

• Create a puzzle by taking poster board and cutting it into different shapes. In small groups, the students draw or write their ideals, and then put them back together into a complete puzzle. Hold a couple of blank pieces out so the class can add more to the puzzle as they go along.

Finally, the FVC needs to be reevaluated periodically in order to keep it up to date with the developing community. With experience, group members may choose to add a quality to the FVC, or they may even choose to remove one if it is no longer relevant.

Word Meaning Chart: One of the difficulties in discussing issues with students is that they may try to give the "correct answers" without giving them much thought. Another concern is knowing whether or not the words carry much meaning for the students. One strategy is ask the students what a particular action looks like, sounds like, and feels like. Chart it so that everyone can see the results. It may look like this:

Topic	Looks Like	Sounds Like	Feels Like
Cooperation	Reaching out to help someone. Sitting close together. Looking at each other. Not talking when someone else is talking.	Saying, "Thank you." Saying, "Sorry." One person talking at a time. Saying, "I'll help."	Safe Not crazy Comfortable Happy

32 Five Finger Contract

Focus: Initiating and exploring a Full Value Contract, establishing norms
Materials: Writing materials (optional)
Levels: Grades K–6

Suggested Procedure

1. Teach the class the **Five Finger Contract**. Each of the fingers is a reminder to us about points that will make this class a safe and respectful place for everybody:
   - **Pinky**: Safety – it's the smallest and most vulnerable finger.
   - **Ring Finger**: Commitment – willingness to let things go (and not hold grudges).
   - **Middle Finger**: Awareness of put-downs.
   - **Pointer Finger**: Taking responsibility instead of pointing blame.
   - **Thumb**: Agreement to work toward group goals.
2. Write about or discuss each one to agree on what it means to this class at this time.
3. Have small groups address each point with a pi chart (see example Word Meaning Chart preceding this activity) and report to the class.

4. Another strategy is to write these on poster board and ask everyone to add their thumbprints to denote agreement (once everyone indicates that they understand them).
5. Revisit the Five Finger Contract periodically to learn more about what each point means. For example, talk about one or more points after an activity or as an evaluation at the end of a class. Talk about one or more points before a class begins to remind students about creating a safe environment.

Sample Processing Questions for Five Finger Contract
- How would you define each of these points?
- Considering we're not perfect, and that we are working toward these goals, what should we do when one (or more) of these points is ignored?
- How can we celebrate when we are adhering to these goals?

Connections for Five Finger Contract
Life Skill Links: caring, choice and accountability, citizenship, communication, cooperation, effort, forgiveness, integrity, justice, positive attitude, purpose, respect, responsibility, safety, self-discipline
Academic Applications: • Putting a Full Value Contract into place (and making it come alive in the classroom) creates an atmosphere where students feel comfortable learning, thus increasing academic achievement.
Variations/Modifications: • Draw a hand on a large piece of paper or poster board. Have students decorate it. Write specific examples of each ideal on or around the hand.
Extensions: • Have each student create his or her own Five Finger Contract by tracing their own hands on a piece of paper. They can write in some goals and ideals they have for themselves, and then post it on their desks or in a notebook where they will see it every day as a reminder.

Facilitation Notes
Many times it is difficult to know where to begin when attempting to create a safe and respectful community. The Five Finger Contract is a good place to start. It is important to set the right tone at the beginning of the process, and this can help. After the class has been together for a while, students can move into another phase in which they can create a Full Value Contract of their own.

Adaptations for Students with Disabilities: Five Finger Contract

Cognitive Disabilities	No major modifications necessary.
Orthopedic Impairment	No major modifications necessary.
Hearing Impairment	• Have an interpreter available if necessary.
Visual Impairment	• Revisit verbally at regular intervals to act as a reminder.

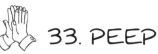 # 33. PEEP
Focus: Initiating and exploring a Full Value Contract, establishing norms, sharing responsibility
Materials: Writing materials (optional)
Level: Grades 6 and higher

Suggested Procedure
1. Teach the class about safety using PEEP as described below:
   Physical: Be aware of physical limitations; take care of yourself. Watch out for the physical well-being of others. When outside, use sunscreen, drink water, and wear appropriate clothing.
   Emotional: Use and respect Challenge by Choice; only volunteer yourself; no-put downs. Be aware of peer pressure.

Environmental: Move in a controlled manner; follow safety protocols/directions; be aware of weather, insects, etc. When inside, be aware of furniture. Take care of the environment by cleaning up and being gentle with equipment and natural things.

Personal: Take responsibility for one's needs; wear appropriate clothing for the task (e.g., if outside, wear close-toe shoes); nothing in mouth, etc. (In some programs this can also focus on refraining from use of drugs or alcohol.)

2. Have small groups address each point with a pi chart and report to the class.
3. Another strategy is to write these on poster board and ask everyone to sign it to denote agreement to work toward these ideals.
4. Tell students that if they see, feel, or hear a safety issue at any time, they are to "PEEP" it. That way safety issues can be avoided, or the whole class can stop and learn from what has happened.
5. Revisit PEEP periodically to learn more about what each point means.

Sample Processing Questions for PEEP
- How would you define each of these four points?
- What are some situations that can be "PEEPED"?
- How should we handle hearing a "PEEP"?

Connections for PEEP
Life Skill Links: caring, choice and accountability, cooperation, effort, forgiveness, integrity, justice, positive attitude, purpose, respect, responsibility, safety, self-discipline

Academic Applications: • Putting a Full Value Contract into place (and making it come alive in the classroom) creates an atmosphere where students feel comfortable learning, thus increasing academic achievement.

Variations/Modifications: • For fun, bring in the little marshmallow chickens called Peeps™. Assign a safety point for each one and put them on display in the room. When a "PEEP" is called, choose the little chicken that needs to be talked about.

Extensions: • Give each student a chart with PEEP written on it. Have each student label one or two things they would like to remember about each point. For example, someone may write "no put-downs" next to emotional safety. Then post it on their desks or in a notebook where they will see it every day as a reminder.

Facilitation Notes
PEEP is a wonderful way to involve everyone in personal and group safety. Explain that, as the teacher, you are ultimately responsible for everyone's safety and will step in when a situation seems unsafe. This applies to emotional as well as physical safety. As one person, however, it is impossible to monitor all situations all of the time. Therefore, it is important that each member of the class take responsibility for safety and not always wait for the teacher to step in. If an unsafe situation presents itself, all one has to do is say "PEEP." At that point everything stops until the matter is dealt with. Here are three examples:

1) Someone in the class calls another student a name. Those who hear it say "PEEP." Action stops, and the students are questioned. One says, "She called me a name!" The other says, "I was just teasing." You ask, "Did you think she was teasing?" "No, it seemed as if she meant it." The first student then says that she won't do it again. Although this may not solve the problem, it is a beginning. Having those around recognize the put-down, and then having a short discussion, allows all to learn from the incident.

2) Someone in the class calls another student a name. Those who hear it say "PEEP." Continue with the activity. It might be enough just to recognize the put-down for this behavior to stop.

3) The class has moved the furniture to do the activity Neighbors. There is a table right behind one of the place markers. Just as the activity is about to start someone says "PEEP." Action stops, and that person (who is across the circle from the table) says, "That table is really close to the place marker; I'm concerned that we'll run into it." The table is moved and action continues.

This is all about sharing responsibility. Generally, people are reluctant to "PEEP" others at first. You can model this response to unsafe situations. Later, "PEEPING" becomes more shared as students become more comfortable. A norm has been established.

Adaptations for Students with Disabilities: PEEP

Cognitive Disabilities	• Modify PEEP to just Physical (body) and Emotional (feelings) at first.
Orthopedic Impairment	No major modifications necessary.
Hearing Impairment	• Have an interpreter available, if necessary. • Have a visual signal for PEEP to go with the verbal signal.
Visual Impairment	• Use tactile representatives for each part of PEEP.

34. Play Hard, Play Safe, Play Fair, Have Fun

(Thanks to the New Games Foundation for this concept.)
Focus: Full Value Contract, creating definitions for each concept, perspective taking
Materials: Writing materials
Level: Grades K and higher

Suggested Procedure

1. Divide the class into smaller groups.
2. Give each group one of the phrases (e.g., Play Hard), and ask them to define it.
3. Have each small group present their definition to the class.
4. Discuss the definition – make any additions or changes as the discussion progresses.
5. Post and revisit the definitions periodically to revise the contract.

Sample Processing Questions for Play Hard, Play Safe, Play Fair, Have Fun

- Why might different people have a different concept of "fun" or playing "hard"?
- How would you define "cheating" (a concept that regularly comes up when discussing playing fair) or "playing by the rules"?
- What are some examples of Play Safe?

Connections: Play Hard, Play Safe, Play Fair, Have Fun

Life Skill Links: caring, choice and accountability, cooperation, effort, empathy, honesty, imagination, initiative, integrity, justice, perseverance, positive attitude, purpose, respect, responsibility, safety, self-discipline
Academic Applications: • Putting a Full Value Contract into place (and making it come alive in the classroom) creates an atmosphere where students feel comfortable learning, thus increasing academic achievement.
Variations/Modifications: • *For younger students:* It might be necessary to take one of these concepts at a time. Explore it in depth over a few weeks, and then add the next one.
Extensions: • This Full Value Contract lends itself well to Physical Education. Have these phrases posted next to the exit. On the way out, have each student touch the one that they thought the class did best, or the one that they think the class needs to work on more. That way you can get a quick indication of how they think things are going and can address it in the next class.

Facilitation Notes

The definitions for these concepts are extremely important. I might think "fun" means using sarcastic humor; the receiver of that humor may think otherwise. As the class spends more time interacting, these definitions will change.

Adaptations for Students with Disabilities: Play Hard, Play Safe, Play Fair, Have Fun

Cognitive Disabilities	• Deal with only one concept at a time.
Orthopedic Impairment	• Use cutouts with Velcro™ backing to stick to the board. • Instead of using tagboard, use magnets to make words or write words on small pieces of paper and put them up with small magnets. • Use magnetic strips that can be stuck to the back of paper.
Hearing Impairment	No major modifications necessary.
Visual Impairment	• Create a symbolic tactile representation for each value/concept being discussed.

MPS

 ## 35. The Being (Adapted from The Peaceable Being, *Adventures in Peacemaking*, p. 14)

Focus: Full Value Contract, describing attributes
Materials: Butcher paper and markers
Level: Grades K–5

Suggested Procedure
1. Divide the class into groups of four to six.
2. Give each group a long piece of butcher paper and various nonpermanent markers.
3. Have each group trace the body of one person in their group.
4. On the inside of the outline, they should draw or write behaviors or qualities that are safe and respectful of self, others, and the class (e.g., sharing, humor, a picture of people shaking hands).
5. On the outside of the outline, they should draw or write behaviors or qualities that damage people's sense of respect and safety (e.g., prejudice, a picture of someone hitting another).
6. Post the beings and have each group present theirs to the class.
7. Have all students sign their work.
8. Refer to them over time.

Sample Processing Questions for The Being
- What is the class like when it is peaceful?
- What is the class like when it is not peaceful?
- How might these Beings help remind us about making this a safe and respectful class?
- When there are issues that occur from outside your beings, how should we handle it?
- How can the class use the inside attributes while working to diminish the outside attributes?

Connections: The Being
Life Skill Links: caring, choice and accountability, cooperation, empathy, peacefulness, positive attitude, purpose, relationships, respect, responsibility, safety, self-discipline
Academic Applications: • Putting a Full Value Contract into place (and making it come alive in the classroom) creates an atmosphere where students feel comfortable learning, thus increasing academic achievement.
Variations/Modifications: • *For younger students:* Do this as a whole class, where one person is traced, and the whole class brainstorms the attributes that go on the inside and the outside of the being.
Extensions: • Have each student create their own being. Give them an outline of a body on an 8 1/2 by 11-inch piece of paper. Have them decorate it and put a few things on the inside that they would like to work on, and a few things on the outside that they the would like to not do.

Facilitation Notes
The Being is a nice activity because it allows people to be physically engaged while discussing the qualities of a safe and respectful place. Encourage people to be creative with their outlines – dress them up a

bit. Of course, the person who is being traced must volunteer. The students must have some trust built up before allowing themselves to be traced by others.

Adaptations for Students with Disabilities: The Being

Cognitive Disabilities	• Create and use a bank of words for values, impediments to our goals, etc.
Orthopedic Impairment	• Use cutouts with Velcro™ backing to stick to the board. • Instead of using tagboard, use magnets to make words or write words on small pieces of paper and put them up with small magnets. • Use magnetic strips that can be stuck to the back of paper.
Hearing Impairment	No major modifications necessary.
Visual Impairment	• Create a symbolic tactile representation for each value/concept being discussed.

MPS

 # 36. The Village

Focus: Full Value Contract, determining goals and ideals
Materials: Flip chart paper or butcher paper, markers
Level: Grades 8 and higher

Suggested Procedure

1. Split the class into groups of four to six. Have each group follow these directions to create a "village."
2. Determine, at most, 20 ideals your village will use to make it work well (e.g., respect, sharing). You should write, draw, or otherwise mark these ideals inside your village.
3. Decide on what hinders you from sticking to your ideals or drags your village down (e.g., racism, sarcasm). These go on the outside of your village.
4. Each person should draw his or her own dwelling (aka personal goal) on the village map. This is a goal for how each student wants to act in class. For example, if I think I talk too much, I may draw a mouth that says, "Let others talk."
5. Each group should be prepared to present their village to the class.

Sample Processing Questions for The Village

- What process did you use to decide on how to create your village?
- Did you agree on what the ideals should be? Why do you think it was so easy/difficult to reach agreement?
- Are there some ideals that we already are achieving?
- Which ideals do you think we need to work on more?

Connections for The Village

Life Skill Links: caring, choice and accountability, citizenship, effort, integrity, justice, organization, peacefulness, positive attitude, purpose, relationships, respect, responsibility, safety, self-discipline
Academic Applications: • Use as a connection to how governments organize themselves using constitutions. Connect the idea of choice and accountability to the U.S. Bill of Rights. Create a constitution and bill of rights for the class. • Putting a Full Value Contract into place (and making it come alive in the classroom) creates an atmosphere where students feel comfortable learning, thus increasing academic achievement.
Extensions: • Ask students to keep a journal about how they believe they are living up to the ideals of the village.

Facilitation Notes

The Village takes considerable discussion about what students envision their class to be. Encourage groups to use drawn symbols as well as written words to describe their ideals and hindrances. Each of the villages will look different, and many times a group will use their village as a metaphor. For example, a group might draw a river around their village to keep the hindrances out, and then draw paths between the dwellings to represent communication and shared goals.

Adaptations for Students with Disabilities: The Village

Cognitive Disabilities	• Create and use a bank of words for values, impediments to our goals, etc.
Orthopedic Impairment	• Use cutouts with Velcro™ backing to stick to the board. • Instead of using tagboard, use magnets to make words or write words on small pieces of paper and put them up with small magnets. • Use magnetic strips that can be stuck to the back of paper.
Hearing Impairment	No major modifications necessary.
Visual Impairment	• Create a symbolic tactile representation for each value/concept being discussed.

MPS

 # 37. Hands All Around

Focus: Full Value Contract, identifying attributes and vocabulary
Materials: Flip-chart paper or butcher paper, water soluble markers or crayons
Level: Grades 4 and higher

Suggested Procedure

1. Break the class into groups of four to six.
2. Have students brainstorm a list of words or phrases that describe how they want to be treated – and how they want to treat each other, in order to make your class a safe and respectful place to be.
3. From this list, choose 10 that are most important to you as a group.
4. Make sure that everyone understands what each of the words means. For example, if someone says "cooperation," define it so that everyone agrees what cooperation means for your group.
5. Have everyone trace their hands around the edge of a large piece of paper (decorate hands).
6. Write your 10 words in the middle of the paper, so that your traced hands form a frame around them.
7. Read the 10 words out loud, and decide if you can agree to live by these ideals while in this class.
8. If so, sign your hands. If not, discuss your concerns and modify your words to make it possible for everyone in your group to sign.
9. Choose one or more spokespersons to share your contract with the larger group.

Sample Processing Questions for Hands All Around

• Did you all agree on how to create your product? What did and did not work for you?
• How did you decide on which words to use? Was it easy to agree?
• Do you understand all of the words that are used here?
• Give an example of each word. What do these actions look, sound, and feel like?

Connections for Hands All Around

Life Skill Links: caring, choice and accountability, citizenship, communication, cooperation, effort, positive attitude, relationships, respect, responsibility, safety, self-discipline

Academic Applications: • This is a good strategy to use when you have some established cooperative learning groups, as they can create one for their own group. • Putting a Full Value Contract into place (and making it come alive in the classroom) creates an atmosphere where students feel comfortable learning, thus increasing academic achievement.

Extensions: • Once the posters are up, give students an opportunity to indicate how they think they are doing. Keep small sticky notes colored green and red. Periodically, ask the students to consider how they are meeting the parts of their contract. Hand out the sticky notes. If they think they are doing well with one, choose a green note and write what happened. If there was a problem with one, they write on the red one. The note can then be posted next to the word that it connects to. Keep the sticky notes handy in case a student would like to post one at any time. At the end or beginning of the day, you can check to see if there are any posted to discuss as a small group or as a whole class. (Thanks to Nancy Constable for this idea.)

Facilitation Notes
For younger students, the brainstorming can take place as a whole class. Then have each small group pick their top 5 or 10 to put on their group sheet. Older students can have more time in their small groups to discuss what is important to them. It is also possible to be less structured with older students about what to draw on the paper.

Adaptations for Students with Disabilities: Hands All Around

Cognitive Disabilities	• Create and use a bank of words for values, impediments to our goals, etc.
Orthopedic Impairment	• Use cutouts with Velcro™ backing to stick to the board. • Instead of using tagboard, use magnets to make words or write words on small pieces of paper and put them up with small magnets. • Use magnetic strips that can be stuck to the back of paper.
Hearing Impairment	No major modifications necessary.
Visual Impairment	• Creating a symbolic tactile representation for each value/concept being discussed.

MPS

38. What Do I Need, What Can I Give?
Focus: Full Value Contract, creating ground rules
Materials: Adhesive Notes, flip-chart or butcher paper, markers
Level: Grades 9 and higher

Suggested Procedure
1. Hand two sticky notes to each student.
2. Ask students to think about what they need in order to feel safe and respected in this class. Each idea should be written on a separate note.
3. Ask them to think about what they can give to make others feel safe and respected in this class. Each idea should be written on a separate note.
4. Give them time to think and write.
5. Divide the class into groups of four to six. Ask them to share what they wrote on their sticky notes.
6. Have them combine their ideas. (e.g., If someone wrote, "I need people to take me seriously," and someone else wrote, "I need people not to laugh at me," these could be combined.)
7. Give each group a turn to share one of their ideas, in a round-robin fashion. If an idea has already been suggested, they do not need to repeat it. As each idea is stated, write it on the flip-chart or butcher paper.
8. After all the combined ideas are written publicly, ask students to read them out loud. Ask them to think about three things: a) Do they need clarification about any of the ideas? b) Can they agree to work toward doing what's written? c) Is there anything missing?
9. Hold a discussion to clarify, negotiate, and add.

Sample Processing Questions for What Do I Need? What Can I Give?
• How did you like this process? Was it helpful?
• Are you surprised about anything on our list?
• What will it take for us to live by these ground rules?
• How will we handle it when there is a problem – when one or more of the ground rules is ignored?

Connections for What Do I Need, What Can I Give?

Life Skill Links: caring, choice and accountability, cooperation, effort, empathy, positive attitude, purpose, relationships, respect, responsibility, safety, self-discipline, wisdom

Academic Applications: • This is a good strategy to use when you have some established cooperative learning groups, as they can create one for their own group. • Putting a Full Value Contract into place (and making it come alive in the classroom) can help create an atmosphere where students feel comfortable learning, thus increasing academic achievement.

Variations/Modifications: • Use the Affinity Group Process: Once students have their ideas on the sticky notes, break into groups of six to eight, and give each group a large piece of flip-chart or butcher paper. They stick their notes onto the paper, and then silently arrange the notes into categories. If someone disagrees with where someone puts a note, he or she can move it. It is possible to make a category of one. Once done, have them label the categories. As they present their categories, it can be written like an outline, with a heading and then subcategories as descriptors below. For example, a broad category might be "Communication." Under it are descriptors from the sticky notes like, "People listen to each other," and "Be open-minded."

Facilitation Notes

This process gives students an opportunity not only to discuss external rules but also what they can give and receive internally to make the classroom a good teaching and learning environment.

This process can be done in 45 minutes to an hour. Encourage discussion about clarifying the ideas. Sometimes students are reticent about asking what they think are obvious questions. Model how this might be done by choosing one that is unclear to you and asking for clarification. This usually gets the discussion rolling. Also, make sure you fill out your own sticky notes and add them to the mix.

Adaptations for Students with Disabilities: What do I Need? What Can I Give?

Cognitive Disabilities	• Brainstorm as a large group.
Orthopedic Impairment	• Use cutouts with Velcro™ backing to stick to the board. • Instead of using tagboard, use magnets to make words or write words on small pieces of paper and put them up with small magnets. • Use magnetic strips that can be stuck to the back of paper.
Hearing Impairment	No major modifications necessary.
Visual Impairment	• Creating a symbolic tactile representation for each value/concept being discussed.

MPS

Codes, Missions, and Values: Many organizations have mission statements, codes of conduct, or value statements. The YMCA, for example, holds dear the values of "caring, honesty, responsibility and respect." Create a Full Value Contract by presenting the mission statement, values declarations, or code of conduct. Ask group members to define what it means to them.

TRIBES Community Agreements: In the same vein as codes, missions, and values, you can use the TRIBES agreements of attentive listening, appreciations/no put-downs, the right to pass, and mutual respect as a full-fledged Full Value Contract. After the students have been together for a while and you have been operating with the agreements, invite them to define them more deeply and completely.

Community Standards: Older students might not enjoy an activity that seems "juvenile." If this is the case, ask them to create community standards that make the class a place for everyone to feel safe and be respected. These might begin as general qualities that the students define and agree upon (honesty, sharing, listening). Later it may get more specific (taking turns when speaking, spending time discussing before diving into a project, etc.).

Signing a Contract: A contract denotes a legal obligation to fulfill the terms of the contract. We ask students to indicate an agreement to the Full Value Contract in a variety of ways: nodding, thumbs up, signatures, thumbprints, initials, etc. The reason for requesting an active token of agreement is to make the process concrete and show that it is important to the process as a whole.

What about those who do not wish to sign? Although this is a rare occurrence, these folks generally have valid reasons for not wanting to put their mark on the FVC. Usually it means that they are taking the process quite seriously and truly believe that they cannot live up to the spirit of the contract.

My experience includes a student who was diagnosed with attention deficit disorder. His history included little success with behavior programs, and he saw his signature as a symbol of future failure. Since I already had a rapport with the student, we were able to talk privately about the matter. We discussed that these were goals – not reasons for punishment – and that messing up meant we could learn from the situation. We agreed that he would participate without a signature for a while, and check in after two weeks. Within a month he felt comfortable enough to sign the contract.

Another solution is to spend time as a group negotiating the ideals and points on the contract until everyone feels comfortable signing it. This can take awhile, especially with a large class, so it may take many small discussions over a longer period of time to establish the contract. We must remember that it is not the product but the discussion process that allows each of us to learn and understand the ideals. It is time well worth taking.

As the contract develops, the students gain a deeper appreciation for individual needs and create a document that is useful for all involved.

Summary: When to Move on to Trust

Assessment of a group is both an art and a science. You can look to the Cooperation issues on the Community-Building Model (page 27) as a guide to determine if group members have made progress. With time together, students will have the opportunity to know which Cooperation issues need to be addressed and which ones are already in place. When students are encouraging of each other, rather than degrading – in essence, kind to each other – then it is possible to move into issues of Trust.

It is not necessary to be 100 percent successful with every issue. There will always be times when people put themselves or others down, for example. Having some history with the issues, though, offers a frame of reference for dealing with them later. Many times, all it takes is a reminder to help students get back on track. At other times, it may be necessary to back up and do more Cooperation activities in order to deal with specific issues.

It is important to include your students in the decision to move on. Talk about what attributes they need to make sure that trust can, in fact, flourish in the class. Ask them if they are ready to meet the challenges in order to make it safe for everyone to build trust.

One way to approach moving from one step to another is to decide to try a low-level trust-building activity. There are many Trust activities that do not put people at risk for injury if group members prove to be unprepared. Once you try the activity, the group can assess how it felt to put trust in other group members. Your observations can be added to the mix to determine if the students are ready to "dive" into Trust.

Moving to Trust: Some Observations

	Move On	Stay with Cooperation
Put Ups/ Put Downs	• You notice a decrease in put-downs over time. • Students notice when a put-down occurs. • When a put-down occurs, students are willing to discuss it, and then let it go. • You notice an increase in put-ups, both verbal ("thank you," compliments) and physical (more sharing, helping others). • Laughter is shared, and people can laugh at themselves.	• You notice no change in the number and kind of put-downs. • Students seem to ignore put-downs altogether, as if it's just part of the way things are. • Students seem to only say "the right" things so that they can avoid talking about put-ups/put-downs. • Put-ups, when they do occur, seem superficial. Although a beginning, it may not be time to move to Trust. • Students laugh at each other, especially when someone makes a mistake.
Hidden Agendas	• Students are able to state needs rather than sneak to get an individual need met. • No matter who is in the class, people are willing to participate and discuss issues. • You notice that people are more willing to take turns, rather than monopolize playing and talking time.	• You find students "opting out" of activities in the name of Challenge by Choice on a regular basis. • You notice that students are more willing to participate and talk when one or more individuals are gone. (This can indicate fear of reprisal or bullying.)
Active Listening	• Active listening skills have been taught and practiced. • You notice that active listening skills are being used (at least sporadically) at other times.	• Students constantly talk out of turn. • There is an unwillingness to "hear" another person's point of view. • Even when focusing on active listening, students cannot seem to use the skills.
Mixing	• Students are willing to work with everyone in the class on an activity. • Students notice when there is a segregation (e.g. all the boys on one side, all the girls on the other) even if they do nothing about it. • When gathering spontaneously, there is not always a gender, race, or clique segregation.	• There is a student who is constantly scapegoated, and no one will work with her/him. • Students complain about their partners when paired with others. • Students refuse to mix, even when it is focused on.
Perspective Taking	• Students have had an opportunity to explore other perspectives besides their own. • Students are willing to compromise when necessary. • When someone is hurt or upset, students show concern. • People are willing to solve conflicts when they occur. • Students are willing to take responsibility for their actions.	• Students hold grudges and seek revenge. • When someone is hurt or upset, students tease or show little concern for the individual. • Students constantly blame others. • Students make fun of others' cultures or customs.

[1] Kreidler, William and Lisa Furlong. *Adventures in Peacemaking.* (p. 8)
[2] *Beyond Discipline*, by Alfie Kohn (pp. 113-114)
[3] Adapted from Luckner and Nadler, *Processing the Experience*, (p. 20)

5 Trust

Making Mistakes • Empathy • Trustworthiness • Risk Taking • Physical/Emotional

ACTIVITIES

Trust Builders
Feelings Literacy
Behavioral Goal Setting
Low Ropes Course

The Cornerstone of Community

Without trust, a community cannot survive. It is the foundation on which relationships are built, and community is all about building and maintaining relationships. Trust is also fragile in that it is painstaking to establish, yet easily broken. Once broken, it is even more difficult to reestablish.

By necessity, after the laughing, joking, and teasing of Deinhibitizers, the mood of the class must change. Students need to switch gears to a more thoughtful frame of mind. Trust building has to be taken seriously if it is to be a safe experience.

Students are now asked to become partners in keeping track of safety. Everyone is responsible for speaking up if a potential or actual safety hazard is spotted. At this stage, too, they must use humor with care. If, for example, someone jokes that she is going to run her partner into a wall during a Trust Walk, trust is already on shaky ground. If no one speaks up to protect a class member, trust can easily be shattered, and the class may have to go back to square one.

Along with this added group responsibility is a focus on personal responsibility. People are encouraged to make "I" statements and reflect on their own behavior, especially as it relates to being trustworthy. It is also a time to delve into the world of feelings so as to become more self-aware. Goleman states that "self-awareness – recognizing a feeling *as it happens* – is the keystone of emotional intelligence .... An inability to notice our true feelings leaves us at their mercy."[1] The myriad of emotions that we feel during an activity that requires giving up some of our own control to others is fertile ground for the development of a feelings vocabulary. The more we can identify our feelings, the more literate we are when working through conflict and the other dynamics of relationships.

Challenge by Choice is highlighted during trust building. Choosing to trust others is a personal decision. An individual's past experience has a huge effect on his or her willingness to trust others. It is risky to varying degrees, depending upon history and frame of reference. Personal goal setting can also be initiated at this point, as students begin to explore the meaning of risk taking and setting personal goals. These goals can be self-monitored with support from other students.

Trust Issues and Skills

Making Mistakes

Every group must answer the question, "Is it okay to make a mistake?" Invariably, students answer in the affirmative. "Of course it's okay because everyone makes mistakes, and we can learn from our mistakes!"

The trouble is, when someone actually does make a mistake, the first reaction from many is to tease or degrade that person. Therefore, it is necessary to ask this question outright and then to have some practice with it. The ultimate goal is that people's actions are consistent with their words.

If students work through this issue, a tangible change occurs in the atmosphere of the group. People are able to take greater risks without fear of reprisal. The level of trust among students soars because people don't have to worry that others are lying in wait to catch them in a mistake. Once a class gets over this bump, it can truly thrive.

Activities can help you focus on this question of making mistakes. My favorite is Turnstile (p. 98).

Empathy

To truly identify with someone else's feelings is to care. It makes sense to trust someone who cares about you. This is why focusing on empathy is so important at this stage of community building. We display empathy by taking care of each other, by asking questions about how people want to be treated during the Trust activities, and by making sure we all take responsibility for everyone's physical and emotional safety. If someone is uncomfortable, we try to make it right, because that person's discomfort causes us discomfort. "I feel your pain" is more than a cliché.

Perspective taking is a precursor to empathy. The first step is to understand that others have different perspectives from one's own. The next step, empathy, allows people to recognize the feelings of others. Goleman calls it the fundamental people skill. The beauty of using activities to explore these concepts is that real things happen. When someone reports that he could not keep his eyes closed during the Trust Walk, there is real fodder for discussing emotional safety. Since everyone has an easier time with some activities and a harder time with others, your class can investigate how people have different reactions to different experiences. Covering your eyes and allowing someone to lead you around can be difficult for one person and easy for another. The roles may be reversed, however, when choosing to fall backwards and be caught by others.

The ability to make **mistakes** is vital not only to establishing trust within a class, but also to learning. Learning from one's mistakes is a powerful way to gain experience. It can be encouraged during community-building time – and all the time. Spend time talking about mistakes from which you have learned and inviting students to tell stories about their mistakes. Create an environment where learning from mistakes is a norm, not something to hide.

As students become more comfortable with making mistakes, emphasize a few points:

- Making mistakes is meaningless unless we can glean learning from them.
- There is a difference between making a mistake and gross negligence. It is the difference between forgetting to turn on your turn signal and getting into the driver's seat after drinking. Spend time clarifying the difference and brainstorming examples.
- Making mistakes implies consequences. If I stay up too late and sleep through my alarm, I will have to deal with the consequences of being late to work or school. The idea is to learn from this mistake in order to prevent others like it in the future.
- Along with the consequences comes responsibility. Sometimes it is enough to throw up one's hands and say "oops!" At other times, the mistake may have caused hurt feelings – like forgetting someone's birthday or borrowing something and losing it. In these cases it is important to find a way to "make things right."

Since "90 percent or more of an emotional message is nonverbal,"[2] reading another's feelings accurately requires noticing nonverbal cues. *How* a message is conveyed can be more telling than the actual words. Help students key into tone of voice, gestures, and facial expressions – the body language we all transmit.

Process what it feels like to be cared for and supported by another person to whom we have entrusted our safety. Discuss what it was like to be responsible for another's well-being. Discover what it is like to empathize and care about another's welfare.

What do we do now?

You have just spent the last month or so creating a place where trust can be built. You have developed a Full Value Contract and worked through Cooperation issues. Now it is time to "step up" to Trust, so you choose a beginning activity like the Trust Walk to begin this part of the journey. After talking about how to lead someone with closed eyes and how to get into pairs, students lead each other around tables, desks, and bookcases. Then it happens: One student leads another into the wall. Now what?

After checking if everyone is okay, you can frame this incident as a higher level of put-down and deal with it accordingly. As with put-downs, it *must* be acknowledged and processed. Was it on purpose or was it an accident? No matter what the motive is, how does it affect a student's ability to trust or be trusted? If it was a mistake, how can it be made right?

This can take a minute or the rest of class, depending upon the severity of the incident and the hurt feelings involved. If there is time after the discussion, ask the person who was being led if she or he feels up to trying it again, and then respect the decision. Next time, revisit the incident briefly as a way to learn from a mistake, then try the whole activity again. Usually the person who was run into the wall will be ready to try again after some time has passed, and the person who was leading will be ready to be more attentive.

During this stage of trust building, it is your responsibility to be alert to possible safety issues. Watch the students' body languages to ascertain their empathy level. Offer reminders to those who are moving too fast or seem to be unaware of how their partners will fit through a door or between tables. Sometimes shorter students forget to look up for the barriers that only affect taller students.

This incident provides an after-the-fact way to discuss empathy. Empathy is best taught through experience, and although we have been learning these lessons since we were toddlers, it is something that cannot be overemphasized. Choosing activities carefully is a way to make sure that students can learn about empathy without being put at undue risk. Address the mistakes that occur at the lower levels so that everyone will be prepared to care for each other's physical and emotional safety as you introduce higher-level activities.

It's all about behavior.

Being trustworthy has everything to do with behavior. Saying one thing and doing another is a sure way to break trust, while aligning one's beliefs and deeds proves that one can be trusted. Being trustworthy means looking at the big picture to work toward positive outcomes and then matching those intentions with actions. Sounds like an exercise in integrity and ethics ....

Trustworthiness

One way to show empathy is to be trustworthy in taking care of another's needs. To be "worthy of trust" means that one's behavior toward another is consistent, supportive, and caring.

Consistency is a key factor in establishing trust. When giving up some of our control and entrusting our personal safety to another, it is important to know what to expect. If, on the other hand, that other person behaves in unpredictable ways, it is difficult for us to trust him or her.

Clear communication is another way to engender trust and prove trustworthiness. For example, encourage participants who are guiding someone during a Trust Walk to paint pictures with words about the environment they are entering. There is no need for them to withhold information. This can lead to a discussion about keeping secrets, or sharing information so that everyone is included. These are big trust issues for a community.

Another trust-related behavior involves consulting with a person who appears to be in need. Before simply assuming that someone has needs to be met (or needs rescuing), it is important to ask if she or he *wants* help. It can be maladaptive to encourage everyone to jump in to help others without invitation. Conversely, we want students to recognize when someone is in danger and act to keep that person from getting hurt. Encourage students to ask for help if they need it. Yet, as with so many other instances in life, we must learn to deal with ambiguity. The important thing is to bring the issue out into the open so that people can grapple with it.

Risk Taking

In our quest to make life as safe (and as litigation-free) as possible, we sometimes err on the side of encouraging *less* risk taking. Certainly, the words "safe" and "safety" are used frequently in this book. However, risk taking is the stuff of growth. To risk is to push one's limits, to expand boundaries, to learn.

There are two main schools of thought about risk taking. One is to push people outside their comfort zones. By doing so it is believed people will learn and grow from the experience. The other approach is to create an environment where it is safe for people to *step* outside their comfort zones. Within the context of Challenge by Choice, people are given opportunities to try things they never thought possible. The group encourages and supports the goals that individuals set for themselves. The second approach is much more conducive to the creation of community, where the empowering aspects of self-determination and personal responsibility are highly valued and reinforced.

To trust is to risk. What better time to begin an exploration of risk taking than when involved in a series of trust-building activities? Themes around risk taking include: What is a safe or unsafe risk? What does "healthy" risk taking mean? When is it appropriate to say no? What role does peer pressure play in risk taking, and what is the difference between peer pressure and encouragement? All of these questions – and more – will emanate from the activities described in this chapter and subsequent discussions of trust building.

Blindfolds?

Pete Albert, a social worker, longtime adventure educator, and originator of the Madison Metropolitan School District Stress/Challenge program in Wisconsin, tells a story about the use of blindfolds when he was working with a group of high-school English as a Second Language students some time ago. At least a half-dozen cultures were represented in this group, including students from Mexico, Laos, Viet Nam, and the United States. When the blindfolds were brought out to use for a trust activity, Pete describes the atmosphere in the room as getting suddenly colder. Not understanding what was going on, he put them away and went on to another activity. Later, he learned that the last time many of the students had seen blindfolds they had been on the faces of people about to be executed. Pete brought in strips of white cloth for the students to decorate as their own, thus turning them into personal works of art that happened to be eye coverings, instead of blindfolds.

Many of the trust activities we do involve the use of "blindfolds." Pete's story prompted me to reassess my use of them. I now offer "eye coverings" for those who wish to use them, with the other option being to close one's eyes. If people peek, it is simply another exercise in Challenge by Choice.

Physical and Emotional Trust

Most of the activities we do involve some sort of physical trust – activities in which participants' eyes are covered, falling and catching, walking on cables, and spotting. These concrete examples open doors to the abstract concepts around emotional trust. Although there may be an apparent difference between trusting someone to keep your body safe and trusting that same person to keep your feelings safe, they are really two sides of the same coin. As issues come up for discussion around physical trust, they can be used as metaphors for other emotional trust issues such as entrusting someone with confidential information, helping someone meet personal goals, or not passing on rumors.

Trust Activities

The following trust activities must be chosen carefully with much thought given to sequence. Each class will need to follow its own path of Trust. Some classes take baby steps, while others leap through the process as if it is no problem at all. Whatever pace your class takes, it can be enlightening for all involved.

Role of the Teacher

The teacher's role changes from leader to guide at this point. On an expedition, a guide is needed because the group of people going on the trek are unfamiliar with the area or may not have the necessary experience to undertake the journey on their own, and it is understood that the guide has been down this path before. A guide teaches the necessary skills to accomplish the tasks required for the trek. The guide helps the group decide which route to take, works with participants to take care of their own needs, and watches out for the general safety of the group.

During Trust activities, the teacher takes the guide role by planning a sequence of activities to help the students develop a history that will engender trust. He or she teaches the necessary spotting skills along with appropriate communication to make the activities safe and discusses behavior that is consistent with trustworthiness. The teacher/guide helps the students develop a feelings vocabulary with which to communicate and take care of their emotional needs. These physical and behavioral skills will be used during the rest of the journey.

While in the middle of the sequence, the teacher may consult with the students about which activity to move to next. Although the sequence is important, it is not so hard and fast that it is inflexible. Giving students an opportunity to make some decisions encourages them to begin the transition into becoming a more self-determining body.

Processing is important during the trust phase. People need a chance to discuss their feelings about trusting others and being trusted. What does trust even mean? When might trusting someone be appropriate, and when might it be too risky? All students must have the opportunity to answer questions like these for themselves. The answers will differ for each person, depending on his or her background and experiences with trust.

Trust Activities

These activities require people to give up a little control while entrusting others to keep them safe, both physically and emotionally. Care must be taken to brief your class about the activities in such a way that everyone knows what is expected and how to keep their colleagues safe. Discussion about behaviors that prove trustworthiness is essential before embarking on these activities.

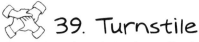 # 39. Turnstile

Focus: Making mistakes, aligning beliefs and actions, dealing with frustration, emotional trust
Materials: Long jump rope (15 feet or longer)
Levels: Grades 4 and higher

Suggested Procedure

1. This activity can be done in a classroom if the furniture is moved out of the way. However, more room is desirable, so a gym, all-purpose room, hallway, or outside area is a better option.
2. Ask the class how they feel about making mistakes. Is it okay? Why or why not? Discuss how to show support when a mistake is made.
3. Ask for two volunteers to turn the rope. These people can also jump, or they can choose only to turn. Everyone else is asked to stand on one side of the rope. *The turners spin the rope "front door," or toward the jumpers as it arcs over the top.*
4. The object is to get everyone from one side of the rope to the other. Tell them that they are trying to get everyone to graduate from high school. Once they get everyone through one level, they will advance to the next, more challenging level.
5. **Level I: Preschool** – Everyone must get through the rope without it stopping or touching them (this means that some people may choose to run through without jumping). If the rope stops or touches them, then that person goes back to try it again.
6. **Level II: Kindergarten** – One person at a time runs in, jumps once and runs out. If the rope stops, or the person does not jump, then that person goes back to try it again.
7. **Level III: Elementary School** – People jump through in groups of two or three – run in together, jump once, and run out. If even only one person misses, the little group of two or three goes back to try again.
8. **Level IV: Middle/Junior High School** – Same as Level II, except that if anyone misses the whole group goes back and tries again.
9. **Level V: High School** – Same as level IV except that each time the rope hits the ground, another person must be jumping. This means that people continuously follow each other in and out of the jump rope. If the rope stops, or no one is in the rope when it comes around, then the whole group must start over.

Sample Processing Questions for Turnstile

- Is it really okay to make a mistake in this class? How do you know?
- How did it feel when you missed?
- What did you say and do when someone else missed?
- How can making mistakes help us?
- What kinds of mistakes are okay to make? Give some examples.
- Did you ever feel like quitting this activity? Why did you choose to continue?
- Which level was the most satisfying to complete? Why?
- How did your attitude affect your performance with this activity?
- On a scale of 1 to 10 (1 low, 10 high), how much frustration did you feel during this activity? Why?

Connections for Turnstile

Life Skill Links: caring, choice and accountability, communication, cooperation, courage, effort, empathy, flexibility, integrity, leadership, patience, perseverance, positive attitude, problem solving, respect, responsibility, safety, self-discipline

Academic Applications: • This activity can be used as a metaphor for how many people have persevered in history (e.g., Thomas Edison, who had a learning disability; Harriet Tubman, who struggled to free herself and others during slavery in the U.S.; people who worked in the underground against the Nazis in Germany during World War II).

Variations/Modifications: Once a group "graduates," you can offer "postgraduate" challenges: Everyone can try to jump at the same time, do level V in pairs, or repeat level V – except that everyone should run back to the end of the line after jumping to see how many in a row can make it through before the rope stops.

Extensions: • Identify signals that frustration is occurring: checking out of the activity, saying this is stupid or boring, blaming others, etc. Then identify causes of frustration: task too hard, group unorganized, unrealistic goals, in a rut, etc. Finally, identify ways to deal with frustration: Stop and reevaluate, practice individual calming strategies (e.g., count to 10), go to another activity and return to this later, etc.

Facilitation Notes

A discussion about making mistakes is important before attempting this activity because someone will miss. Being prepared for this inevitability helps develop the norm that making mistakes is acceptable. Ask the students if it is okay to make a mistake. With few exceptions, they will answer as expected: "Yes, because we learn from our mistakes" or "Nobody's perfect." We are taught to pay lip service to this notion, yet we rarely see that making mistakes is truly fine. Adults model this inconsistency by chiding others (and themselves) or laughing at people when a mistake is made. This is not to say that mistakes cannot be funny. Learning how to be gentle when someone makes a mistake does not mean we can't have a good chuckle with them when something funny happens.

Turnstile is perfect for dealing with this very issue because mistakes will be made. This activity can be presented as a way to practice both making mistakes and reacting to others who have made mistakes. It can set the tone for the rest of the year. Later, if students tease or blame others for mistakes, all you need say is, "Is it really okay to make a mistake?" That phrase alone will act as a reminder.

Another nice element of Turnstile is the built-in sequence. If students are struggling with one level, then stop at the end of that level. Later, return to the activity and continue with the sequence when students are ready for a bigger challenge.

This activity almost always guarantees a struggle. Few groups can accomplish every level of the Turnstile without missing more than a few times. Once worked through, students celebrate getting through the challenge, and the stage is set to discuss tenacity and dealing with frustration.

Another issue that can arise during Turnstile (especially with elementary students) is one of taking turns. Developmentally, these younger students are more concerned with getting a turn than in accomplishing the group task. If the group must all come back, varying levels of pushing and shoving can occur as students jockey for position. Ask them to develop a ground rule for this so that the need for pushing and shoving is diminished. Generally they will institute a norm assuming that those who have just gone through go to the back of the line to give others the next chance.

Turnstile can also be done by students in wheelchairs; they can be required to get through the rope without it touching them. These students can either do it themselves or have someone help by pushing them through on their signal.

Adaptations for Students with Disabilities: Turnstile

Cognitive Disabilities	• Use the rope swinging method, whereby the rope does not make full circles, but only swings back and forth (cradles). • Make sure that the rope is swinging at a slow pace. • If timing the jump is difficult, allow people to stand next to the rope before it is turned.
Orthopedic Impairment	• This activity may not be appropriate for orthopedically impaired students. • People in wheelchairs can either try to figure out the timing of this activity themselves or have someone push them on their signal to try to get through the rope without it touching them. • These students can turn the rope.

Adaptations for Students with Disabilities: Turnstile (cont.)

Hearing Impairment	• Have a visual signal when the whole team is jumping.
Visual Impairment	• Use brightly colored rope or something that makes noise when it hits the ground. • This activity may not be appropriate for severely visually impaired students.

MPS

40. Paired Trust Activities

Focus: Physical and emotional trust, trustworthiness, empathy, risk taking
Materials: Eye coverings (optional), soft throwable objects (Search and Rescue)
Levels: Grades 2 and higher

Suggested Procedure

1. Depending on the age and maturity level of your students, these activities can be done inside or outside (see facilitation notes).
2. Have your students get into pairs, either by choice or by a random method.
3. Describe the activity (see below) and go over all safety guidelines: speed, making sure both people can fit through a space, looking up for obstacles, giving one's partner as much information as possible, making sure people know what is around them before asking them to bend down, etc.
4. Teach the "bumpers up" position: Hands out in front with palms facing out.
5. At any time either person in the partnership can stop the activity if he or she feels too much discomfort. This must, of course, be communicated to the partner before stopping.
6. Offer eye coverings to those who want them; others can close their eyes.
7. Set up boundaries.
8. Allow enough time for each person to have a turn guiding and a turn being led.

Activity A Trust Walk

The partner who is guiding can give both verbal and nonverbal directions.

Show the class different methods for leading someone who cannot see. The person being led can hold hands with the guide, hold the elbow of the guide, or have the guide hold his or her elbow. Or he or she may not wish to be touched at all, but may opt for verbal directions only. The important thing is that this be discussed. Each person *must* be given the opportunity to choose if or how to be touched.

Remind students that there are no secrets about what is in the area. Partners should feel free to describe what or who is around the people they are leading. Encourage them to take their partners to an object (tree, chair, etc.) and have them feel it. Later they can try to guess what and where it was.

Adaptations for Students with Disabilities: Trust Walk

Cognitive Disabilities	• Keep the space open with few barriers, such as in a gym.
Orthopedic Impairment	• Make sure there is a large amount of space. • Remind students to hold on to individuals as balance is more difficult when sight is taken away.
Hearing Impairment	• Have hearing-impaired students be guides and only be led if they choose.
Visual Impairment	• No major modifications necessary. • Do this in groups of three with at least two sighted people per group.

Activity B 🔗 Search and Rescue

The partner who is guiding can only give verbal instructions. Make sure each pair has a soft throwable object.

Once the partner has closed or covered eyes, the guide throws the object. After the object is thrown, only the person who cannot see can touch it. His or her task is to retrieve the object and get it to the "hospital" (e.g., spot on the floor, trash can, bag). When that has been achieved, the two partners switch roles.

A word of caution: If the object is thrown near a wall or other barrier, the guide must tell the partner that the barrier is there before asking the person to bend down.

Adaptations for Students with Disabilities: Search and Rescue

Cognitive Disabilities	• Teach a few concrete verbal directions that can be used. • Keep the space open with few barriers, such as in a gym.
Orthopedic Impairment	• Make sure there is a large amount of space. • Allow students to help their partners keep their balance. • Allow partners to pick up the item for the person whose eyes are closed.
Hearing Impairment	• Have hearing-impaired students be guides and only be led if they choose . • Students can physically guide partners who have a hearing impairment.
Visual Impairment	• Do this in groups of three with at least two sighted people per group.

Activity C 🔗 Car and Driver

The partner who is guiding can only give nonverbal instructions.

The person whose eyes are closed is the "car," and the guide is the "driver." Since we do not talk to our cars when we drive them, the same applies here. The "car" stands in "bumpers-up" position, and the "driver" stands behind him or her. The signals go like this:

> Hands on shoulders: **stop**
> Hands off shoulders: **go**
> Hand on right shoulder: **turn right**
> Hand on left shoulder: **turn left**
> Two taps on shoulder: **reverse**

Speed is an issue here since the driver's hands are off the shoulders when the car is moving. It is important that the car not outrun the driver. Also remind the drivers not to wait until the last minute before avoiding a collision and to look behind them when going in reverse.

If someone does not wish to be touched at all, offer the option of having the driver give verbal directions.

Adaptations for Students with Disabilities: Car and Driver

Cognitive Disabilities	• Keep the space open with few barriers, such as in a gym.
Orthopedic Impairment	• Make sure there is a large amount of space. • Change the rules so that hands on shoulders means "go" to aid in balance.
Hearing Impairment	• Have hearing-impaired students be guides and only be led if they choose . • Students can physically guide partners who have a hearing impairment.
Visual Impairment	• Do this in groups of three with at least two sighted people per group.

Sample Processing Questions for Paired Trust Activities

- What did your guide do to gain your trust? Be specific.
- Did you feel your guide took care of your safety? Why or why not?
- What did your partner do that made you feel more comfortable? Less comfortable?
- Were you more comfortable being led or being the guide?
- When you were guiding, did you feel responsible for your partner? Why or why not?
- How risky was this for you? What would have made it more/less risky?
- Were there times when you peeked or wanted to peek? What was going on when you had that feeling?
- If we did this activity again, what would you do differently to help your partner trust you more?
- What does it mean to trust someone?
- What does it mean to trust yourself?

Connections for Paired Trust Activities

Life Skill Links: caring, choice and accountability, communication, cooperation, courage, empathy, leadership, loyalty, patience, relationships, respect, responsibility, safety

Variations/Modifications: • *For younger students:* Try this first with eyes open to experience leading and being led.

Extensions: • Create an image of the ideal trustworthy person. Draw or provide small groups with a picture of a person. Have them add qualities and attributes that would make this person trustworthy. • Have students draw about experiences in which they have either trusted someone or been trusted by someone else.

Facilitation Notes

At first, have your students try these activities in a large open area like a gym or empty lunchroom. It will give them an opportunity to understand all that is expected. It will also give you the opportunity to assess their readiness to accept the responsibilities that go along with building trust. Next, add obstacles in the large room. Then try these activities in a smaller space, like your classroom or outside, where the terrain is uneven and less predictable.

It is also important to think about how you want your students to pair up. In the beginning, it may be helpful to have your students pick their own partners so they are comfortable with their guides. As their comfort level increases, have them pair up in a more random fashion so they have an opportunity to build trust with people they do not know as well.

It is not necessary to do all of these paired activities. Age and developmental level play a huge part in the decisions you make during this step in the sequence. Elementary students will need more practice because they are at a different developmental level (and thus more egocentric) than high-school students. Since each activity requires something different from the students (nonverbal versus verbal directions, for example), you may choose to combine all into a mini-sequence, or choose one that you feel will challenge students at the highest level.

During the debriefing, students generally talk about how it helped to know that their partners were there by hearing their voice or feeling their hand on their shoulder. This is a good metaphor for communication. Good communication can give rise to a higher level of trust.

41. Hog Call

Focus: Risk taking, physical/emotional trust, trustworthiness
Materials: Eye coverings (optional)
Levels: Grades 4 and higher

Suggested Procedure

1. Find a large open area, like a gym or field.
2. Have the students get into pairs.
3. Ask each pair to create two words that go together, like salt and pepper, or fire and hydrant.

4. Ask students to share their words out loud to make sure no two pairs are alike.
5. Tell students that they will be split up and that they must all find their partners without using their sense of sight. They can only call the "name" of their partner (e.g., "salt" calls "pepper").
6. Split the pairs up so that one person from each pair is lined up on one side of the large space and the other person from each pair is lined up on the other side.
7. Explain that everyone will have closed eyes or be wearing an eye covering, and that your job is to make sure no one runs into a wall or barrier.
8. Remind everyone to move slowly and with bumpers up.
9. Everyone closes their eyes or puts on an eye covering.
10. On a signal they start calling their partner's name.
11. Continue until all partners are reunited.

Sample Processing Questions for Hog Call

- Was it necessary to trust everyone around you? Why or why not?
- Did you feel at risk during this activity? How?
- What strategies did you use to find your partner? Did you plan in advance?
- What did you do to keep yourself safe?
- What did you do to keep those around you safe?
- How did you react when someone bumped into you?

Connections for Hog Call

Life Skill Links: caring, choice and accountability, communication, cooperation, empathy, endurance, flexibility, forgiveness, organization, patience, respect, responsibility, safety

Academic Applications: • This activity can be used to teach and explore compound words, synonyms, antonyms, etc., by assigning students a word and having them find their assigned partner. • Use as a way to practice or connect math concepts. Have students choose a number or computation out of a hat (e.g., one person chooses 10, another person chooses 2 x 5). They then try to find their partner. • Use with different songs. Secretly give each student a song to sing. Those who are singing the same song get together. • Match artists with genre. • Students are given or choose an animal. They then get together according to the type of animal: mammal, reptile, amphibian, bird, etc.

Variations/Modifications: • Have groups get together instead of pairs. • *For older students:* For a greater challenge, make the area smaller, or larger. • A more challenging variation of Hog Call is to have people spread out around the designated area instead of lining up in straight lines.

Facilitation Notes:

Hog Call is a nice, albeit less structured, way to begin looking at issues of trust. It is less intimate than having one person lead another, offering a more game-like atmosphere. Students must be cautioned about moving too fast. Let the class know that the likelihood of being touched by someone is high in this activity. You can invite those who are worried about being touched to act as spotters.

Adaptations for Students with Disabilities: Hog Call

Cognitive Disabilities	• Keep the space open with few barriers, such as in a gym.
Orthopedic Impairment	• Make sure there is a large amount of space. • Have assistants help balance students who need help, or make this a partner activity so students can support each other.
Hearing Impairment	• Make this a partner activity. • Make sure students with a hearing impairment are choosing to close their eyes.
Visual Impairment	No major modifications necessary.

42 Shakers

Focus: Risk taking, physical/emotional trust, spotting
Materials: Eye coverings (optional), noise makers (maracas, juice cans with beans, whistle), soft item for tagging (soft foam ball, stuffed animal)
Levels: Grades 2 and higher

Suggested Procedure

1. Clear desks away and have students form a circle.
2. Ask for a volunteer to be "the bat" and another volunteer to be "the moth." These two stand in the middle of the circle. Everyone else is a spotter.
3. The bat and the moth each get a noisemaker. They can choose to close their eyes or wear an eye covering. Also, give the bat the soft item so that she or he can tag the moth without fear of violating the other person's space.
4. The object is for the bat to tag the moth by using echolocation. To do this, the bat shakes her noise maker. At this point the moth must respond by shaking his noisemaker.
5. Give the bat a minute or so to tag the moth. If she does (or if the time runs out), they both choose people to take their places in the middle.
6. The role of the spotters is to keep the bat and moth in the middle of the circle so that they do not stray.

Sample Processing Questions for Shakers

- Did you have to think much about your own safety, or did you feel comfortable with your spotters? Why or why not?
- When you were the bat, what strategies did you use to find the moth?
- When you were the moth, what strategies did you use to stay away from the bat?
- What did you do when you were spotting to keep the players safe?
- Why did you choose the role of bat/moth/spotter?
- Was it an easy or difficult choice to be in the middle?

Connections for Shakers

Life Skill Links: caring, choice and accountability, communication, cooperation, effort, empathy, resourcefulness, safety
Academic Applications: • This is a great way to learn about echolocation from the "inside out."
Variations/Modifications: • *For older students:* Have the moth keep his or her eyes open. This results in a greater challenge for the bat.
Extensions: • Discuss different ways to be trustworthy in school and at home. Have students set a goal to try to practice one way of being trustworthy for the next week. At the end of each day, have them evaluate how they are doing with their goal (they might keep track in a journal).

Facilitation Notes

This is a good starting activity for younger students. It is very controlled, and it offers the opportunity to try out moving without the sense of sight. It also puts the rest of the class in a position to act as spotters. If the class is larger (over 15), try splitting into two groups so more people get an opportunity to be in the middle.

Caution people to move slowly. The spotters should put their hands up to keep the players from straying outside of the circle. Remind them that they are a boundary and should not push students who are in the middle.

Adaptations for Students with Disabilities: Shakers

Cognitive Disabilities	• Students can practice making and responding to sounds before trying the activity.

Orthopedic Impairment	• Make the circle big enough to accommodate a wheelchair. • Assign a partner if help with balance is needed.
Hearing Impairment	• Use drums as the noisemakers.
Visual Impairment	No major modifications necessary.

43. Everybody Up

Focus: Risk taking, physical/emotional trust, trustworthiness
Materials: None
Levels: Grades K and higher

Suggested Procedure

1. Clear an area and have people get into pairs.
2. Ask for two volunteers so that you can show how this is to be done.
3. Ask the volunteers to sit down on the floor facing each other. They should put the bottoms of their feet together.
4. Have them get a good grip with their hands (this looks as if they are going to do a rowboat stretch).
5. Now ask for two spotters; one should stand behind each seated person. The spotters' job is to protect the two in the middle in case something goes wrong. They especially need to make sure that the participant's head does not touch the floor. (Although this rarely happens, it is important to have spotters ready.) Spotters stand with one foot behind the other and hands out behind the person they are spotting. They are not to help, only to protect.
6. Tell the two who are sitting that their responsibility is **not to let go of their partner's hands**. After a count to three, they should pull with their hands and push with their feet. In this way, they will use tension to stand up.
7. Once these volunteers have successfully stood up, have pairs join together to stand and spot for each other.
8. Once everyone has tried it with their partner, have students mix up and try it with different people.

Sample Processing Questions for Everybody Up

- What worked and didn't work for you and your partners?
- Were your partners trustworthy? What did they do to make sure you were safe?
- Were you trustworthy? How do you know?
- What responsibility did the spotters have? Why do you think it was important to have them there even if they did not have to act?
- How did it feel to know that you had people ready to help you if you needed it?
- When you were a helper, were you ready to be there if they needed you?
- Can you think of other times when we prepare for trouble and hope not to use the skills (e.g., CPR, first aid)? Why do this?

Connections for Everybody Up

Life Skill Links: caring, choice and accountability, communication, cooperation, empathy, endurance, perseverance, respect, responsibility, safety, self-discipline
Academic Applications: • Use to teach the concept of opposites. Once students get the hang of this, have them choose opposites (e.g., up and down, night and day). They say one word as they stand up, and the other word as they sit back down.

Variations/Modifications: • *For younger students:* Enlist the help of some volunteers before you try this and have them practice it to act as models for the class. • Have students sit down again using tension. • For those who have trouble physically sitting down, have them lean back and do a slow 360° as they are holding hands with their partners.

Extensions: • Discuss other ways to show trustworthiness – in class, in school, at home, on the bus. • What is trust? Do a T-chart for trust if you haven't done one yet – what does it look like, sound like, feel like? • Have a "trust" poster and stickers. Anytime someone sees a time when someone demonstrates trust, have them call attention to it and put a sticker on the poster. Have your class carry the trust poster to their other classes and ask the teachers to add stickers to it when students call attention to acts of trust, trustworthiness, and support.

Facilitation Notes

This is another activity that can be tried early on to assess the students' commitment levels. It is also a nice warm up activity for the next activity, Dream Catcher.

One issue that can occur with Everybody Up is body image and size. Larger individuals have a more difficult time with this. If there are some comparatively large people in the class, ask them to pair up according to people about the same size. Generally this is not a problem, because the students quickly figure out that the smaller folks compensate by leaning farther out. Introduce the 360° turn as an option for the whole class (see variations/modifications above). If a pair is having difficulty due to differences in size, you can suggest that the larger person stand, while the smaller person sits. He or she can then lean forward and then back to help the other person stand.

Adaptations for Students with Disabilities: Everybody Up

Cognitive Disabilities	• Give hints as necessary to facilitate success.
Orthopedic Impairment	• Play could be on mats, soft grass, etc. • Participants in wheelchairs can stay in their chairs. They can lean forward with their partner and come back as their partner stands. • Participants who are not in wheelchairs need the ability to hold onto their partner's hands and stand up with assistance from the group.
Hearing Impairment	• Agree on visual signals for the partners to use ahead of time to indicate when they will be sitting and standing.
Visual Impairment	No major modifications necessary.

MPS

44. Dream Catcher*

Focus: Risk taking, physical/emotional trust, trustworthiness, goal setting
Materials: 1-inch tubular webbing: 10- or 12-foot pieces (can be found in climbing stores like REI or Eastern Mountain Sports)
Levels: Grades 1 and higher

Suggested Procedure

1. Find a large space free of furniture and have everyone pair up.

---

* Dream Catcher is an adaptation to Dr. Tom Smith's Raccoon Circles, which are described in Karl Rohnke's *FUNN Stuff III* on p. 60 under the title, Miniature Yurt Circles. Tom also has co-written a book with Jim Cain called *Raccoon Circles*. See bibliography.

2. Give each pair a piece of webbing. This should be pre-tied in a circle using a water knot, or teach the participants to tie the water knot themselves (see figure 5.1)
3. Have some extra webbing circles available.
4. After doing Everybody Up, ask students to figure out at least three new ways to sit down and stand up together by using tension. They may choose to use the webbing as a prop. Teach the girth hitch as a way to put two or more pieces of webbing together.
5. After people have tried this for a while, have volunteers show their creations to the class.
6. Then take one of the webbing circles and girth-hitch enough pieces of webbing on it so that everyone has a place to hang on – one or two people per piece of webbing. This now looks like circle with spokes extending from it.
7. On an agreed-upon count, everyone should sit down and stand up together.

Sample Processing Questions for Dream Catcher
- How difficult was it for you to trust the large group as opposed to just your one partner?
- Did your responsibility change when more people were added to the Dream Catcher?
- What would have happened if even one person had let go in the middle of the activity?
- Have you been affected by the actions of someone else? Have you affected others by your actions?
- What dreams do you have? What are your goals?
- What are some goals for this class? What do we want this place to be like? What do we want to accomplish?

Connections for Dream Catcher
Life Skill Links: caring, choice and accountability, communication, cooperation, effort, empathy, loyalty, positive attitude, problem solving, purpose, relationships, respect, responsibility, safety, self-discipline, wisdom
Academic Applications: After doing this activity, have students write down academic goals for the semester or year. Ask them to write an action plan for accomplishing these academic goals.
Variations/Modifications: • *For younger students:* Instead of putting all of the webbing circles together, have small groups get together around single circles. On a signal, everyone should sit down and stand up together. • *For older students:* Tell students that if a dream or a goal is shared, it is much more likely to happen. Ask each person to share a dream or a goal they have in their lives. When ready, have everyone sit down and stand up together in order to "catch" the dreams to help make them realities. • For those people who have difficulty sitting and standing, offer the variation of leaning back while holding the webbing and doing a 360° circle when working with their partners. When the group does this as a whole, they can lean forward when the group sits, and lean back when the group stands up.
Extensions: • Bring in adults from the community to talk about their dreams and how they are working to accomplish their goals.

Facilitation Notes
During a Project Adventure workshop in Vermont, we were doing an activity called Raccoon Circles (developed by Dr. Tom Smith). Without warning, the participants took their webbing and girth-hitched them all to one circle, so it looked like a wheel with spokes. Then everyone hung on to a spoke and we all sat down together. It looked like a Native American dream catcher, so the name stuck.

There is a natural sequence to Dream Catcher which is quite engaging. Once everyone gets the hang of sitting down and getting up together, come up with a cheer that can be yelled while doing the activity. You can also use the cheer as a transition after a debriefing session later on. After a period of talking, bring out the Dream Catcher. Yell your cheer as you sit down and stand up together. Now you're ready for another activity.

This activity offers a wonderful time to talk about dreams and goals while one is part of a human dream catcher. What are students' goals both here in class and later on in life? What do we want to accomplish as a class?

As with Everybody Up, remind students never to let go of their webbing while doing the activity. Cause and effect are very real here. If someone lets go, the others will have no way to hold themselves up. This is a great metaphor for community – what one person does affects everyone else.

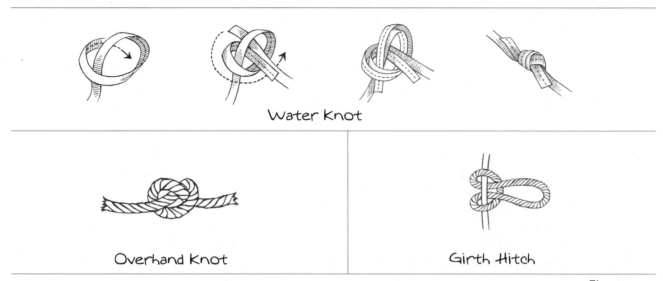

Water Knot

Overhand Knot

Girth Hitch

Figure 5.1

Adaptations for Students with Disabilities: Dream Catcher

Cognitive Disabilities	• Give hints as necessary to facilitate success.
Orthopedic Impairment	• Play could be on mats, soft grass, etc. • Participants in wheelchairs can stay in their chairs. They can lean forward with their partner and come back as their partner stands. • Participants who are not in wheelchairs need the ability to hold onto the webbing and stand up with assistance from the group.
Hearing Impairment	• Agree on visual signals for the group to use ahead of time to indicate when they will be sitting and standing.
Visual Impairment	• Design tactile signals for the group to use ahead of time (e.g., "I will take my hand off your shoulder when we should stand up").

MPS

45. Yurt Circle

Focus: Risk taking, physical/emotional trust, trustworthiness
Materials: None
Levels: Grades 4 and higher

Suggested Procedure

1. Find a space that is big enough for the whole class standing in a circle facing the middle, with some room to spare. Have everyone then take a step back so that the circle isn't too close.
2. There must be an even number of people in the group. If there isn't, then you should step out to make the number even.
3. Determine what your state bird and state flower are. (In Wisconsin they are the robin and the wood violet.)

4. Every other person is labeled the bird (a robin); all the others are the flowers (wood violets).
5. The object for this activity is for all of the birds to lean in one direction while all the flowers lean in the other direction. You will determine which group leans in and which group leans out.
6. When people lean, they should keep their bodies as stiff as possible, trying not to bend at the waist.
7. Ask everyone to hold hands so that they have a good grip. Remind everyone to not let go during the activity.
8. Count to three, and then have people slowly lean in their given direction – either in or out.
9. Try this a couple of times, then have them reverse directions. When people get really good at this, they can start leaning in one direction, then switch to the other direction seamlessly.

Sample Processing Questions for Yurt Circle
- What made this work?
- What would happen if someone let go?
- Was it easier for you to lean in or out? Why?
- How might a community work in this way – where everyone is connected, even when it might not be obvious?
- How did you work with the people around you to make sure no one was pulling too hard? What adjustments did you make?
- What kind of adjustments (give and take) do we make with members of our class to make sure they are taken care of?
- How did you prove you were trustworthy in this activity?

Connections for Yurt Circle
Life Skill Links: caring, choice and accountability, citizenship, communication, conservation, cooperation, effort, empathy, flexibility, loyalty, perseverance, problem solving, relationships, respect, responsibility, safety, self-discipline

Academic Applications: • Use as a way to address the concept of citizenship, democracy, and responsibility for all in a community. • Use as a way to demonstrate leverage and balance.

Variations/Modifications: • *For younger students, or large classes:* Have them get into smaller groups of 8 to 12 for this. Once they have mastered small groups, try getting everyone together for the ultimate cooperation challenge. • Try this first with one group (the birds, for example) all turned around so that their backs are facing the middle of the circle. In this way, everyone leans back – the birds leaning back toward the middle of the circle, and the flowers leaning away from the middle of the circle.

Extensions: • Make the connection between this activity and being part of a team. How are people connected when playing a team sport? How can they make sure they really are a team, and that one or a few people aren't carrying the load for everyone (or hogging the ball)? Part of being trustworthy is pulling your share of the load. • Monitor the concept of "positive interdependence" when students are engaged in cooperative learning groups.

Facilitation Notes
It may be necessary to address the issue of squeezing hands. Students are often embarrassed to hold one another's hands, so you must first determine if they are ready to do so. Another outcome is for someone to squeeze his or her partners' hands too tightly, causing them to cringe. Ask students, or remind them, about trust. You might also suggest that they try holding each others' wrists, which gives a better grip.

As with the Dream Catcher activity, this one demonstrates how people are connected even when they do not think they are. If one person moves too fast, or is not in sync, then everyone feels it. It usually takes a few tries to get the Yurt Circle to work well. Once people get it, then it seems almost easy.

Adaptations for Students with Disabilities: Yurt Circle

Cognitive Disabilities	• Use smaller groups (four to six students each). • Have every other person turn around. Then have them all lean back (they will be leaning in opposite directions but facing each other).

Orthopedic Impairment	• Play could be on mats, soft grass, etc. • Participants in wheelchairs can stay in their chairs. Have someone hold each chair. • Participants not in wheelchairs need the ability to hold onto someone's hand tightly.
Hearing Impairment	• Agree on visual signals for the group to use ahead of time to indicate when they will be leaning.
Visual Impairment	No major modifications necessary.

46. 60-Second Speeches

Focus: Risk taking, emotional trust, empathy
Materials: 3" x 5" note cards and writing utensils
Levels: Grades 6 and higher

Suggested Procedure

1. Everyone is given a set amount of time (5–15 minutes) to prepare a 60-second speech of his or her choosing.
2. Offer note cards for those who wish to take advantage of them.
3. Set up a forum for the speeches – auditorium-like, circle, etc.
4. Students are then given 60 seconds for their speeches, no more and no less.

Sample Processing Questions for 60-Second Speeches

• What was the most difficult part of this activity for you?
• How did the audience treat you? Were they helpful?
• What strategies did you use to get through this challenge?
• Did you consider this a risk or not? What do you think makes it risky for some and not so risky for others? What things do you find risky?
• Did you want to get this over with, or were you content to put it off as long as possible? How do you usually handle situations that are difficult or risky for you?

Connections: 60-Second Speeches

Life Skill Links: caring, communication, courage, empathy, flexibility, imagination, organization, patience, respect
Academic Applications: • This activity can be used as a warm up for more formal speeches. • Speeches can be given on just about any topic. Give students a theme on which to focus their speeches that aligns with a course of study.
Variations/Modifications: • For even more spontaneity, have students choose a letter of the alphabet at random. Their speech must be about something that starts with that letter.
Extensions: • Create a way to show appreciation for people when they take a risk. It can be a special cheer, standing ovation, or having one or two people stand up and say how much they appreciate what this person has attempted.

Facilitation Notes

Speaking in front of a group is one of the riskiest endeavors for people in the United States. Take the time to acknowledge this fact, and then talk about what the class can do to make it easier for each speaker. To give a speech is to risk embarrassment. How do people show their trustworthiness with other people's feelings?

Since this activity can take some time, split it up over a few days. Have a few people give a speech at the end of a class period or as a warm up to another activity. It is a great change-of-pace activity.

One year I did the 60-Second Speech activity with a 6th-grade class. One student was terrified and said that he could not do it. Challenge by Choice was, of course, in effect, and I asked him to talk with me after class. He shared that he would really like to do the activity, but it was too much of a risk for him, so we talked about alternatives: taping it, speaking in front of a smaller group, or giving the speech to one other person. None of the options seemed to work, so he remained part of the audience and did not give a speech.

Later in the year, we had a high ropes course experience. Climbing was easy for this student who had so much difficulty giving a speech. During the last week of school, this student asked if he could give his speech to the class. He stood up there and stammered his way through it. We cheered.

Adaptations for Students with Disabilities: 60-Second Speeches

Cognitive Disabilities	• Have students work with partners. • Do not hold fast to the time limit. • Consider having students tell a story together instead of giving a speech.
Orthopedic Impairment	No major modifications necessary.
Hearing Impairment	• Have an interpreter if necessary.
Visual Impairment	No major modifications necessary.

47. Sherpa Walk

Focus: Risk taking, physical/emotional trust, trustworthiness
Materials: Long rope, like clothesline (optional), eye coverings (optional)
Levels: Grades K and higher

Suggested Procedure
1. Outside in a wooded area is the most interesting place for Sherpa Walk, but it can be done almost anywhere.
2. Have the entire class line up one behind the other.
3. Either have the students put their hands on the shoulders of the person in front of them, or have them all hang onto one long rope.
4. Ask for two volunteers to be the guides, or have the class choose two people to act as guides. These people leave the line.
5. Everyone on the line either puts on an eye covering or closes her or his eyes.
6. One of the guides stays toward the front, while the other takes up the rear. The catch is that the guides may not talk.
7. The guides lead the line of people through a course that is either predetermined, or they make it up as they go along.
8. You act as a spotter, but you may not talk either.

Sample Processing Questions for Sherpa Walk
• How much did you rely on the guides? On those around you? On yourself?
• How did it feel not to be in control of where you were going?
• How did it feel to keep your eyes closed? Was it hard?

- Whom did you have to trust in this situation?
- What did the guide have to do to make sure everyone was taken care of?

Connections for Sherpa Walk
Life Skill Links: caring, choice and accountability, communication, cooperation, courage, empathy, flexibility, patience, respect, resourcefulness, responsibility, safety, self-discipline

Academic Applications: • Use as a simulation and metaphor for the Underground Railroad or other instances where people have to rely on someone else to guide them.

Variations/Modifications: • *For younger students:* Do this in smaller groups of four to six students. • There are many variations to a Sherpa Walk. Set up an obstacle course in a gym, or string clothesline around a bunch of trees for people to follow. The more people must go through, under, over or around, the more interesting the activity will be. You can also fill a hat with pieces of paper, some of which are blank and others have an X. Whoever draws an X is able to talk. Whoever draws a blank must be silent. This can produce some good discussion about dealing with different challenges.

Extensions: • Look for teachable moments when someone is showing trustworthiness by being safe around others. Either discuss it individually with the student involved, or have a group discussion if it involves everyone. • Give students opportunities to practice being safe with each other and taking care of each other, rather than relying on you to take on that role all the time. • Periodically reflect on times when people showed trustworthiness and keep a chart in the class of these examples.

Facilitation Notes
Although the guides are not allowed to talk, the people being led can. There are instances where people forget this detail and it makes the activity more challenging. If this happens, it can bring up good discussion about assumptions that people make and how these assumptions can affect us.

Remind students about moving slowly and watching out for those around them. It may be necessary to practice walking with eyes open first.

Adaptations for Students with Disabilities: Sherpa Walk

Cognitive Disabilities	• Have extra spotters for students. Practice with a "hands-on" experience first.
Orthopedic Impairment	• Rope should be attached or arranged so that participants can feel the rope and still have both hands free to use manual wheelchairs. • Students in wheelchairs should be in the front of the line or have an individual spotter. • The guide can use verbal cues to warn people in advance to stop.
Hearing Impairment	• The spotter should be readily available to give tactile cues to stop, go, etc. • Make sure hearing impaired students know they have a choice to close their eyes or not. • Hearing impaired students can be the guides.
Visual Impairment	No major modifications necessary.

MPS

48. Trust Lean
Focus: Risk taking, physical/emotional trust, trustworthiness, empathy
Materials: None
Levels: Grades 5 and higher

Suggested Procedure

1. You will need space for many groups. Use the hallway, school lawn, gym, or all-purpose room if possible. A classroom is feasible but tight.
2. Have students get into groups of three or four. Ask for one group to volunteer as models. Make sure to show the whole activity before having everybody do it.
3. One person in the small group is the "faller." This person assumes the falling position:
   - Stand with feet together.
   - Arms are crossed over the chest.
   - Hold body as stiff as a board (squeeze buttocks – not only is this good exercise, but it keeps the body from bending).
4. The other two or three people are spotters and stand behind the faller. They assume the spotting position:
   - Stand shoulder to shoulder.
   - Put one foot in front of the other to provide a stable base. (If two people are spotting, their outside foot goes in front – the person on the faller's left puts her left foot forward, and the person on the right puts his right foot forward. If there is a third spotter, the middle person can put either foot in front.)
   - Keep knees bent.
   - Keep hands up with fingers pointing toward the sky.
5. The spotters stand very close to the faller.
6. Teach a communication sequence between faller and spotters:
   - Faller: "Spotters ready?"
   - Spotters: "Ready!"
   - Faller: "Falling!"
   - Spotters: "Fall on!"
7. At this point, the faller tips back into the waiting hands of the spotters, who gently set the faller upright.
8. If everyone feels comfortable, then the faller chooses to step a bit forward, and the whole process is repeated a couple more times.
9. Remind the spotters that each time the faller steps forward she or he will fall back lower, so they should squat down a little more each time. They should **not** turn their hands so that their fingers point toward the floor. This creates poor leverage and does not work well.
10. If something should go wrong (faller bends or tilts to the side), the spotters' responsibility is to keep the faller's head, neck, and shoulders from touching the floor.

Sample Processing Questions for Trust Lean

- Were you more nervous as a spotter or as a faller? Why?
- What did the spotters do that helped keep the faller as safe and comfortable as possible?
- Did you feel your spotters were serious about keeping you safe? How could you tell?
- What were some of the things that went through your head when you were falling/spotting?
- How did you choose how far to step each time? Did you think about it?
- Did you trust your spotters? Why or why not?
- Did you trust yourself? Why or why not?

Connections for Trust Lean

Life Skill Links: caring, choice and accountability, communication, cooperation, courage, empathy, flexibility, loyalty, respect, responsibility, safety, self-discipline

Variations/Modifications: • *For older students:* This activity can be done in pairs, with one person spotting and one person falling.

Extensions: • Talk about what it means to "lean on someone." What are ways we can be there for our friends and family? What are ways we can be there for each other in class?

Facilitation Notes

Trust Lean is the beginning of a classic trust sequence that signals a quantum leap when dealing with issues of trust. Up to this point you have focused on situations that are more controlled. Now you are sure that students truly care about each others' safety and are able to make choices freely about what they are willing to do and not do.

Spotting is now very active. Spotters truly have someone's welfare in their hands, and it must be taken seriously. This is no time for joking about dropping someone or pretending to not be there. These types of jokes can break trust as surely as allowing someone to fall. It is also good to remind people that not all accidents can be prevented. Sometimes people bend and the spotters cannot do anything about that. What a spotter can do, though, is keep people from hurting themselves by protecting the head, neck, and shoulders. Some teachers prefer to do this activity on mats as an extra safety precaution.

One point to make with the students is to remind them that anyone – faller or spotter – can stop the activity at any time. If someone is not comfortable falling or catching, he or she can stop, and the group moves to the next person.

Adaptations for Students with Disabilities: Trust Lean

Cognitive Disabilities	• Make sure that spotters understand their role. Stand nearby, ready to assist, when this activity is first tried.
Orthopedic Impairment	• An adult can tip the wheelchair if it is a manageable weight and the participant feels comfortable being tipped. • Check to see if the participant can come out of the wheelchair with assistance to more fully experience the activity.
Hearing Impairment	• Use tapping cues to indicate when the participant should "fall on." • Have someone stand in front of the faller to facilitate communication between spotters and fallers.
Visual Impairment	• These spotters should touch the back of the faller so they know how far away the faller is. • When spotting, visually impaired students should be paired with others who are comfortable spotting. • Add an extra spotter if necessary.

MPS

49. Pendulum Trust Lean

Focus: Risk taking, physical/emotional trust, trustworthiness, empathy
Materials: None
Level: Grades 5 and higher

Suggested Procedure

1. You will need space for many groups. Use the hallway, school lawn, gym, or all-purpose room if possible. A classroom is feasible, but tight.
2. Get into groups of five or six. Ask one group to volunteer as models. Make sure to show the whole activity before having everybody do it.
3. One person in the small group is the "faller." This person assumes falling position:
   • Stand with feet together.
   • Arms are crossed over the chest.

- Hold body as stiff as a board (squeeze the buttocks – not only is this good exercise, but it keeps the body from bending).
4. The other four or five people are spotters. Two stand in front of the faller, and the other two or three stand behind the faller. They assume spotting position:
   - Stand shoulder to shoulder.
   - Put one foot in front of the other to provide a stable base. (If two people are spotting, their outside foot goes in front – the person on the faller's left puts her left foot forward, and the person on the right puts his right foot forward. If there is a third spotter, the middle person can put either foot in front.)
   - Keep knees bent.
   - Keep hands up, with fingers pointing toward the sky.
5. The spotters stand very close to the faller. The faller indicates in which direction she or he will fall first – forward or backward.
6. Teach a communication sequence between faller and spotters:
   - Faller: "Spotters ready?"
   - Spotters: "Ready!"
   - Faller: "Falling!"
   - Spotters: "Fall on!"
7. At this point, the faller tips into the hands of the spotters, who gently push the faller back into the waiting hands of the other.
8. This swaying back and forth stops when the faller stands up and says, "I'm on my own."
9. If everyone feels comfortable, then the faller asks the spotters to take a step back, and the whole process is repeated a couple of more times.
10. Remind spotters that each time they step farther away from the faller, she or he will fall back lower, so they should squat down a little more each time. They should **not** turn their hands so that their fingers point toward the floor. This creates poor leverage and does not work well.
11. If something should go wrong (faller bends or tilts to the side) the spotters' responsibility is to keep the faller's head, neck, and shoulders from touching the floor.

Sample Processing Questions for Pendulum Trust Lean
- How was this one compared with the one-direction trust lean?
- How did your role as a spotter change?
- What does it take to trust others with your physical safety?
- What did you do as a spotter to help the person in the middle?

Connections for Pendulum Trust Lean
Life Skill Links: caring, choice and accountability, communication, cooperation, courage, empathy, flexibility, relationships, respect, responsibility, safety, self-discipline
Variations/Modifications: • *For older students:* This activity can be done in triads, with one spotter in front and one behind.
Extensions: Have students write about their experience with trust and trustworthiness in their journals. They can then choose to share parts of their journal with the class to spark discussion.

Facilitation Notes
The Pendulum Trust Lean ups the ante by having the faller go in two directions. **Caution** students about the urge to push too hard, thus almost throwing the faller back and forth. This can be unsettling for the faller.

It is also helpful to talk with the class about where to touch a person when spotting in the front. The faller has her arms crossed over her chest. This means that the elbows and upper arms are good places to touch.

Adaptations for Students with Disabilities: Pendulum Trust Lean

Cognitive Disabilities	• Reiterate directions to ensure understanding. • Make sure that participants are in correct spotting positions.
Orthopedic Impairment	• This activity may not be appropriate for orthopedically impaired students.
Hearing Impairment	• Use visual cues to indicate when the participant is going to "fall on."
Visual Impairment	• Have an assistant help place students in the middle. • When students are spotting, have them stand behind the faller and touch the faller's back to see how far away she or he is. • Add an extra spotter if necessary.

MPS

> Eric Borgwardt and company at Bethel Horizons Adventure Center use the following communication sequence whenever a student is engaged in trust, low, or high ropes activities:
>
> Faller: "I'm going for it!"   Spotters: "We're here for you, _____(name)."
>
> Faller: "Falling."   Spotters: "Fall on, _____(name).
>
> This helps students make a more concrete connection between what they are doing and how they relate to the other people.

 50. Willow in the Wind

Focus: Risk taking, physical/emotional trust, trustworthiness, empathy
Materials: None
Level: Grades 5 and higher

Suggested Procedure

1. You will need space for one, two, or three groups – use the hallway, school lawn, gym, or all-purpose room if possible. A classroom is feasible, but tight.
2. Have students get into groups of eight to ten. Ask for one group to volunteer as models. Make sure to show the whole activity before having everybody do it.
3. One person in the small group is the "faller." This person assumes falling position:
    • Stand with feet together.
    • Arms are crossed over the chest.
    • Hold body as stiff as a board (squeeze the buttocks – not only is this good exercise, but it keeps the body from bending).
4. The other people are spotters and stand in a tight (shoulder-to-shoulder) circle around the faller. They assume spotting position:
    • Stand shoulder to shoulder.
    • Put one foot in front of the other to provide a stable base (it doesn't matter which one).
    • Keep knees bent.
    • Keep hands up, with fingers pointing toward the sky.
12. Teach a communication sequence between faller and spotters:
    • Faller: "Spotters ready?"
    • Spotters: "Ready!"
    • Faller: "Falling!"
    • Spotters: "Fall on!"

5. At this point, the faller tips backward into the waiting hands of the spotters, who gently push the faller to another part of the circle. This continues until the faller chooses to stand and says, "I'm on my own."
6. There should be at least three hands on the faller, which means that nobody is having to hold the entire weight of the faller alone.
7. Remind the spotters that they should **not** turn their hands so that their fingers point toward the floor. This is poor leverage and does not work well.
8. If something should go wrong (faller bends or tilts to the side) the spotters' responsibility is to keep the faller's head, neck, and shoulders from touching the floor.

Sample Processing Questions for Willow in the Wind
- How did it feel to be surrounded by so many people during this activity?
- Did you feel like the spotters were taking care of your safety? How could you tell?
- Compared to the other leaning activities, how was this one?
- For those who chose to fall, what made you take that risk?
- For those who chose not to fall, what made you take that risk?

Connections for Willow in the Wind
Life Skill Links: caring, choice and accountability, communication, cooperation, courage, empathy, forgiveness, patience, respect, responsibility, safety, self-discipline
Academic Applications: • Use as a way to develop academic support in the class. Discuss ways in which people in the class can support each other when engaged in learning. Have each student select a short-term academic goal. Then ask them to come up with three things that would be helpful and supportive to them in accomplishing that goal. In small groups, share the goal and the support strategies. The task of each small group is to offer the necessary support. At the end of the assigned time for the goal completion, have the small groups and individuals evaluate how much support they gave and received.
Variations/Modifications: For an added sequence, try this first in smaller groups of five to six. As students become comfortable, create bigger groups until you reach the maximum of about 12 or so.
Extensions: • Discuss the role of support in the development of trust. How much support does one need? How can too much support (especially when not wanted as in the form of rescuing) actually break trust? In this activity, there are many hands holding someone up. Can that be intimidating? How can people make sure that the support they are offering is invited? • Communication during Willow in the Wind is necessary to make sure everyone is on the same page. What happens when some people have the information and others don't? How can we make sure that people are on the same page when working together in class?

Facilitation Notes
At this point in the sequence, people are asked to fall in all directions. Willow in the Wind can be very difficult for some people because of all the touching that is involved. Make sure to remind people about Challenge by Choice; individuals must be sure to make the choice that is right for them. It can also help to acknowledge that touching is an issue for some people.

For the most part students enjoy this activity. Encourage people to close their eyes, which offers a different dimension to the activity. As with the Pendulum Trust Lean, remind students to monitor how hard they are pushing people. It can get out of hand very quickly.

With some classes, it may be useful to have an adult join each of the groups for the first couple of tries until students understand exactly what is expected of them.

Adaptations for Students with Disabilities: Willow in the Wind

Cognitive Disabilities	• Reiterate directions to ensure understanding. • Make sure that participants are in correct spotting positions.
Orthopedic Impairment	• This activity may not be appropriate for orthopedically impaired students.
Hearing Impairment	• Use visual cues to indicate when the participant is going to "fall on."
Visual Impairment	• Have assistants help place students in the circle. • Tighten the circle.

MPS

51. Airport

Focus: Cooperation, safety, empathy, trustworthiness
Materials: Objects found in room, eye coverings (optional)
Level: Grades K and higher

Suggested Procedure

1. Clear furniture from the middle of the room.
2. Have students form two lines, standing side-by-side. The two lines should be facing each other about 8 feet apart. This is the "runway."
3. Place objects from the room on the "runway" (e.g., things like chairs, books, boxes, shoes).
4. Choose two people; one is the "pilot" and the other is the "air traffic controller." The pilot stands at one end, and the air traffic controller stands at the other end of the runway.
5. The pilot closes his or her eyes or puts on an eye covering.
6. The task is for the air traffic controller to help the pilot move down the runway without touching any of the obstacles or any of the people lining the runway. She or he may only use verbal directions to help the pilot land the plane.
7. Allow everyone in the class to be either the pilot or the air traffic controller.

Sample Processing Questions

- How did it feel to be the pilot?
- How did it feel to be the air traffic controller?
- What did your air traffic controller do to keep you safe?
- Did it seem like the air traffic controller cared about the pilot's safety? How could you tell?
- How did you have to change the way you communicated with the pilot (when you were the air traffic controller)? What did you learn as you went along?

Connections for Airport

Life Skill Links: caring, choice and accountability, communication, cooperation, courage, effort, empathy, respect, resourcefulness, responsibility, safety
Academic Applications: • This activity can be used as an introduction to a communications unit to help students think about what communication is and how it changes depending upon any given situation.
Variations/Modifications: • *For younger students:* Create smaller groups so that all have an opportunity to have a turn as pilot or air traffic controller without too long of a wait. Have an adult available to monitor each group. • *For younger students:* Have the air traffic controller stand on the same end of the runway as the pilot to facilitate in perceiving "right" and "left." • *For older students:* Try having the pilot walk backwards toward the air traffic controller. This changes the communication between pilot and air traffic controller. • *For older students:* Have the pilots walk backward, and have the air traffic controller face them. The air traffic controller, then, only gives visual signals. • Ask students who are going to be pilots to add or subtract obstacles according to their own comfort levels.

Extensions: • It is human nature to care about other people's safety, even if we don't know them. Read stories about times when people were good Samaritans and helped people they didn't even know.

Facilitation Notes

This activity is useful for younger groups or as an initial trust activity with older groups. It is very controlled in that you are able to observe students' reactions and offer helpful hints if necessary. Watch out for students in the "runway" for signs of boredom. When this happens, discontinue the activity and continue later so that all get an opportunity to try out the roles.

Adaptations for Students with Disabilities: Airport

Cognitive Disabilities	• Start out with few obstacles. Add more as students become comfortable with the activity. • Have the "air traffic controllers" join the "pilots" to lead them physically instead of verbally.
Orthopedic Impairment	• Make sure there is enough room for a wheelchair to move through the "runway." • Have someone available to help students balance when eyes are closed.
Hearing Impairment	• Have "pilots" walk backward with eyes open. The "air traffic controller" uses visual signals.
Visual Impairment	• No major modifications are necessary when the student is the "pilot." • Have students work in pairs as the "air traffic controllers."

52 High Risk, Low Risk (Thanks to Bonnie Goeke-Johnson for this activity.)

Focus: Being put on the spot, support of others, risk taking, Challenge by Choice, trustworthiness
Materials: Two decks of cards: High risk and low risk (see pages 120–122)
Level: Grades 4 and higher

Suggested Procedure

1. Tell the class that anyone who wants to volunteer can choose to take a risk. There are low-risk cards and high-risk cards.
2. The volunteer chooses one of the decks of cards from which to draw. She draws a card and reads it. If she does not wish to do what is on the card, she may draw another.
3. If she still does not wish to take that risk, she can choose to pass and sit down. If she chooses to do the activity, then she does it.
4. The audience's task is to be supportive (this may mean that you have to have a discussion about what that looks and sounds like).
5. After she is done, another volunteer is chosen.

Sample Processing Questions

• Were you glad you had the choice to do this or not? How would it have been different if you had been forced to do it?
• What are some risks you have taken that you wish you hadn't?
• What causes us to choose to do things even when we don't really want to?
• How can we be more thoughtful about our risk taking?
• What does choice have to do with trusting others and yourself?
• How does someone's behavior determine if someone (or how much someone) trusts another?

Sample Low-Risk Cards

Name two things that you think should be taught in school that are not being taught now.

Describe one thing other people told you that you do well.

Describe something you have done that made someone else feel appreciated.

Tell about an act of kindness you have done or have had done for you.

Name a book you've read in the last month and try to convince others to read it.

Hum a sound.

Tell a clean joke.

What would you do if a person accidentally punched you hard?

Sample Low-Risk Cards

Shake hands with each person in the class.	Tell the class about your favorite TV show.
What would you buy if someone gave you $500, no strings attached?	Give a one-minute speech on "How I think my school should be changed."
Tell the class two things that make you angry.	Name at least three things you would like to have adults do that they don't do now.
What is a boring experience you have had?	Tell the class something good that happened to you this week.

Tell five people something positive about them.

Tell the class at least three of your strengths.

Tell the class something about yourself that no one in the room knows.

Do a one-minute dance.

Look one person in the eyes for one minute.

Talk about a time when you were scared.

Sing a song.

Tell the teacher one thing that you like about his/her teaching and one thing that you think could be improved.

Connections for High Risk, Low Risk

Life Skill Links: caring, choice and accountability, courage, curiosity, empathy, patience, respect, safety, truthfulness

Academic Applications: • Use a similar structure with questions from areas of study. Prepare cards with questions that are easier or more difficult. Have students choose which to tackle in public. Of course, choosing an "easier" question and not being able to answer it can be a high-risk endeavor. Make sure to prepare students and the class for this eventuality. Create an expectation that any question that cannot be answered is an opportunity to support a classmate by helping them out.

Variations/Modifications: Have students create the cards.

Extensions: • Ask students to identify things in their lives that are constructive or healthy low-risk and high-risk situations. Ask them to choose one to try during the week and then report and/or write about their experience. • Create a chart about risk taking. Have an action on one side (e.g., sky diving). On the other side, write the conditions, if any, that would encourage a person to take that risk (e.g., instruction by a certified agency, the right equipment). An option, of course, is "never."

Facilitation Notes

This activity is a wonderful tool for exploring the concept of safe, healthy risk taking, but should only be attempted if there is a high degree of trust in the class. If people are teased for trying something (even if they are teased later), it can have a negative impact for that person.

Adaptations for Students with Disabilities: High Risk, Low Risk

Cognitive Disabilities	• Make sure risk ideas are developmentally appropriate for students.
Orthopedic Impairment	• Make sure that physical risks are achievable for students.
Hearing Impairment	No major modifications are necessary.
Visual Impairment	• Read the card to the student in private so he or she can make a personal choice about attempting the risk or not.

53. Integrity Ball (Adapted from Fireball, *Affordable Portables*, p. 23))

Focus: Taking turns, interpreting rules, responsibility, trustworthiness, perspective taking
Materials: A soft, throwable ball
Level: Grades 5 and higher

Suggested Procedure

1. Stand in a circle.
2. The ball will be tossed around the group using the following rules:
   - No one can make any sound.
   - No one is allowed to move except to catch or throw the ball.
   - No one may make a bad throw or a bad catch.
3. Explain that each individual interprets these rules for him/herself. If she feels she broke any of these rules, then she is to step back from the circle and kneel down – take herself out of the game. **No one can decide for anyone else, even if they think that person should or should not go out.**
4. If students want more clarification of the rules, just tell them that they are to decide how to interpret them for themselves.
5. Do this for a few minutes, then ask the following questions:
   - Without using names, was there a time when you thought someone should have pulled themselves out of the game? What happened?

- Was there a time when you weren't sure if you should pull yourself out or not? What happened? What did you end up doing – staying or going?
6. Discuss people's various interpretations of the rules. (Was it okay to even move their eyes? What about laughing – was that okay?) There are no right or wrong answers.
7. Invite everyone back into the game and try another round.
8. Do as many rounds with discussion as appropriate for your group.

Possible Processing Questions
- Why do you think we all interpreted the rules differently?
- Was it easier for you to point out when you thought others didn't follow the rules, or when you thought you broke a rule (blame vs. taking responsibility)?
- Do you feel that you used integrity in interpreting the rules? Why or why not?
- Do you think that others used integrity in interpreting the rules? Why or why not?
- What are some rules that we have here at school that you must interpret?
- What are some rules that you have to interpret every day at home or in the community?
- How does acting with integrity make someone more trustworthy?
- Do you behave differently when people aren't watching, or do you always behave the same no matter what?

Connections for Integrity Ball
Life Skill Links: choice and accountability, citizenship, communication, cooperation, empathy, flexibility, honesty, integrity, justice, patience, problem solving, purpose, respect, responsibility, truthfulness, wisdom
Academic Applications: • Use as a connection to our legal system. How and why are laws enacted? What happens when people break laws? Are all laws appropriate or even useful? • When studying the civil rights movement or the history of social change in various countries, use this activity to highlight why people may choose to disobey their government (violently and nonviolently) and reap the consequences of their actions. • This activity can be a nice connection to the study of ethics.
Extensions: • Discuss how integrity is not about following rules, but about the choices one makes in how to act according to rules they set for themselves and rules that are set for them. • Discuss the school rules and how they can be interpreted in different ways. Which interpretations reflect integrity? • Have students create a personal code of ethics that they will follow. • Create "dilemma cards" to challenge a person's integrity. Have students respond as to how they might handle the situation. Have them create the cards for the class.

Facilitation Notes
There is no way to predict how this activity will unfold. Some groups have people pulling themselves out right and left, while other groups can play for a long time before anyone chooses to withdraw. The ensuing discussions uncover a variety of motives for how someone chooses to stay or go. The important thing to remember is that there is no right or wrong – it is the discussion that is important. Once people realize that everyone sees the world in his or her unique way, then they can begin to ask why someone makes a choice rather than simply jumping to a judgment about that person.

This activity can also act as a bridge for students to take more responsibility for their own choices and lead to increased independence. In many situations, students rely on the adults and the "rules" to dictate how they will act. If, on the other hand, they are making conscious choices about their own behavior, they have a greater chance of making healthy choices. When one's choice and the rules collide, it can lead to a deeper understanding of why a rule is in place. Of course, it can also lead to the changing of a rule to meet current needs.

Adaptations for Students with Disabilities: Integrity Ball

Cognitive Disabilities	• Re-frame activity to talk about what is right and what is wrong.

Adaptations for Students with Disabilities: Integrity Ball (cont.)

Orthopedic Impairment	• Do this activity on a large table and roll the ball. • Instead of throwing a ball, use sounds and eye contact.
Hearing Impairment	No major modifications are necessary.
Visual Impairment	• Pass the ball around the circle. No one may move until they are physically touched with the ball.

54. Zip, Zap, Pop (Thanks to Faith Evans for the "oops" idea.)

Focus: Being put on the spot, choices, making mistakes
Materials: None
Level: Grades 2 and higher

Suggested Procedure

1. Clear an area and stand in a circle.
2. Teach three sounds and motions:
   ZIP: Hand on forehead like a salute (doesn't matter which hand).
   ZAP: Hand at chest/stomach level like a salute (doesn't matter which hand).
   POP: Hands together (like praying motion) pointing out.
3. Start by doing ZIP. **Whichever way your fingers are pointing is the direction you send the message.** (If you use your right hand, you will send the message to the person on your left).
4. That person then says and does the ZAP. Again, whichever way his or her fingers are pointing is the direction the message is sent. (If he or she uses the left hand, the message is sent back to you. If he or she uses the right hand, the message is sent to the person on his or her left).
5. Whoever has the message now does the POP by saying it and pointing to someone else in the circle. **It can be anyone.**
6. The person who receives the POP then starts the whole process over with ZIP.
7. Try this for a while as practice. If someone makes a mistake, simply have them correct it and keep the game moving along.
8. Once people understand how this works, add the following rules:
   • If you make a mistake, you say "oops," and we applaud you for creating a learning opportunity. Then start the sequence going again.
   • If you receive POP (and POP only) but do not want to receive it, you can cross your arms over your chest and say "no." It then bounces back to the person who sent it and he/she starts the next ZIP.
9. Play for a while, and then discuss what happened.

Sample Processing Questions

• How did it feel to make a mistake in front of everyone? How did we treat you when it happened?
• If you chose to say "no," how did it feel to take that risk?
• How did it feel to be told "no"?
• Are there times when you feel like you don't have a choice – when the pressure is high to go along? Describe a situation.
• Why is it important to have a choice about when to trust another person or how much to trust another person? What influences your decision to trust others?
• Does it take courage to say "no" when everybody else is doing something? In what way?

Connections for Zip, Zap, Pop

Lifeskill Links: caring, choice and accountability, cooperation, courage, flexibility, forgiveness, patience, peacefulness, perseverance, positive attitude, respect, responsibility, safety, self-discipline

Academic Applications: • Use as a fun way to memorize something. Instead of using "Zip, Zap, Pop," create new words such as "Roy," "G," "Biv" to remember the order of the colors in a rainbow. Or how about "length," "times," "width" to remember the formula for area.

Variations/Modifications: • Try the game first as an elimination game, and then do it again as an inclusion game so that students simply move to the other side of the circle rather than being "out." Discuss the difference and how they felt each time.

Extensions: • Discuss ways to react when someone makes a mistake. At the end of a class, evaluate how people are responding to mistakes. • How one says "no" is as important as the ability to do so when necessary. Practice exercising one's right to pass in respectful ways. Brainstorm ways to say "no" and role-play them. • Discuss when it is appropriate to say "no" and when it is important to try something one might be nervous about or may just not feel like they want to do.

Facilitation Notes

It generally takes quite a while for people, both younger and older, to get the hang of this activity. At times one or two people will continue to struggle with it. Be patient about speeding up the game too soon.

Although this activity can be viewed as a Deinhibitizer, a group needs a higher degree of trust to attempt this. Many people will make mistakes and it can become quite intimidating if it is not a safe place in which to do so. As such, it is a great activity to use when exploring trust issues around making mistakes. It is also a good time to reinforce the concept of Challenge by Choice, especially in the context of situations when people are asked to place their trust in others.

Adaptations for Students with Disabilities: Zip, Zap, Pop

Cognitive Disabilities	• Use two movements instead of three (e.g., "Hello," where they salute to one side or the other, and "Goodbye," where they point to someone else in the circle).
Orthopedic Impairment	• Create movements that everyone can do.
Hearing Impairment	• Do not require that all do the sound with the motion.
Visual Impairment	• Instead of "Zip, Zap, Pop," use people's names. Give everyone time to learn who is next to them before starting.

55. Help Tag

Focus: Empathy, risk taking, emotional trust, trustworthiness
Materials: 2–4 hand towels or 2–4 other throwable items
Level: Grades 3 and higher

Suggested Procedure

1. This is a tag game, so you will need a large space, such as a gym, cafeteria or outside area.
2. Depending on the size of your group, have two to four throwable items in play. If you have added too few or too many items, play for a while, then stop the action and adjust the number of throwables to meet the level of challenge necessary for your group. If you are using hand towels, tie a knot in each one to make them easier to throw and catch.
3. Identify two people who are the chasers. Their job is to tag people. Once tagged, a person is frozen for the remainder of that round.

4. If a person is holding a towel, that person is safe and cannot be tagged.
5. The only way someone can get a towel is to ASK FOR IT. Agree on a phrase like, "Please, help me," or "I need help," or "I need the towel!"
6. When someone asks for the towel, the person holding it decides if s/he will give it to that person or not.
7. Have each round last about a minute or 2. Each time, change the two people who are the chasers.

Sample Processing Questions
- Did you find yourself asking for help or trying to avoid getting tagged on your own?
- If you were holding a towel and someone asked for it, did you always provide it, or did you find yourself deciding to keep it? What entered into your decisions?
- Is it ever appropriate to NOT help someone when they ask for it?
- Why do you think it takes trust to ask for help?
- How do you prove your trustworthiness when someone asks you for help?
- Are there times when people might ask for help when they don't really need it? What are some examples?
- What do you do when you know someone really does not need help and they ask you for it?
- What do you do when you know someone needs help and they don't ask for it?

Connections for Help Tag
Life Skill Links: caring, choice and accountability, communication, cooperation, effort, empathy, flexibility, purpose, relationships, respect, responsibility, safety

Academic Applications: • After doing this activity, ask students to create a list of people who can help them with their academic work and their homework. • Use as an introduction to community service and service learning projects. Create a list of service projects that can be done inside and outside of the classroom. See if the people who are affected by these require the help before giving it. Choose one and do it.

Variations/Modifications: • Give the chasers a soft item to use to tag people (e.g., foam ball). This minimizes body contact and identifies the chasers.

Extensions: • Keep track of times when people have asked for and/or given help during the class. • Make a point to ask for help from students and other staff.

Facilitation Notes
Make note of when students who are asking for the towels a lot or when students are holding onto the towels (and withholding help). That way, you will have some specific examples to present to the group when processing the information.

Younger students may have difficulty with more than one towel, so see how it works and make modifications as necessary.

Adaptations for Students with Disabilities: Help Tag

Cognitive Disabilities	• Use one towel and one chaser. • Do activity walking instead of running.
Orthopedic Impairment	• This activity may not be appropriate for orthopedically impaired students. • Do in pairs so that one person can be the thrower and catcher. • Do as a walking activity.
Hearing Impairment	No major modifications are necessary.
Visual Impairment	• Do as a walking activity. • Do in pairs so that one person can be the thrower and catcher. • Have brightly colored towels for easier identification.

56. Five Ways to Show You Care

Focus: Cooperation, caring, empathy
Materials: None
Level: Grades K–1

Suggested Procedure

1. Create a list of ways to show caring.
2. From the list of ways to show you care, choose one (e.g., "helping").
3. Ask the students, "How can we act out helping someone to show we care?" You might then pantomime reaching out as a way to show helping.
4. Do the same with four more ways from the list that you created. You will now have five ways to show you care, all acted out in some way.
5. Number the five in the list, and then practice together. Call out "one," and everyone acts it out. Then "two," and so on.
6. Once students are beginning to catch on, call the numbers out quickly, or in a rhythm.
7. Finally, try counting backwards, or randomly.

Sample Processing Questions

- Doing these motions reminds us about caring, but it isn't the real thing. For each of the ways we did caring here, how do we really show caring? (Pick one and have them identify ways they can really show the caring, not just act it out.)
- Why is it important to show people you care about them?
- Do you trust people who show they care about you? Why?
- Who are people who show they care about you?

Connections for Five Ways to Show You Care

Life Skill Links: caring, cooperation, empathy, initiative, peacefulness, positive attitude, purpose, relationships, respect
Extensions: • Every once in a while call out "Caring # 3!" (or 2, or 5) and see who jumps up and acts it out. • Make note of when you see a real act of caring that is similar to one of the five you identified as a class. Call it out for students to act out. Then make a note of what you saw to the class.

Facilitation Notes

At first, students may seem rather lackadaisical about the motions, but if you keep surprising them with the numbers, they become more engaged over time. Don't give up. Soon they will ask why you haven't called out the numbers in awhile.

The doing of the numbers and motions is only that – going through the motions. This activity opens the door so that you can all put these ideas into practice. Doing the motions helps, but it is only the first step.

Adaptations for Students with Disabilities: Five Ways to Show You Care

Cognitive Disabilities	• Start with two or three ways to show you care and build up from there.
Orthopedic Impairment	• Make sure everyone can do the motions.
Hearing Impairment	• Have a visual signal for the numbers.
Visual Impairment	• Talk through the motions as you do them so that everyone knows how to do them.

Emotional Self-Awareness: Feelings Literacy

People can learn to be more self-aware of emotions by developing a feelings vocabulary. Here are some activities that encourage students to learn the names of a variety of emotions, so they can begin identifying them when they occur.

51. Feelings Speed Rabbit

Focus: Feelings literacy, acting silly, being put on the spot
Materials: None
Level: Grades K–3

Suggested Procedure
1. Clear a space and have students stand in a circle. You take the middle.
2. Teach a variety of motions/emotions, each of which will be acted out by three people.
3. Point to someone and say "scared." Ask the class what the facial expression of someone who is scared might look like. Have the person you point to do that. Then ask how someone who is scared might show it with his or her body. The person on each side of the person you pointed to do that motion. Together, the three people embody the word scared.
4. Point to someone and say "angry." Have students create the face and body language to show anger, with the person you pointed to showing the face and the side people showing the body signals.
5. Point to someone and say "excited." Have students create the face and body language to show excitement.
6. Once these are established and practiced, the game begins. Tell them that you will point to someone, say "scared," "angry," or "excited," and count to 10 as fast as you can. If the threesome responds before you get to 10, you continue. If not, the slowest person of the threesome takes your place in the middle.
7. After doing this for awhile, add more. Ask the class to give their suggestions.

Sample Processing Questions for Feelings Speed Rabbit
- Why might it be important to learn about different feelings?
- How can you tell if someone is feeling a certain way?
- What are other ways to express your feelings?

Connections for Feelings Speed Rabbit
Life Skill Links: caring, communication, cooperation, effort, empathy, patience, sense of humor
Academic Applications: • After trying this activity, ask students to identify feelings of characters by the way they talk or look in the pictures of a story you are reading.
Variations/Modifications: • *For younger students:* Create motions that can be done by one person. Then build into working with other people.
Extensions: • Have students draw pictures of themselves showing different emotions, and have them share their pictures with the class.

Facilitation Notes
Sometimes it helps to begin this activity using some of the classic Speed Rabbit animal motions (see p. 59), and then build in the feelings motions as the activity progresses. This strategy allows the students to get into the groove of the activity without adding new content right away. This is also a wonderful activity to repeat throughout the year, adding more feelings to the vocabulary list.

Adaptations for Students with Disabilities: Feelings Speed Rabbit

Cognitive Disabilities	• Create motions that require only one person or pair. • Only do two different emotions/motions at first. Add more later. • Don't time students at first. • You stay in the middle.
Orthopedic Impairment	• Make sure all students can do the motions. Ask for help from the students about how to modify them.
Hearing Impairment	• Use your fingers to count. • Stay with the student in the middle to help say the emotion. • Learn the ASL sign for the emotion to use instead of saying it.
Visual Impairment	• Teach motions verbally and allow students time to practice them. • Stay with students in the middle to help with pointing.

58. Feelings Cards: Charades

Focus: Feelings literacy
Materials: Feelings cards – homemade or commercially made
Level: Grades K and higher

Suggested Procedure

1. Divide the class into groups of four to six.
2. Give each group a stack of feelings cards set face down.
3. The object is for students to take turns choosing a card and acting it out for their group members to guess. When the feeling is guessed, another person takes a turn.
4. If the group is having a hard time guessing the feeling, the person doing the charade can show them the card and pick a new one or ask someone in their group for help.
5. Continue this for 5 minutes or so.

Sample Processing Questions for Feelings Cards: Charades

- How easy/difficult was it to act out the feelings on the cards? Why?
- Is it possible to misinterpret what someone is feeling? How does that happen?
- What body language do you use to show how you are feeling?

Connections for Feelings Cards: Charades

Life Skill Links: communication, cooperation, patience, perseverance
Academic Applications: • Using this activity as a springboard, have students surmise how a character is feeling by his or her actions in the story.
Variations/Modifications: • *For younger students:* Do as a large group. Allow students to see a list of the feelings to help them guess the feeling being shown.
Extensions: • Do some role plays with scenarios using only certain emotions. For example, one student is only allowed to be silly, even when the situation is serious. The other student is only allowed to be angry. Have them role-play a situation in which they find a broken bike. See how these two feelings work together and discuss.

Facilitation Notes

This activity can easily become competitive, with each small group trying to get more cards than the next. Obviously, this detracts from the true focus of the activity, which is to practice and learn about feelings. It is possible to minimize the competitive nature of the activity by publicly stating that each group has a different set of cards and de-emphasizing the competition. Of course, if competition becomes a factor in this activity, it is a topic that is worth processing.

Start with emotions that are familiar to students. Do the activity later in the year, and add more cards by discussing them first. In this way, students can continue to expand their feelings vocabulary throughout the year.

> **Feeling cards** can either be made by the class or purchased (see Adventure/Experiential Education Resources in the appendices). Try brainstorming a list of feelings (supplementing with other common emotions) and having students create the cards with markers and paper. Another strategy is to bring in a digital camera and photograph students showing feelings, then labeling them. It may be necessary for the students to do some research on what a particular feeling is by asking other students and adults how they would describe it. Here is a list of feelings that can be used for making your own cards.

Accepted	Crazy	Friendly	Mad	Sad
Afraid	Curious	Frightened	Meek	Scared
Angry	Depressed	Frustrated	Melancholy	Shocked
Annoyed	Determined	Glad	Mischievous	Shy
Anxious	Disgusted	Happy	Miserable	Silly
Ashamed	Disappointed	Helpless	Moody	Smart
Bitter	Down	Hopeful	Nervous	Smug
Bold	Eager	Hurt	Optimistic	Strong
Bored	Ecstatic	Hysterical	Overwhelmed	Stupid
Brave	Embarrassed	Infuriated	Panicky	Surprised
Calm	Energetic	Inspired	Peaceful	Suspicious
Cautious	Enraged	Irritated	Pessimistic	Tense
Confident	Envious	Jealous	Proud	Tired
Confused	Excited	Lonely	Put Down	Upset
Content	Exhausted	Loving	Relaxed	Vulnerable
Courageous	Flexible	Lucid	Restless	Worried

Adaptations for Students with Disabilities: Feelings Cards Charades

Cognitive Disabilities	• Choose three to six feelings to start and have them repeated in the piles of cards. Practice them in advance. Add more later. • Have a list of feelings posted for students to choose from.
Orthopedic Impairment	• No major modifications necessary.
Hearing Impairment	• Teach the signs for all the emotions so that people can guess by using signs as well as verbally.
Visual Impairment	• Use words or sounds instead of pantomime. • Have the cards written in Braille.

59. Feelings Cards: Stories

Focus: Feelings literacy
Materials: Feelings cards – homemade or commercially made
Level: Grades K and higher

Suggested Procedure
1. Divide the class into pairs.
2. Give each pair three feelings cards.
3. Ask them to create a short story (one paragraph) using those feelings words.
4. Have each pair read and/or act out their story.

Sample Processing Questions for Feelings Cards: Stories
- Which feelings were easier to write about? Why do you think they were easier?
- Which ones were more difficult? Why do you think they were more difficult?
- What are different ways to express how you feel? (Writing is one way.)

Connections for Feelings Cards: Stories
Life Skill Links: communication, cooperation, imagination, resourcefulness
Academic Applications: • Aside from writing a story, try creating a poem using the words.
Variations/Modifications: • *For younger students:* Do this as a whole class, and create a shared story. • *For older students:* Have them see how many different emotions they can weave into a longer story. • Try giving each pair just one card and having them create a story about that single feeling. • Give each person a card and go around the circle asking them to create a sentence using that feeling word, or describe an event (real or created) where that feeling occurred.
Extensions: • Have an ongoing journal writing assignment that has students periodically record one or more feelings they have had that day.

Facilitation Notes
The idea with these emotions activities is to encourage the students to examine a myriad of feelings so they can better communicate their feelings and needs. Once the more common emotions have been explored, start on similar ones. For example, you may deal with families of emotions, such as mad, angry, enraged, infuriated, etc. As students develop a more complete feelings vocabulary that goes past "mad, sad, glad," they can better articulate what it is they are feeling. These stories can help them make these connections.

Adaptations for Students with Disabilities: Feelings Cards Stories

Cognitive Disabilities	• Make sure everyone knows what each feeling is before starting. • Give assistance as needed.
Orthopedic Impairment	No major modifications necessary.
Hearing Impairment	• Provide interpreters as needed.
Visual Impairment	• Have the cards written in Braille.

60. Crossing the Feelings Line

Focus: Feelings literacy, communicating feelings
Materials: Rope or tape to make a large circle on the floor
Level: Grades 3 and higher

Suggested Procedure

1. Clear an area. Place the rope or tape in a large circle so everyone can stand around it.
2. Tell the class that each person is going to cross the line differently from anyone else.
3. Each person is to cross the line by showing either a) a different feeling or b) the same feeling as someone else, but exhibited in a different way.
4. Demonstrate by stepping over the line with hands clenched and a scowl on your face, then step back.
5. Have each student tell the class what the emotion is when it is being shown, or have the class try to guess.
6. After everyone has had a turn, have students pair up.
7. This time, each pair is to cross the line differently from any other pair. Give them 30 seconds or so to plan.
8. After pairs, go in groups of four, then eight, and so on, until the entire class is crossing the line together.

Sample Processing Questions for Crossing the Feelings Line

- Were you concerned about running out of feelings to share? Did that happen? Why or why not?
- How was it working with other people on this? Were the ideas easier or more difficult to come by?
- Which feelings do you see as "positive," and which do you see as "negative?" Why?
- What ways did you use to express your feeling? What are other ways you could have used?
- Which are the feelings that seem to be the most commonly mentioned? What are some other feelings that we have?
- How might it be risky to express your feelings to others? What can we do to reduce the risk so that people feel comfortable sharing their feelings here?

Connections for Crossing the Feelings Line

Life Skill Links: choice and accountability, communication, cooperation, courage, imagination, organization, patience

Academic Applications: • After studying a particular section of history, have students brainstorm feelings people may have had during that period and only use those in this activity. For example, during the Great Depression, they may come up with: frustrated, frightened, nervous, generous, etc.

Variations/Modifications: • *For younger students:* Have them work alone and in pairs only. Then jump to the whole class crossing the line. • *For older students:* Add the rule that once a feeling has been used, it cannot be used again. In this way, they will need to dig a little deeper to demonstrate a similar emotion. If "anxious" is used, they might have to use "nervous" or "tense."

Extensions: • Keep a "wall of emotions" by presenting a new feelings word each day or each week. Have students use the word all day or week as much as possible. Then see if they can identify if they have had that feeling during the day or week.

Facilitation Notes

Generally, as the groups get bigger in this activity, the students have an easier time coming up with ideas. With the addition of people options are expanded. The first time around, it may be necessary to help individual students come up with ideas toward the end of the activity, so make sure you have a few feelings ideas available (e.g., concerned, shy, or hysterical). These are feelings that are usually forgotten in favor of the more common "mad," "sad," "glad."

Adaptations for Students with Disabilities: Crossing the Feelings Line

Cognitive Disabilities	No major modifications necessary.
Orthopedic Impairment	No major modifications necessary.
Hearing Impairment	• No major modifications necessary. • Have an interpreter available, if necessary.
Visual Impairment	• Have the boundary clearly defined.

61. Emotion Motions

Focus: Feelings literacy, active listening, making mistakes
Materials: None
Level: Grades 3 and higher

Suggested Procedure

1. Have students sit in a circle.
2. Start by showing – only through motions – an emotion (e.g., hitting your hand in your fist to show frustration). Then have everyone practice it.
3. The person next to you shows another feeling using motions only (e.g., crossing his arms and sitting tall to represent pride). The next person may signify "bored" by placing her chin in her hand and sighing. This continues until everyone has a unique motion and everyone has practiced all of them.
4. The game is now ready to begin. Start by showing your motion (fist in hand), and then showing another one (crossing arms and sitting tall). You have just passed it to the person who is "pride."
5. "Pride" now does his own motion – crossing arms and sitting tall. Then he puts his chin in his hand and sighs, thus passing to "bored." This continues until someone makes a mistake (taking too long, forgetting a motion, doing a motion incorrectly, etc.).
6. That person then becomes your motion ("frustration") and takes your spot. Everyone else moves over one spot until the empty spot is filled. Many times this means that only part of the group moves, while the others stay put.
7. The catch is that the feeling motion stays in the same spot; it does not move with the person. So, those who have just moved have to take on a new motion.

Sample Processing Questions for Emotion Motions

- What are some nonverbal signals that show how someone might be feeling?
- How might you treat someone differently depending on the nonverbal signals he or she is sending out?
- What are some actions you can take to help your situation when you are feeling mad, sad, anxious, etc?
- Is it possible to "listen with your eyes"? How?

Connections for Emotion Motions

Life Skill Links: communication, imagination, patience, relationships
Academic Applications: • After doing this activity, identify nonverbal signals that are being used in stories, works of art, and videos that are used in class.
Variations/Modifications: • *For younger students:* Do not move when someone makes a mistake. Acknowledge it and continue the game.
Extensions: • Introduce the concept of mixed signals: when one's body language, tone of voice, and what one says do not match. Practice noticing mixed signals through role playing. • This activity helps open the door to talk about nonverbal communication and body language. You can then transition the discussion into what to do when feeling depressed, angry, and so on. Encourage students to talk to others and seek out help when they are feeling hurt, angry, frustrated, or depressed. Creating different strategies for these situations helps students become more aware of their feelings and learn how to take appropriate actions.

Facilitation Notes

Before trying this activity it is important to make sure the students feel okay about being put on the spot and that it is okay to make mistakes in the class.

This is a variation on King/Queen Frog (Ice Breakers/Acquaintance activity # 8, p. 50 in Chapter 4). Try that activity first to lead into this one.

Adaptations for Students with Disabilities: Emotion Motions

Cognitive Disabilities	• Do this in small groups. • Have the motion stay with the person, so that when everyone moves, they all still do the same motion.
Orthopedic Impairment	• Make sure all motions can be done by all students in the class. • Allow a longer time to complete motions.
Hearing Impairment	• Have everyone learn the sign for their chosen emotion and use sign language.
Visual Impairment	• Use sounds instead of motions. • Do this in smaller groups.

62 Blue JellyBeans

(Adapted from the activity Mashed Potatoes, *Adventures in Peacemaking, Early Childhood Edition*, p. 5–18)
Focuses: Taking turns, feelings literacy, listening, right to pass/Challenge by Choice
Materials: Talking stick or an item to pass
Level: Grades K–1

Suggested Procedure

1. Have everyone sit in a circle.
2. Choose any phrase, such as "blue jellybeans."
3. Then choose a certain feeling – say, excited. Practice being excited.
4. The object is for everyone in the circle to say the phrase in the way of the emotion. In this case, each person will say "blue jellybeans!" in as excited a manner as possible.
5. Pass the talking stick around, giving each person an opportunity to say the phrase.
6. As the talking stick goes around the group, each person has the right to say "pass," or show the emotion in their face instead of their voice.
7. Go around as many times as you wish using a different emotion each time.

Sample Processing Questions

• Was it fun to show different emotions with the words "blue jellybeans?" What made it fun?
• Did you find it easier to show the emotion with your voice or your face? Let's try doing both.

Connections for Blue JellyBeans

Life Skill Links: choice and accountability, communication, imagination, patience, respect
Academic Applications: • Use any words or phrases from students' sight word lists or wall of words.
Extensions: • Brainstorm a list of emotions. Every week add a new one to the list and practice it with "blue jellybeans." • During reading aloud, encourage students to use their voice to show different emotions.

Facilitation Notes

Some students have difficulty with this activity either because they are not sure what the feeling word is or because they are shy about acting in front of the group. Practicing the feeling sound as a group before doing it individually can be helpful. If a student chooses to pass, he or she will have had some experience with it and will also be able to see other students modeling the feeling sounds.

This is a great activity to use as a way to introduce new feelings words to the class. You can model it, and then everyone gets an opportunity to practice it.

Adaptations for Students with Disabilities: Blue Jellybeans

Cognitive Disabilities	• Practice the same emotion words for many days in a row before trying a new one. • Do body movements along with sound.
Orthopedic Impairment	No major modifications necessary.
Hearing Impairment	• Act out the feelings along with sound. • Teach the sign for the feelings words and use them along with the sound and body motions.
Visual Impairment	No major modifications necessary.

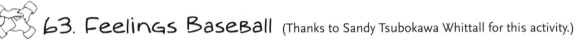

63. Feelings Baseball (Thanks to Sandy Tsubokawa Whittall for this activity.)

Focus: Cooperation, taking turns, feelings literacy
Materials: Four bases arranged like a baseball diamond
Level: Grades K–1

Suggested Procedure

1. You will need a large area, like a gym, a cafeteria, or outside.
2. Have the students sit or stand in a circle behind home plate.
3. Consult with the students about three feelings on which to focus (e.g., excited, sad, surprised).
4. Work together to come up with theatrical ways to act out each feeling. You might choose to jump up and down for "excited," put hands over your face for "sad," and raise arms in the air with eyes wide and mouth open for "surprised."
5. Assign a feeling to each base: First (excited), second (sad), third (surprised). Home plate is left open.
6. Tell the students that there are two parts to this activity: a) each person will have an opportunity to run the bases and act out each feeling, and b) everyone else cheers for the runner.
7. Have them choose a fair way to establish an order for who goes first, next, etc. If this is too difficult for them to establish, have them go in alphabetical order.
8. Each student then runs the bases individually with the support and cheering of everyone else. Each time a person gets to a base, he or she acts out the feeling for that base. In this case, students will jump up and down at first base, put hands over their faces at second base, and raise their arms in the air with eyes wide and mouth open at third base. They then run on home to the cheering crowd.
9. Make sure you take a turn as well (but not necessarily first).

Sample Processing Questions for Feelings Baseball

• How did we show that we cared?
• How did it feel to be cheered on?
• What are other ways to show we care about someone?

Connections for Feelings Baseball

Life Skill Links: caring, choice and accountability, communication, cooperation, flexibility, patience, positive attitude, relationships, respect
Academic Applications: • Either read a story or have students make up a story using the three words. Each time a word is used, a student runs to that base and acts out the word (make sure the bases are close together for this one). • Use as a way to teach and practice base running in physical education.
Variations/Modifications: After students have gotten good at the basic version, create a new challenge by having them act out a feeling of their choice at each base and see if others can guess what it is.

Extensions: • Brainstorm some ways to show caring with each other in your class and make a plan to try some of them for the day/week. • At the end of a day, ask the students to reflect back to times when they felt cared for by other students or when they showed caring toward another.

Facilitation Notes

As you can imagine, this activity can take awhile and it is necessary for students to be patient and wait their turn. This can be challenging for some. Keep the bases fairly close together, and have more than one student run the bases at a time to speed things up a bit.

Adaptations for Students with Disabilities: Feelings Baseball

Cognitive Disabilities	• Have one or two feelings initially. Add more later. • Run back and forth between home plate and one base.
Orthopedic Impairment	• Give assistance as necessary to those moving around the bases. • Have people move around the bases in pairs.
Hearing Impairment	• Have a visual signal to show who goes next.
Visual Impairment	• Have people move around the bases in pairs.

64. Morpheelings

Focus: Feelings literacy, acting silly, mixing
Materials: Stopwatch (optional)
Level: Grades K–5

Suggested Procedure

1. Clear a small area in the room. Have everyone stand in a circle.
2. Make sure everyone knows the game Rock/Paper/Scissors, and agree on the rules for that game.
3. Show everyone the following motions: confused (hands on head), disgusted (tongue out, finger pointing at mouth), surprised (hands on face, mouth open), happy (hugging oneself), silly (dancing around).
4. The object is to get as high up in the chain as possible in a given amount of time (I usually go for two minutes or so).
5. Everyone begins as confused. Everyone then finds another person showing confused and does Rock/Paper/Scissors until a winner is established. Whoever wins gets to move up the chain to disgusted. He or she must then find another persons showing disgusted with whom to do Rock/Paper/Scissors.
6. The winner moves up to the next step (surprised), while the loser goes down a step (confused).
7. This continues for the allotted time. When someone makes it up to silly, that person then stands outside of the circle and dances in place.
8. In other words, if you win, you're out.

Sample Processing Questions for Morphing

• How did you feel about doing these silly motions for feelings?
• What are different ways that people show their feelings?
• How do you usually show each of the feelings we did here?

Connections for Morpheelings

Life Skill Links: communication, patience, perseverance
Academic Applications: Use this activity to jump-start thinking about similarities and differences between certain feelings. Create a chart showing feelings that are similar to and different from others.

Variations/Modifications: As with the Morphing activity you can add a choice and risk-taking elements to this activity by giving those who make it to silly the opportunity to take the "ultimate risk." If they choose, they can do Rock/Paper/Scissors with another person showing silly. Whoever wins stays at that level. The person who loses, however, starts over as confused. It can be interesting to discuss why some people chose to take that risk while others were comfortable where they were.

Extensions: • *For older students:* Teach a sequence of feelings that are similar, but subtly different (e.g., annoyed, irritated, frustrated, angry, irate, enraged). Discuss the differences between them, then come up with sounds and motions to signify each and play the game again.

Facilitation Notes
This is a modification of the activity, Morphing (see p. 56). Have students make up their own motions to go with a sequence of feelings.

Adaptations for Students with Disabilities: Morpheelings

Cognitive Disabilities	• Use fewer stages in the chain. • Teach Rock/Paper/Scissors first and play it for a while before attempting to add this variation.
Orthopedic Impairment	• Create motions that all students can do.
Hearing Impairment	No major modifications necessary.
Visual Impairment	• Do this in pairs; each partner takes a turn doing the Rock/Paper/Scissors.

Behavioral Goal Setting

The Trust phase of the sequence is a great time to begin looking at personal goal setting. Goals are better achieved when people have help and encouragement from the outside. It is risky to entrust others with the contents of a personal goal that is near and dear to one's heart. These trust activities give people experience with the art of goal setting and strategies to use in order to meet those goals.

A behavioral goal has to do with just that: behavior. Ask students to assess their own behavior in class. What might they want to change or reinforce? What personal goals do they have in regard to trusting other students and being trustworthy? Have them first write up a goal that can be accomplished in a very short period of time — maybe even one that can be accomplished in an hour or less. After processing what worked and did not work with that goal, try another goal-setting exercise that requires a longer period of time. This type of goal setting is invaluable as a way to encourage self-reflection, a skill that can be used for an entire lifetime.

65. The River of Life
Focus: Personal goal setting, risk taking, physical/emotional trust, trustworthiness
Materials: Two long ropes for boundaries (clothesline works fine), lots of "stuff" to put inside the boundaries (wadded-up pieces of paper, stuffed animals, shoes, etc.), a sticky note and writing utensil for each person, eye coverings (optional)
Level: Grades 6 and higher

Suggested Procedure
1. Clear the middle of the room, or find a large area like a gym or all-purpose room. You can also go outside.

2. Place the two ropes on the ground parallel to each other, about 10 to 15 feet apart. Make them wavy to simulate a river.
3. Distribute the "stuff" randomly inside the river boundaries.
4. After presenting the concept of Smart Goals (below), ask each student to think about a personal behavioral goal – something they wish to work toward in this class. For example, maybe someone is very quiet in a large group and wishes to be more vocal. That person may set a goal to contribute to a group discussion at least once per day. Another student may have trouble getting her homework in on time. Her goal may be to finish all her homework and hand it in for at least 27 of the next 30 school days.
5. Have them write their goals on their sticky notes.
6. Divide the class into pairs and have them stand around the "river of life."
7. Explain that the river of life is full of accomplishments and frustrations. One way to navigate through the river of life is to set goals for oneself. This helps to provide direction. Many times, though, there are obstacles to achieving goals – some external, some self-imposed. For example, if a goal is to get one's homework in on time, some obstacles would be: procrastinating by choosing to do other things first (like playing games or watching TV), other responsibilities at home, or leaving it at school by mistake. The obstacles are represented by the "stuff" that is strewn about.
8. Have each pair choose who will be the goal-getter first. The other is the guide. The goal-getters place their goals in the river of life. The object is to get to the goal, pick it up, and get out the other side of the river while touching as few obstacles as possible.
9. Goal-getters then don eye coverings or close their eyes. The guides then verbally direct the goal-getters to their goals. If the goal-getters touch an object, they must tell their guides about an obstacle that might be encountered when trying to achieve their particular goal.
10. After goal-getters reach the other side, they switch roles with the guides.

Mary Henton, in *Adventure in the Classroom*, describes "SMART" Goals. **A SMART Goal** is:

• **S**pecific: Goals are not either/or situations. They should focus on one behavior that a person wants to increase, decrease, or change in some way.

• **M**easurable: In order to know if a goal has been achieved, it must be measurable according to quantity and time.

• **A**chievable: A goal needs to be realistic. If we continually make goals that cannot be accomplished, it is more an exercise in frustration than goal setting.

• **R**elevant: This refers to the larger group. The goal must offer an overall positive outcome within the context of the group. Although the goal may carry over into a person's life outside of the group, it cannot be damaging or harmful to the person, group or society as a whole. It is also important that the person making the goal wants to accomplish it. In this way it is relevant to the individual setting the goal.

• **T**rackable: It must be possible to see if you are heading toward your goal at any particular time. If half of the time has expired to your stated goal, you should be able to see how far you have come and what else you need to do to achieve the goal.

(Adapted from *Adventure in the Classroom*, p. 81, as adapted from Blanchard, Sharp and Cox).

Sample Processing Questions for The River of Life
• What did your guide do to help you achieve your goal?
• What are some resources that can help you achieve your goal? (These can involve things or people.)
• What are some obstacles you are likely to encounter when working toward your goal? What can you do to keep the obstacles from preventing you from achieving your goal?
• How will you know when you have achieved your goal? How will you keep track? Is there anyone who can help you track your goal?
• Why is it important to work toward goals rather than set goals that you have no intention of accomplishing?

Connections for River of Life

Life Skill Links: caring, choice and accountability, communication, cooperation, effort, empathy, initiative, integrity, organization, perseverance, positive attitude, purpose, responsibility, self-discipline

Academic Applications: • After trying behavioral goals, have students set academic SMART Goals.

Variations/Modifications: Offer a different challenge by not allowing the guides to join their partners in the river. They must stay on the outside and call out directions to their partners. • A fun variation is to make this a 3-D activity. Hang things from the ceiling so that students must not only avoid obstacles on the ground, but ones in the air as well.

Extensions: • Have students keep a record of their goals in a journal. Periodically have them evaluate how they are doing with their goals. At the end of the year, ask them to write a report about their goal achievement for the year. Then ask them to write about their goals for the summer and for their future academic career. • Create a way for the students to report on how they are doing with their goals (e.g., check in with their partner every day or chart their progress). When someone achieves a goal, have a celebration. Then have that student create a new goal.

Facilitation Notes

Make sure you have done some sightless activities before so that students are already used to the concept of being guided by someone else. Also, remind goal-getters to keep their hands in the bumpers-up position.

This activity can get loud and confusing for the students. Some teachers prefer to have the guides stay on the outside of the boundaries, while others permit the guides to accompany the goal-getters on the inside of the river. Base this decision on the maturity and experience of the students. Also, the amount of "stuff" in the river will be determined by the ability of the class. The more items, the more difficult the activity.

If someone is not progressing with his or her goal, have a private conference to ascertain the issues. Revisit the SMART Goals checklist to make sure the goal is appropriate. Help the student decide on strategies to either recreate a goal or make progress on the given goal.

Adaptations for Students with Disabilities: River of Life

Cognitive Disabilities	• Try to make partners a "safe" match (i.e., one partner should be responsible).
Orthopedic Impairment	• Leave more space between obstacles for participants in wheelchairs. • Use poly-spots (or other flat objects) for participants in wheelchairs (poly-spots work well for ambulatory participants as well).
Hearing Impairment	• The partner can give directions using hand taps, hands on the shoulders, etc. • Make sure hearing-impaired students feel comfortable closing their eyes.
Visual Impairment	• Students could not give directions but could be the goal-getter.

MPS

66. Three-Person Trust Walk

Focus: Personal goal setting, risk taking, physical/emotional trust, trustworthiness
Materials: Eye coverings (optional)
Level: Grades 6 and higher

Suggested Procedure

1. After discussing SMART Goals (p. 139), have each person create a goal for him/herself.
2. Find a large open area, like a gym or field.
3. Have the students get into groups of three.

4. Tell them that each person will have a turn to be led (with eyes covered or closed) by the two other people in their group, who are the guides and will keep their eyes open. The person being led will be in the middle. Each group should discuss how the person in the middle wishes to be led (e.g., holding hands, walking next to each other, holding onto the guides' elbows).

5. State the boundaries. Give each person at least 3 minutes of time to be led. During that time, the person being led is the center of attention for the guides. The one being led should share his or her goal and discuss with the guides how he or she expects to accomplish it, what obstacles may occur, how to celebrate achieving the goal, and what to do if it turns out the goal is unrealistic. All during this time, the guides are leading this person around the stated boundaries.

6. After 3 minutes, have participants switch. Do this a third time to make sure everyone gets a turn.

7. Have students write and post their goals in the classroom.

Sample Processing Questions for Three-Person Trust Walk

- How did it feel to be led by two people?
- What did your partners do to keep you safe and prove that they were trustworthy?
- As guides, how did it feel both to lead and to listen to your teammate? How did you deal with the safety aspects of this situation?
- How did it feel being the center of attention?
- What were some things you shared with your group about your goal?
- What will you do if you find that your goal is unrealistic?

Connections for Three-Person Trust Walk

Life Skill Links: caring, choice and accountability, communication, cooperation, empathy, patience, perseverance, positive attitude, purpose, relationships, respect, responsibility, safety, self-discipline

Academic Applications: • Try having the students create personal goals that relate to their academic work. For example, if the class is working on a research project, what do they want the outcome to be? How might it look? What quality level are they aiming for? If, on the other hand, they are working on some math concepts, what level of accuracy do they wish to accomplish? Or, if their handwriting or keyboarding needs work, what goal can they set to begin the process of improving it?

Extensions: • Ask students to identify someone to whom they can be accountable for their goals. Create a rubric for the "accountability partners" to fill out to evaluate the progress and goal of their partners.

Facilitation Notes

Make sure the students have practiced with other sightless and guiding activities before attempting this one, because the combination of leading and listening can be difficult. Make the terrain as obstacle-free as possible so that guides can put more of their attention into listening to the person they are guiding rather than watching out for their safety.

Adaptations for Students with Disabilities: Three-Person Trust Walk

Cognitive Disabilities	• Discuss goals in advance and offer suggestions when needed. • Use an open area, such as a gym, to minimize obstacles.
Orthopedic Impairment	• Make sure there is a large amount of space. • Remind students to hold on to individuals whose eyes are covered as balance is more difficult when sight is taken away.
Hearing Impairment	• Have hearing-impaired students be guides and only be led if they choose.
Visual Impairment	• Do this in groups of threes with at least two sighted people per group.

67. Anonymous Goals

Focus: Personal goal setting
Materials: Paper and pens for each student
Level: Grades 5 and higher

Suggested Procedure

1. Hand out paper and pen to each student.
2. Tell them not to write their names on their papers.
3. After discussing SMART Goals (p. 139), ask each person to write an example of a SMART Goal. It does not need to have personal meaning to them, but it can if they wish.
4. When done, they should crumple their papers and throw them in a pile on the floor.
5. Mix the papers up, then have each person take one at random. It doesn't matter if students get their own.
6. Divide the class into groups of three to four students.
7. Each group's task is to read the goals and evaluate them in relation to how SMART they are (see below for an evaluation sheet). Students then make any corrections necessary.
8. Each group presents one of their SMART Goals to the class.

Sample Processing Questions for Anonymous Goals

- Why is it helpful to create goals for yourself?
- How might SMART Goals help you?
- What part of SMART Goals is most difficult for you to create? Why is that?

Connections for Anonymous Goals

Life Skill Links: choice and accountability, organization, purpose, responsibility, self-discipline

---

SMART Goals
Peer Evaluation

Evaluators:

Criteria	Evaluation+/o/-	Comments
Is this goal Specific?		
Is this goal Measurable?		
Is this goal Achievable?		
Is this goal Relevant?		
Is this goal Trackable?		

Other Comments:

Variations/Modifications: • *For younger students:* Do this activity with the entire class rather than breaking into small groups.

Facilitation Notes

Although less action-oriented, Anonymous Goals is a low-risk way to determine if students understand the concept of SMART Goals. Not only do they practice writing goals, they also practice evaluating them. Use this activity as an assessment tool to see if your students understand the notion of goal setting.

Adaptations for Students with Disabilities: Anonymous Goals

Cognitive Disabilities	• Help students with their writing.
Orthopedic Impairment	• Allow students to use computers or scribes to write their goals.
Hearing Impairment	• No major modifications necessary.
Visual Impairment	• Allow students to use computers or scribes to write their goals.

 ## 68. Goal Toss (Thanks to Sarah Shatz for this activity.)

Focus: Cooperation, communication, problem solving, making mistakes, goal setting
Materials: Soft throwable object for each person
Level: Grades 6 and higher

Suggested Procedure

1. Stand in a circle.
2. Tell the group that you all are going to count to 10 and do something with the object for each number.
3. Practice each number with the motion that goes with it. Here is an example:
    1—Throw object and catch it
    2—Throw object in air, clap once, and catch it
    3—Throw object in air, clap twice, and catch it
    4—Throw object in air, touch toe or knee, and catch it
    5—Throw object in air, spin around, and catch it
    6—Pass object to person on the right
    7—Pass object to person on the left
    8—Pass object to person across the circle
    9—Throw object in air, do a little dance, and catch it
    10—Throw object in air, throw arms over head and yell "Hey ho, way to go!" and catch it
4. After the pattern is set and practiced, ask everyone to silently set a goal for themselves about how many times they will catch the object during the sequence.
5. Go through the whole sequence, allowing time for people to pick up dropped items between throws.
6. After finishing the sequence, ask people to think about whether or not they met their goal. Then have them create a new goal based on this information.
7. Go through the sequence one more time.

Sample Processing Questions

• Did you feel self-conscious when you dropped your object? Why or why not?
• Was your first goal realistic? Was it too easy or too hard to meet?
• Did you change your goal the second time through? How did it change?
• When setting goals, what do you do if you find out they're unrealistic?
• What happens if a goal is too easy or too hard?

Connections for Goal Toss

Life Skill Links: choice and accountability, cooperation, effort, integrity, organization, patience, perseverance, positive attitude, responsibility, self-discipline

Academic Applications: • When students set academic goals, both short- and long-term, require that they give a rationale for how realistic the goals are. Is it about taking the easy way out just to have a product? Is it about making a goal so difficult to reach that they cannot possibly achieve it? Or is it about setting goals to help us accomplish what is important to us?

Variations/Modifications: • Allow students to publicly declare their goal for themselves to offer a higher degree of accountability.

Extensions: • Invite students to constantly evaluate how realistic their goal setting is and modify accordingly.

Facilitation Notes

Goal setting is a tricky business. It takes practice and experience to learn how to set realistic goals that are actually advantages rather than obstacles to getting something done. If a goal is too easy, it allows an "easy exit" for the goal-setter and is of very little value. If a goal is too difficult, then it invites the goal-setter to give up.

An appropriate and realistic goal can be a wonderful tool for focusing attention and energies. An unrealistic goal is, in itself, a barrier to goal attainment. A useful phrase for goal setting is: "Progress, not perfection." (Dev Pathik, May workshop 2002)

Adaptations for Students with Disabilities: Goal Toss

Cognitive Disabilities	• Shorten the sequence. • Make the throwing and catching appropriate to the ability level of the students.
Orthopedic Impairment	• Be sure the throwing and catching motions can be done by everyone. • Use objects that are easier to throw and catch (e.g., mesh balls). • Roll items in different ways on a tray or table. • Create motions that don't require throwing and catching, allowing students to hold on to the items.
Hearing Impairment	• Use visual prompts when counting.
Visual Impairment	• Create motions that don't require throwing and catching, allowing students to hold on to the items.

69. Goal Challenge

Focus: Personal goal setting
Materials: Goal Challenge sheet (p. 146), 5-foot pieces of rope, six cups, jump ropes, tape measure, 12-inch rulers, stopwatches, Wordplay sheet (p. 147)
Level: Grades 5 and higher

Suggested Procedure

1. Spread out the goal-setting stations by placing the items for a particular activity at various places around the room or outdoor setting.
2. Have the students pair up, and give each student a goal challenge sheet.
3. Tell the students that the idea is to try some things and then set personal goals for themselves to try to accomplish.
4. The partners choose which things to try and have 15 minutes to try as many as possible.

5. Visit the groups and monitor progress. Offer comments and hints if things bog down. (e.g., "Maybe its time to move on to another challenge," or "Have you both had an opportunity to try this?" or "Let me see you both try this one. I'll time you.")

Sample Processing Questions
- Did you achieve your goals? Why or why not?
- Were your goals realistic? Why or why not?
- Did you find any of these challenges particularly difficult? Which ones?
- Were any of them way too easy? Which ones?
- Why do you think these were difficult or easy for you?
- How might you get the support you need to accomplish your personal challenges?

Connections for Goal Challenge
Life Skill Links: choice and accountability, cooperation, effort, initiative, organization, perseverance, problem solving, purpose, resourcefulness, responsibility, self-discipline

Academic Applications: • Instead of using the Goal Challenge sheet, create your own challenges according to what you are studying. Make sure to include a mixture of verbal, analytical, and physical challenges.
• Create challenges that fit the multiple intelligences as a way to allow students to explore their spectrum of intelligences and engage in metacognition.

Variations/Modifications: • Give everyone a certain amount of time at each station, then have them move to another one so they get the opportunity to try everything.

Extensions: • Have everyone (including you) create a goal for him/herself to accomplish during the semester. Post them and monitor progress. If a semester-long goal is too large, have everyone set a daily or weekly goal and check to see if the goals have been reached.

Facilitation Notes
Goal Challenge is a fairly unstructured activity that allows people to make choices, try some things out, and challenge themselves. It is also an opportunity for you to make some informal observations about goal-setting styles of individual students. Are there some who are always setting their goals low so they can be ensured of "success"? How about others who have such high expectations that they can never meet their goals? Still others seem to be able to set goals that push them, but not too far. These observations can be useful in other areas of the learning environment, and this activity can help to set a tone.

I find that it is difficult for me to watch the students struggle with these tasks. My first inclination is to give them obvious hints to get "the right answer." The activity, though, is much more satisfying for them if they are allowed to struggle and get the answer the hard way: A good lesson for me and for them.

Here are a couple of answers from the goal challenge sheet: F. Cups: The most common solution is to simply take one cup from the longest line and place it over the top of the middle cup. F. Overhand knot: The trick is not to change the rope, but to change oneself. Before picking up the rope, cross your arms. Then you can pick up the rope and pull. There's your knot.

Adaptations for Students with Disabilities: Goal Challenge

Cognitive Disabilities	• Have fewer choices. • Choose challenges that fit the developmental levels of the students.
Orthopedic Impairment	• Make sure there are a variety of challenges that students can do.
Hearing Impairment	No major modifications are necessary.
Visual Impairment	No major modifications are necessary.

Goal Challenge

This activity encourages you to challenge yourself. Work with a partner. For each activity:
- set goals for yourself
- practice as much as you like
- participate (# of times listed below)
- try to meet or exceed your goals

A. Standing Broad Jump: Stand on a line and jump as far as you can. Measure the distance from your heels to the starting line. Try this three times and take your average.

Goal (feet and inches)	Try # 1	Try # 2	Try # 3	Average

B. Wordplay Puzzles: Answer as many of the Wordplay Puzzles as possible in 5 minutes. Give yourself a point for each correct answer.

Goal	# of correct answers

C. Holding breath: How long can you hold your breath?

Goal	Length of time breath held

D. Reaction Time: Have someone hold a ruler, vertically, so that your fingers are just underneath it. When they let go, catch it, and note at what centimeter your fingers are. Try this three times and take an average.

Goal (centimeters)	Try # 1	Try # 2	Try # 3	Average

E. Jump Rope: Number of jumps in 20 seconds. Try it three times and take the average.

Goal (#of jumps)	Try # 1	Try # 2	Try # 3	Average

F. Puzzles: Try to solve the following puzzles.

The Cups: Set up six cups so that four are in a line vertically and the other two are lined up horizontally with the second cup in the vertical line (a cross). Now can you make two equal lines by moving fewer than two cups?

Overhand Knot 2: You have been given a piece of rope. Holding one end of the rope in your right hand and one end in your left, can you tie an overhand knot without letting go?

Wordplay Puzzles

Directions: Each of the words or pictures represents a common phrase. For example, **DEAL** means "big deal."

1. KNEE
   LIGHT

2. HIJKLMNO

3. BJAOCKX

4. YOUJUSTME

5. DICE
   DICE

6.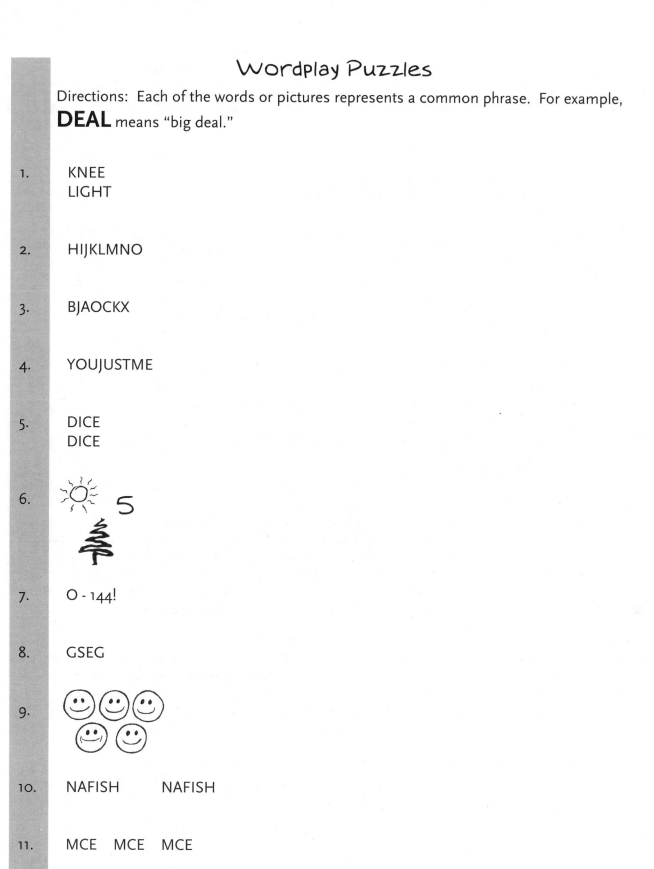

7. O - 144!

8. GSEG

9.

10. NAFISH   NAFISH

11. MCE MCE MCE

Wordplay puzzle Answers: 1. Neon Light 2. Water (H to O) 3. Jack in the Box 4. Just between you and me 5. Paradise 6. High Five 7. Oh Cross! 8. Scrambled Eggs 9. Cheerios 10. Tuna Fish 11. Three blind mice (they don't have any I's)

10. Clean and Messy (Thanks to Kathy Hellenbrand for this activity.)

Focus: Working together, goal setting
Materials: About 20 small cones (the Physical Education teacher should have some)
Level: Grades K–2

Suggested Procedure

1. Clear a large space in the room or go to a large space.
2. Spread the cones out in the space, with half of them standing and the other half lying down.
3. Randomly identify half of the students as the mess makers and the other half as the cleaners.
4. Tell the students that if they are mess makers, they are trying to tip all the cones over. If they are the cleaners, they are trying to stand the cones back up. This is all to be done with walking feet. For safety reasons, no one is to run.
5. Tell the students that you will give them one minute either to make messes or to clean them up.
6. Remind the students to use walking feet.
7. Yell "go" and begin the time. (If they are having fun, extend the time.)
8. After one round, have everyone switch roles and try it again.

Possible Processing Questions

- Did you like the messy or the clean role best?
- Did you get frustrated when you saw someone try to change what you had done?
- What can we do in here to keep the room organized?
- What is one thing (a goal) you can do every day to keep your stuff organized?

Connections for Clean and Messy

Life Skill Links: cleanliness, cooperation, effort, initiative, organization, perseverance, responsibility, self-discipline

Academic Applications: • Having an organized work area, desk, and classroom can be helpful for students when trying to work. Teaching them organizational strategies and having them set organizational goals helps them create good study and work habits. This activity can help set the stage to begin that process.

Extensions: • Identify what constitutes a mess (some students aren't aware of what disorganization looks like). Discuss ways to help each other clean up messes (rather than leaving it for someone else). • Set a goal to take 5 minutes every day to address clutter in the classroom (including desks).

Facilitation Notes

Goal setting is different for younger students. Developmentally they need to focus on concrete examples and then set goals according to that, as opposed to setting a goal for some abstract future vision. In essence, they do not have much experience with which to judge what a goal is or how to base a goal. An activity such as this gives them a bridge into what is a very real and current situation in the classroom. They can practice setting goals with this and then generalize to other, less tangible, goals.

Adaptations for Students with Disabilities: Clean and Messy

Cognitive Disabilities	• Have everyone be "messy" first, and knock the cones over. Then have everyone be "clean" to pick them up.
Orthopedic Impairment	• Use the mini cones and place them on a table within everyone's reach. • Give students a tool, such as a hockey stick, to use on the cones. • Have students do this in pairs to help each other with balance.
Hearing Impairment	No major modifications are necessary.
Visual Impairment	• Have students do this in pairs to find the cones together.

71. Giving and Receiving

Focus: Sharing, helping others, put-ups, goal setting
Materials: A few small items to pass (marble, pebble), music
Level: Grades K–2

Suggested Procedure

1. Sit in a circle and show everyone the small items.
2. Tell the students that the objects are gifts, and that the task is to try to give them away.
3. They are to pass the items around the circle as the music plays. When the music stops, the people with the items will have received a "gift" from those next to them.
4. Start the music and have students pass for a short time.
5. When you stop the music, see who has the "gifts." Ask each of the people who has a "gift" to thank the person who passed it to them.
6. Continue play for a few more rounds so that more people have an opportunity to give and receive gifts.
7. After processing the activity, have each student create a goal for giving a "gift" of a put-up or helping another person for that day.

Sample Processing Questions: Giving and Receiving

- Were you able either to give or receive a gift?
- How did it feel to give a gift and be thanked for it? How did it feel to receive a gift and thank someone for it?
- Do gifts have to be things? What other kinds of "gifts" can we give each other?
- How does it feel when you do things for others?
- How does it feel when people do things for you?

Connections for Giving and Receiving

Life Skill Links: caring, empathy, initiative, kindness, positive attitude, purpose, relationships, respect
Academic Applications: • Use the activity to help students focus on helping each other with class work. Before they come to you for help, have them ask at least two other people first.
Variations/Modifications: • Along with saying "thank you" to the person who gave them the "gift," ask students to offer an appreciation as well.
Extensions: • Talk about the concept of "random acts of kindness." Brainstorm a list of things that are nice to do for other people, even if there is no recognition for it. At the end of every day, give students a chance to acknowledge acts of kindness that they witnessed throughout the day. • Read books or sing songs about people who help others.

Facilitation Notes

Again, younger students need a clear focus to set goals. What better situation than to have them set goals about helping others and accepting help? Watch carefully during this activity for a couple of things: a) that everyone has a chance to receive a "gift," and b) students who may hold on to the "gift" so they can get it. If the latter occurs, stop the action to problem solve how everyone can have an opportunity to get a "gift."

Adaptations for Students with Disabilities: Giving and Receiving

Cognitive Disabilities	No major modifications are necessary.
Orthopedic Impairment	No major modifications are necessary.
Hearing Impairment	• Have an interpreter if necessary.
Visual Impairment	No major modifications are necessary.

Low Challenge Ropes Course

A low-challenge course contains activities that develop trust between students. Ropes courses can be indoors or outdoors and require personnel who have specific training on the use of the elements. Many school districts have their own courses, but if there is no course in your district, many are privately run in most areas of the United States.[*]

Although using a low challenge ropes course is not essential to further the community building process, it is a wonderful and unique tool for helping a group push its limits. If a course is available, it can be a group-changing experience.

Generally, any activity that involves spotting of participants involves trust. (Later Problem-Solving activities involve trust, too, but also require the group to solve a dilemma in the process.) The following low challenge ropes activities focus on an individual taking a risk to trust the other students to act as his or her safety net. Each of these elements is described below, along with sample processing questions. **Note: It is necessary to have the proper training before doing any ropes course elements. If you do not have the necessary training, contract with a reputable provider of ropes course services** (see Appendices). **This book is not a substitute for proper training and does not give you enough information to safely run these activities.**

The term "**challenge course**" is commonly used to refer to a low ropes course. These courses involve the use of special equipment designed to encourage the development of trust and group problem-solving skills. These elements are secured to trees, poles, or walls or are designed to be free-standing. Some are even portable.

When building any challenge course, it is important to make sure that the elements are safe and built to industry standards. The Association for Challenge Course Technology (ACCT)[**] has developed challenge course standards in the areas of installation, operations, and ethics. It is an integral resource for any organization interested in building a low or high ropes course.

These activities are included here so that, if used, a class can continue the community-building process at the low challenge ropes course. In this way, the challenge course does not become an isolated event or an end in itself, but rather part of the existing program. If your group is using outside facilitators, make sure to communicate with them about what has already been accomplished, including the stage of group development. Also, bring your Full Value Contract to the course. You may wish to talk with the facilitators about your level of involvement during the experience. Are you interested in bringing in classroom issues during processing time; do you wish to participate with the students; or are you more interested in observing? These decisions will be made according to the maturity level of both the individuals and the class in their group process, along with the goals that you and they have set.

If you choose to participate with the students, it can be a rich experience for all involved. Seeing you take some risks, express nervousness, and share feelings models these very attributes for the students. The danger, of course, is that they see you as the person with the answers and fall back on your experience. If participation is in the plan, make sure you communicate your motives and vision of your involvement. The most difficult part of the day could just be keeping thoughts and ideas to yourself.

---

[*] For more information on ropes courses in your area, contact AEE, ACCT, or Project Adventure (see Adventure/ Experiential Education Resurces in the Appendices).

[**] See Adventure/Experiential Education Resources in the Appendices.

72. Wild Woosey

Focus: Risk taking, physical/emotional trust, trustworthiness, spotting and support
Level: Grades 5 and higher

Description
Sometimes called the Commitment Bridge, the Wild Woosey consists of two cables strung between three trees or poles in the shape of a V (figure 5.2). Two participants stand on the narrow (pointed) end of the cables (one per cable) and support each other as they move down the cables. As the cables move further apart, they must adjust their strategy to get as far as possible.

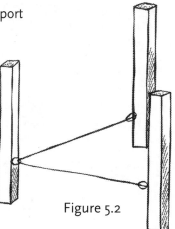

Figure 5.2

As a pair works together to get as far down the cables as possible, the rest of their group act as spotters. They are taught special spotting techniques to ensure a safe experience for the students on the cable.

Sample Processing Questions for Wild Woosey
• What did you do to support your partner on the cable? What worked? What didn't work?
• How did the rest of your group support you and make sure that you were safe?
• How can you support each other in class? What are some examples of ways to support each other?
• How can you ask for help if you need it?
• For you, is it easy or difficult to ask for help? How can we make it easier to ask for help in our class?

Facilitation Notes
Participants on the Wild Woosey generally go farther down the cables when they resist the urge to pull away from their partners, and instead lean in on them. This reality creates a nice metaphor for support by talking about how one can "lean" on others, and, in turn, allow others to "lean" on them. When is it appropriate to offer help to others? How does one ask for help when it is needed? To whom does one go for help? **Caution: It is necessary to have the proper training before doing any ropes course elements. If you do not have the necessary training, contract with a reputable provider of ropes course services.**

 ## 73. Walk of Life (AKA: Mohawk Walk)

Focus: Risk taking, physical/emotional trust, trustworthiness, spotting and support
Level: Grades 4 and higher

Description
The Walk of Life is a series of cables strung between poles or trees (figure 5.3). These cables vary in length, and some have different types of ropes nearby to be used as support. The object is to get the entire group safely from one end of the series to the other. This generally is accomplished in two ways. Either half the group attempts the element while the other half spots, or each leg of the element is accomplished together – whoever is not on the cable spots the others. Once everyone finishes one leg, the entire group moves to the next.

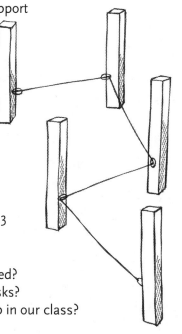

Figure 5.3

Sample Processing Questions for Walk of Life
• What did you need to do to help each other across the cables?
• How did you communicate your needs? How did you ask for what you needed?
• Is it risky to ask for help, or to communicate personal need? What are the risks?
• Given the risks, what can we do to help people take the risk of asking for help in our class?
• Given the risks, what can you do to reduce your personal risks?

Facilitation Notes

It is common for students to begin this activity by trying to walk the cables alone. Although some of the shorter cables allow for this solution, it does not take long for students to figure out that they need to give and receive help to get across the longer cables.

The Walk of Life version of this element involves the use of a metaphor for our journey through life. Each leg of the cable series can be identified with a stage of life. The first can be birth, the second preschool, etc. The final cable might be graduation, with a stated goal that we are working to help everyone graduate. **Caution: As with any ropes course activity, do not try the Walk of Life without proper training.**

74. Tension Traverse

Focus: Risk taking, physical/emotional trust, trustworthiness, spotting and support
Level: Grades 3 and higher

Description

The Tension Traverse is another cable activity that can either stand alone or be part of a Mohawk Walk. It incorporates one cable attached between two trees or poles, with a long rope attached to one of the trees or poles (figure 5.4). The object is for a participant to use the rope for support while traversing as far down the cable as possible. Meanwhile, the rest of the group act as spotters.

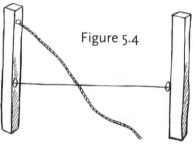

Figure 5.4

Another version of Tension Traverse involves three cables attached to trees in the form of a triangle. Two ropes are attached to the same tree or pole, and two people traverse at the same time in opposite directions.

Sample Processing Questions for Tension Traverse
- How did you use the rope for support? What strategies did you use?
- What are other supports for you in your life – both internal and external?
- Did you feel like your spotters were there for you? How could you tell?
- How did your spotters help you on this element?

Facilitation Notes

As an individual activity, the Tension Traverse allows a participant to challenge himself. Ask each person to set a goal, and ask spotters to support the accomplishment of that goal by offering suggestions and encouragement as needed. Have the student traversing the element state what she needs from the spotters. For example, the spotters can only guess what she needs, and may offer loud words of encouragement unless the traverser states that she needs quiet.

The rope in a Tension Traverse is very important. How it is used (there are various ways) can be as important as using it at all. It opens the door to a discussion about different kinds of support – both internal and external. Confidence, for example, can be a powerful internal source of support for someone. Encouragement from others can be an equally powerful external source of support. **Caution: As with any ropes course activity, do not try the Tension Traverse without proper training.**

Trust Fall From Height

A fall from height can be a useful and powerful tool for developing trust and support within a group. Some schools have chosen to ban the activity because of a concern that the Trust Fall is more dangerous than other activities. This is a prudent course of action, especially when dealing with staff who may have little or no training in adventure activities.

If, however, the Trust Fall is facilitated by someone with the necessary training, and the group of students is prepared to handle the responsibility of catching their classmates, the Trust Fall from Height can help a class reach new levels of support and empathy. This, in turn, creates an atmosphere where students are willing to take new risks with their learning. **As with any ropes course activity, do not try the Trust Fall from height without proper training.**

Summary: When to Move on to Problem Solving

Cooperation and Trust are part of group formation. People care about each other and are concerned for everyone's well-being. The Full Value Contract is now well established; the students have a history together that includes trusting each other and taking risks. People understand what it means to make a mistake and how to handle a situation where mistakes occur. Individuals have established personal goals that can continue into the group challenge arena.

Students are now ready to face challenges together. This readiness means that they are willing to struggle with conflict, because solving problems almost always involves differences of opinion and style. These issues will be discussed in greater depth in Chapter Six: Problem Solving, Branching Out.

Moving to Problem Solving: Some Observations

	Move On	Stay with Trust
Making Mistakes	• The class has explored and discussed the concept of making mistakes. • Students begin to acknowledge mistakes they make rather than attempting to hide them. • Students begin to articulate what they have learned from a mistake. • When a mistake is made, other students refrain from teasing or put-downs. • Both in individual and group situations, students are willing to try something new – even if it may not be perfect or falls below expectations.	• Students laugh at each other when someone makes a mistake. • When a mistake is made, students tease or use put-downs. • Students hide mistakes for fear of being put down. • Students blame others or external factors for mistakes that are made. • Students balk at trying something until it is "perfect."
Empathy	• Students perform simple random acts of kindness for each other without prompting (e.g., helping to pick up dropped items). • Students show concern for each other's physical and emotional safety. • When engaged in conflict, students express understanding for another's feelings. • During class meetings, students acknowledge others' ideas even if they do not agree.	• Students actively do things to harm others – physically and/or emotionally. • Students do not recognize when others are at risk – physically or emotionally. • Students are passive when others are at risk; they do nothing to prevent harm.
Trustworthiness	• Students can identify what it means to be trustworthy. • When engaged in trust activities, students take their responsibility seriously. • Students show through repeated practice that they know how to keep others safe from physical harm. • Students can articulate how to support others through words and actions. • Student's words and actions are generally consistent.	• Students accuse others of trying to harm them, either physically or emotionally. • Students seem to be reticent about sharing ideas for fear of reprisal from others (this is common if there is someone known as a bully in the class). • Students must be closely monitored during trust activities due to inconsistent follow-through on safety directions. • Students cannot express what it means to be "trustworthy." • Students consistently say one thing and do another.

	Move On	Stay with Trust
Risk Taking	• Students support other's choices about taking risks. • Students can express the difference between a healthy and unhealthy risk. • Students show they understand that risks are different for different people. • Students can set goals about the types of healthy risks they choose to take. • Students understand that there is a difference between encouragement and pressure when supporting others' taking of risks. • Students can articulate how to decrease risk by using thought, resources, and education (e.g., using a bike helmet and learning the rules of the road before riding a bike).	• Students heckle or tease others into taking risks (e.g., calling someone "chicken"). • Students think that all risk taking is good or bad; they cannot differentiate. • Students do not feel free to try new things for fear of being put down. • Students engage in impulsive risk taking without examining consequences.
Physical/ Emotional	• Students can explain the differences and similarities between physical and emotional trust. • Students show an ability to spot others during increasingly demanding activities. • Students agree to and practice confidentiality when asked. • Students can talk about how to take care of others' feelings and why it is helpful.	• Students have little or no regard for others' feelings or physical well-being. • Students cannot articulate the difference between emotional and physical safety.

---

[1] Goleman, D. 1995. (p. 43)
[2] Goleman (p. 97)

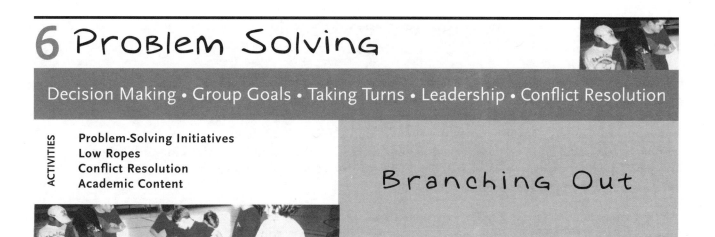

6 Problem Solving

Decision Making • Group Goals • Taking Turns • Leadership • Conflict Resolution

ACTIVITIES

Problem-Solving Initiatives
Low Ropes
Conflict Resolution
Academic Content

Branching Out

When the class arrives at the Problem Solving stage, it is an indication that they are ready to branch out into more complex tasks and interactions. As the teacher, you offer them group challenges to solve together. You also act as a process observer to help them make sense of how they are working together as a class.

Conflict is a hallmark of problem solving because people are now comfortable asserting themselves by sharing opinions and taking on leadership roles. Sometimes the conflict is between individual students. Other times the source of the conflict rests with you, the teacher, as students attempt to make sense of their roles within the class. Since you have been seen as the expert up to this point, it is not uncommon for students to challenge your authority. This is a sure sign that the class is entering the storming stage, and students are searching for ways to have influence in the class. It is time to quietly celebrate that the process is moving along and that relationships are growing to meet the additional challenges that wait.

You can offer students strategies for dealing with conflict without actually solving their conflicts for them. Through activities that focus on conflict-resolution skills, students can learn how to work through the rough spots and begin to develop class norms in challenging situations.

More complex operating norms for the class are developed during Problem Solving. A common scenario is this: During the first problem-solving initiative, very little planning occurs. The class appears disorganized, forming into many small groups – all of which are attempting to come up with a solution to the challenge. A small argument breaks out between members of the mini-groups about which solution to attempt. Meanwhile, a third group begins a solution. People stop arguing and join in.

After the activity is over, the students discuss what happened. You ask if everyone felt included in the decision. Some say yes, others say no. They discuss why they felt included or not and what they think caused this to happen. If no one brings it up, you offer the observation that you saw many small groups discussing solutions, and you wonder how that influenced the planning process.

The discussion continues for a while until someone suggests that the class stand in a circle to strategize solutions to the challenges, thus making sure that everyone is part of the planning process. The students agree to try it during the next challenge. As they gain more experience, students begin to monitor class planning, calling people together to form a circle in order to keep everyone involved. A norm has been born.

As long as issues are dealt with, the class continues through the process of norming. They learn more about how this group works, as well as particular strengths of each student. Leadership begins to ebb and flow with the strengths of individuals, and students become more interdependent when working together. This class has come of age.

Problem-Solving Issues and Skills

Decision Making

Every group must consciously decide how to decide. There are various ways to make decisions. Without discussion, it can become autocratic, where the person seen with the highest status charges ahead and everyone else follows. At other times the "rule of loud" comes into effect. This happens when many people talk at once, and the loudest person gets heard. Another strategy involves the "arbitrator approach," in which students ask the teacher to choose between conflicting sides. None of these methods are very useful to an inclusive community.

Many groups choose to use a majority-vote method because students are used to this type of decision making. As a rule, majority vote is exclusive because only 51 percent of those voting need to agree. Those who "lose" the vote may either go along with the decision, choose not to participate, or hide their agendas and even sabotage the group process.

Consensus is an inclusive – albeit sometimes time consuming – alternative. One myth of consensus decision making is that it is an either/or situation. A strategy that can easily be taught is "five-finger consensus." When a decision is to be made, it should be articulated so that everyone understands what they are deciding. Then everyone holds up the appropriate number of fingers to show agreement:
  • Five Fingers = This is the best thing since sliced bread.
  • Four Fingers = It's really great.
  • Three Fingers = It's an okay thing to do.
  • Two Fingers = I'll go along with it.
  • One Finger = I won't block it.
  • A Fist = Block.
This method includes five ways to agree with a decision and one way to block it. If even one person blocks it, the students must discuss alternatives in order to meet the objections of that one person.

Learning why a decision is being blocked is important because it cannot be resolved otherwise. Part of the Full Value Contract is that people will work toward class goals. If someone is blocking a decision for a self-serving reason that cannot be addressed by the students no matter how hard they try, then a block can be overruled. If, however, the blocker has articulated principled, well-thought-out objections, the block stays in place, and the class must find another way to meet their challenge together.

Five-finger consensus can also be used to determine the quality of a decision. If everyone holds up only one finger, then it is probably best to re-evaluate the decision. (If everyone holds up their middle finger, you have another issue to deal with.)

Deciding how to decide can be accomplished through the normative process by working through challenges and gaining experience together. As different types of decision making occur, help the class sort through what is going on and how it is working for them. Help them develop decision-making strategies that work for them, and offer skills that will help them be as inclusive as possible.

Group Goals

One way to practice the art of consensus is to embark on a process for arriving at group goals. Since people are working together to solve problems, you need to focus on group goal setting. This can be an arduous process or it can be totally painless, depending on the goal to be set. It is sometimes difficult for people to compromise on an opinion, but it is a necessary skill when working with others. Noticing if the same people are "giving in" all the time, while others are forever "getting their way," is important. This is an issue of influence that needs to be addressed.

You can help students practice group goal setting by asking them to start with a small goal. Many Problem-Solving initiatives are uniquely suited for group goal setting, especially if the activities are being timed. Once a base time has been set, ask the class to set a new time goal they would like to achieve during the next round. Observe how they arrive at the decision and help them scrutinize their decision-making process during the discussion following the activity.

Looking for the Win-Win Solution

Take some time to discuss the concept of win-win solutions. It is not always enough to compromise; a compromise can mean arriving at a solution where one – or all – parties feel as if they lost or have given in to keep the process moving. Help your students recognize that win-win solutions are better long-term responses to problems or conflicts that arise.

As they gain experience with group goal setting and decision making, students will set norms for how to arrive at group goals. Depending on the goal to be determined, they might need you to mediate a discussion; at other times students will take on that role. Asking the students if they want your assistance is important before diving in to mediate.

Taking Turns

The subject of taking turns can be an issue of influence, outright enthusiasm, or a trust issue disguised as enthusiasm. During the Cooperation and Trust activities, everyone has a chance to do everything. While solving problems together, however, people must take on roles depending on the needs of the class in relation to the task at hand. Some parts of the task are glamorous, like being the first one to try something or being the one to bring over the imaginary "serum" to save the world. Other tasks are commonplace, like being one of the middle people to get to the other side.

According to the age and maturity level of the class, taking turns can be quite an issue. Physical fights can occur between people who are pushing to be the first to attempt an activity. Feelings can get hurt when people argue over who gets to carry the "serum."

The first step is to sort out the underlying reason for the conflict. It could simply be that a few people are overflowing with enthusiasm. In this case, it is only a matter of slowing down to make a more conscious decision, including how to share the more attractive tasks over time. If the issue is one of influence, then the students need to discuss how decisions are to be made. On the other hand, it could be a trust issue, because someone may feel the only way to do the task right is to do it him/herself. This issue needs to be addressed during processing time in order to revisit emotional trust issues.

Whatever the motive, the issue of taking turns is common in the beginning stages of Problem Solving. If it is not resolved, it will return in force time and again until a solution is worked out.

Leadership

It is difficult to find a word that carries more baggage than leadership. In our society, being in the lead is almost always seen as positive, while following is negative. But in a community, leadership must be shared. By definition, communities are places where people arrive at the table as equals, able to collaborate to accomplish mutual goals.

Historically, leadership has variously been defined as autocratic, democratic, and laissez-faire. These definitions all see leadership as a static role in which someone is considered a leader if he or she is in a position of authority. Increasingly, though, people are asked to take on leadership roles as members of small groups or communities. These roles take place within the group rather than above or separate from the group.

Given this change in focus, it is vital that young people learn how to work as group members, taking initiative when necessary and stepping back to help others when appropriate. This type of collaborative leadership means that students learn how to develop relationships with those around them. They take turns sharing leader and follower roles according to the strengths of those in the group.

Camp Manito-wish YMCA in Northern Wisconsin has developed Seven Qualities of a Collaborative Leader. These qualities were articulated from the staff's 75 years of combined experience in working with teenagers and young adults:

A Manito-wish Collaborative Leader:
- **Builds a shared vision:** Works with others to create group goals so that everyone can head in the same direction.
- **Shares a common space with others:** Gets together in a circle, around a table, in a classroom – wherever. Students must sit down together at some point in order to open lines of communication for true collaboration.
- **Builds models – tries it … changes it … tries it again:** Has the ability to try something, learn from his or her mistakes, and then improve the next time. Sometimes groups get into "analysis paralysis" because members are trying to perfect an idea even before they try it. At other times, groups get into a rut by trying something over and over without changing.
- **Lets others amplify her/his abilities:** Recognizes that the combined strengths of everyone allow a group to accomplish more than one could alone. This is known as synergy – where $1 + 1 = 3$.
- **Remembers that followership and leadership go hand-in-hand:** Leadership "percolates" in a class depending on the strengths of individuals. It is an act of leadership to consciously take a step back to allow someone else to move ahead.
- **Doesn't collaborate to turn out the lights:** Collaboration is not always useful, as in the case of an emergency (such as a fire), or when a task is so simple that it can be done by someone taking the initiative.
- **Celebrates successful collaborations:** It is important to acknowledge and celebrate collaborations, as well as individual effort. Sometimes, when a class has come through a particularly grueling process, it is even more important to celebrate.[1]

These qualities can be explored while students work together to accomplish tasks. They offer some direction when examining the concept of collaborative leadership.

Conflict Resolution

My partner, Bert, is a school counselor. One day he came home from a meeting with a new insight. His group had been discussing conflict resolution, and another counselor shared the belief that conflict resolution can only take place in the context of community. Without community, there is no reason to resolve the conflict. Why should anyone care?

Given that conflict is an inevitable part of problem solving, this is a perfect time to teach conflict-resolution skills. There is usually much opportunity for practice. A wonderful resource is *Adventures in Peacemaking* by William Kreidler and Lisa Furlong. This book, a joint venture between Educators for Social Responsibility and Project Adventure, is an Adventure-based approach to teaching conflict resolution. Even though the book is geared toward children ages 5 to 12, its concepts are universal. It contains many activities that give participants a chance

Symptoms of Frustration: checking out, blaming, taking control, saying "this is stupid or boring," etc.

Causes of Frustration: disparity between expectations and outcome, exclusion from the process, task is too difficult, decision making gets bogged down (conflicting opinions, power struggles, class is in a rut), etc.

Solutions: look at causes instead of symptoms, take time out to reassess, go to another activity with the option of coming back later if students feel it is necessary, etc.

to learn about how conflict escalates and to practice conflict-resolution skills.

In general, being able to resolve conflict involves building cooperation and trust, along with becoming more emotionally aware. These attributes are the focus of the Cooperation and Trust levels in this community-building sequence. Once students have reached a certain degree of cohesion, they can tackle a conflict-resolution process[*]:
- Asking: What's the problem?
- Brainstorming possible solutions
- Choosing the best solution
- Doing it
- Evaluating and adjusting

Conflict-resolution skills are invaluable both in and out of class. The only way to practice them is to be involved in conflict – a thought that makes many of us shiver. In the community that allows conflict to take place in a safe environment, people are committed to resolution rather than perpetuation.

Problem-Solving Activities

Role of the Teacher

When you see students struggling to come up with solutions to a challenge, it is essential that you back off. As much as you might want to jump in and help the class through a frustrating moment, it does not help them learn how to deal with frustration. Unless they are considering an unsafe solution to the challenge or close to an outright fight, they must be allowed to struggle.

As a **mentor**, you can act as a process observer. Sometimes a well-placed time-out for an observation from you is all your students need in order to refocus. For example, maybe the students have been using the "rule of loud" to make decisions, and then during the processing session they have decided to use a stick as a prop to show who is talking. During the next activity, the stick is forgotten; the class reverts to the "rule of loud." If no one in the class points this out, you can stop the class in order to hold up an imaginary mirror. Ask them what they see in regard to decision making. Most of the time, people will see that they have not been following their own resolution. If not, you can point it out.

A mentor offers feedback by sharing observations and suggestions with the people who are being mentored. These can help make students aware of strategies they may not have known about before.

Problem-Solving Initiatives

"Initiative" implies ingenuity, motivation, and taking the first step. Therefore, the rules for the following activities are kept to a minimum to allow for creativity. Most of these activities have open-ended solutions. In fact, I have learned that as soon as I think I have seen everything, someone comes up with another way to solve a problem. These activities require few or no props, and many can take place right in the classroom.

> **Thinking "Outside of the Box"**
>
> Problem-Solving initiatives give us an opportunity to play with solving problems creatively. As teachers/facilitators, we often see students locking themselves into one way of viewing a problem because of the assumptions they make. Even if a rule is not stated, past experience dictates how they will view the activity, and a rule is somehow conjured up in one or more minds.

---

[*]Adapted from a model by the Mediation Center, Asheville, NC.

I once heard, "If a rule is not stated, it does not exist." Encourage the students to think "outside of the box" and address their problems with creativity and imagination. The community you have created is a safe place in which to experiment. Many of the ideas will not work, but some will. Future challenges will then be addressed with open minds and make the chances for success that much greater.

15. Warp Speed

Focus: Group goal setting, decision making, leadership, creative thinking, trial and error
Materials: One soft throwable object (fleece ball, foam ball, wadded-up paper ...), stopwatch
Level: Grades 5 and higher

Suggested Procedure

1. Clear the desks or tables away. Have students stand in a circle.
2. Ask everyone to raise one hand to show that they have not had the object yet.
3. Call someone's name and throw the object to her. She puts her hand down to show she's had the object. Then she calls the name of someone whose hand is up and throws him the object. This continues until everyone has had the object and it is returned to you.
4. Figure out who has the first birthday of the year in the class. Give that person the object.
5. Tell the class that this is a timed activity. They must send the object to the same person they threw it to before. The object must begin and end with the person who starts it (in this case, the person with the first birthday). Try this, and get a baseline time.
6. Now reiterate the rules: The item must touch everyone in that same order, and it must begin and end with the same person. Then give them time to discuss strategies.
7. Try the activity multiple times to arrive at a mutual solution.

Sample Processing Questions for Warp Speed

- What was your group goal for this? Did you know what you all wanted to accomplish together?
- How did you decide which idea to try?
- How did your solution change each time? Were you willing to learn from each attempt?
- Do you feel you took a leadership role in this activity? How?

Connections for Warp Speed

Life Skill Links: common sense, communication, cooperation, effort, flexibility, imagination, leadership, organization, patience, perseverance, problem solving, self-discipline

Academic Applications: • Use the "try it, change it, try it again" process as a metaphor for the editing process. • Use this activity as a model of circle writing, where the story begins, weaves around, and then ends up where it all started. Have students create a sentence where each person contributes a word. Make sure it connects with the first person (who is also the last) so that it makes sense. When each person passes the ball, he or she also says their word.

Variations/Modifications: • Have an item going in both directions at the same time. • If students have done this before and arrive at a quick solution that they used before, try it again. The second time, however, they may not use that same solution.

Extensions: • Remind students that it is okay to make mistakes and learn from those mistakes. Model this by sharing mistakes that you made and how you learned from them. Post a list of mistakes that have been made throughout the week and what was learned as a result. • Make a list of possible tasks and problems to solve during a unit/semester/year. Determine as a class which ones lend themselves to trial-and-error problem solving and which ones need more planning before attempting them. For example, figuring out the best and most fair system for bathroom passes can be trial and error, but carrying out a fire drill needs to be done in a certain, prescribed way.

Facilitation Notes

It is fair to say that Warp Speed has an almost limitless number of solutions, which makes this activity popular. It can also be accomplished in a relatively short amount of time.

Watch for who is doing most of the talking and who is hanging back during the discussion about solutions. Neither is necessarily good nor bad, as different people have different leadership styles. It can become a problem if there is a pattern of the group mindlessly following one person. It is a good issue to bring up during processing time to make sure everyone felt that they were part of the solution.

Many groups decide to stand next to each other rather than stay in their original configuration. Other groups stay where they are and play with different ways to get the object around without moving themselves. One class was together on an overnight weekend, and they decided that their group goal was to get the object around as slowly as possible. They figured out how long each person would keep the object, then began sending it around during the rest of the 3-day experience. Students were setting their alarms in the middle of the night just to pass off "Mr. Corn" to the next person in the sequence.

Adaptations for Students with Disabilities: Warp Speed

Cognitive Disabilities	• Use a slower playing ball such as a Boingo™ ball or Balzak™.
Orthopedic Impairment	• Drop a beanbag on one student's tray; he or she then drops the beanbag on someone else's tray. This can work for students that have reasonable hand control. • Use a Boingo™ ball or a Balzak™ to slow the pace. • Use a larger item to throw.
Hearing Impairment	• The thrower must make eye contact before throwing the ball. • The leader can stand behind the hearing impaired student and give a physical cue when his or her name is called. • Have interpreters available to facilitate communication if necessary.
Visual Impairment	• A group member hands off a beanbag to the visually impaired student; he or she then hands the beanbag off to the next participant. • Use brightly colored/larger objects for improved tracking.
General Notes	• Do not require a crisscross pattern; allow students to hand the ball to the person next to them if necessary. • Have participants roll the ball instead of throwing it. • Use larger balls. • De-emphasize the ball drops.

MPS

76. Moon Ball

Focus: Group goal setting, leadership, taking turns, trial and error
Materials: A beach ball
Level: Grades 2 and higher

Suggested Procedure

1. Clear the desks or tables away. Have students stand in a circle.
2. Tell the students that the object is to hit the beach ball into the air. Each time the ball is hit, it counts as a point. The ball cannot be hit by the same person twice in a row. If that happens or if the ball stops or

touches the ground, they must start over. Throw the ball in the air for them to start. (You don't want them to have any planning time at first).

3. After students have tried some rounds, adjusted their strategies and had some success with this, stop the action. Ask them to set a goal for how many points they would like to get.

4. Try a few attempts. If the goal is obviously too easy, they will achieve it quickly. Then ask them to set another, more challenging goal. If the goal is obviously too difficult, they will encounter some frustration. Stop the action and ask them to reassess.

Sample Processing Questions for Moon Ball

- What goals did you set for yourselves? Did it help to set goals? Why or why not?
- If you did not set goals, what goal were you personally striving for? Were these individual goals compatible?
- What were some strategies you used to achieve your goals? Did you feel you were included in this activity? Why or why not?
- What kind of leadership role did you take in this activity? (Remind students that there are many ways to show leadership).
- How did your strategy change over time? How did you make those decisions?

Connections for Moon Ball

Life Skill Links: choice and accountability, communication, cooperation, effort, flexibility, leadership, organization, perseverance, problem solving

Academic Applications: • *For younger students:* Each time a person hits the ball, they must skip count by 2's, 5's, etc. (i.e., starting with 2's, the first person says "2," the next person says "4," the next "6," and so on).

Variations/Modifications: • If the class meets or exceeds their goal, give them a moment to celebrate. Then add a new rule: Everyone must hit the beach ball once before anyone can hit it a second time. • Try this game first in smaller groups.

Extensions: • Have students set goals for themselves during class. Have the students write their goals down and revisit them periodically. See if they feel that they are putting in an effort toward achieving a goal. • Create group goals. They can be aimed at behavior (we want to make sure everyone feels included in this class) or skill-oriented (we want everyone to learn their multiplication tables).

Facilitation Notes:

Moon Ball is a great activity to try once in awhile because it offers the class an opportunity to assess their progress. After working together on other initiatives, they will approach this activity differently.

The rules to Moon Ball are vague by design. This provides an opportunity for the class to discuss a variety of strategies and interpretations. Generally they will begin with the "chaos method." Sometimes this actually works once, but replicating the results is another issue altogether. Finally, students will begin to arrive at an agreed-upon scheme to become more consistent.

A common influence issue that must be addressed is one of ownership – making sure that everyone has the chance to be involved rather than a few people hitting the ball while others stand around and watch. Encourage your class to set some goals. If they do, they might find that a goal gives them a place to go rather than hitting a beach ball for no other apparent reason.

Adaptations for Students with Disabilities: Moon Ball

Cognitive Disabilities	• Use balloons instead of balls to slow the activity down and help students remain focused.
Orthopedic Impairment	• Use a Balzak™ (a cloth fabric that covers a balloon) or a balloon. They will float in the air more slowly, aiding students with slower reaction times.

Adaptations for Students with Disabilities: Moon Ball (cont.)

Hearing Impairment	• No major modifications necessary. • Have interpreters available to facilitate communication if necessary.
Visual Impairment	• This activity may not be appropriate for the severely visually impaired. • Try it in smaller groups with brightly colored balloons. Everyone in the small group could hold hands to keep the balloon up.
General Notes	• Have students who are less mobile form the center part of the circle and students who are more mobile form the outside of the circle. • All students can be limited in their movement by standing on a poly-spot or other identified spot.

MPS

> **Moon Ball-a-thon**
>
> The middle school class of Gus Pausz, who was an art teacher and adventure educator in Skokie, Illinois, decided to use the Moon Ball initiative as a fund-raiser for Play for Peace (whose mission is to "bring children of conflicting cultures together through cooperative play"). The students got pledges of a penny a hit. After they were done, they had collected hundreds of dollars for the organization. We miss you, Gus.

 ## 11. Balloon Frantic

Focus: Group goal setting, decision making, leadership
Materials: Two balloons per person, stopwatch
Level: Grades 8 and higher

Suggested Procedure

1. Clear the desks or tables away. Have students stand in a circle.
2. Give everyone including yourself two balloons to blow up and tie off. Each person keeps one balloon; the others are put in a pile near you.
3. Tell the class that this is a timed activity. The rules are:
   a) Everyone must start with a balloon.
   b) On a signal they are to hit the balloons into the air (they must be hit in the air – not held or stuck anywhere with static electricity!).
   c) Every 5 seconds you will add another balloon.
4. The time starts when the signal is given. Time stops when the group has amassed six penalties. A penalty is called when a balloon touches the ground (desk, table, etc.) or is stopped. Students have 5 seconds to get the balloon back in play, or another penalty is called on the same balloon.
5. On the sixth penalty, the time stops and the round is over. Give students five rounds to get their "best" time (however they define it).
6. They can strategize between rounds for the next round.

Sample Processing Questions for Balloon Frantic

- Did you discuss a group goal for this activity? What were your goals?
- Describe how you feel you improved (or did not improve) your strategies for solving this problem.
- How were decisions made? Did you feel you had input into the decisions?
- What leadership roles were taken and by whom?

Connections for Balloon Frantic

Life Skill Links: communication, cooperation, effort, flexibility, imagination, initiative, leadership, organization, patience, perseverance, problem solving, purpose, self-discipline

Academic Applications: • Connect to population density and sustainability. Label the balloons as different herbivores. When a balloon touches the floor, count it as a penalty, but don't return it to the game; simply add another balloon. At the end, see how long the herbivores made it. As students get better at keeping the balloons going, and herbivores survive longer, come up with ways that the habitat can be more sustainable for wildlife (e.g., sufficient rainfall in a year).

Variations/Modifications: • Using indelible markers, have students write a role, task, or responsibility on each balloon (e.g., "homework" or "volleyball practice"). Use these as a metaphor for how many things students need to do. Process how to give and receive support rather than try to handle everything alone. • *For younger students:* Modify the initiative by having them work in smaller groups to see how long they can bounce a balloon per person without any of them hitting the ground. Give them a stopwatch to monitor themselves. Once they are proficient, have them add just one more balloon. It makes a huge difference.

Extensions: • Ask students to discuss ways they can juggle all the things they need to do. What can they control? Who can help them (as they helped each other here)? How does one prioritize tasks (i.e., "drop" one thing in order to do another, more important, thing)?

Facilitation Notes

This is one of my favorite indoor initiatives. There are so many elements to consider that it is impossible to predict how it will go. Some people focus on the time element, others on the reduction of mistakes. Some believe that the class should split up and handle the balloons individually, while others think they should join hands, pile them up, and keep the balloons moving like a popcorn popper. Without a stated goal, students will generally head in a variety of directions, causing greater conflict and frustration.

Deciding on a group goal can help. Many times a group goal is related to time or mistakes. Some classes, however, decide their goal should have nothing to do with time or mistakes. They want to try hitting the balloons as creatively as possible. They have fun and learn much about goal setting in the process. Different types of goals are appropriate for different situations (e.g., a creativity goal would work for a computer software designer, but would not be as effective for someone working on the line creating the computers).

Adaptations for Students with Disabilities: Balloon Frantic

Cognitive Disabilities	• Start with each person having one balloon, then add one or two more to make it challenging. Work up to more balloons over time.
Orthopedic Impairment	• Students should work in pairs to keep one or two balloons going. Add more balloons to increase the challenge.
Hearing Impairment	• Agree on visual cues in advance to enhance communication. • Have interpreters available to facilitate communication if necessary.
Visual Impairment	• This activity may not be appropriate for the severely visually impaired. • Students should work in pairs to keep one or two balloons going. • Students in small groups can join hands to keep the balloons in the air.

 ## 18. Pathfinder

Focus: Taking turns, asking for help

Materials: A large tarp with a 10 x 10-foot grid drawn on it with permanent marker (a grid taped to the floor works just as well, though is obviously less portable), drawn map of the "correct" path for your eyes only

Level: Grades 4 and higher

Suggested Procedure

1. Clear the desks or tables away. Have students stand around the laid-out tarp on the floor.
2. Tell the class that their task is to get everyone from one side to the other. The problem is that there is only one solid path, and it is invisible (see figure 6.1). The other parts are quicksand.
3. To get across, only one person can be on a horizontal row at any given time (this means that there can only be, at most, 10 people on the tarp at a time – if it is a 10 x 10 grid). No one may skip a row or column; students must move only to a square directly to the front, front diagonal, or side positions (no backward moves).
4. They may not place any markers (other than their own bodies) on the tarp.
5. If someone steps on a solid point in the path, she or he will be signaled a "thumbs up" (by you). If someone steps in a quicksand section, she or he will be signaled a "thumbs down" and must return to the starting side.
6. No one may offer help to anyone unless that person asks for it. To do so, he or she asks someone directly for help, and by name.

One possible path:

Start

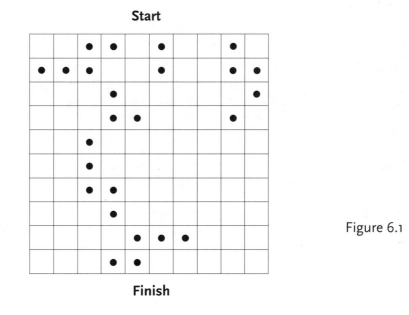

Figure 6.1

Finish

Sample Processing Questions for Pathfinder
- How easy or difficult was it for you to watch people on the path and not be able to help?
- Did you find it necessary to ask for help? Was that an easy decision for you, or did you find it difficult to ask for help?
- When are appropriate times to ask for help?
- Are there times when you ask for help, but don't really need it? When?
- Do you feel that people waited their turns and were helping each other through the path?

Connections for Pathfinder
Lifeskill Links: caring, choice and accountability, common sense, communication, cooperation, courage, curiosity, effort, empathy, flexibility, forgiveness, initiative, kindness, leadership, organization, patience, perseverance, problem solving, purpose, respect, resourcefulness, responsibility, self-discipline

Academic Applications: • Use this as an introduction to mapping or orienteering to illustrate the need for tools and assistance in finding one's way. • Use as a metaphor for hidden information in math problems, logic problems, and literature. • Start a unit with this activity. For every square students find that is "solid," give them a clue about what you are about to study. When all the clues are assembled, see if they can solve the mystery of the next course of study. Once it is "discovered," have them each write guiding questions about what they would like to learn during the unit.

Variations/Modifications: • *For younger students:* Make the grid smaller. • Have students create paths for each other. • This activity can be done in a fishbowl format by having half the class do it while the other half of the class observes. Before the second group attempts the activity, ask students what they learned from the first group. • For an easier challenge, allow them to use place markers.

Extensions: • Make a point of reminding students to ask for help when they need it. Model this by asking for help when necessary. • Remind students that rushing through their work will increase the likelihood of mistakes. Create a ground rule that everyone asks someone else to check their work before turning it in.

Facilitation Notes

Pathfinder is a slow, yet engaging activity that takes thought and focus. If students rush through this, it can become quite an exercise in frustration. Another difficult aspect for some is not being able to give help spontaneously to someone in the middle of the path. This condition alone can bring up many metaphors about giving and receiving help.

Sometimes a group discovers the path quickly but runs through it, thereby stranding a few people at the beginning. Although these people have gotten through it, they have forgotten that they were responsible for helping others.

Adaptations for Students with Disabilities: Pathfinder

Cognitive Disabilities	• Use a smaller grid (4 x 4 at first) and work up to larger ones. • Allow students to use markers for their path. • Start with easier paths and work up to more challenging ones.
Orthopedic Impairment	• Create a grid on the floor that is large enough to accommodate a wheelchair.
Hearing Impairment	• No major modifications are necessary. • Have interpreters available to facilitate communication if necessary.
Visual Impairment	• Create a 3-D grid by using ropes. • Have a hand-held grid that is raised so that students can follow along. • Mark the grid with numbers and letters to facilitate communication about squares (e.g., A1, A2, B1, B2).

79. All Aboard

Decision making, leadership

Materials: A tarp

Level: Grades K and higher

Suggested Procedure

1. Clear the desks or tables away. Have students stand in a circle around an open tarp.
2. Tell students they are scientists who are stuck in a huge pit. Their only hope is to get everyone onto the "growth machine pad" together (although it is still in its testing phase). Once they have enough weight (the weight of the entire team) on the pad for five seconds, they will grow one size bigger. This must be done over and over again, until they are big enough to get out of the pit.
3. Start with the tarp open wide. When the students get the entire group on the tarp, count to five. Then ask them to step off.
4. Fold the tarp by a third. Try this again.
5. Continue folding and standing until it is a bit of a struggle. Then fold it one more time ....

Sample Processing Questions for All Aboard
- How did your strategy change during this activity? Why did it change?
- How did you listen to each other in order to make a group decision? Did it work?
- Were you a listener, a talker, or both during this activity? How do these enter into being a leader?

Connections for All Aboard
Life Skill Links: caring, communication, cooperation, effort, empathy, initiative, leadership, organization, patience, perseverance, problem solving, responsibility, safety, self-discipline

Academic Applications: • Use as a way to explore the idea of bringing different perspectives and skills to different problems. Some problems are easily solved, while others require thought, persistence, and discipline. Examine different problems to be solved, and discuss the strategies that might be necessary to solve each of them.

Variations/Modifications: • Modify this activity according to the trust level of your students. If they are not willing to stand too closely to each other, only fold the tarp a few times. The more they are willing to share space, the more challenging it will be.

Extensions: • Discuss that it is necessary to try new ways of solving problems if the one that is being tried doesn't work. • Have students keep track of their leadership activities during a day or a week (this can range from offering suggestions and helping others to organizing a large project for the whole school). Have them write about it in their journals.

Facilitation Notes
As the tarp gets smaller and smaller, the solution to the problem changes. At first, students can simply step on the tarp. As the space tightens, they need to coordinate their efforts. Make sure that you are spotting this activity by watching for students who might fall over. Warn students to step off the tarp slowly, rather than in a large, uncontrolled clump.

Adaptations for Students with Disabilities: All Aboard

Cognitive Disabilities	• Work more gradually to a smaller-size tarp.
Orthopedic Impairment	• Start with a very large tarp to accommodate a wheelchair. • Add extra spotters for balance issues.
Hearing Impairment	• Have interpreters available to facilitate communication if necessary. • Agree on a visual signal for counting to five and stepping off the tarp.
Visual Impairment	• Agree on verbal cues so students know when and where to go.

80. Turn Over a New Leaf
Focus: Decision making, leadership, taking turns
Materials: A tarp for every 8 to 12 people
Level: Grades 5 and higher

Suggested Procedure
1. Clear the desks or tables away. Break the class into smaller groups of 8 to 12.
2. Have each small group stand on an open tarp.
3. Tell them that the object is to turn the entire tarp over without anyone stepping off the tarp.

Sample Processing Questions for Turn Over a New Leaf
- How did you decide who was going to move and when? Was this important?

- Why did you choose to do the task in that way? Are there other ways?
- Did you find this task easier or harder than you first thought? What made it easier or harder?

Connections for Turn Over a New Leaf

Life Skill Links: common sense, communication, cooperation, effort, flexibility, justice, kindness, leadership, organization, patience, perseverance, positive attitude, problem solving, purpose, responsibility, safety, self-discipline

Academic Applications: • Use as a metaphor: turning over a new leaf. What does this mean? Who in history has shown that they actually did turn over a new leaf by changing their ways from doing harm to doing good? What did it take for these people to change that radically?

Variations/Modifications: • Use different size tarps for every group. The smaller the tarp, the more challenging the activity will be. Processing can then include the fairness of giving people the same problem with different tools. • Once they have accomplished the task one way, challenge them to find an alternate solution.

Extensions: • Discuss how to handle a problem that proves to be more difficult than expected. • Brainstorm ways to "turn over a new leaf" by being intentional about performing acts of kindness for others.
• Plan and carry out a service learning project. • If doing the variation above, connect it to the idea of privilege. Do we all have the same opportunities? Is this fair? How do we work to give everyone similar opportunities – both in the larger world and in the smaller world of this classroom?

Facilitation Notes

This activity is more difficult than it seems. At first, students think they can simply step to one side and turn the tarp over. Quickly, they realize that it is more complicated than that, necessitating the movement of people from one place to another and possibly back again. Not everyone can be moving at once. Some groups fold the tarp diagonally, others twist it. Still others roll and shuffle. No one way is the best.

Adaptations for Students with Disabilities: Turn Over a New Leaf

Cognitive Disabilities	• Use a larger tarp; work gradually to a smaller one. • Try it in smaller groups first.
Orthopedic Impairment	• Use larger tarps.
Hearing Impairment	• No major modifications are necessary. • Have interpreters available to facilitate communication if necessary.
Visual Impairment	• Make sure that students are communicating effectively about where and when to move.

81. Setting the Table

(Thanks to Jim Dunn and Candace Peterson for inventing this activity.)
Focus: Decision making, leadership, group goals
Materials: A tarp
Level: Grade 5 and higher

Suggested Procedure

1. Clear the desks or tables away. Have students stand in a circle around an open tarp.
2. Ask the students to think about what they "bring to the table" when working with others in a group. What are their strengths and skills? Have each person say a strength/skill out loud and step onto the tarp ("table").

3. Once on the tarp, tell them that even when everything is pulled out from under them, their strengths and skills keep them standing.
4. To test this, they are to choose two "magicians" from the group. These two should step off the tarp.
5. The rest can rearrange themselves on the tarp in preparation for the "magicians" to pull the "tablecloth" out from under them. Their task is to end up in the same place in which they are standing, but with the "tablecloth" gone. This means that they cannot jump off to the side of the tarp while it is being pulled.

Sample Processing Questions for Setting the Table
- How did you decide who would be the magicians? Do you think this was a fair way to decide?
- Did this turn out to be easier or more difficult than you thought?
- What strategies did you use to accomplish this task? How did you decide on which strategy to use?
- What made it possible for you to succeed at this task?
- Were you willing to try this even though you weren't sure it was possible? What made you give it a try?

Connections for Setting the Table
Life Skill Links: caring, choice and accountability, citizenship, common sense, communication, cooperation, courage, effort, empathy, flexibility, initiative, leadership, organization, perseverance, positive attitude, problem solving, purpose, responsibility, safety

Academic Applications: • Risk taking is a part of learning. Sometimes people quit because they believe a task is impossible. Use this activity as a way to illustrate that a task may not seem possible, but through persistence and effort, it can be achieved. At worst, a seemingly impossible task will prove to be unattainable. Without the effort, it would continue as an unknown. • Research political, historical, and social acts that seemed impossible, but were accomplished. What caused them to be attainable? Were there sacrifices? If so, who or what had to be sacrificed in order to attain the "impossible"? • Have students interview acknowledged leaders in the community. What skills and strengths do these people "bring to the table"? Have the students write a profile about their chosen community leader.

Variations/Modifications: • A 10 x 10-foot tarp can accommodate a maximum of 25 people for this activity. If you have a larger class, divide the group in half and use two smaller tarps.

Extensions: • Create a list of all of the attributes people in class "bring to the table." Have students choose one that they would like to develop. Ask each student to write a goal about how they will develop their chosen attribute.

Facilitation Notes
Setting the Table has a higher perceived risk than actual risk. People, therefore, tend to over-analyze the situation. Generally, the group will decide to jump at the same time and have the "magicians" pull quickly. Sometimes they will choose to have everyone jump continuously while the tarp is pulled slowly.

Adaptations for Students with Disabilities: Setting the Table

Cognitive Disabilities	• Work in small groups with four to five students per tarp.
Orthopedic Impairment	• This activity may not be appropriate for orthopedically impaired students. • Offer the opportunity to help pull the tarp.
Hearing Impairment	• Have interpreters available to facilitate communication if necessary. • Agree on a visual cue for students to jump.
Visual Impairment	• Provide spotters for visually impaired students.

82 Marshmallows

Focus: Taking turns, decision making, leadership
Materials: Two boundary markers (ropes work well) set about 20 feet apart, 8 to 10 "marshmallows" (carpet squares, poly spots, or bathmats cut up into 12-inch squares)
Level: Grades K and higher

Suggested Procedure

1. Clear the desks or tables away. Set up the boundary markers. Have everyone stand on one side of the markers.
2. Tell the students that they are standing on one side of a very large vat of hot chocolate. It is so hot that, if they were to step in, it would scald their legs badly. The trouble is, they are being chased by a pack of wild boars, and they must get to the other side.
3. Luckily, they have some "marshmallows" with them. They can use these to float in the hot chocolate, but there are a few rules:
   - If students lose contact with a marshmallow, they lose that marshmallow. (Model this by throwing a marshmallow to someone – tell her that she would lose the use of this marshmallow because no one was touching it while it was in the air.)
   - They must get as many of the marshmallows to the other side as possible.
4. If anyone should touch the hot chocolate during the traverse, they must all start over.

Sample Processing Questions for Marshmallows

- Were you happy with your role in this activity? How were the people chosen to be the first and last?
- How did you make sure that people stayed in contact with the marshmallows and that no one fell in?
- What happened when a marshmallow was lost? Was it okay to make a mistake?
- What leadership roles did you take during this activity – what did you do to help complete this task?

Connections for Marshmallows

Life Skill Links: caring, choice and accountability, common sense, communication, conservation, cooperation, effort, empathy, flexibility, forgiveness, initiative, kindness, leadership, loyalty, organization, patience, perseverance, positive attitude, problem solving, purpose, respect, resourcefulness, responsibility, safety, self-discipline

Academic Applications: • Have students "earn" marshmallows by answering questions related to a topic of study. If they lose a marshmallow, they can earn it back by answering another question. • Label marshmallows with math signs. At the end, have them create math problems or formulas with the ones they have left. If they are missing essential parts, have them answer math problems to get them back.

Variations/Modifications: • *For younger students:* Try doing this without the rule of having to touch the marshmallows all the time. • You can also insert a rule that people must be connected at all times. • For a bigger challenge, have half the group on either side of the boundary markers with half the marshmallows. Their task, then, is to end up on the opposite sides. • Every two minutes or so, stop the action and have a student pick a "choice and consequence" from a pile that you wrote up in advance. Some examples include:
- You choose NOT to go to a drinking party, which kept you from being arrested for underage drinking like everyone at the party was. You did not go to court and do not have a record. (Gain a stepping stone.)
- You choose to cheat on a final exam, which caused you to fail the class. You must now go to summer school. (Lose a stepping stone.)
- You choose to go through a red traffic light while riding your bicycle You got hit by a car and are now in the hospital. (Lose two stepping stones.)
- You choose to try smoking and got hooked. You develop a cough and lose some of your friends because you smell. (Lose a stepping stone.)
- You tried smoking marijuana once and decided it was not for you. This helped you stay in school, and now you are ready to graduate and looking forward to going to college. (Gain two stepping stones.)

• Your friend dared you to drink some hard liquor and you did it, causing you to get drunk. You lose your way home and end up sleeping in a park and getting frostbite. (Lose 2 stepping stones.)

Extensions: • Revisit this activity periodically to assess improvement in working together. • Create a list or add to an existing list of cooperation strategies that apply to working within large and small groups at school.

Facilitation Notes

Marshmallows is a wonderful initiative for people of all ages. Even adults can struggle with getting across the vat of hot chocolate. There are many details that cannot be overlooked, like making sure that someone is always stepping on a marshmallow or supporting each other so that no one falls in. If someone steps off a marshmallow, then the idea of making mistakes is brought into focus.

Usually, a group will choose to set up a path of marshmallows, with everyone following. The tendency to rush causes mistakes to be made, and frequently marshmallows are lost along the way – especially the closer people get to the other side. This allows for a discussion about how sometimes, if one focuses too much on the goal, we lose sight of the process.

Adaptations for Students with Disabilities: Marshmallows

Cognitive Disabilities	• Allow some flexibility for the marshmallows to be in the hot chocolate without contact.
Orthopedic Impairment	• One of the front wheels of any wheelchair must be touching a spot. As the student's wheelchair passes over to the next spot, the rear tire should touch the previous spot (one wheel on a spot at all times). • Allow students in wheelchairs a stick or extension to use to stay on the marshmallows. • Allow students in wheelchairs to be in the hot chocolate, but they can only move forward (no backtracking). • Have extra spotters for those that may have balance issues.
Hearing Impairment	• Use a visual signal to let hearing impaired students know when the group is going to move to the next spot. • Have interpreters available to facilitate communication if necessary.
Visual Impairment	• Students can be paired with sighted students who can help guide them across the marshmallows. •Use poly-spots or other flat objects as the marshmallows.

MPS

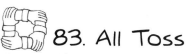

83. All Toss

Focus: Taking turns, group goals, decision making
Materials: A soft throwable object for each person
Level: Grades 9 and higher

Suggested Procedure

1. Clear the desks or tables away and stand in a circle.
2. Give each person an object. Ask students to put it at their feet.
3. Tell students that the goal of this activity is to see how many items can be thrown and caught all at the same time. When throwing an object, they must all be thrown at the same time. They cannot be thrown to oneself or to the person on either side of the thrower.
4. Start with one object. Count to three, and throw your object in the air. If no one catches it, then try again until someone does.

5. Ask someone else to pick up his or her object. Now there are two items in play. Count to three and both people should throw their objects simultaneously. If both objects are caught, have a third person pick up an object to throw along with the other two.

6. Whenever an object is dropped, it is taken out of play for the next round. Whatever is caught is thrown again. For example, if five objects are thrown and two dropped, the next round involves the three that remained in play. If those are caught, then a fourth one is picked up for the round after that.

7. As the task becomes more difficult, allow time for the students to create strategies.

8. If time is running low, or if frustration or boredom are running high, ask the class to set a goal for how many attempts they have to throw all of the items at the same time.

Sample Processing Questions for All Toss
- When did you decide to really begin to communicate? What made you decide to do that?
- Why did your strategies change?
- What did you need to do to make this work?

Connections for All Toss
Life Skill Links: common sense, communication, cooperation, effort, endurance, flexibility, forgiveness, imagination, initiative, leadership, loyalty, organization, patience, peacefulness, perseverance, positive attitude, problem solving, purpose, respect, resourcefulness, responsibility, self-discipline

Academic Applications: • This activity can be used to illustrate anything that is scaffolded or builds one thing upon another. In math, long division is a good example: In order to perform long division, it is necessary to know how to add, subtract, multiply, estimate, and line up the numbers.

Variations/Modifications: • With a large class, try dividing into two groups for this activity. Once both groups have had a chance to try, then combine the two into one large group for more challenge. • For an even bigger challenge, add the rule that every time an item hits the floor, students must totally start over. This variation generally moves into a discussion about perseverance and frustration, but can also lead into a discussion about how problems change when the stakes are raised.

Extensions: • Create strategies for working on projects. Many times projects begin with a simple idea and then become more complicated as they progress. How can students create a plan so that projects have a structure, ensure quality outcomes, and remain interesting and fun?

Facilitation Notes
At first, most groups do little planning when attempting this task. As more items are added, however, and items begin to hit each other, then the need arises to communicate and collaborate more closely. Although it is unstated, many groups decide to stay in a circle to complete this task. Some groups, though, decide to get into two lines and throw across from each other, especially when items begin to hit each other in the middle of the circle.

Some of the more interesting conversations after this activity surround the goal-related issues: Is it more important to be organized or have fun? Is it possible to organize the fun right out of an activity? Can one be organized and still have fun?

Adaptations for Students with Disabilities: All Toss

Cognitive Disabilities	• Use an item for every two people. • Use larger throwing objects. • Use throwing objects that are slower to fall (beach ball, Balzak™).
Orthopedic Impairment	• Allow a certain number of people to pass their object to the person next to them. • Use larger throwing objects. • Use throwing objects that are slower to fall (beach ball, Balzak™).

Hearing Impairment	• Have interpreters available to facilitate communication if necessary. • Agree on a visual cue to use when throwing items.
Visual Impairment	• This activity may not be appropriate for visually impaired students. • Use larger, brightly colored objects to throw. • Allow some students to pass their object to the person next to them. • Use objects that beep.

84. Basic Group Juggle and Variations on a Theme

Focus: Decision making, leadership, taking turns, group goals
Materials: Many soft throwable objects
Level: Grades K and higher

Suggested Procedure: Basic Juggle

1. Clear the desks or tables away. Have students stand in a circle.
2. Tell students they need to know the name of the person on their right. Give them time to see who that is.
3. Take one item and throw it around the circle to the right. Each person calls the name of the person to his or her right before throwing the object. Go around a couple of times.
4. Tell students to notice the person they have been passing to – what are they wearing? This is important because they will always pass to this same person, no matter where he or she is in the circle.
5. Now ask students to mix up and re-form the circle.
6. Ask each student to identify where the person who used to be on his or her right is now. He or she should continue to throw to that person.
7. Pick up an object and begin the pattern by calling the name of the person who used to be on your right and throwing your object to that person.
8. Now tell students that, as a group, they will juggle all of the objects. Everyone must always throw to the original throwing partner. Then throw the objects one after the other and watch chaos reign.

Group Juggle Variation A: You're in or You're Out

(Thanks to Carla Hacker for creating this variation.)

1. This variation needs more room, so using the gym or going outside are the best options.
2. Do a Basic Group Juggle to teach the activity, then divide the class into groups of four to six.
3. Give each group an object, and have them set their own juggle pattern in their small groups.
4. Each time they complete a full pattern without dropping the object, they should take a step back.
5. If an item is dropped during the pattern, they take a step in.
6. After they have tried this for a while, give each group more items to juggle.

Facilitation Notes

This variation of Group Juggle is particularly well suited for younger students. It allows them to assess how they are doing by seeing how far back they are standing after a given amount of time. • *For older students:* Ask them to choose how many items they think they can handle. This is a good way to deal with the issue of realistic versus unrealistic goals.

Group Juggle Variation B: Low-Drop Juggle

1. Do a Basic Group Juggle. After setting the pattern (but before going through the first round with all the items), tell the students that each person must count his or her own misses.
2. Demonstrate what a miss looks like: Throw your item toward your catching partner, but deliberately throw it on the floor. Even if it is your fault, the catcher must count it as a miss. Then throw it to some-

one who is not your catcher. Your catching partner must count it as a miss because she didn't catch it – someone else did.

3. All misses will be counted and added up for a group total of misses.
4. Try the activity with everyone throwing to their original catching partners. Make sure to throw the items quickly, one after the other. Remember, we want some chaos here.
5. If someone finds an item on the floor nearby, he must pick it up and throw it to his catching partner.
6. Either the items will all return to you or they won't, and you will have to stop the action. Go around and ask each person for her or his total misses. Add them up. This number is generally quite high.
7. After announcing the total, ask the class how they can reduce the number of misses without moving from where they are already standing and using the same number of items to throw. Get specific strategies.
8. Try the activity again to see if the class can put their strategies into action.

Facilitation Notes
The results of this activity are generally quite impressive. All it takes is adding a group goal, thus changing from an individual point of view to a group orientation.

Ask older students what kind of a goal they would like to set for themselves rather than stating the goal for them. This could be anything from fewer misses, to a fixed number of misses, to a goal unrelated to the number of misses. Help them settle on one goal, then ask them for strategies to achieve it.

Group Juggle Variation C: Juggling for Our Lives
1. Do the Basic Group Juggle through step 7.
2. Divide your throwable objects into two piles – one to go through the pattern forward, the other to go through the pattern backward. Put all the stuffed animals in one pile (for example) and all the fleece balls in another pile.
3. In addition to the two piles, have two wadded-up pieces of paper and a cup of water handy.
4. Start with one pile. Tell students that these objects represent their lives – what they do every day, their roles, their responsibilities. Ask them to call out some of the things they do every day (e.g., homework, sports teams, baby-sitting).
5. Take a few items and go through the pattern with everyone still throwing to the same person.
6. Next, take the other pile. Tell students that these objects represent all those curve balls in our lives – the unexpected (e.g., illness, car accidents).
7. Try sending a few of these items through the pattern backwards. With these, everyone throws to the person who was just throwing to them.
8. Take out the two wadded-up pieces of paper. Tell them that these are rumors, which can go anywhere. When in play, students can throw these to whomever they wish.
9. Finally, take out the cup of water. Tell students that this represents their school responsibilities. You will be passing it around the circle, hand to hand.
10. Then start the Juggle – sending items out in all the various directions. Either they will all come back to you, or you will need to stop the action. Be prepared for confusion and a bit of chaos (hence the need for soft objects).
11. Ask students how they felt about this round. Generally, you will get answers like "crazy," "overwhelming," "exciting."
12. Now ask them for strategies to bring their "life" into a semblance of order. The two uncontrollables are needing to use the same items and needing to stand in the same place. What can they control?
13. After eliciting strategies – like slowing down, communicating better by making eye contact, or waiting until someone is ready before loading on more objects – try it again. The results can be impressive.

Facilitation Notes
This variation works well for high-school students. The metaphor resonates with many of them, creating an avenue to issues about leadership, decision making, and goal setting in their lives. It is also a way to focus on the behaviors in life that can be controlled, as opposed to pointing fingers at others who are outside

one's sphere of influence. It is truly amazing how much people can effect change if the focus is strong enough. By the way, see what happens if people choose not to pass on the rumors ....

Sample Processing Questions for Group Juggle
- What skills/qualities did you need in order to juggle all of the objects successfully?
- How did setting group goals affect the activity?
- What made the difference between the first and second attempts?
- What parts of this were you able to control? What was outside of your sphere of influence?
- In your life, what parts are you able to control? What parts are outside your sphere of influence?

Connections for Group Juggle
Lifeskill Links: caring, choice and accountability, common sense, communication, cooperation, effort, empathy, flexibility, forgiveness, initiative, integrity, kindness, leadership, organization, patience, perseverance, positive attitude, problem solving, purpose, relationships, respect, resourcefulness, responsibility, safety, self-discipline, wisdom

Academic Applications: • Use the Group Juggle to teach about circular storytelling. (Thanks to Cindy Shaw for this idea.) The person who starts gives a sentence to begin a story. Each person adds a sentence in turn. By the time it returns to the first person, he or she says their sentence and it should make sense. Write the story down. • Use as a way to sequence anything (e.g., dates, letters, numbers, events). Everyone is assigned one part of the sequence. The class must figure out who throws to whom in order of the sequence.

Variations/Modifications: • Any Group Juggle can be made more or less challenging depending upon the number of items that are thrown.

Extensions: • Group Juggles are a safe way to explore the concept of making sense out of chaos. Once we take control of a situation by noticing the problems, coming up with solutions, and enacting the solutions, things can become much calmer. Use this example as a way to make sense of classroom dynamics. Sometimes students become so focused on their own needs that they forget they are part of a community. It can be rather chaotic when everyone is only looking out for themselves. Brainstorm ways to make the class a calmer and more inviting place to be. • Set group goals for the class with the stated outcome of having everyone achieve more. • If using the Juggling for our Lives variation, have students write about things they can control in their own lives to make them more manageable.

Adaptations for Students with Disabilities: Group Juggle

Cognitive Disabilities	• Speed/time should not be an issue. • Use a slower playing ball such as a Boingo™ ball or Balzak™.
Orthopedic Impairment	• Drop a beanbag on a student's trays; he or she then drops the beanbag on someone else's tray. This should work for students with reasonable hand control. • Use a slower playing ball such as a Boingo™ ball or Balzak™.
Hearing Impairment	• Throwers need to make eye contact with students before the ball is thrown. • The leader can stand behind hearing impaired students and give a physical cue when his or her name is called. • Have interpreters available to facilitate communication if necessary.
Visual Impairment	• Group members could hand off a beanbag to visually impaired students. They then hand the beanbag off to their "catching" partners. • Use brightly colored/larger objects for improved tracking.

Notes	• Do not require a crisscross pattern; allow participants to hand the ball to people next to them if necessary. • Have participants roll the ball instead of throwing it from participant to participant. • Use larger objects. • De-emphasize the ball drops.

MPS

Controlling Chaos

In order to make sense out of chaos, one must experience it. Group Juggles are a unique and safe way to get at the issue about controlling what one can, while letting go of the parts that cannot be controlled. Most of these juggles require us to go a little crazy, trying to juggle everything even when it is impossible (which is why the objects must be soft). This "controlled" chaos allows us to look at the situation and manage the parts that are controllable – our speed and communication, for example. The uncontrollables – number of objects or where we are standing – can be left alone.

85. Puzzles

Focus: Taking turns, group goals, decision making, leadership
Materials: Legos™, eye coverings (optional)
Level: Grades 8 and higher

Suggested Procedure

1. Divide the class into groups of four to five. Have each group sit around a table.
2. Give each group a handful of Legos™. Student groups are to create a sculpture using no fewer than 15 pieces and no more than 20 pieces. Give them 10 to 15 minutes to create their sculpture.
3. When everyone is done, give them 5 to 10 minutes to create a plan to put the sculpture back together with their eyes closed (or wearing eye coverings). During the planning session, they may not take the sculpture apart.
4. When the time is up, groups should take their sculptures apart, mix up the pieces, then close (or cover) their eyes.
5. Give them 10 to 15 minutes to put the sculpture back together.
6. When done, give each group an opportunity to share their sculpture with the class. They should talk about some of the successes and challenges they had with the task.

Sample Processing Questions for Puzzles

• What plan did your group come up with to re-create your sculpture? Did it work for you? Why or why not?
• What roles did you take on? Were you the one in there putting things together, or did you wait until your pieces were needed?
• How did you communicate when your eyes were closed? What strategies did you use?
• Was it easier for you to create or re-create the sculpture? What made it easier or harder for you?
• What would have happened if someone had deliberately hidden or withheld a piece of the puzzle when you were trying to recreate it?

Connections for Puzzles

Life Skill Links: caring, choice and accountability, common sense, communication, cooperation, effort, empathy, flexibility, forgiveness, honesty, imagination, initiative, integrity, kindness, leadership, loyalty, organization, patience, perseverance, positive attitude, problem solving, purpose, resourcefulness, responsibility, self-discipline, truthfulness, wisdom

Academic Applications: • Use this activity as a way for students to connect with being intentional about planning their high-school career. Have them write a retrospective autobiography of their high-school years. Then ask them to write about what they need to do and what support they need between now and then to make that vision a reality.

Variations/Modifications: • Have one person from each group keep their eyes open as an observer. They may not help in any way during the process, but can offer their observations to their group afterwards.
• Instead of having the groups mix up their pieces when they are ready to re-create their sculpture, allow them to arrange the pieces.

Extensions: • Create a vision for the quarter/semester/year. At the end of their time together, what do they want to have accomplished as a class and as individuals? Then set goals to try to achieve that. • A mission is what you are about. A vision is where you hope to be. Have students spend some time writing in a journal about what their vision is for themselves 20 years from now, and what their mission is right now. How can they take the initiative to act on their mission and vision?

Facilitation Notes

This is a nice activity to use when exploring the idea of creating a common vision or group goals. People often think that re-creating the sculpture will be easy and then quickly learn otherwise. Your discussion can transition to the idea that creating a goal or vision is really the easy part; making it happen is where people usually get bogged down.

Adaptations for Students with Disabilities: Puzzles

Cognitive Disabilities	• Use large Legos™ with fewer pieces.
Orthopedic Impairment	• Use large Legos™. • People can pair up with students to help them place puzzle pieces.
Hearing Impairment	• Allow students to keep their eyes open but not touch the puzzle pieces. They can offer help through physical touching (not of Legos™), sounds, and yes/no signs. • Have interpreters available to facilitate communication if necessary.
Visual Impairment	No major modifications necessary.

86. Hidden Polygon

Focus: Taking turns, group goals, decision making, leadership
Materials: A large rope for every six to eight people (cotton clothesline works well), eye coverings (optional), cards with the words of different shapes on them (e.g., square, triangle)
Level: Grades K and higher

Suggested Procedure

1. Clear the desks or tables away. Break the class into smaller groups of six to eight.
2. Give each group a rope tied in a circle. Have everyone stand around their rope, holding on with at least one hand.
3. Ask them to either close their eyes or put on eye coverings.
4. The task is to create different shapes with the ropes. Everyone must keep at least one hand on the rope at all times. When they think they have made a shape, they can look.

5. Start with a circle for everybody, just to get the idea. Then hand out cards to each group. Groups are to create the shapes, one at a time, at their own pace.

Sample Processing Questions for Hidden Polygon
- How did you communicate while doing this? What worked?
- Did anyone stand silent and just do as instructed? Was this a useful strategy? Why or why not?
- With people talking and not being able to see, how did you make decisions? How did you take turns talking?
- What kind of leadership qualities helped in this activity?
- Did you find yourself being frustrated at any time? How did you exercise patience? What did you do?

Connections for Hidden Polygon
Life Skill Links: caring, common sense, communication, cooperation, effort, empathy, flexibility, honesty, kindness, leadership, organization, patience, perseverance, positive attitude, problem solving, purpose, respect, responsibility, safety, self-discipline

Academic Applications: • This is a good way to teach basic shapes to young children. You can also have them create numbers or letters with their ropes.

Variations/Modifications: • *For younger students:* Do this while having them hold hands instead of with a rope. • *For very young children:* Have them keep their eyes open.

Extensions: • Bring in some strategies about body language and how we can tell things about people from body language. • Have students get into pairs. Ask them to find out three things about each other without saying anything. They can only communicate non-verbally. Then go around the group to report what they learned. See how accurate they were in interpreting the non-verbal communication. • Play a clip from a television show without the sound on. See if the students can interpret what the show is about.

Facilitation Notes
The creation of these shapes varies in difficulty depending upon the number in the group and how picky the small group members are about the correctness of the shape. For example, a square is easy to make with a group of four, but difficult with a group of five. If the students want to make an exact rhombus, then each side must be the same length. Some groups struggle with one shape, while another speeds through them all.

Adaptations for Students with Disabilities: Hidden Polygon

Cognitive Disabilities	• Have helpers with open eyes help direct students with closed eyes.
Orthopedic Impairment	• Students in power wheelchairs should not have their eyes closed or covered. • Students in wheelchairs may need assistance, but no major modifications should be necessary.
Hearing Impairment	• Use sign language to inform the students which shape will be made. • Make sure students know that closing their eyes is a choice. • Allow students to keep their eyes open. • Have interpreters available to facilitate communication if necessary.
Visual Impairment	No major modifications necessary.

MPS

81. Collaborative Numbers
Focus: Group goals, collaboration
Materials: A numbers sheet for each person (figure 6.2)
Levels: Grades 5 and higher

Suggested Procedure

1. Give each student a number sheet and tell them to turn the sheets face down. They may not write on or tear them.
2. Tell students that when you give the signal, they are to turn the paper over and touch the numbers in order from lowest to highest. They will have 60 seconds to get to the highest number possible.
3. After the minute is up, they are to turn the paper face down again.
4. Try this a few times. Each time have the students write down the last number they touched.
5. Now tell students they may work with as many people as they wish, but they cannot work alone.
6. Together, using one number sheet, they are to do the same task. On a signal, turn the paper over and touch as many numbers as possible, in 60 seconds, in order from lowest to highest. The same rules apply – they may not write on or tear the paper.
7. After a round with the groups, give them a minute to set a group goal and create a strategy.
8. Try this a few times. Each time have the students write the last number they touched.
9. Give the groups a few minutes to compare the results between working alone and working in groups.

Sample Processing Questions for Collaborative Numbers

- Did you prefer working alone or working with at least one other person? What made it preferable for you?
- How were your results? Where they the same or different when working alone versus working with a group? What do you think made the difference?
- What tasks work best for you when collaborating? What tasks work best for you when working alone?

Connections for Collaborative Numbers

Life Skill Links: common sense, communication, cooperation, effort, leadership, organization, patience, perseverance, positive attitude, problem solving, purpose, relationships

Academic Applications: • This activity can be used as an introduction to collaborative groups. Along with a shared grade comes shared responsibility. How can these groups work well together so that one person does not end up doing all of the work, and everyone has an opportunity to share in the tasks?

Variations/Modifications: • After trying this a couple of times, ask each group to tell you the highest number they attained. Add all the group numbers together and see if they can surpass it. Have small groups share their strategies.

Extensions: • Identify attributes that allow groups to work together efficiently (e.g., group goals, sharing of the work). Before beginning a collaborative group project, have each group create an action plan for how they will work together using the identified attributes. • Create ground rules for working together to solve problems. Discuss what works best when a group of people is trying to problem solve (e.g., take turns talking, accept all ideas, stand or sit in a circle so everyone can see each other).

Facilitation Notes

This is a great activity that takes very little time and has a big message: On certain tasks, working together creates a synergy (see sidebar). Generally, the groups get much further than the individuals on this task – especially if the small groups work out a strategy to make each person responsible for a smaller piece of the whole paper of numbers. This focus allows each person to be more efficient. Many groups choose to fold the paper to delineate between the areas of focus for each individual. By the way, experience shows that having four people in the small group generally produces the best results.

Cooperation or Collaboration? Cooperation is simply working together. Following directions is a form of cooperation. Sitting quietly in the desks during a discussion is a form of cooperation. Helping someone with a task is a form of cooperation. Working together (1+1) gets the job done (=2).

Collaboration allows a group of people to accomplish more than anyone could do on his/her own or when simply cooperating. Collaboration needs cooperation, but cooperation doesn't mean collaboration exists. Working together by including everyone and using everyone's strengths (1+1) causes things to happen that cannot necessarily be predicted or expected (=3). Another word for this is "synergy."

Collaborative Numbers Sheet

Newstrom, John W., Scannell, Edward E., *Games Trainers Play*, 1980, McGraw Hill, Inc.

Figure 6.2

Adaptations for Students with Disabilities: Collaborative Numbers

Cognitive Disabilities	• Have a paper with fewer and larger numbers on it. • Do not time it at first to let them find all the numbers.
Orthopedic Impairment	• Have students work in pairs so partners can help point to the numbers. • Allow for more time, or do not time the activity. • Time this to see how long it takes, then have students try to reduce the time.
Hearing Impairment	• No major modifications necessary. • Have interpreters available to facilitate communication if necessary.
Visual Impairment	• Have some number sheets available in Braille or in raised letters. • Allow more time, or time it to see how long it takes. • Have fewer numbers on the sheet.

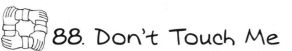

88. Don't Touch Me

Focus: Group goals, decision making, leadership
Materials: A Hula Hoop™ or short rope to make a circle, stopwatch
Level: Grades 6 and higher

Suggested Procedure

1. Clear the area and have students stand in a circle. Ask everyone to identify a partner across the circle. Have students point to the feet of their partners; they should be pointing at each other's feet.
2. Place the Hula Hoop™ on the floor in the middle of the circle.
3. Have students trade places with partners without touching anyone else. At some point in the switch, each person must put his or her foot in the Hula Hoop™. This can be done simultaneously or alone; it is up to the students.
4. This is a timed activity. The time will start when the first person moves from his or her spot. The time will stop when the last person has assumed his or her place on the other side of the circle.
5. Try this a number of times, allowing for some strategizing between attempts.

Sample Processing Questions for Don't Touch Me

- Did you set a group goal for this activity? What was it?
- How did you arrive at this goal?
- Can you think of other solutions for this task?
- How did your solution change over time? What do you think caused you to change your solution?
- How did we know when we arrived at a satisfactory solution?
- What caused us to stick with this task (or not)?
- Did you experience any frustration during this activity? Why or why not?
- Can you think of any other solutions that we did not try?
- Did we choose not to do any solutions that were suggested? Which ones? Why did we choose not to use them? How do we know unless we try them?

Connections for Don't Touch Me

Life Skill Links: common sense, communication, cooperation, effort, flexibility, honesty, initiative, integrity, leadership, loyalty, organization, patience, perseverance, positive attitude, problem solving, purpose, responsibility, self-discipline
Academic Applications: • On small pieces of paper, write the names of people or places you are studying. Then write a short description of each of these people or places. Randomly hand them out to students.

Before starting the task, they must figure out who they are matched up with. This will determine with whom they are to switch places. This can also be done with vocabulary words and definitions.

Variations/Modifications: • If your class is large, try this in smaller groups first.

Extensions: • Many times the first suggestion for a problem is the one that is tried, yet the first suggestions are usually the weakest ones. Encourage students to brainstorm at least a few solutions before trying one, and then choose one that they think might work best. If it doesn't work, they can then return to the other suggestions for a try. • Another group problem-solving issue is that many times a suggestion is discounted even if no one has seen it work or not before. Encourage students to try solutions that they have not tried before so that they, in fact, know that the solution does not work. They may be in for a surprise. • Use this activity to enter into a discussion about personal space. How did we avoid people's personal space in this activity? How did we feel about people being in our space? Talk about it in relation to how people may invade someone's space and then discuss how to deal with it.

Facilitation Notes

As with many of these initiatives, there are a variety of ways to accomplish the task. Some groups remain in the circle formation, while others rearrange themselves to improve their efficiency. Most groups will choose to set a goal to lower their time, but a few have chosen to see how many different solutions they can find.

Adaptations for Students with Disabilities: Don't Touch Me

Cognitive Disabilities	• Start with two lines of students facing each other. See how long it takes to just switch with a partner.
Orthopedic Impairment	• Allow people to stand next to their partners if it is difficult to move quickly across the circle.
Hearing Impairment	• Agree on a visual cue to signal students when it is time to move. • Have interpreters available to facilitate communication if necessary.
Visual Impairment	• Have partners help guide the students to their spots.

It's All in the Doing

Remember, it's not just what a group does to solve a problem, it's also how they solve it. Our own biases as teachers/facilitators come out loud and clear when we observe a class in action. Many times our brains tell as that students are going about this all wrong, when in fact they are just doing it another way. Before intervening, take a step back to survey the scene and examine your own biases about how things should be done. Step in only when safety is an issue or the frustration level surpasses the students' abilities to deal with it.

Processing the experience, too, is more about how things were handled rather than what was done. It may start with the what, but the group should continue to look for the connections with the bigger issues of how and why. Otherwise our students leave with only an understanding of what to do if they happen to stumble upon some throwable objects or a beach ball, but have little understanding of the general principles of leadership, decision making, conflict resolution, and the like.

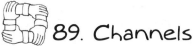

89. Channels

Focus: Taking turns, goal setting, decision making, leadership

Materials: Purchase Pipeline (available from Project Adventure: 1-800-796-9917), make channels using 1/2-inch PVC pipe (cut lengthwise with a band saw in 12" to 18" sections), use paper towel tubes cut lengthwise, or use corner molding found in supply stores (cut into 12" to 18" sections). You will also need a tin can, ball bearings, or marbles.

Level: Grades 2 and higher

Suggested Procedure

1. Clear the desks or tables away so there is an aisle through the classroom at least 5 feet wide.
2. Every student is given a channel. The task is to move the ball bearing across a predetermined area and into the can. The area needs to be longer than the length of the group standing next to each other. (This means that you may have to create a route that starts at one end of the room, heads into a corner and goes back to the other end of the room.)
3. Explain all the rules to the students:
   - No one may touch the ball bearing with their skin or clothing.
   - The ball bearing may not touch the floor.
   - If either of the above happens, the group must start over.
   - When an individual has the ball bearing in his or her channel, they may not walk.
   - Channels may not be made into tunnels by putting two channels on top of the other.
   - Each person must remain in possession of his or her own channel.
4. After the students have gotten the ball bearing into the tin can once, try increasing the challenge by adding more ball bearings. Ask them to set a goal for how many they think they will get into the can. If a ball bearing hits the floor or touches a person, then that one is taken out of play.
5. Try other items such as marbles, ping-pong balls, golf balls, and even raw eggs.

Sample Processing Questions for Channels

- How did you organize your group in order to accomplish this task? Why didn't you spread out more?
- Given the nature of the task, could this have been accomplished alone?
- How were you able to accomplish this task in a group, when you could not have done this easily alone?
- How was each person a leader and a follower in this activity?
- What strategies worked for you? What did not work? How did you make adjustments?

Connections for Channels

Life Skill Links: choice and accountability, citizenship, common sense, communication, cooperation, courage, effort, empathy, flexibility, forgiveness, integrity, kindness, leadership, organization, patience, perseverance, positive attitude, problem solving, purpose, relationships, respect, resourcefulness, responsibility, self-discipline, wisdom

Academic Applications: • This activity can be used to illustrate how the parts make up a whole. Each person can be identified as a part of something (e.g., a formula, government, flower, human body systems). If they are all present, then something is formed. Without even one part (if the marble falls), then the entity may not function.

Variations/Modifications: • Try doing this in a circle. See how many times you can get the ball bearing around the circle before it drops. • Sometimes it is helpful to try this activity in smaller groups first; then combine the groups for a "grand finale" attempt when everyone has had an opportunity to practice. • *For younger students:* Have them work in small groups.

Extensions: • Here's a philosophical question you can pose to your class (from my friend Dan Creely): "Are you controlling the marble, or is the marble controlling you?" This can lead into other areas where individuals may get drawn into things because they do not think about the ramifications of their choices.

Facilitation Notes

This task is harder than it appears, and a group must have the capacity for patience. It is common for the ball bearing to fall more than once, causing the group to start over many times. The frustration level can get high, especially when communication breaks down and people stop working together. If this happens, it provides good fodder for discussion with a focus on how to recognize the need for, and provide structure for, group effort when facing a difficult problem.

If you choose to "raise the stakes" by introducing raw eggs (best done outside), the processing can turn into a discussion about how students reacted to the increased challenge. Did people find themselves focusing more or less? When have the stakes been raised for them at school? How have they reacted?

Adaptations for Students with Disabilities: Channels

Cognitive Disabilities	• Work in pairs first for practice. Then try it in groups of three, and then groups of four, etc. • Use paper towel centers and ping-pong balls to slow down the pace. • At first, just practice moving the ball from one place to another. Work up to having a specific goal.
Orthopedic Impairment	• Pair students up with one channel so that they can help each other. • Use paper towel centers and ping-pong balls to slow down the pace. • If students are unable to hold the channel steady, allow them to pass the ball by hand.
Hearing Impairment	• Agree on communication signals for when the action speeds up. • Have interpreters available to facilitate communication if necessary.
Visual Impairment	• Have partners help guide students to the end of the line when it is necessary to move.

90. Stargate

Focus: Working together, helping, safety, encouraging others
Materials: One or more Hula Hoops™
Level: Grades K–1

Suggested Procedure

1. Practice some words of encouragement (e.g., nice job, you're doing good, keep going).
2. Ask the group to stand in a line.
3. At one end of the line, have two students hold the Hula Hoop™ vertically between them. These are the only two students who are allowed to touch the Hula Hoop™.
4. Everyone else holds hands and goes through the Hula Hoop™ (Stargate) without letting go of hands.
5. Anyone who is not going through the hoop can give words of encouragement or physically help the others through.
6. If anyone touches the Hula Hoop™, count it to get a score.
7. Try timing it to see if they can get through faster.
8. Try doing this with two people going through at a time without touching.

Sample Processing Questions for Stargate

- Did it help to have people offering words of encouragement?
- What did we do to cooperate? Give examples.
- How did we handle it when someone touched the hoop? Were we encouraging, or did we use put-downs?
- Did we cooperate better or worse when we were timing ourselves? How? Why?

Connections for Stargate

Life Skill Links: caring, communication, cooperation, effort, forgiveness, kindness, leadership, organization, patience, perseverance, positive attitude, problem solving, respect, responsibility, safety
Academic Applications: • As each student goes through, have them count or say the alphabet in sequence. They can also spell sight words or recite a poem that they know.

Variations/Modifications: • Using a rope instead of a Hula Hoop™, have the class decide on different shapes to try and traverse through, such as triangle, square, and rectangle. Agree on what the shape looks like before going through. They will also need to figure out how to hold the rope in order to hold its shape. • As students get more comfortable with this activity, try timing it. Then set goals to see if they can reduce their time and maintain their ability to be safe and helpful to those around them.

Extensions: • Talk about and choose encouraging phrases that can be used during the day. At first it may sound contrived, but the students will use encouraging words more naturally over time. • Have a cooperation show-and-tell. Have the students share stories from that day or the day before about cooperating with others or times when they saw other people cooperating. • Create a list of ways to cooperate with each other throughout the day. Post it.

Facilitation Notes

This is a great activity to help younger children practice keying in to other people. Because it is not enough to get oneself through the Stargate, one must help the people in front and behind as well. Try this activity once without much preparation. You will probably notice that some students naturally notice those around them and offer help. Others, though, may take little notice of those around them and even hinder those from getting through because of their inattention. Remember that they are not doing this on purpose, but are in need of awareness and direction. Help students analyze what worked and didn't work. Come up with a few concrete strategies and try it again. With practice, students will show an increased awareness of others.

Adaptations for Students with Disabilities: Stargate

Cognitive Disabilities	No major modifications are necessary.
Orthopedic Impairment	• Use a rope that is large enough for a wheelchair to get through. It can be cinched in for ambulatory students and opened wider for those in wheelchairs. • Provide extra support for those who need help with balance.
Hearing Impairment	• No major modifications necessary. • Have interpreters available to facilitate communication if necessary.
Visual Impairment	• Allow students to feel the size of the hoop before attempting to step through.

91. Knots

Focus: Working together, decision making, leadership
Materials: 2- to 4-foot lengths of rope for each person (optional)
Level: Grades 4 and higher

Suggested Procedure

1. This activity can be done with groups of 8 to 12 participants. The difficulty level rises with the number of participants.
2. The addition of a short rope (2 to 4 feet) for each person is optional, but helps to spread the group out for ease in discussion and allows people who are uncomfortable with touching to participate.
3. Divide the class into smaller groups. Ask each small group to stand in a circle.
4. Ask students to grasp the hand (or rope) of two other people in the group – they must be different people, and they cannot be on either side of the participant. No one moves from their original place when grasping hands. (If using ropes, tell them to grasp the rope of one other person and someone else will grasp their rope.)
5. The object is to untangle the knot without letting go of hands or ropes. Participants are allowed to change an uncomfortable grip.

Sample Processing Questions for Knots
- How did you go about solving this problem? How did you decide who would move and when?
- Did you think this through or just move at random? Did it work for you? Why?
- Do you think you used common sense to solve this problem? Why or why not?

Connections for Knots
Life Skill Links: common sense, communication, cooperation, effort, flexibility, imagination, initiative, kindness, leadership, organization, patience, perseverance, positive attitude, problem solving, purpose, respect, resourcefulness, responsibility, safety, self-discipline, wisdom

Academic Applications: • Use this activity as a way to explore the concept of unraveling a historical mystery (e.g., What happened to Medgar Evans? or What happened at the Alamo?). Use the Knot problem as a way to show that there is a whole story (the knot), but the clues (each individual person) are not necessarily lined up. Have students then choose a topic, pose questions, seek out clues, and see if they can come up with an answer based on the clues. Some mysteries, of course, have many different "answers," and some will never be solved. • After doing Knots, ask students to respond to the following in the their journals: "Life is like a rope full of knots; you have to untie them one at a time."

Variations/Modifications: • To allow for a feeling of success, try this with smaller groups first and then work up to larger groups.

Extensions: • Create a strategy for solving problems together as a class. When a problem arises, use the strategy. • Keep track of decisions that the class makes together. Analyze how they worked together or used common sense to make the decisions.

Facilitation Notes
This is a classic adventure activity dating back to the early New Games era. One reason it continues to be used is that the outcome is never assured. Sometimes groups end up in a circle, but sometimes they end up in two or more circles. There are even cases where two circles are joined in the middle like a figure eight, and it is impossible to form one complete circle. If you do this in smaller groups, you may have one group that just cannot seem to unravel the knot, while the others speed through it.

In a case where there seems to be no obvious solution, the option of "knot aid" can be offered. The group can choose one hand connection to be unclasped, and re-clasped in a different place.

Adaptations for Students with Disabilities: Knots

Cognitive Disabilities	• Do in smaller groups. • Try it in a line first (where two people do not hold hands).
Orthopedic Impairment	• Use ropes so that it is easier to go over and under. • Use longer ropes to increase the size of the holes people must go through to accommodate wheelchairs. • Provide extra support for those who need help with balance.
Hearing Impairment	• No major modifications are necessary. • Have interpreters available to facilitate communication if necessary.
Visual Impairment	No major modifications are necessary.

 ## 92 Alphapong (Adapted from Alphabet-Pong, *Play It!*, p.103)
Focus: Working together, group goal setting, success/failure, making mistakes, communication
Materials: A ping-pong ball for each small group of three to five; a book (or notebook) for each person
Level: Grades 4 and higher

Suggested Procedure

1. This is best done in a larger space.
2. Divide the class into smaller groups of three to five.
3. Give each person a book or a notebook (something to use as a ping-pong paddle) for bouncing the ping-pong ball back and forth.
4. The object of the activity is for each small group to get as far down the alphabet as possible.
5. Every time the ball is bounced, another letter of the alphabet is called out.
6. If the ball touches the ground or is bounced twice in a row, the group starts over.
7. Allow the small groups to do this for a while without setting a conscious goal.
8. After a few minutes ask each group to set a goal for themselves. How far down the alphabet do they think they can go?
9. If a group gets all the way through the alphabet, suggest that they come up with a phrase they want to spell out and see how far they can get.

Sample Processing Questions for Alphapong

- How did your strategy change as you experienced this activity?
- How did you cooperate to get the task done?
- How did you feel when you reached your goal (or did not each your goal)?
- Did having a goal help? Why or why not?
- What role did communication play in this activity? How did we communicate?
- How did we react when the ball was dropped? Was it okay to make a mistake?
- Was everyone included in both the planning and the solving of the problems?

Connections for Alphapong

Life Skill Links: choice and accountability, communication, cooperation, effort, empathy, flexibility, forgiveness, honesty, kindness, leadership, loyalty, organization, patience, perseverance, positive attitude, problem solving, purpose, respect, responsibility, safety, self-discipline

Academic Applications: • This activity can be done with any sequence, or can be used to remind us of anything we may need to classify. For example, give each group a topic, such as "mammals." Each time they bounce the ping-pong ball, they must name a type of mammal or an attribute that makes it a mammal.
• Have groups create a story by adding a word each time the ping-pong ball gets bounced. Write down the story as it stands, and keep adding to the story each time. • Try this while reciting and then creating haikus.

Variations/Modifications: • Do this first with a partner to allow people to practice. Then join pairs into groups of four to six.

Extensions: • Set some class goals for the week/month/year. Keep track of your progress.

Facilitation Notes

Although this activity can be done in a regular-sized classroom, it is better to have more space if it's available. If done in a classroom, students must be more controlled with their actions. Caution students to keep their "paddles" below their own heads so that they don't accidentally hit someone else. Also, tell students to allow errant ping-pong balls to go. If they chase them, they may run into a table or desk. This is a good metaphor for "picking one's battles." Sometimes we just have to "let things go."

I have a crate of old novels that I use for this activity. Students are asked to choose a book that they connect with in some way. After the activity, have them share why they chose that particular book. Sometimes it's because they read it, or they like the author, or there was some word in the title that caught their attention. This can provide some interesting connections for processing.

Adaptations for Students with Disabilities: Alphapong

Cognitive Disabilities	• Do this in pairs. • Use balloons to slow the action down. As students improve their technique, graduate to foam balls before attempting ping-pong balls.

Orthopedic Impairment	• This may not be appropriate for the orthopedically impaired. • Use balloons instead of ping-pong balls to slow down the action.
Hearing Impairment	• Do this in a large space (e.g., gym, all-purpose room, cafeteria, outdoors) so students have time to move out of the way when necessary. • Have interpreters available to facilitate communication if necessary.
Visual Impairment	• This may not be appropriate for the severely visually impaired. • Use brightly colored foam balls to slow down the action.

93. Catch as Catch Can

Focus: Problem solving, cooperation, leadership, goal setting
Materials: Many soft throwable items (two to three per person), wadded-up pieces of paper work well.
Level: Grades 6 and higher

Suggested Procedure

1. Two people are chosen to stand in the middle of a circle, back to back.
2. Everyone else is holding two soft throwable items.
3. On the count of three, everyone throws the items in the air (at the same time), and the two people in the center try to catch as many as possible.
4. The group then strategizes to beat its own record.
5. Every time a goal is met, it is increased. It is even possible to have a goal of trying to catch all of the items.
6. Do this for a given amount of time (5 to 10 minutes) to see how high a goal the group can accomplish.
7. The rules that must remain are that the objects must be thrown simultaneously, the two in the middle may only use props that they are wearing, and the objects must be thrown, not handed.

Sample Processing Questions for Catch as Catch Can

• What different strategies did you try? How did it change from beginning to end?
• How did the larger group help the two in the middle to improve?
• What did you consider successful?
• How might goal setting help in recognizing when you have been successful?
• How did you as individuals persevere and stick with it during this activity?

Connections for Catch As Catch Can

Life Skill Links: caring, choice and accountability, citizenship, common sense, communication, cooperation, courage, curiosity, effort, empathy, flexibility, forgiveness, imagination, initiative, justice, kindness, leadership, loyalty, organization, patience, perseverance, positive attitude, problem solving, purpose, relationships, respect, resourcefulness, responsibility, safety, self-discipline

Academic Applications: • Use this activity as a way to help students focus on homework. Label the items as all the things they have to get done. Have a few of them labeled as "homework." Almost all of the wadded-up pieces of paper may be white, while three of them are colored paper. See how difficult it is to get one's "homework" done with everything else that is going on. Brainstorm ways to support getting the work done so that academic achievement can be maintained.

Variations/Modifications: • Do a number of rounds first where they must only use their hands and arms to catch the objects and are not allowed to use clothing to catch the objects. Then allow them to use other "resources" that they are wearing.

Extensions: • When students are involved in activities that require perseverance, encourage them to set a goal so that they have a measure of when they feel successful. This helps them to keep their eyes on the prize. • Identify people (either known personally by the students or famous individuals) who have persevered through difficult times and struggles. • Participate in high ropes course activities where it is necessary for the students to struggle through anxiety to accomplish the task to the best of their abilities.

Facilitation Notes
When setting up this activity, make sure the people in the middle have some space between them so they do not bump heads when they are attempting to catch all of the items. As you can imagine, it is not possible to catch all of the items without some help and planning.

One key to success in this activity is that the throwing people work in partnership with the catching people. The more they make throws "catchable," the more success the two in the middle (and consequently, the group) will experience. Make note of when students continue to make throws at, rather than to, the catchers. This offers good information for processing and can be used as a metaphor for teasing (i.e., laughing at, rather than with, someone). It can also lead into a discussion about group goals versus individual goals and how they are sometimes at odds. How do both individuals and groups deal with this situation? How should this group deal with a situation in which individual goals and group goals don't mesh?

Adaptations for Students with Disabilities: Catch As Catch Can

Cognitive Disabilities	• Do this in smaller groups with fewer items. • Start out with a couple of items, then add more as students understand the activity and improve their technique.
Orthopedic Impairment	• Someone who is in a wheelchair and has a tray attached may be an asset as a catcher in this activity.
Hearing Impairment	• Agree on a visual signal when throwing. • Have interpreters available to facilitate communication if necessary.
Visual Impairment	• Have students pace off the distance for throwing before starting so they know how far to throw the items. • Use brightly colored objects for throwing.

94. Who's the Leader?
Focus: Awareness of conflicts, taking responsibility, positive and negative leadership
Materials: None
Level: Grades 1–6

Suggested Procedure
1. Sit in a circle so that everyone can see each other.
2. Choose one person to be the "detective." That person goes out of the room.
3. Choose someone in the circle to the "leader."
4. The object is for everyone to do what the leader is doing. Start this before the detective is called back into the room.
5. The detective now has three guesses (or 1 minute, whichever comes first) to guess who the leader is.

Sample Processing Questions for Who's the Leader?
• How did it feel to be the leader? The detective?
• How did it feel to be a participant without being able to say anything? Was that easy or hard for you? What did you do to keep from showing who the leader was?
• As the detective, did you find it hard to figure out who was the leader? Why?
• Can you think of a time when you were a leader?

- Is being a leader always positive? When are there times when someone can be a negative leader?
- What are examples of positive leadership? Negative leadership?
- How is being an instigator an example of negative leadership?
- Do we have choices about what kinds of leaders we want to be? In what ways?

Connections for Who's the Leader?

Life Skill Links: choice and accountability, citizenship, communication, curiosity, effort, empathy, honesty, initiative, integrity, justice, leadership, loyalty, patience, peacefulness, positive attitude, problem solving, relationships, respect, responsibility, self-discipline

Academic Applications: • After doing this activity, read examples of positive and negative leadership in current events. What makes a leader positive or negative?

Variations/Modifications: • *For younger students:* Do this first as a whole group without the detective to practice leading and following. Emphasize that the leader should change what he or she is doing fairly often and that people should not stare at the leader.

Extensions: • Have students identify instances of positive and negative leadership in class. Without using names, keep track of examples of each. Talk about how they affect individuals and the class as a whole.
• Give the students an example of a conflict where leading (or instigating) is an issue:

> "Beth told everyone on the playground that Jolene liked a certain boy in the class. Even though it wasn't true, Beth was having fun talking about it. Later, Jolene heard about what Beth had done and was really embarrassed. She got a bunch of her friends to wait for Beth after school. When Beth and her friends came out of school, Jolene and her friends yelled and threw snowballs at them. Jolene called Beth some names. There wasn't a fight, but everyone knew something would happen the next day."

Discuss what the problems are, who the instigators are, and how the whole thing could have been solved before it got out of hand. Brainstorm many solutions. • Try using classroom conflicts as examples of leadership opportunities for the whole class to brainstorm possible solutions. • When mediating classroom conflicts with individuals, ask them to determine who the instigator of the conflict is. What could have been done differently to prevent the problem from ever happening?

Facilitation Notes

Different issues arise depending upon the age of the participants in this activity. With younger students, getting a turn is extremely important. Although it may not be possible for everyone to get a turn at this time, students need to know how they will get their turn, even if it occurs at a later date. Creating a fair way to choose who will be the detective and who will be the leader for each round is a good way to start with younger students. Most older students are more willing to wait their turn, and some are even willing to not have a turn at all.

As people gain experience with this activity, they become savvier about hiding the leader. This can create an opportunity to talk about how bullying can be hidden, especially if people are following a leader who is instigating a situation. The more people involved, the easier it is to hide in the crowd because "everyone is doing it."

Adaptations for Students with Disabilities: Who's the Leader?

Cognitive Disabilities	• Do this without the detective first to practice leading and following. • Have two people be the detective together. • Allow more time for guessing.
Orthopedic Impairment	• Make sure any motions can be done by everyone in the group.
Hearing Impairment	• No major modifications are necessary. • Have interpreters available to facilitate communication if necessary.
Visual Impairment	• Use sounds instead of (or in conjunction with) motions.

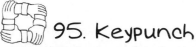# 95. Keypunch

Focus: Working together, leadership, cooperation, taking turns, identifying problems
Materials: 30 spot markers numbered from 1 to 30, boundary marker (rope, tape, gym lines), stopwatch
Level: Grades 6 and higher

Suggested Procedure

1. A large space is necessary for this activity. In the far end of a room or field, mark off an area about the size of a basketball key with rope or tape.

2. Inside the marked area, put down 30 markers (gym spots, paper plates, tape) with a number from 1 to 30 on each one. This should be done randomly. The group should not be able to see this from where they are gathered.

3. Inform the class that they have been chosen to participate in a computer debugging exercise. Their job is to figure out the sequence from lowest to highest, and actually touch all of the keys (markers) on the keyboard (marked off area), in order from lowest to highest. They have five attempts or 20 minutes (whichever comes first) to get their best time. The time will start when the first person leaves the starting line and will stop when the last person returns. In between each round, the group has time to strategize. Here are the rules:

    a. The keys must be touched in sequence (a 10-second penalty will be assessed for each one touched out of sequence).
    b. Only one person may be on the keyboard at a time (a 10-second penalty for more than one).
    c. A person's whole body must be within the keyboard boundary in order to touch a key (10-second penalty if only part of a body is within the keyboard boundary). This means that people can't stand outside of the boundary and simply reach in with a foot and touch the number.
    d. When someone is on the keyboard (inside the marked-off area), he or she may step between the keys at anytime – it is not necessary to leap from one key to another.

4. Points of clarification: The keys must be touched in sequence only once. It is not necessary for each person to touch each number. Also, the group may not look at the keyboard between rounds. If they so choose, they may use their first round as a fact-finding mission, but may not go over to look at it before the clock starts.

Sample Processing Questions for Keypunch

- How did you figure out what the problem was?
- How did your solution evolve as you moved through your attempts? Did the finite number of attempts influence your decisions?
- When people had ideas, how did you make space for them to be heard (or not)?
- Did you include each member of the group to accomplish this task?
- What might have happened if everyone had wanted to be on the keypunch pad at once? How did you settle who would be on the pad, and when?
- How did you know when you were successful?
- How did you work together to make this successful?

Connections for Keypunch

Life Skill Links: common sense, communication, cooperation, curiosity, effort, endurance, flexibility, forgiveness, honesty, initiative, integrity, leadership, organization, patience, perseverance, positive attitude, problem solving, respect, resourcefulness, responsibility, safety, self-discipline

Academic Applications: • Instead of numbers, use vocabulary words that need to be touched in alphabetical order. • Put the words to sentences on the plates. Students must touch them in a logical sequence, including punctuation. • Put the symbols for some of the more common elements of the periodic table. Then give each student an atomic number. The group must figure out whose atomic number matches the element, and each person must touch his or her element. • Give each person a short biography of someone you are studying. Place pictures of these people on the keyboard. They must match their biog-

raphy with the person. • Place a variety of words on the keyboard. Make a rule that students can only touch the nouns, and then have them do it in alphabetical order. Do the same with verbs, adjectives, etc.
Variations/Modifications: • Make a rule that everyone has to touch at least one number. This will keep everyone involved in the activity.
Extensions: • When there is a conflict, group task, or decision to be made, spend time on determining what the decision or problem is before trying to solve it.

Facilitation Notes

Keypunch is a high-level Problem-Solving activity because there are so many variables to consider. Some groups try to figure out who is the most athletic and send only one or two people to solve the problem for everyone else. This begs the question about whose responsibility it is to get a task done. It can be good discussion for cooperative/collaborative learning group work. If only the ones who are already proficient at a certain skill do all the work, what does that mean for those who are less proficient? When and how is it appropriate to use people's strengths to accomplish a task?

Other groups try to solve the problem with everyone's involvement. At first, this is quite unwieldy, with people being on the keyboard at the same time. With experience, though, the group comes up with systems to make their work more efficient that include better communication, paying attention to what others are doing, etc. If they can stick with this, students see that it is not a matter of being able to work together, but of how they work together.

Keypunch can be done with a large group, but the bigger the group, the harder it is to discuss solutions. You may need to help facilitate ground rules so that everyone can have a chance to hear and speak; otherwise, the loudest in the class will be the only ones heard.

Adaptations for Students with Disabilities: Keypunch

Cognitive Disabilities	• Do this in smaller groups and with fewer numbers.
Orthopedic Impairment	• Give students an extension to touch the number without having to bend down. • Allow helpers to push a wheelchair onto the keypad so students can touch the numbers. • Allow those with limited speed to start and end at the Keypunch pad.
Hearing Impairment	• No major modifications are necessary. • Have interpreters available to facilitate communication if necessary.
Visual Impairment	• Do this in pairs so that everyone can get to the numbers.

 96. Tabletop Puzzle

Focus: Problem solving, cooperation, planning, patience
Materials: A set of index cards for every group of three to five students with the numbers 1 to 10 written on them (one number per card), a stopwatch for each group
Level: Grades 1–5

Suggested Procedure

1. Divide your class into groups of three to five, and have each group sit around a table.
2. Before handing out the cards, give the following directions: You will get a stack of 10 cards. Each card has a number on it from 1 to 10. Begin by placing the cards face down on the table. Do not look at the cards. On a signal, turn them all over and have each person in your group touch the cards in order from 1 to 10.

3. Have them try to beat their own best time. They should start the clock when they turn the cards over and stop it when the last person touches the last number (10).
4. They will need to designate a timekeeper for each round (a different person each time).
5. They should keep track of their time by writing it down.
6. They then pick up the cards, mix them up, and start the process over again. They are allowed to plan between rounds.
7. Cards cannot be put in a particular order. They must be randomly shuffled at the beginning of each round.
8. Continue until they are sure that they cannot beat their time (it is up to them to determine this). Some groups may quit quickly, while others keep going and going and going.

Sample Processing Questions
- What made you quit?/What made you keep going?
- Was there a time when you just knew you couldn't get a quicker time? Did you agree on that, or did you have different ideas about when to quit?
- What strategies did you use to better your own time?
- Perseverance can be helpful when you have something challenging to do, but it can also become a problem when you get stuck in a rut. What do you think that means?
- What does it mean to test your limits?
- How can we test our limits in a safe way? How do we test our limits in unsafe ways?
- Was this about getting better as a group or about winning? What's the difference?

Connections: Tabletop Puzzle
Life Skill Links: choice and accountability, common sense, communication, cooperation, curiosity, effort, empathy, endurance, flexibility, integrity, justice, kindness, leadership, organization, patience, perseverance, positive attitude, problem solving, purpose, resourcefulness, responsibility, self-discipline, truthfulness
Academic Applications: • This is a great activity for reinforcing counting and number recognition.
Variations/Modifications: • *For younger students:* Do this first as a whole class. Put students in groups. You be the timer. Start the time when you say go, and end the time when the last person is done. Graduate to more independent practice when students are ready.
Extensions: • It takes perseverance to test oneself and to meet challenges. If we give up too easily, we may never know what we are really able to do. Have students identify things that are challenging for them in school. In a journal, ask them to write about how they can persevere to meet those challenges. Discuss the idea of safety and common sense when it comes to perseverance. For example, testing my limits by seeing how long I can tease someone before he or she hits me is neither safe nor sensitive. Perseverance is most meaningful when doing something to better oneself – it is a way to help each of us grow as human beings.

Facilitation Notes
The maturity level of your students will determine how much independence they can have with this activity. You may need to start by having each student or pair of students work with a set of cards. Then graduate to a larger group. Once they have gotten the idea, give them more freedom to test their limits independently as small groups.

One of the issues that can arise in this activity is competition. It is possible to lose sight of working on one's own time and competing with other groups. This situation can lead to put-downs of students who are perceived as "slow." Foreshadow this dynamic by talking about the difference between winning by putting in your best effort, and winning by beating others.

Before starting, create a system for how to share the task of timing since it is a very popular activity.

Adaptations for Students with Disabilities: Tabletop Puzzle

Cognitive Disabilities	• Make sure students know their numbers before attempting this activity. • Do this independently at first.
Orthopedic Impairment	• Have someone hold the student's hand over the numbers. On a signal, they help students touch the number. • Give students an extension with which to reach the numbers.
Hearing Impairment	• No major modifications are necessary. • Have interpreters available to facilitate communication if necessary.
Visual Impairment	• Do this in pairs so that everyone can get to the numbers.

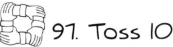 ## 91. Toss 10

Focus: Cooperation, communication, problem solving, making mistakes
Materials: A soft throwable object for each person (wadded-up paper works fine)
Level: Grades 5 and higher

Suggested Procedure

1. Stand in a circle.
2. Tell the class that you all are going to count to 10 and do something with their object for each number.
3. Practice each number with the motion that goes with it. Make up anything you want, but here is an example:
   1 – Throw object and catch it
   2 – Throw object in air, clap once, and catch it
   3 – Throw object in air, clap twice, and catch it
   4 – Throw object in air, touch toe or knee, and catch it
   5 – Throw object in air, spin around, and catch it
   6 – Pass object to person on the right
   7 – Pass object to person on the left
   8 – Pass object to person across the circle
   9 – Throw object in air, do a little dance, and catch it
   10 – Throw object in air, throw arms over head, yell "Hey ho, way to go!" and catch it.
4. After the pattern is set and practiced, introduce a second part – try to count to 10 as a group.
5. No planning is allowed, and each number must be called, in order, by someone in the group. When the number is called, everyone does the motion for that number.
6. Here's the catch. If more than one person says a number at the same time, then you must all start over.

Sample Processing Questions for Toss 10

• Did you feel self-conscious when you dropped your object? Why or why not?
• How did we solve this problem? Did we communicate in any way? How?
• How was your frustration level? What made you keep wanting to try? What kept you from trying?
• What strategies did you personally use to help achieve the task?

Connections for Toss 10

Life Skill Links: choice and accountability, common sense, communication, cooperation, effort, flexibility, forgiveness, initiative, organization, patience, perseverance, positive attitude, problem solving, self-discipline
Academic Applications: • Instead of random motions, have the motions relate to a process, such as the water cycle, or dynamics equations (Newton's 2nd Law: Acceleration = Force/Mass). Agree on motions for each part, and then do them in order. • For P.E., do choreographed dance motions or skill movements that your class is working on.

Variations/Modifications: • Instead of group counting, have students silently set individual goals for themselves when they do this (i.e., make all or a percentage of their catches or enjoy the activity no matter how many mistakes are made). Check in afterward to see if they met their goals.

Extensions: • Discuss how the class works together even when rules are unstated. How do we make things go smoothly in here? What do we do to make things not-so-smooth at times? What unwritten rules (or norms) do we have that give this class its personality? Do we like these unwritten rules/norms? Do they work for us? If not, what can we do to change them to something that does work for us?

Facilitation Notes

This activity is really two activities combined into one — first the pattern of throwing and catching the object, and then the count-to-10 activity. Interestingly enough, many groups get through the counting to 10 on the first try. If this happens, ask them to repeat it. Many times the second time through is more difficult.

Assessing the frustration level of the group is also important if they are unable to get to 10 and have to keep starting over. Some groups handle that easily, while others begin to cross the line into being overly frustrated. For this reason, this activity can be a good assessment of problem-solving ability, and can help you decide if the class is ready to move on to other, more challenging tasks, or continue with Ice Breaker/ Deinhibitizer activities.

Adaptations for Students with Disabilities: Toss 10

Cognitive Disabilities	• Count to three or five instead of 10. • Do not include the counting part of this activity until they are ready for a greater challenge. • Use items that are easier to catch – beanbags or semi-inflated beach balls.
Orthopedic Impairment	• Make sure that throwing and catching movements can be done by everyone to some degree. • Use items that are easier to catch. • Do this with partners who can help each other with the motions and catching. • In partners, have one person throw the item, while the other person does the motions and catches it. • Do this with sounds and hand motions instead of throwing and catching.
Hearing Impairment	• Have a visual signal in conjunction with calling out the number. • Have interpreters available to facilitate communication if necessary.
Visual Impairment	• Do this with sounds and hand motions instead of throwing and catching. • Use bright objects that are easier to catch.

98. Metaphorical Tableaus (Thanks to Chris Cavert for metaphor ideas.)

Focus: Flexibility, decision making, collaboration
Materials: List of metaphors (below)
Level: Grades 9 and higher

Suggested Procedure

1. Explain that a metaphor is an indirect comparison between two things. In this case it is a figure of speech that means one thing and is used to suggest a likeness to something else. For example, "I'm all ears" does not mean that someone has ears all over their body, but it means that they are listening very intently.
2. Tell them that you have 20 metaphors that have something to do with being flexible.

3. Divide the large group into groups of three or four.
4. Have each group choose a letter between A and T. Every group must have a different letter.
5. The letter they choose is the metaphor they analyze:

A. It will all come out in the wash.
B. No strings attached.
C. Bend the rules.
D. Bite your lip.
E. Water under the bridge.
F. Wipe the slate clean.
G. Every cloud has a silver lining.
H. We'll cross that bridge when we get to it.
I. There are many ways to cook an egg.
J. Don't judge a book by its cover.

K. Get off the fence.
L. Jumping in feet first.
M. Turning over a new leaf.
N. Mind over matter.
O. Look outside of the box.
P. Pull out all stops.
Q. Read between the lines.
R. Make hay while the sun shines.
S. Take the good with the bad.
T. Breaking down the barriers.

6. Their task is to discuss their metaphor and what it has to do with being flexible. Then they are to present their metaphor and what they think it means to the large group in a creative way that is not simply a mini-lecture. Encourage creative presentations – skits, infomercials, songs, poems, etc.
7. If a group is struggling with their metaphor and it is going nowhere, model flexibility by allowing them to choose another one.

Sample Processing Questions for Metaphorical Tableaus
• How might phrases like these help remind us to be flexible when necessary?
• Did you learn anything about yourself and your style of dealing with new and different things from this activity and the discussion you had with your group?
• Did you have to be flexible when deciding how to present your metaphor? If so, how?
• What does it mean to be flexible?
• How do you know when you are being flexible?
• What does flexibility have to do with working in a group, or being part of a community? How can it be helpful, or not be helpful?

Connections for Metaphorical Tableaus
Life Skill Links: choice and accountability, citizenship, common sense, communication, cooperation, flexibility, forgiveness, honesty, leadership, organization, patience, peacefulness, perseverance, positive attitude, problem solving, purpose, relationships, respect, resourcefulness, responsibility, self-discipline, sense of humor, truthfulness, wisdom

Academic Applications: • Research shows that metaphors are a wonderful teaching and learning tool.* Help students create metaphors for their own learning by asking them to look for patterns as they study. Have them answer questions such as: "The human nervous system is like the steering wheel of a car because ..." or "The human circulatory system is like what part of a car?" With practice they will get better at creating their own metaphors.

Variations/Modifications: • Have people present non-verbally. See if people can guess which metaphor they are representing. • See if students have sayings from their parents or grandparents to share.

Extensions: • Make up a phrase or motion to help people remember to be flexible. For example, sometimes it is necessary to be able to let go and move on. You can use the phrase or choose a non-verbal way to show this by throwing both arms in the air. • Choose a new metaphor each week to discuss and then try to use it in appropriate situations.

---

*See Marzano, R.J., Pickering, D.J., and Pollock, J.E. (2001). *Classroom Instruction that Works*, p. 16.

Facilitation Notes

Metaphors are abstract concepts, so it is important that your class is ready to grapple with them. Bring in some metaphors to see if they are ready. A good resource is *Games for Group: Book 2* by Chris Cavert. He has a whole section just on "Metaphors for Life."

Adaptations for Students with Disabilities: Metaphorical Tableaus

Cognitive Disabilities	• This activity may not be appropriate for students with cognitive disabilities. • Try choosing some metaphors to discuss and act out as a whole class.
Orthopedic Impairment	No major modifications are necessary.
Hearing Impairment	• No major modifications are necessary. • Have interpreters available to facilitate communication if necessary.
Visual Impairment	No major modifications are necessary.

99. Human Machines

Focus: Resourcefulness, decision making, leadership, teamwork
Materials: None
Level: Grades 4 and higher

Suggested Procedure

1. Divide the class into smaller groups of 8 to 10 students.
2. Give each group time to agree on a machine they want to create (e.g., washing machine, blender, lawn mower, bicycle). It can be anything with moving parts.
3. Give them time to figure out how to portray their machine. For example, if they decide to be a car, some people will be the moving tires, someone else is the engine, another person stretches their arms to be come the windshield, etc.
4. Their next task is to add sounds to go with their moving machine.
5. When ready, have each group show their machine in motion to the large group.

Sample Processing Questions for Human Machines

• How was it possible to make a machine without any of the real parts? What did you have to consider?
• Could you make the same machine in a totally different way? How?
• What are some other things that you have created using very few resources?
• When have you had to create something new?
• What happens when you are trying to create something but don't have everything you need? How do you handle that?

Connections for Human Machines

Life Skill Links: choice and accountability, common sense, communication, conservation, cooperation, effort, flexibility, imagination, initiative, leadership, organization, problem solving, purpose, resourcefulness
Academic Applications: • Once students understand how this works, have them represent anything that has parts to it (e.g., an amoeba, plate tectonics, the banking system) • Students can also represent what happens through the digestive or circulatory system from beginning to end.
Variations/Modifications: • Do this with subjects that are not machines, such as brushing one's teeth (i.e., some people are the teeth, some the toothpaste and tube, others the brush. Show how toothpaste comes out of the tube onto the brush and then is brushed onto the teeth.)

Extensions: • Choose something to go without for a day (e.g., paper, belts, reading materials). At the end of the day, check in to see how everyone adapted to being without this one thing. Was it replaced by something else, or was it simply ignored for the day? • Talk about the three Rs – reduce, reuse, and recycle. Brainstorm ways to do these so as to be less wasteful at camp and at home.

Facilitation Notes

Students may need some understanding of how to represent something as a group. Try it first with a group of volunteers in front of the class. Help them go through the process of figuring out what to do by soliciting ideas from the whole class, then have them act it out. It may also be helpful to name the machine that everyone will do first, then have them invent their own.

Adaptations for Students with Disabilities: Human Machines

Cognitive Disabilities	No major modifications are necessary.
Orthopedic Impairment	No major modifications are necessary.
Hearing Impairment	• No major modifications are necessary. • Have interpreters available to facilitate communication if necessary.
Visual Impairment	No major modifications are necessary.

 # 100. Fusion

Focus: Making assumptions, leadership, resourcefulness
Materials: Different size lengths of rope (3 to 12 feet in length)
Level: Grades 5 and higher

Suggested Procedure

1. Clear a large space in the room.
2. Each student is given a length of rope and asked to tie it into a circle using any type of knot.
3. Then have them put the circle on the ground and stand in it so that their feet are entirely within the circle.
4. Tell the students that there are only two rules for this activity.
    A. On a signal, everyone in the group must move to another circle.
    B. Each round, everyone must have their feet entirely within the new circle.
5. The catch is that each time the group moves, one circle is taken out.

Sample Processing Questions for Fusion

• When did you realize that you would need to share circles? Did you feel it might be necessary to eliminate people instead?
• If this was an elimination exercise, how might it have been different?
• Was this activity about competition, cooperation, or both?
• When does competition get in the way of accomplishing tasks?
• In your life, where do you think competition is useful, and where might it be detrimental?
• When did you know that everyone would fit inside the circles?
• When the group all fit, how did you feel?
• How did you work together to make this successful?

Connections for Fusion

Life Skill Links: caring, choice and accountability, citizenship, common sense, communication, cooperation, empathy, flexibility, initiative, justice, kindness, leadership, loyalty, organization, patience, problem solving, purpose, resourcefulness, safety, self-discipline, wisdom

Academic Applications: • This activity encourages "out-of-the-box thinking." It can be used as a way to model creativity before embarking on creative writing, visual, dramatic, or musical arts projects. • Use as a way to help any team focus on what it means to be a team.

Variations/Modifications: • *For younger students:* They may not make the cognitive leap to putting only one's feet in the circles, so focus on the competition/cooperation part of this activity by keeping enough circles out there so that it is a challenge to stand in them, but not impossible (like cooperative musical chairs).

Extensions: • Decide on how people can work together so that everyone has the same opportunity to succeed in class. If we see everyone's gifts as resources, how can we share our gifts?

Facilitation Notes

A group must make two main changes in this activity. One is that they must share circles. The other is the realization that their whole body does not have to fit in the circle, but only their feet. This means that people can sit on the ground outside of the circle, placing only their feet in the circle. At the end, everyone will be crowded around one circle.

It is important to make sure the larger ropes are available toward the end. If the final rope is too small, give the group the option of choosing any rope they wish. It is not, however, necessary to leave the biggest rope as the final one. The more challenging the task, the more the group must strategize.

This is a good activity for the end of a group's time together or if a group is feeling the need to compete with others in the group. It can serve is a useful metaphor for joining together and sharing of space because they must figure out how to deal with the diminishing resources.

Adaptations for Students with Disabilities: Fusion

Cognitive Disabilities	• Focus on the cooperation aspect of this activity.
Orthopedic Impairment	• Make the circles large enough to accommodate wheelchairs. • Have extra spotters for those that may have balance issues.
Hearing Impairment	• No major modifications are necessary. • Have interpreters available to facilitate communication if necessary.
Visual Impairment	• Do this in pairs to help students find the open circles.

Low Challenge Ropes Course Activities

A challenge course has many activities that require more specific equipment. These courses are generally stationary, and teachers/facilitators need formal training to run the activities safely. It is necessary to have the proper training before doing any ropes course elements. If you do not have the necessary training, contract with a reputable provider of ropes course services. (See Questions to Ask Ropes/Challenge Course Providers in the Appendices.)

The following activities offer a representative sample of low ropes course elements.

 ## 101. Islands

Focus: Decision making, taking turns, leadership
Materials: See figure 6.3
Level: Grades 5 and higher

This element consists of three separated platforms ("islands"), either forming a line or forming an L shape (figure 6.3). Everyone is asked to stand on an end platform and is given one or two boards to use as tools. (Each board, by the way, does not span the entire space between the platforms.)

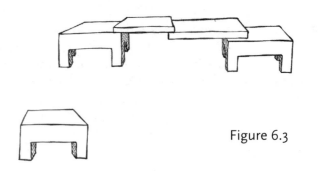

Figure 6.3

The object is to get the entire group to the farthest "Island" without touching the ground. Students are not allowed to jump.

Sample Processing Questions for Islands
- Since there is only one way to solve this problem, how did you decide to use this method?
- What did you do when you were not physically involved in getting someone over to another island? Did you feel you were still part of the process?
- What did you take into consideration when choosing who should go first/next/last?
- What roles did you assume during this activity? Did your role change at all?

Connections for Islands
Life Skill Links: caring, choice and accountability, citizenship, common sense, communication, cooperation, courage, effort, empathy, flexibility, forgiveness, initiative, kindness, leadership, organization, patience, perseverance, positive attitude, problem solving, respect, responsibility, safety, self-discipline

Academic Applications: • This is one of the few challenge course activities with one solution. Use it as a way to show that certain types of math and science problems have only one solution. How does one go about systematically searching for that one solution? How do you know when you have found that solution?

Variations/Modifications: • Divide the class into three groups, and have each group start on a different Island. The object is to have everyone move to a different island. • To raise the stakes, you can set a time limit. Only use a time limit if your group is already very attuned to safety issues so that they do not trade safety for finishing quickly.

Extensions: • Talk about different levels of involvement. Not everyone could be physically doing something at all times during this activity. How can one still be engaged and involved even as a spectator or in a support role? How can this idea be transferred to class? When are there times when we can support someone without doing a task for them?

Facilitation Notes
Unlike most Problem-Solving initiatives, there is a single answer for Islands – using the boards to build a bridge between the platforms. How this is done depends on the decisions made by the students. At first they will devise a diving board-like structure, where some people stand on one end, and have a smaller person go out to place the second board on top of the first, thus creating a bridge. Since students are not allowed to jump, once the bridge is built, they must make choices about the order in which people go across. Eventually, the bridge must be moved between the second and third islands.

Considerations include body size and type, which can be uncomfortable for some people. Body type, though, is not the only consideration. Much depends on how many people are standing on the end of the board, and where the person crossing places his or her weight. Leverage is a key component, which can be discussed during the debriefing time – especially in relation to how, when working together, people can accomplish different (and often more) things than when acting alone.

Another issue that can arise during this element is the down time for people. Only a handful of people can be actively involved in the solution at any given time. The rest must watch and wait. How does one stay engaged in the process, even when not physically active in it? How can the solution be constructed to maximize involvement of all participants? The discussion can then evolve to the "real world," as when people work together in cooperative groups, or on a project with others. How can the way they work together keep everyone involved so that a few people are neither doing all of the work nor being excluded from the task?

Adaptations for Students with Disabilities: Islands

Cognitive Disabilities	• Allow the board to touch the ground. • Help students figure out how to set up the boards to maximize safety.
Orthopedic Impairment	• There is a version of Islands that can be built as a universal element and can accommodate wheelchairs.
Hearing Impairment	• No major modifications are necessary. • Have interpreters available to facilitate communication if necessary.
Visual Impairment	• Have extra spotters to make sure students get across without falling and do not step off an island.

102 Nitro Crossing

Focus: Decision making, leadership, taking turns
Materials: See figure 6.4
Level: Grades 3 and higher

Nitro Crossing consists of a rope hung from a cable or a beam (see figure 6.4). Boundaries are set, with the rope hanging between the boundaries. The class should stand behind one of the boundaries. Their task is to get over to the other side without touching the ground between the boundaries (usually described as a chasm at least a mile straight down ...). They also are given a bucket of water (commonly called nitro, serum, or magic potion), which must be transported to the other side without spilling a drop. Sometimes, a platform (or an area marked with Hula Hoops™) is set on the other side, where everyone must end up together (called Prouty's Landing).

Figure 6.4

Sample Processing Questions for Nitro Crossing
• How did you choose who would take certain roles? Why were these people chosen?
• Do you feel you were listened to during this activity? Why or why not?
• How did you support each person who was going to the other side? Did some people need more support than others? How did you know?
• Name at least one thing you did to help accomplish this task. How might what you did be described as a leadership role?
• How well did you communicate during this activity?

Connections for Nitro Crossing
Life Skill Links: caring, citizenship, common sense, communication, cooperation, courage, effort, empathy, endurance, flexibility, forgiveness, imagination, initiative, justice, kindness, leadership, organization, patience, perseverance, positive attitude, problem solving, respect, resourcefulness, responsibility, safety, self-discipline
Academic Applications: • Create a real "serum." For example, have them get some baking soda over, followed by vinegar. To end the activity, they combine the parts and observe what happens. As a group they write down their observations of the experiment. Later, in class, they can revisit the notes, and you can teach them about the making of solutions.

Variations/Modifications: • The age of your class and how well students are working together will dictate how many variables to add to this activity. If they are young or this is one of their first initiatives, then it may be enough to get the rope and swing to the other side. If they are older and functioning well together, increase the challenge by adding the water and/or the platform. • Allow some touches on the ground in between the boundaries for the group. Only start over after the agreed-upon number of touches has been reached. • If you have some people who do not have the arm strength to make it all the way to the other side, include a Hula Hoop™ in the middle so that they can swing to the "island" and then do another swing to the other side. • Allow a certain number of people to walk across. The group can decide who these people will be.

Extensions: • Create ways for the class to have group discussions and work in groups so that everyone is included in the process. Brainstorm strategies, post them in the classroom, and check in to see if students are using the strategies they devised.

Facilitation Notes

Nitro Crossing is really a series of problems to solve. It begins with having to get the rope, which is just hanging there. Since students cannot jump for the rope, they must find an alternate way to get it. Sometimes they are told that they can only use their clothing to get it; at other times they are given more leeway.

Other problems include getting the people over, getting the "serum" over, or even having everyone fit onto a platform or into Hula Hoops™. Consequences for spilling the serum or stepping off the platform range from just getting back on the platform to having the whole group come back and start over.

Taking turns can become a big issue, especially with elementary and middle-school students. It can become a competition about who gets to go first or who gets to take the "serum." Some students may get hurt feelings, check out, or even sabotage the situation if they feel excluded. Sometimes it helps to stop the process for a moment to discuss the immediate issues. Focus on what is working and what is not, and develop some quick strategies. Then start the process again. Later, during the debriefing session, a wider-angle view can be used to see how that incident fit in with the whole activity.

It is also common for smaller groups to form, each discussing their own solution to a problem but neglecting to communicate between the groups. Conflict can arise when different groups or individuals spar about which idea to try and when. This scenario can expand into a discussion about cliques, playground disputes, etc.

Adaptations for Students with Disabilities: Nitro

Cognitive Disabilities	• Allow students to have the rope at the beginning (save that challenge for another time). • Do not include the bucket of water as an added challenge.
Orthopedic Impairment	• There is a universal version of this element called the Nitro Trolley.
Hearing Impairment	• Agree on a visual cue so students know when they should come over and when other people are on their way. • Have interpreters available to facilitate communication if necessary.
Visual Impairment	• Have extra spotters to make sure students do not fall off the element.

103. Spider Web

Focus: Decision making, taking turns, leadership
Materials: See figure 6.5
Level: Grades K and higher

The Spider Web stands about 6 feet high and can be either stationary or portable. It looks like a giant web with a rectangular frame that is attached to trees, poles or moveable supports (figure 6.5). The inner frame is made up of small bungee cords or string, with a variety of openings in different sizes and shapes. The object is to pass everyone through these holes without touching any part of the web. Usually a hole can be used only once or twice. This requires that some people must be lifted and passed through the upper holes, while others will step or crawl through the lower holes.

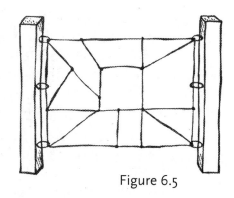

Figure 6.5

Consequences for touching the web vary from having the group count the number of touches to having everyone go back and start over – for only one touch.

Here are a couple of variations:
Jim Dunn of the Madison (Wisconsin) Public Schools has younger students use only one bottom hole. However, they must all get through it without touching the web, while maintaining contact with at least one other person.

Karl Rohnke introduced a variation that Project Adventure has used with its portable game frame at the TEAM Conference in Chicago. Students take a 50-foot piece of rope and weave it through the entire web without touching the web. My experience with this is that it gives the brain a great workout and everyone wishes they had at least one more arm each.

Create a vertical Keypunch (see p. 191) by hanging numbers on each hole. Instead of stepping on the numbers, have students throw a ball through the holes in order without touching the web with either their bodies or the ball. This is a variation on an activity called Millennium Bug by Tom Heck Learning Systems.

Sample Processing Questions for Spider Web
- What role(s) did you take during this activity? Were there other roles you could have assumed? Why or why not?
- Why did you choose the order that you did? Did you have a rationale?
- Did you feel you had a choice about which hole you would go through and how you would go through it?
- What did you do to keep each other safe when going through the web?
- If you could do this activity over again, what would you do the same way? What would you change?

Connections for Spider Web
Life Skill Links: caring, choice and accountability, common sense, communication, cooperation, courage, effort, empathy, flexibility, forgiveness, initiative, integrity, kindness, leadership, organization, patience, perseverance, positive attitude, problem solving, purpose, respect, resourcefulness, responsibility, safety, self-discipline, truthfulness
Academic Applications: • This activity takes a lot of planning and requires everyone to be on the same page in order to complete it successfully. Connect this experience to the creation of the U.S. Constitution. That document did not suddenly appear. It took time to come together on ideas and meet a variety of needs.
Variations/Modifications: • A few variations are cited above. This element can be set up to meet just about any age of group and must be structured to meet each group's particular stage of development.
Extensions: • Use this activity as a metaphor for graduation. Everyone starts on one side; the other side represents graduation. The goal is to get everyone to graduate, but everyone has different challenges (holes) they must deal with to get to the other side. Have students identify a challenge for them. Someone might say, "passing geometry," while another may say, "getting my homework done." During the debriefing session, focus on the support that students can seek out, or offer to help them through their particular challenge.

Facilitation Notes

The Spider Web takes a great deal of planning in order to get everyone through. Body size and type are emphasized, which can be uncomfortable for some people. It is also necessary to ascertain how comfortable individual students are with being picked up and passed through the web. Past experience with trust activities and discussion will help in determining how willing people are. As the teacher, you can model asking if someone is willing to be lifted, especially if the other students are making the assumption that it is okay.

It is common to see the "rule of loud" come into play during this activity. Since there is so much planning involved, many ideas begin to flow. Sometimes many people talk at once and only the loudest are heard. It is helpful in these situations to call a time-out, mention your observation that many people seem to be talking at once, and let students process that piece of information.

There is no one, right way to do this activity. Almost every challenge course has a Spider Web, and it is a nice element to revisit. Sometimes a person is the smallest in the group, while the next time he or she happens to be one of the largest. It gives people a chance to take on different roles.

Due to the size considerations, many students assume that the "big" people must do all the lifting, while the "smaller" people should be lifted. This is a good time to show that size is not the only consideration and that people working together can lift more than anyone working alone.

Adaptations for Students with Disabilities: Spider Web

Cognitive Disabilities	• Have fewer holes to choose from. • Be lenient about touches.
Orthopedic Impairment	• There is a universal version of this element called the Universal Spider Web, which is attached underground. There are holes a wheelchair can fit through. • If students are willing, they can be lifted out of their wheelchairs to go through a hole.
Hearing Impairment	• Agree on visual cues so students know when people are going through the Spider Web. • Have interpreters available to facilitate communication if necessary.
Visual Impairment	• Have an assistant available to help students know where to be to help with spotting.

 # 104. The Wall
Decision making, taking turns, leadership
Materials: See figure 6.6
Level: Grades 8 and higher

The Wall stands 10 to 12 feet high (see figure 6.6). The object is to get everyone over the sheer face to the other side. When people are not helping on top, or going over, they are part of the spotting team.

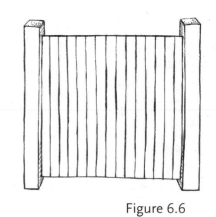

Figure 6.6

Sample Processing Questions for The Wall
- What role(s) did you take during this activity? Were there other roles you could have taken? Why or why not?
- Why did you choose the order that you did? Did you have a rationale?
- Did you feel you had a choice about what role you took in this activity?

- Did you feel you had a choice about going over or not?
- What did you do to keep each other safe?
- If you could do this activity over again, what would you do in the same way? What would you change?

Connections: The Wall
Life Skill Links: caring, choice and accountability, citizenship, common sense, communication, cooperation, courage, effort, empathy, flexibility, initiative, kindness, leadership, organization, patience, perseverance, positive attitude, problem solving, purpose, respect, resourcefulness, responsibility, safety, self-discipline

Academic Applications: • Use The Wall as a metaphor for a large undertaking, such as writing a term paper. It might seem daunting at first. We did not try to get everyone over the wall at once, but sent people over one at a time. In the same way, how can the task (term paper) be broken down to make it manageable?

Variations/Modifications: • Allow some people to climb the ladder to help the first person over, or allow someone to help the last person up. • Some challenge ropes courses have a rope or allow the use of a piece of webbing to assist climbers. • Some challenge ropes courses require that a wall over 10 feet be belayed. In other words, all climbers wear harnesses and are attached to a climbing rope for additional safety.

Extensions: • Have students identify personal barriers (or walls) they encounter in their lives. Give them time to write in their journals about these barriers and how they might approach a barrier to make it scalable.

Facilitation Notes
Although The Wall is a simple problem, the solution is far from easy. This is a high-level activity that requires a large amount of cooperation and trust between students. Proper spotting is critical in this activity. Many emotions, questions, and skill requirements arise when doing The Wall, and it is important to revisit the concept of Challenge by Choice. Make sure that each person is acutely aware that they have a variety of choices about how they participate in this activity.

A challenge such as this, when a group is ready to meet the challenge, can be both taxing and rewarding. It is physical. People are required to physically support each other by lifting, pulling, and spotting. It can also be quite an emotional challenge. The anxiety level for some can be quite high, especially if they are dealing with a fear of heights or a fear of trusting others with their safety. When finished, people feel they have accomplished something that has challenged them to a fuller degree than most of the other elements.

Body size, again, can be an issue here. Watch for people objectifying each other by talking about "getting the small person over," or saying "we have to get the big person over first ...." When this happens, it is important to call attention to it right away, as objectification can be hurtful. Stopping the process for a quick discussion can help the students refocus their intent. Encourage students to call each other by name. Later, during the debriefing session, the idea of objectifying or stereotyping others can be addressed using this experience as an example.

> There are many **ways to measure success**. One day, Lee Gillis and I were working with a group of adults. They had successfully gotten everyone else over The Wall, but could not get the last person over. Try as they might, they could not figure out a way to get that last person over, but they wouldn't quit. Finally we asked them, "What do you need in order to close this chapter?" Their answer was, "We need to all be together." They then proceeded to send everyone else back over The Wall (from back to front) to join their companion. We all learned a valuable lesson that day.

Adaptations for Students with Disabilities: The Wall

Cognitive Disabilities	• Allow everybody to help anyone going over The Wall. • Place two people at the top from beginning to end to assist.
Orthopedic Impairment	• This activity may not be appropriate for the orthopedically impaired.

Hearing Impairment	• Agree on visual cues so students know when to spot and when to go over The Wall. • Have interpreters available to facilitate communication if necessary.
Visual Impairment	• Provide assistants to help students when they are spotting so they do not get kicked by anyone going over The Wall, and they know where to be.
Notes	• This is a high-level activity. It is best attempted when a group has shown high levels of trust and a high ability to spot each other. Groups of mixed abilities can do this activity, but must be ready for it. • Provide extra spotters when attempting this element with groups of mixed abilities.

Conflict-Resolution Activities

When people come together to solve problems, conflict is inevitable. It can arise from miscommunication, unwillingness to compromise, or an intolerance for diversity. It can also arise simply because people have differing ideas or have little practice working with others. The one sure bet is that there will be conflict. Resolving it is another matter, of course. Activities can be used to teach specific conflict-resolution strategies and concepts. *Adventures in Peacemaking* by Kreidler and Furlong contains many such activities and provided the spark to create these that follow.

 ## 105. Butter Battle Escalator

Focus: Conflict resolution, awareness about how conflict can escalate[*]
Materials: *The Butter Battle Book* by Dr. Seuss, escalator graphic (see figure 6.7)
Level: Grades 3 and higher

Suggested Procedure

1. Read *The Butter Battle Book* by Dr. Seuss out loud as a group. Pay attention to how a conflict escalates between the Yooks and the Zooks. On a large sheet of paper or on the board, chart six steps of the escalation following the model in figure 6.7.
2. Discuss the following questions:
   • What was the original conflict?
   • What do you think caused the conflict to escalate?
   • Read the last page again and brainstorm at least five possible ways to resolve the conflict.
   • What could the Yooks and Zooks have done to de-escalate and not end up as they did?
3. Ask students to think of a conflict they had with at least one other person. Then have them chart how it escalated using their own escalator sheets. With partners, they should discuss the conflicts they have charted. Ask the following questions:
   • If the conflict was resolved, how was it resolved?
   • If the conflict was not resolved, how could it have been resolved?
   • When you become angry or upset, what are some de-escalators that help you calm down so that you can deal with the conflict? Write each one on a sticky note (e.g., listen to music).

---

[*] See *Adventures in Peacemaking*, p. 241, Conflict Escalates.

4. Post your de-escalators (sticky notes) on a sheet of paper. Create and label categories so that those that are similar are together.

Sample Processing Questions for Butter Battle Escalator
- What are some causes of conflict?
- Why do you think conflicts tend to escalate?
- What are some strategies we can use in this class to de-escalate conflicts?
- Once a conflict is de-escalated, what are some strategies to resolve the conflict?
- How can we help each other de-escalate a conflict so that it can be resolved?

Connections for Butter Battle Escalator
Life Skill Links: choice and accountability, citizenship, common sense, communication, cooperation, effort, empathy, flexibility, forgiveness, honesty, initiative, integrity, justice, kindness, patience, peacefulness, perseverance, positive attitude, problem solving, purpose, relationships, respect, resourcefulness, responsibility, safety, self-discipline, sense of humor, truthfulness, wisdom

Academic Applications: • Study conflicts that are in current events, or study some historical conflicts. How were they escalated and de-escalated, or how are they escalating or de-escalating right now?

Variations/Modifications: • *For older students:* Some older students may not want to read a children's book. You can make up a short story to illustrate the point. Here is an example:

Road Rage

One day I was driving on the highway and one of my tires blew. It was scary for a moment because I started fishtailing, but was able to get it under control and move off to the side of the road. After I stopped shaking, I started to think about the next steps. That's when I noticed that there was a car behind me. A big guy was getting out of the car, and it was obvious that he was irate. When he got to my window, I opened it just a bit. He yelled, "What do you think you were doing out there?! Where did you learn to drive?"

I felt my face get hot, and before I knew it I was out of the car and in his face, "You have some nerve! My tire blew and I almost got killed. You should be ashamed of yourself!"

He got into my face then, and even gave me a little shove when he shouted, "People like you shouldn't be allowed out of your house, never mind behind the wheel of a car!"

"You bald-headed idiot," I shouted back. "Get out of my face so I can fix my car!"

In response, he grabbed me and shoved me up against my car. I kicked and hit anything in my way. That's when the red lights came up behind us. When the officer approached, she asked, "What's going on here?"

Both of us were bleeding and hurt, but we were able to point at each other and say, "You started it!" Both of us were cited for disorderly conduct.

• Use news items that are occurring at the moment. Unfortunately, there are plenty of conflicts to choose from (e.g., the Middle East or the U.S. political arena during an election year).

Extensions: • Brainstorm and post ways to de-escalate a conflict. Check in periodically to ascertain how students are doing. Write about conflicts they have and how they were handled.

Facilitation Notes
The Butter Battle Book can be used with students of all ages. It is a perfect allegory for the idea of escalating conflicts. There are many other ways to use children's literature for addressing conflict-resolution concepts. This is just one example.

Conflict Escalator

Conflict:

_____

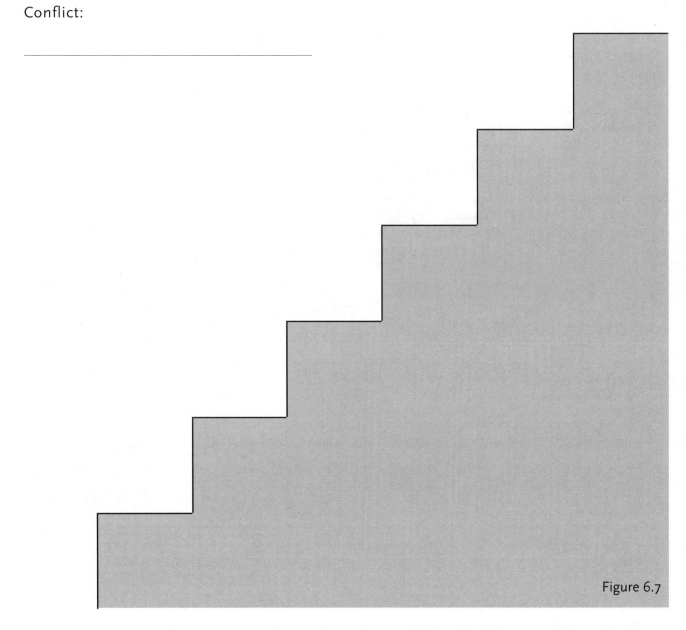

Figure 6.7

	How was the conflict resolved?
	How could the conflict have been resolved?
	De-escalators for you:

It is important to give the students an opportunity to explore how to deal with conflicts at a time when they are not involved in a conflict. Later, when a conflict inevitably occurs, they will have heightened skills to deal with it. De-escalation is important because conflicts cannot be resolved when people are thinking and acting in an enraged state.

As the teacher, it is helpful for you to float between the pairs or small groups to help guide discussion about de-escalators. Some students may have difficulty identifying personal de-escalators because they have little experience even trying to de-escalate a conflict.

Adaptations for Students with Disabilities: Butter Battle

Cognitive Disabilities	• Provide examples of conflicts for students to consider (maybe ones that occur in class).
Orthopedic Impairment	No major modifications necessary.
Hearing Impairment	• Provide an interpreter if necessary.
Visual Impairment	• Provide materials in Braille and graphics that are textured so students understand the concept of the conflict escalator.

106. Brainstorming

Focus: Conflict resolution, brainstorming solutions
Materials: An ordinary household or classroom item for each group, paper and pencil
Level: Grades 3 and higher

Suggested Procedure

1. Divide the class into groups of four to five.
2. Tell the students they are going to do a brainstorming activity. Rules for Brainstorming:
   • Every idea is accepted. No matter how outlandish the idea, it is written down.
   • Ideas are not evaluated. Even if you think an idea won't work, it is written down.
   • Go for as many ideas as possible – quantity of ideas is important. Choosing the appropriate ideas comes later.
3. Give each group an ordinary item. Have them brainstorm as many uses for it as possible in three minutes.
4. Ask each group to circle the following categories from their list:
   • The three most likely uses of the object
   • The three most unusual uses of the object
5. Have groups share their object and circled words with the class.
6. Present the class with the following conflict to test their Brainstorming skills:
   Tirana was unhappy with the look of the backyard. She had been looking at those bushes for way too long, and they needed to be cut. Although the bushes were in the neighbor's yard, they were hanging over into hers. One day she went out and started cutting off the top three feet of the bushes. When she was about half done, the neighbor on the other side of the yard came running out the door yelling, "What are you doing? We need our privacy here!" Tirana replied, "What do you care? This isn't even on your side of the yard." This was Tirana's first meeting with this neighbor, and it didn't look like it was going to be a pleasant introduction.
7. Have the students brainstorm possible solutions to this conflict. Share solutions with the class.

Sample Processing Questions for Brainstorming

• How does brainstorming solutions help in a conflict situation?
• If two people are arguing about who got in line first, what are some solutions to this conflict?

- How might you choose which solution to try?
- Why do you think it is important to accept all ideas when brainstorming? What difference does it make?

Connections: Brainstorming

Life Skill Links: choice and accountability, common sense, communication, cooperation, effort, empathy, flexibility, forgiveness, imagination, initiative, integrity, justice, organization, peacefulness, positive attitude, problem solving, purpose, relationships, respect, resourcefulness, responsibility, self-discipline, wisdom

Academic Applications: • Brainstorming is a commonly used skill for a variety of academic pursuits. After practicing it here, use it for making decisions about story ideas, research topics, projects, etc.

Variations/Modifications: • *For younger students:* Do this as a whole class first, with you as the scribe, before trying it in small groups.

Extensions: • Have a Brainstorming sheet available for students when they get into conflict situations. Have them brainstorm possible solutions as individuals before coming together to work through the conflict.

Facilitation Notes

Brainstorming is an important skill when working through conflicts. If people are to look for possible solutions, they must be able to produce a variety of options. After the list is made, then an appropriate course of action can be chosen.

Adaptations for Students with Disabilities: Brainstorming

Cognitive Disabilities	• Try Brainstorming as a whole class first. • Take an item and pass it around. Have each person say one thing it could be used for and pass it along. If certain students can't think of anything, they can ask for help from the rest of the group.
Orthopedic Impairment	• Make sure there is someone in the group who can scribe – either on computer or on paper.
Hearing Impairment	• No major modifications necessary. • Have interpreters available to facilitate communication if necessary.
Visual Impairment	• Make sure students know what their item is before starting the brainstorm.

107. Conflicts – the Real ... the Imagined

Focus: Conflict resolution: Using a model for resolving conflicts
Materials: ABCDE Problem Solving* Chart (see below), 3 x 5" note cards
Level: Grades 3 and higher

> **ABCDE Conflict Resolution Model**
> **A**sk what the problem is.
> **B**rainstorm possible solutions.
> **C**hoose One.
> **D**o it.
> **E**valuate and make adjustments.

---

* This is an adaption of the model created by the Mediation Center, Asheville, NC.

Suggested Procedure

1. Ask two students to role-play the following scenario for the class:

   The night before, you asked your brother if you could use the bathroom first in the morning because you had to leave early for a school trip. He agreed. When you woke up, he was in the bathroom, and taking his time, too. You pound on the door and say ...

2. Label this scenario as a conflict. Discuss the concept of conflict. What is a conflict? What are some other examples that people can share (without using names)?

3. Have the students get into groups of four to five. Give each group some index cards. Have each group write down a description of a conflict on each card (again, without using names). Collect all the cards.

4. Introduce the ABCDE problem-solving model.

5. Get some volunteers to role-play a conflict situation. Have them pick a card and role-play how the conflict might go without using the ABCDE model.

6. Have them re-play the conflict using the ABCDE model. Make any necessary clarifications about the model to the class.

7. Pass a card to each group. Have each group role-play with and without the ABCDE model.

Sample Processing Questions for Conflicts — the Real ... the Imagined

- What was the difference between the two role plays for your group?
- What are some instances when using this model could be helpful?
- When is it difficult to use this model?
- Does solving a conflict using this model have to take a long time? Why or why not?

Connections for Conflicts — the Real ... the Imagined

Life Skill Links: caring, choice and accountability, citizenship, common sense, communication, cooperation, courage, effort, empathy, flexibility, forgiveness, health, honesty, imagination, initiative, integrity, justice, kindness, patience, peacefulness, perseverance, positive attitude, problem solving, purpose, relationships, respect, resourcefulness, responsibility, safety, self-discipline, wisdom

Academic Applications: • Apply the ABCDE model to conflicts in history or in current events. How could things be different?

Variations/Modifications: • *For younger students:* Do this as a whole class. Every day apply the model to a different conflict chosen from the cards the students created.

Extensions: • When appropriate, bring an occurring conflict to the attention of the whole class for resolution.

Facilitation Notes

This activity provides an opportunity to practice using a conflict-resolution skill when students are not involved in a conflict. The more practice they have with the model, the more they will be able to use it when the need really arises. Keep some of these cards on hand for times when you have a few moments between tasks or classes. Pick one, and have volunteers role-play the conflict to the class. Then have the class brainstorm some solutions.

Adaptations for Students with Disabilities: Conflicts — the Real ... the Imagined

Cognitive Disabilities	• Brainstorm conflict scenarios as a large group.
Orthopedic Impairment	No major modifications necessary.
Hearing Impairment	No major modifications necessary.
Visual Impairment	No major modifications necessary.

108. Rearrange the Classroom

Focus: Conflict resolution, reaching win-win solutions, consensus
Materials: 11" x 17" piece of paper for each group of three to four students, paper pieces representing room furniture, scissors, glue
Level: Grades 4 and higher

Suggested Procedure

1. Divide the class into groups of three to four.
2. Tell students that you want them to rearrange the classroom using the following guidelines:
   - Have defined areas for individual quiet space, group work space, and group social space.
   - Make sure that windows, bulletin boards, doors, and chalkboards are not blocked.
   - Keep things that go together, together (i.e., the teacher's desk should be near file cabinets, pet supplies should be near the pet's cage).
   - Add one new thing to the classroom to make it a more comfortable place for learning.
3. Go over the concept of win-win decisions, and revisit the idea of five-finger consensus (see p. 156)
4. Give each group a set of materials.
5. When everyone is done, have each group present their concept of the rearranged classroom.

Sample Processing Questions for Rearrange the Classroom

- What were the easy parts to this task? What were the more difficult ones?
- Did you disagree on any part of your vision for the room? What was it? How did you resolve the disagreements?
- Did you look for win-win solutions? What were they? How could they have been win-lose, or lose-lose solutions?
- What are some skills you need in order to arrive at win-win solutions?
- Does compromising always mean that everyone wins?

Connections for Rearrange the Classroom

Life Skill Links: choice and accountability, citizenship, common sense, communication, cooperation, flexibility, forgiveness, imagination, initiative, integrity, justice, kindness, organization, patience, peacefulness, perseverance, positive attitude, problem solving, purpose, relationships, respect, resourcefulness, responsibility, self-discipline, wisdom

Academic Applications: • This activity is a natural for a drafting class in middle or high school or for an art class in elementary school.

Variations/Modifications: • Do as individuals first, and then join up to agree on a combined design.

Extensions: • Remind students to search for the win-win solution when necessary. • Have students create an organizational design for their desks/lockers/cubbies and then use it. • After using a design for a while, discuss how useful it is. Decide what worked and what didn't work well. Keep track of the things that worked well, and toward the end of the year, combine the suggestions for a final room arrangement. • Have students organize a part of their space at home and report back on what they did and how it worked.

Facilitation Notes

This activity can take some time because the students are basically starting from scratch. Each individual must first have a vision of the room, and then they must find ways to blend their visions into something each can appreciate. It is amazing how tenacious of their own ideas people can be, even when the consequences are imaginary. Practice in looking for the win-win solutions can help students learn a skill that is useful when the consequences are real. For fun, you can actually rearrange the room periodically using students' designs.

Adaptations for Students with Disabilities: Rearrange the Classroom

Cognitive Disabilities	• Have each group design just one part of the classroom. They can physically rearrange it right then and there.
Orthopedic Impairment	• Have larger, 3-D objects to move around instead of paper.
Hearing Impairment	• No major modifications necessary. • Have interpreters available to facilitate communication if necessary.
Visual Impairment	• Have larger, 3-D objects to move around instead of paper. • Have students work in small groups on one part of the classroom – moving the real furniture. • Make sure students have an opportunity to become familiar with the new arrangement.

 # 109. The Winless Zax

Focus: Conflict resolution, win-win solutions, decision making, taking turns, perspective taking
Materials: The Zax Story by Dr. Seuss (found in the book *Sneetches*)
Level: Grades K–3

Suggested Procedure

1. Read the The Zax Story, up to the last page (save that for later).
2. Ask the students to get into pairs.
3. Introduce the win-win grid. It looks like this:

	Win	Lose
Win	Win - Win	Win - Lose
Lose	Lose - Win	Lose - Lose

4. Ask students to decide what is happening with the Zax at this point and recognize that they are involved in a lose-lose situation.
5. In their pairs, ask them to create as many win-win solutions as they can in 90 seconds.
6. Have them each choose one to share with the large group.

Sample Processing Questions:

• How many win-win solutions were we all able to come up with in just 90 seconds? How is it possible that we can come up with so many in just a short period of time?
• How did the Zax show disrespect for each other?
• How does a win-win solution show mutual respect?
• When you have a conflict with someone, how do you usually react (e. g., get quiet, yell, walk away)? Use yourself as an example – share your style of dealing with conflict.
• Have you ever tried figuring out a win-win solution? When?

Connections for The Winless Zax

Life Skill Links: caring, choice and accountability, common sense, communication, cooperation, empathy, flexibility, forgiveness, health, imagination, initiative, integrity, justice, kindness, patience, peacefulness, positive attitude, problem solving, purpose, relationships, respect, resourcefulness, responsibility, self-discipline, wisdom

Academic Applications: • Read other books about conflicts and have students come up with win-win solutions.

Variations/Modifications: • *For younger students:* Instead of working in pairs, come up with win-win solutions as a large group.

Extensions: • Create a list of possible issues, decisions, and problems that you, as a group, may have to face today. Choose one and think of possible strategies that can help to either prevent the problem or address it should it arise. • Use the concept of win-win when necessary during the day. If a conflict arises, stop the action and take 90 seconds to brainstorm win-win solutions.

Facilitation Notes

The Zax Story is a succinct illustration of a lose-lose situation. It gives students an opportunity to think about these situations on a cognitive level when they are not involved in a conflict.

If your students are not yet ready to work independently in pairs, have them share ideas in a large group. When they have an idea of a win-win solution, have them come up with a partner and show it. Or have them do it with you.

110. Batten Down the Hatches

Focus: Conflict resolution, reaching win-win solutions, consensus
Materials: A list of household items like the one shown here
Level: Grades 6 and higher

List of Supplies		
Matches	Car keys	3 pounds of cheese
5 gallons of gasoline	Flashlight with new batteries	Family photo album
Tent with stakes and poles	Suitcase with a change of clothes for each person	Video game
Case of dog food		Road atlas of the United States
Rain coat for each person	Winter coat for each person	5 gallons of water
10-pound bag of oranges	Five boxes of Pop Tarts®	Jack knife
Charcoal grill	Gallon of milk	Box of 10 candles
Charcoal	Matches	Cell phone
Package of toilet paper	Weather radio	Emergency flares

Suggested Procedure

1. Tell the class that they are living in southern Florida, and there has just been news of a large hurricane heading their way. The evacuation notice has just gone out. They have 15 minutes to gather up everything they need before leaving. Due to limited space, they can only take 15 items with them, not including people and pets. The family consists of two kids, parents, and the family dog, Juno.
2. Give each person a list of supplies. Have students rank their top 15 items.
3. Divide them into groups of four to six.
4. Review the idea of win-win solutions and reaching consensus.
5. Ask each group to reach consensus and list at least their top five items. If they get that far, then have them continue to rank the other 10.
6. Have each group report their top 5 to 15 items to the class.

Sample Processing Questions for Batten Down the Hatches
- Which items were easy to agree on? What were some of your disagreements about?
- How did you reach a consensus on the items? What strategies did you use?
- Did you feel that you arrived at win-win solutions? Why or why not?

Connections: Batten Down the Hatches
Life Skill Links: choice and accountability, citizenship, common sense, communication, cooperation, empathy, flexibility, forgiveness, health, integrity, justice, organization, patience, peacefulness, perseverance, positive attitude, problem solving, purpose, relationships, respect, resourcefulness, responsibility, self-discipline, wisdom

Academic Applications: • Use this process as a way to study material. Give students a sheet of questions to be answered, and then come to consensus in small groups about the answers.

Variations/Modifications: • *For older students:* Instead of giving them a list, have them each come up with their own top 10 to 15 items. Then come to consensus on which 10 to 15 items to take.

Extensions: • Discuss issues and instances in which the students might be unwilling to be flexible. These can be issues of principle or values that are near and dear to them.

Facilitation Notes
Consensus activities like this can really be a struggle for some people. Many times it is relatively easy to choose the 15 items to keep; the interesting part is attempting to rank those items. Here are a few hints that might make the reaching of consensus a little easier:

1. Avoid arguing. Try to present ideas logically.
2. Listen to others. They may just convince you to change your mind.
3. It isn't necessary to win or lose. If agreement stalls, look for the next best alternative.
4. Don't agree just to avoid conflict. Yield only if other sides make sense.
5. Avoid conflict-reducing tactics. Don't flip a coin to decide. Look for the win-win through compromise.
6. Disagreements are healthy. Everyone has a different opinion. Work through disagreements and, possibly, you'll find a great solution.

Adaptations for Students with Disabilities: Batten Down the Hatches

Cognitive Disabilities	• Have fewer items to consider. • Do not insist on consensus for all things. Have students agree on a few and talk about why they picked these items.
Orthopedic Impairment	No major modifications necessary.
Hearing Impairment	• No major modifications necessary. • Have interpreters available to facilitate communication if necessary.
Visual Impairment	• Have the list of supplies written in Braille. • Have 3-D representations of each item.

III. Choice and Consequences

Focus: Conflict resolution, making informed choices
Materials: Index cards with a choice written on each one, pen/pencil for each group of three to four
Level: Grades 2–5

Suggested Procedure
1. Divide the class into groups of three to four, and have each group sit together.

2. Give each group one index card with a choice written on it and a pencil. Here are some examples of choices:
   - Helping a friend with his or her homework.
   - Sassing to the principal.
   - Asking your elderly neighbor if she needs help shoveling snow.
   - Yelling loudly in the car when someone is driving.
   - Not wearing a seatbelt.
   - Wearing a seatbelt.
   - Picking up litter when you see it on the sidewalk.
   - Seeing a younger kid who is crying and finding out what is wrong.
   - Throwing things at moving cars.
   - Doing all your homework.
   - Volunteering at the neighborhood or community center.
   - Seeing an argument between your friends and walking away.
3. Have each group brainstorm as many consequences of that choice as they can think of. Give them a reasonable amount of time to complete that task. Remind them that there may be positive and negative consequences.
4. Have each group share three ideas from their list.
5. Discuss which of the choices from the above list could be described as "responsible" and which ones could be described as "irresponsible."
6. Next, pass out two index cards to each group.
7. Ask them to come up with one responsible choice and one irresponsible choice. Write one on each card.
8. Periodically choose one of the cards to discuss as a whole class – what are the possible consequences of the choice? Why is it responsible or irresponsible?

Sample Processing Questions for Choice and Consequences
- On the board write "responsible choices" and brainstorm possible consequences of that. Do the same with "irresponsible choices."
- If being responsible is a choice, how do you know when you are making a responsible choice? An irresponsible choice?
- Share a responsible and irresponsible choice you have made in your life to show that everyone does it. What do you think I learned from my irresponsible choice? From my responsible choice?
- Is it possible to change irresponsible choices to responsible ones? How?
- What are some choices you make every day?
- How do you know these are choices?

Connections for Choices and Consequences
Life Skill Links: choice and accountability, citizenship, common sense, effort, flexibility, forgiveness, health, honesty, initiative, integrity, justice, organization, peacefulness, positive attitude, problem solving, purpose, responsibility, safety, self-discipline, wisdom
Academic Applications: • Using a story from current events, analyze the choices that were made and the consequences of the choices.
Variations/Modifications: • Do an analysis of choices and consequences as a class first, as an example.
Extensions: • Revisit your Full Value Contract and discuss how each person is responsible to each other and the community. • Ask students to journal about choices they make that are responsible or irresponsible.

Facilitation Notes
Many times we do not discuss the consequences of choices with students until they have made a bad one. This activity offers an opportunity to discuss the making of choices and the ensuing consequences when students are in a rational frame of mind. When students are subsequently held accountable for choices, they are then more likely to learn from their situations. They may also have a better chance of making responsible choices and prevent some conflicts and disagreeable situations from occurring.

Adaptations for Students with Disabilities: Choice and Consequences

Cognitive Disabilities	• Have fewer items to consider. • Use examples from their daily routines.
Orthopedic Impairment	No major modifications necessary.
Hearing Impairment	• No major modifications necessary. • Have interpreters available to facilitate communication if necessary.
Visual Impairment	No major modifications necessary.

Academic Content Activities

In her article, "The Virtue of Not Knowing,"* Eleanor Duckworth speaks of creating classrooms in which the "quick right answer" is not the norm. Instead, students are encouraged to explore in realms in which the right answer is unknown. Dr. Duckworth sums it up with the statement: "The virtues involved in not knowing are the ones that really count in the long run. What you do about what you don't know is, in the final analysis, what determines what you will ultimately know."

Although that statement has the ring of a paradox, a closer examination speaks to the process involved in real learning. Academic content can be approached much like working through problem-solving initiatives. Giving students an opportunity to explore content without narrowly looking for one "right" answer can be a great gift, especially since there are few simple answers in daily living. Most of our great "life" lessons are not handed to us on a platter.

Adventure can be woven right into your existing school curriculum. A community of learners means that students can set academic goals, take risks to push their own cognitive limits, and work with and support others while they struggle with concepts. Here are a few examples of how students can approach academic tasks as a class challenge.

112 Venn Diagrams

Focus: Venn diagrams, mixing, perspective taking, leadership, organization
Materials: Rope or tape
Level: Grades 2–5

Suggested Procedure
1. Clear a large space in the room or go to a large space.
2. Put down the ropes or tape in a large Venn diagram. It should look like this:

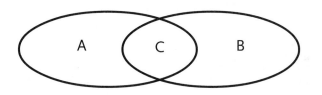

3. Give the students three choices and designate each of the areas of the life-size Venn diagram as each of the choices. On a signal, have them go to the area that represents them. Here are some examples:

---

* From National Elementary Principal, volume 54, number 4, March/April 1975.

- Who is wearing blue (A), red (B), or both (C)? If you are not wearing red or blue, do not move.
- Who has at least one sister (A), brother (B), both (C)?
- Who has a cat (A), dog (B), both (C)?
- Who likes chocolate ice cream, vanilla ice cream, both?
- Who has lived in a house, an apartment, both?

4. When they seem to get the hang of a Venn diagram, have them get into small groups of three to four.
5. Give them a few minutes to make a list of things they all have in common in their small group, then a list of things they do not have in common. If they are not ready for this, you can do it as a whole class.
6. Finally, ask them to choose one thing from their list that they would like to make a Venn diagram from, and have them formulate a question from both of their lists. They need to have two choices. For example, if they all have in common that they like to play basketball but only one of them likes to play baseball, they can formulate a question like this: Who here likes to play basketball (A), baseball (B), both basketball and baseball (C)?
7. Have them draw a Venn diagram using their question and the names of the people in their group.
8. They then bring their question to the large group and try it out on the life-size Venn diagram.
9. After doing the activity, teach students how to create Venn Diagrams on paper.

Sample Processing Questions: Venn Diagrams
- We used two organizational strategies for organizing our thoughts (making lists and Venn diagrams). What are some other strategies for organizing your thoughts?
- How do you organize your thoughts when you are reading something? What helps you remember the story?
- How do you organize your thoughts when you are doing math? How do you keep the numbers straight so that you can add or subtract them?
- What are some strategies to organize your thoughts so that you remember things?

Facilitation Notes
This is a great way to help kinesthetic learners feel the Venn diagram. The moving around also helps young students get the idea that things can be categorized in different places. It is then easier for some to make the abstract leap to the actual diagram on paper.

Adaptations for Students with Disabilities: Venn Diagrams

Cognitive Disabilities	• Have fewer items to consider.
Orthopedic Impairment	• Make sure there is enough space in the 3-D Venn diagram for wheelchairs. • Help students with balance if needed.
Hearing Impairment	• No major modifications necessary. • Have interpreters available to facilitate communication if necessary.
Visual Impairment	• Help students move to the place where they belong in the diagram.

113. The Compass Walk

Focus: Math skills, problem solving, peer teaching and learning, reading directions
Materials: Simple orienteering compasses (enough for half the class), directions on how to take a bearing (should come with the compasses), eye coverings (optional)
Level: Grades 4 and higher

Suggested Procedure
Set the stage with a compass walk. You will need to do this in a large field.

1. Have students get into pairs. They can use eye coverings if they wish.
2. Standing on one end of the field, point out an object on the other end of the field (e.g., tree, pole, home plate of a ball field). That is everybody's goal.
3. One of the students in each pair volunteers to go first. His or her task is to attempt to get as close to that goal as possible without using the sense of sight. With either closed eyes or eyes covered, this person has two minutes to see how close he or she can get.
4. The sighted partner's job is to keep his or her partner safe. Caution students not to help guide their partners, only stop them from running or falling into anything. Suggest that sighted partners walk a little behind their other partners, so as not to influence them in any way. Finding the goal is a task only for the sightless partner. Helping takes the sense of exploration away. If students reach the goal, ask them to remain quiet until time is up so that others do not use their noise as a homing signal.
5. After the 2 minutes, give a signal to stop. Let the students see how close they are to the goal. They can then talk with their partners about the route they took.
6. Have everyone return to the beginning and switch roles.
7. Discuss what it was like to be searching for something with no direction. What strategies did students use? What might it be like to be lost in the woods without one's bearings?
8. Now give each pair a compass and the directions (below) on how to take a bearing. Give everyone time to explore what it means to take a bearing. Applying any previous knowledge, using the written directions, and asking questions of you, let them play with the concept for a while.

How to Take a Bearing
A bearing is a horizontal angle fixing a direction in respect to north. You would use a bearing if you were lost and needed to walk in a straight line.

A. Hold the compass so that the "Read Bearing Here" arrow points away from you.
B. Turn the dial so that it points to north (360°).
C. Place the compass baseplate in your belly button so that the arrow is pointing away from you. The "Read Bearing Here" arrow should be pointing forward.
D. Holding it tightly, turn your whole body until the magnetic needle housing is lined up with the magnetic needle (put the dog in the dog house). You are now facing due North (or 360°).
E. Look up. Find a stationary landmark that is close to where your compass is pointing. That is the direction you can walk. You can put away your compass and walk there.
F. Reorient your bearing by repeating B. Look up again for another landmark. Walk to it.
G. You are now sure that you are walking in a straight line due north.
H. Take another bearing using a different direction. Try 60°, for example.

9. Float around to check up on each pair. Answer questions, and guide them in the directions to get their questions answered.
10. Try the Real Compass Walk Activity below with students.

A Real Compass Walk
A. Place a marker on the ground between your feet.
B. Set your compass for a direction between 0° and 120°.
C. Face this bearing as outlined in B above.
D. Walk this bearing for 20 paces and stop.
E. Add 120° to your last setting. Reset your compass.
F. Head this direction for 20 paces and stop.
G. Again, add 120° to your last setting and walk 20 paces. Your marker should be very nearby.

Facilitation Notes

This lesson can be integrated into a larger unit on geometry along with activities such as the Hidden Polygon (p. 177) and Puzzles (p. 176). Using the theme of finding one's way, read poetry or stories about being lost. Have students write about a time when they were lost or felt lost. This can also be folded into a school, neighborhood, town, or city search.

114. Books and Quilts*

There are many project-based experiences that provide avenues for students to explore their world without looking for one right answer. Students can research topics, then write and illustrate their own books. These books can be shared with, and even given to, the school library. If the books are written for a younger audience, older students can visit younger classes and read their books out loud.

Quilting is a project that can help students explore their own heritage. Have students research their own backgrounds. If a student is adopted, she or he might research the adoptive parent's (or parents') background and traditions, and then make some educated guesses about her or his own background.

Once people have a sense of what their ethnic heritage might be, they can create a class quilt. Have each ethnic group identified by a certain type of fabric. For example, purple might represent South African (or African in general, if students cannot get that specific), green could be German, floral might be Native American, paisley Cambodian, etc. Each student should be as specific as possible about what percentage he or she is of each of these ethnic backgrounds and create a quilt square depicting this. When done with their squares, students can sew them together into a quilt depicting the ethnic heritage of the entire class. This quilt could, in turn, be donated to an organization or raffled off to raise money for a nonprofit group of the class's choosing.

Summary: When to Move on to Challenge

The class is now a full-fledged community. People are interdependent, taking care of their own needs and working through conflict when it arises. It is a safe place where ideas are shared freely, and people know what it means to collaborate. When a problem comes up, students turn to each other to solve it rather than running to you. Risk taking is part of the everyday scene, where one person who struggles with reading might risk reading out loud to the class, and another who is testing her math skills might ask another for help. People feel comfortable challenging themselves within this community. The next step is to take on personal challenges with community support.

Moving to Challenge: Some Observations

	Move On	Stay with Problem Solving
Decision Making	• Students consciously work at making decisions. • Students have discussed and tried a variety of decision-making strategies. • When decisions are made, students check in with each other to see if they agree with the decision.	• Students do not seem to be aware of and make no conscious effort to make group decisions. • The "rule of loud" is frequently used to discuss problems. • A small group of students continually makes decisions for the whole group, while others passively wait for decisions to be made.

* Thanks to Leslie Kebbekus and Jane Stimac for the books lesson, and the School Age Parent Program in Madison, WI, for the quilts project.

Moving to Challenge: Some Observations (cont.)

	Move On	Stay with Problem Solving
Group Goals	• Students understand that group goals help everyone work together. • Students consciously try to arrive at group goals while working through problems with little prompting. • When group goals are established, students are willing to work toward them. • Everyone's input is sought when attempting to establish group goals.	• Students make little or no effort to establish group goals. • When group goals are established, they are generally ignored or sabotaged. • Individuals assume that their personal goal is the group goal.
Taking Turns	• Students take turns doing the difficult and/or mundane tasks. • When one student has had a chance to try something, she or he stands back to let others have a turn. • Everyone is given a chance to participate in activities and/or discussions, even if some people exercise the right to pass. • When an attractive task is to be done, students create a win-win situation or a fair way to choose the person for the task.	• Students argue or fight over whose turn it is to go next. • The same person(s) is always first or last. • The more passive students constantly defer to the more assertive or aggressive students. • During discussions, the same people do most of the talking.
Leadership	• Students show they can take the role of both leader and follower, based on what is required of them. • Students can articulate a basic definition of what it means to be a leader. • Students can identify when they have taken a leadership role. • Students can express that there are different styles of leadership and different leadership roles. • Students show they can collaborate when working in small groups, thus sharing the leadership roles.	• Students cannot articulate a basic personal definition of leadership. • Students accept the notion without question that being a leader is "good" while being a follower is "bad." • Students refuse to share leadership roles, even when it runs counter to solving the problem. • Students cannot identify when they have taken leadership positions.
Conflict Resolution	• Students can practice specific conflict resolution skills when not involved in a conflict. • Students can identify that conflict does not need to be "bad," but can be a powerful learning experience. • When in a conflict situation, students begin to use conflict-resolution skills. • Students can identify and use de-escalating strategies to resolve conflicts. • Students work toward win-win solutions.	• Students do not use conflict-resolution skills, even when prompted. • Students are unable to de-escalate in order to resolve conflicts. • Students work only toward win-lose solutions to conflicts. • Students refuse to work at resolving conflicts.

[1] Frank, L. and Stanley, J. (1999) Manito-wish Leadership Manual. (p. 31)

7 Challenge

ACTIVITIES
High Ropes Course
Outdoor Pursuits
Urban Experience
Presentations/Projects

Stepping Out on One's Own

The community that has formed through the sequence of Cooperation, Trust, and Problem Solving is comfortable. People understand the norms and what to expect from each other. This community, though, is not a mobile entity that can follow its members around for the rest of their lives. Although it can be duplicated, it must stay in this place and time. How, then, do people take necessary risks as individuals outside this community?

Challenge is the time to look inward and outward. With the support of the community, individual students look deep into themselves to explore what risk taking means to them. It is also a time when individuals and small groups leave this smaller community to venture out into the larger one through community service projects, urban experiences, and public presentations. If they run into rough spots, the community is there for support and encouragement.

Interdependence takes on new meaning as students learn about being independent. The community is still there; people with whom one can consult are available for information, ideas, encouragement, and the like. Now, though, the accountability rests with the individual. If, for example, a small group decides to plan a fund drive to raise money for a local food pantry, the end result is theirs, not the whole community's. In an urban experience, where students may be asked to design and execute a survey, individual students must take the risk to approach people to ask questions. The whole community is not physically there to do it with them.

Along with this new independence and accountability comes a whole new meaning to success and failure. The stakes are higher now. If someone drops the ball in a group juggle activity, it hits the floor, gets picked up and thrown back in the game. If, however, someone "drops the ball" when planning the fundraiser, the fund-raising goal is not met. A sense of reality is now in place.

Another issue at this stage is the "us" and "them" mentality that can occur when a group of people has formed specific class norms and has had an opportunity to bond. From the beginning, this class has explored diversity as it relates to the people in its own community. It is important to explore issues of diversity outside as well and appreciate the wonderful variety of race, culture, customs, religion, size, age, sexuality, and so on. It would be a mistake to create a "caring" place in which those on the inside are suspicious of those outside the community.

Throughout this process, you have had the opportunity to watch a group of nervous students grow into more caring, confident community members. The life cycle of this group is almost complete. Watching them struggle toward independence is a final phase of this journey.

Challenge Issues and Skills

Individual Goals

Up to this point, students have been asked to set behavioral goals and group goals. Now it is time to focus on individual goals. In the beginning these goals can be more behavior-oriented, such as how far one might climb on a high ropes course element. Later, task-oriented goals are added, like how much time it will take to get a community service project completed.

One tool to help structure this type of goal setting is action planning. When taking action, it is important to consider many variables. Questions to ask are:
- How would you describe your vision for the project?
- What are three to five goals to meet along the way?
- What is your time line?
- What resources will you need? (Consider people, time, money, etc. Be specific!)
- What might be some barriers to getting this project accomplished? Describe how you might deal with each barrier should it come up. How will you address unforeseen barriers?
- How will you evaluate your project?
- How will you celebrate when the project is complete?

Ideas flow with relative ease compared to getting down to the tasks at hand. Taking action is one of the hardest parts of planning any project. One of the most valuable experiences a student can have is to see a project through from beginning to end. The sense of accomplishment is priceless, and the fact that it has been done once means it can be done again.

When engaging in action planning, it may be useful to have students begin with something they are already involved in, rather than inventing new projects to undertake. In this way, they can integrate this action orientation into their existing lives.

Stating Needs

Part of being independent in an interdependent community is to be able to assess one's own needs and communicate them to others. It may mean asking for help, which can be difficult for some people, but necessary when striking out into new territory. It could take the form of asking someone to stop talking because it distracts from work. It could be asking for advice or encouragement, or asking someone to tell a joke to cheer somebody up.

Needs are often stated in a demanding or angry way. This can occur when people have kept silent until the need is too strong to hold in any longer. It can happen when people are unaware that a need exists until it is at a crisis point. It can also happen when people are not used to having their needs acknowledged by others. A classic example is when someone is up on a high ropes course element and is scared. People are encouraging that person by yelling up to her. Suddenly she yells back, "Shut up!" Under the circumstances, this is a natural reaction – she is scared, and the yelling is only making it worse. Had she been able to anticipate this by reflecting on what she needed in advance by examining her prior experience, she could have stated on the ground, "When I get scared, I need it to be quiet. Yelling encouragement only makes me more scared." In a caring community, students will try to offer what they think the individual needs unless it is communicated differently by the individual.

Time must be spent engaged in self-reflection to become more attuned to personal needs. As teachers, we need to set time aside for students to think, draw, or write, especially if a challenging situation is just around the corner. They can write individual goals to help them put their thoughts into action.

Encouragement/Support

People naturally want to offer encouragement and support to those they care about. So far, it has been a highlight of this community-building process. The students went from focusing on put-ups and put-downs to becoming interdependent when solving problems together. There have been times of celebration and times of frustration. Through it all, they have been encouraging and supportive.

When people begin the process of taking individual risks and stepping outside the community, they tend to focus so much on themselves that class support and encouragement wanes. This is one reason why assessing and stating needs becomes more important, since others aren't always around to ask what individual needs exist. It is important, though, for the community to take time to come together to communicate needs, celebrate successes, and provide support for those individuals who are struggling.

Fear/Anxiety

We began the process with fear and anxiety, and we end with it as well. This is just one cycle in the un-ending spiral. As we come full circle, it is apparent that we are in a different place than when we began. Individuals are no longer approaching anxiety alone; they have a supportive community to help them through it. As they become better at stating needs and setting goals, they develop strategies with which to deal with the fear. Fear is no longer an enemy but a signal that something is happening – a moment of risk taking that, if ridden through, creates a potential for growth.

The challenges are more personal and real now, and the connections to one's life become more apparent. If someone can jump off a pole to hit a bell 30 feet in the air (see p. 227), with a pounding heart and maybe a scream of – relief? delight? – then certainly that same person can write the essay that has been put off again and again, or take that driver's test, or give that speech. Calling merchants to ask for donations for a fund-raiser is intimidating, but the risk is worth the momentary discomfort to reach a stated goal.

Fear and anxiety are not seen as barriers anymore, but as necessary parts of a process. If learning involves risk, then it involves fear. It is all part of the process.

Success/Failure

Much of the risk, fear, and anxiety we face is tied into the concepts of success and failure. Fear of failure can be debilitating. If a task seems overwhelming, it is easier for some people not even to start rather than finish with what they consider an inferior product. Frozen in place, goals are left unmet. When it comes right down to it, though, this is a very personal issue, tied to the experience of a lifetime.

Goal setting, action planning, and stating needs are all strategies to help deal with the issues of success and failure. People must have ways to assess whether they have been successful or not, which is where goal setting comes in. Action planning helps break a larger vision down into more manageable tasks. Stating needs in order to get expertise and support from the community gives people a sense that they are not alone. All of these strategies offer a structure to help people manage success and failure.

Challenge Activities

Role of the Teacher

You are now a consultant. You are part of the community and seen as having a certain expertise, but you are no longer the sole expert. You provide the individuals with a connection to the larger arena and offer suggestions that may be helpful. They can choose to take your advice or not. It is their agenda, not yours, that is the primary focus now.

At this point, it is most important to encourage independence. If students approach you for advice that is readily available to them through other means, help them find the resources. These might include other students, written materials, people outside the community, or even the individual students themselves.

Challenge by Choice makes an overt resurgence now because people are, again, in a place of taking risks. The risks of the past seem minor in comparison to the new challenges ahead. Failure may mean public humiliation or letting oneself down. You can help people determine what types of challenges are appropriate for them by asking pertinent questions and helping them create meaningful goals. You can also provide time for the community to get together in order to meet individual and group needs.

High Ropes Course

A high ropes course is an invaluable tool at the beginning of the Challenge sequence. It is a place where the community can be self-contained while individuals choose their level of risk taking from a variety of elements. These elements are 20 to 40 feet off the ground (or even higher in some cases). Trained personnel provide special equipment (climbing harnesses, ropes, and helmets) in order to ensure a safe experience. When someone is ready to climb, one end of the rope is attached to the climber. The rope goes up through a "shear reduction" system that looks like a pulley, while the other end is fed through a friction device and is held by a "belayer." The belayer is a person who is specially trained to take the slack out of the rope as the participant climbs. If the climber slips, the belayer holds the rope in the friction device to brake the fall. The climber then decides to continue on the element or come down. Climbers are always on belay during these elements, eliminating the risk of anyone taking a significant fall.

Some high ropes course elements require balance, others strength, others just plain guts. As you can imagine, all of them induce anxiety and fear. This is by design. A high ropes course is the perfect place to examine these issues. The safety equipment is state-of-the-art, and training is available to make the experience safe and exciting.

High ropes courses can either be indoors in a gym, or outdoors in trees or on poles. Before contracting with an organization for a ropes course experience, it is prudent to research its history. Make sure it has had a safety inspection within the past year, and determine if its course was built to ACCT (Association for Challenge Course Technology) standards. Ask what kind of training is required for the staff, who provided it, and what qualifications the trainers have. Ask for references from organizations that are similar to yours. For information on ropes courses near you, contact the Association for Experiential Education, Project Adventure, or ACCT (see appendices).

High Ropes Elements and People with Disabilities
In the early years (about 35 years ago) ropes courses were only built for the able-bodied. Any modifications were invented on the spot. Since then, many professionals in the field have focused on changing this. Today elements can be built that are universal – usable by a variety of people, both able- and non-able-bodied. Ask your local ropes course providers if they have universal elements. If not, maybe it's time they had some built.

Following is a representative sample of high ropes course elements. **This book is not a substitute for proper training and does not give you enough information to safely run these activities. If you do not have the proper training, contract with a reputable provider of ropes course services.**

 The Centipede

This element consists of a series of 4' x 4' boards, attached end to end (see figure 7.1). There are attachments for the climber (who is on belay) to use in order to climb as high as she or he chooses. Since the Centipede is only attached at the top, the element swings as the student climbs, making it more difficult.

Some people scamper to the top, while others struggle to make it partway. It is helpful to encourage students to set personal goals for themselves. Later, as they reflect on their climbs, they can assess whether their goals were realistic, if they met their goals, and what motivated them to choose those particular goals. The motivations behind their choices on high ropes course elements tend to mirror their motivations with other challenges in their lives – which can give them insight into how they deal with real-life challenges.

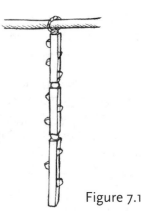

Figure 7.1

Two Line Bridge

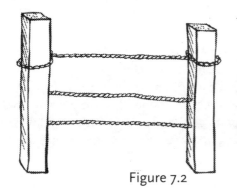

Figure 7.2

The Two Line Bridge (see figure 7.2), also called the Postman's Walk, is less physically strenuous than the Centipede. Participants are on belay and can climb up to the two bottom cables via a ladder or staples in the poles or trees. The task, then, is to traverse the cables, walking on the bottom one, and hanging onto the next one above. The top cable holds the belay system, which is attached to the climber for safety. Since the climber has something to hang onto, this element is a good first try for many.

The Catwalk

The Catwalk is simply a log attached between two trees or poles (see figure 7.3). Sometimes it is set at an angle and is called the High Inclined Log. Most of us have tiptoed along a log on the forest floor. There is a huge difference, however, when that same log is 20 or more feet in the air. The climber goes on belay and gets up to the log via a ladder, staples, or rope ladder. The seemingly simple task of walking across the log takes on a whole new meaning when one is faced with little to hang onto. Many a decision has been made on the Catwalk to push one's limits. These limits are very personal. One person may attempt to cross without touching the belay rope. Others inch out with a firm grip on the rope. Some people dance, do jumping jacks, or walk backwards with their eyes closed. Other people muster up the courage to climb back down.

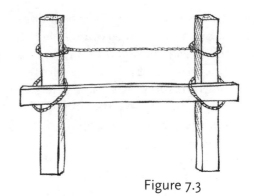

Figure 7.3

It is said that there can be no courage with the absence of fear. The Catwalk embodies this concept. Standing up on the Catwalk gives people much to ponder, philosophically and otherwise.

This element can be designed for two people to share the experience. Together, they help each other across the log, offering advice, encouragement, and a shared sense of accomplishment.

 # Pamper Pole

The Pamper Pole consists of a utility pole stuck in the ground. Participants clip into a belay system, climb the pole, stand on top, and then attempt to dive for something hanging six or more feet away. The object can be a trapeze bar, a bell or ball to hit, or even a bandanna for the taking (see figure 7.4).

Many people describe doing the Pamper Pole as "a rush." It is another place where people make very personal decisions about what they will and will not do. The first choice, of course, is whether or not to even attempt the element. Once made, that choice leads the student to climb the pole. Another decisive moment is reached at the top of the pole. Many people describe this point as the most difficult – how does one get on top of the pole? There is nothing to grab but air when one is at the top. (Climbers are asked not to grab their belay rope.) The climber must now rely on his or her sense of balance, the ability to be calm and centered, and a willingness to push through the fear.

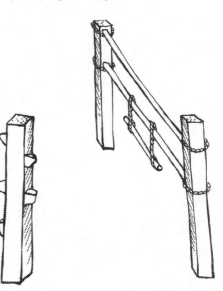

Figure 7.4

Getting on top of the pole can be quite a feat, yet the climber is not done yet. Hanging in front of the climber is a goal (trapeze, bell, etc.). Ask students to name that goal, either out loud or silently. They should name it something that has meaning for them, and which may seem out of reach to them at this point in their lives. When they do jump from the pole, they may or may not reach it. They may not even try to reach it. This metaphor can give people the opportunity to reflect upon those goals in life that may be difficult to achieve. Sometimes we push hard and still do not achieve our goal. Other times we do not even give it our best shot.

The Pamper Pole is a wonderful activity to use toward the end of a ropes course experience. After people have struggled through a myriad of challenges, the class can come together to cheer on each individual as she or he attempts the challenge.

The Fear Occurs Before the Action

High ropes course activities engender fear and anxiety. Since these experiences are designed to offer safe places for people to challenge themselves, this element of fear must be acknowledged. Although each person will deal with it in a different way, there seems to be a universal reaction to fear in the sweaty palms, dry mouth, and butterflies we all experience. Once action is taken, the fear ebbs. The moment of truth for us all is at that decision point.

This phenomenon is clearly seen at the top of the Pamper Pole and on the Zip Line platform. The individual must choose a course of action – to jump or not. For most, the moment passes quickly. A decision is made, and action taken in a moment or two. For some, it is all but debilitating. Frozen in indecision, they can wait 15 minutes or more before acting.

When someone becomes stuck in indecision, it can tax the patience of both the students and teacher. Patience, though, is the key. A decision must be made because it is the only way for the student to get down. The student is given options: climb down or jump. No matter what the decision is, a powerful lesson has been learned.

Zip Line

Since the ride is so exciting, the Zip Line is an element that many will try even if they have chosen to observe for the rest of the day. Once a student goes on belay and climbs up to the platform, he or she is clipped into a pulley that is attached to the cable (see figure 7.5). When ready, this person communicates with a team of people who are prepared to help him or her off the cable and disembarks from the platform. The resulting ride can be quite exhilarating.

Figure 7.5

Lessons to Be Learned

As with much of this process, the high ropes course gives students opportunities. What each individual student does with those opportunities is a significant part of the process. A ropes course experience is a safe and powerful metaphor for how one travels through life. It gives people the chance to explore their hearts, minds, and spirits. The lessons they learn and the insights they gain can help each person travel her or his path with a bit more focus and direction. It encourages students to make choices which, in turn, help them to embrace and trust their decision-making abilities. The result is an increased sense of confidence.

Outdoor Pursuits

Another way to begin the challenge sequence is through outdoor pursuits like snowshoeing, cross-country skiing, rock climbing, canoeing, kayaking, caving, or hiking. Given the time and resources, these endeavors can even be turned into extended trips in the back country.

In general, many people have not spent much time engaged in these types of activities. The novelty of the experience, along with the focus on getting basic needs met, can be the cause for much excitement and anxiety. Questions about where to go to the bathroom, how much effort it takes to get from one place to another, and what to do about insects or the cold inevitably come up. This is part of the adventure — not to know what is going to happen next. A class must be ready to undertake a trek into the wilderness, even if the "wilderness" is the county park. Everyone must deal with different levels of anxiety, set individual goals, receive and offer support to other students.

Any time we take students into the great outdoors, it is our responsibility to teach stewardship. In this way we do not perpetuate the notion that the natural world is just another resource to be used. The following are revised **Leave No Trace Principles** developed by the Leave No Trace organization.*

1. Plan ahead and prepare
2. Travel and camp on durable surfaces
3. Dispose of waste properly
4. Leave what you find
5. Minimize campfire impacts
6. Respect wildlife
7. Be considerate of other visitors

Along with the outdoor experiences comes the notion of stewardship. This is a perfect time to connect the experience of community to the larger realm of the environment. When people are out on the trail, they can learn about minimum-impact camping, keeping the area clean by picking up trash, observing plants and ani-

---

* Leave No Trace can be contacted at 800-332-4100 for more information, along with educational materials.

mals in their natural environment without molesting them, using water wisely, and how to dispose of (or carry out) waste to keep the environment clean. Being in the wilderness allows students to learn about the connections among all types of communities.

When choosing the outdoor experience, you must take into account your own level of expertise. If necessary, contract with an organization that specializes in the particular outdoor pursuit your class is interested in undertaking. Organizations that run ropes courses often offer outdoor pursuit activities, or they can offer suggestions in your area. Check with the nearest outdoor equipment store; look in magazines that specialize in your area of interest. The world is out there, and the expertise is available. It is your responsibility to make sure that your outdoor experience is undertaken in a safe manner, which means involving people with the necessary equipment and qualifications.

> **What Are We Teaching?**
>
> Climbing down into the earth is a unique experience. Caves are amazing places that are homes to bats, long-lived rock formations, tunnels, and absolute darkness. If one really wants to know what if feels like to be alone, sit in the dark in a cave.
>
> There is a cave in Wisconsin that has been used by groups for two decades. At first, a few groups would enter it every year, exploring its nooks and crannies and sharing the sparks of Wintergreen Lifesavers™ in the dark together. Today, literally hundreds of groups make the trek up to the cave every year.
>
> Some of these groups are more prepared than others. I have seen 30 kids run up the hill, widening the trail, trampling flowers, and causing unnecessary erosion. I have seen groups with only a few light sources and no helmets, putting themselves at risk for injury in an unfamiliar place. I have seen bats knocked from the ceiling during hibernation and left to die.
>
> I have also witnessed small groups carefully winding their way up the path, taking the switchback so that the erosion stays with the path. I have seen groups prepared with helmets and a light source for every person – and extra supplies in a backpack, which also contains the first aid kit. I have listened to guides instruct students to feel free to look at the bats and rock formations without touching them, to leave them in their natural state. I have watched as people haul trash from the cave.
>
> Before we head out to the wilderness, we must ask ourselves what it is that we are teaching. Running through a cave with no respect or concern for the habitat, or even for personal safety, is a dangerous lesson. It runs counter to everything that the word community stands for. Part of learning about community means learning about connections to the larger communities of which we are all part, whether it is the larger environment, a neighborhood, or the world.
>
> If you are looking for a place that is exciting, where people can run around at will without regard to noise, and where people are hired to clean up the mess, you may be looking for an amusement park.

Urban Experience

Many times there is no need to take a trek into the wild; it is only a matter of opening the front door. The city wilderness can be as exciting, challenging, and novel as a whitewater rafting trip. Even a small town has much to offer a class that is willing to explore.

An urban experience can be designed to meet the age and maturity level of any class. Even very young children can go out in small groups with an adult chaperone to explore parts of the neighborhoods where they have never been. Searches are explorations of one's community. They can begin in the school itself, then branch out to the larger community. Some look like scavenger hunts, with lists of things to find, while others are more open-ended. Depending on the age of the students, and the targeted skills, any number of searches can be devised. Once students understand the concept, they can create questions to be answered about their school, neighborhood, or larger community.

Here are two examples of searches for the City of Madison, Wisconsin. One is meant for younger students, while the other is geared toward older students.

Urban Experience: City-County Building

Students in grade 2 through 6 get on a city bus. Each group of three to four students, along with an adult who is there just for safety, gets off the bus at a designated stop. From there, they are given a camera (if possible) and a sheet of paper with a series of questions. How they find the answers is up to them.

1. Find the City-County Building. Write down the address.
2. Find the mayor's office. Ask for his or her signature if there, or get the secretary's signature. Take a picture of yourselves in the mayor's office (with the mayor, if possible).
3. Find the Common Council Office. (Make a drawing to show how you got from the mayor's office to the Common Council Office.)
4. Ask for the signature of one of the secretaries.
5. Who is the alderperson for your school?
6. What is an alderperson?
7. On what floor is the jail located?
8. Who is the County Executive? Where does he or she work? What is his or her job?
9. Find the Department of Public Works.
10. Ask for Marilyn's signature at the department of Public Works. What is her job? (Draw a picture of Marilyn.)
11. What do the people in the Department of Public Works do?
12. Find the Municipal Building. There is a statue in front of this building. Who is it? (Take a picture of the statue.)
13. Find the Transportation Department.
14. Inside you will find the Bike Safety Coordinator for the City of Madison. What is his name? What does he do? Ask for his business card to prove you were there.
15. Ask 10 people what they think is the best thing about Madison.
16. What is located at 107 State Street?
17. Perform an act of kindness. Your group must decide what it should be. Describe what you did. (Take pictures of your act of kindness, if possible.)
18. Find the Memorial Union and meet in the lobby by 1:15.

NOTE: If you finish early and have finished lunch, brainstorm with your group members a fun thing to do and report what you did to the class later. Make sure to collect things as you go along. They may come in handy when trying to explain how your day went!

Facilitation Notes

After a city search, students return with brochures, pictures, drawings, and other items they collected along the way. Many of the people they visit give them magnets, business cards, pencils, stickers, and buttons. The students prepare a multimedia presentation for the class, which may include songs, poems, skits, PowerPoint, collages, etc. They also write about their experiences. This experience can be built into larger units on government and social studies.

Each group has an adult along who watches out for safety and helps them sort through conflicts and frustration. Many times parents go along and have as much fun as the students. It is important to emphasize to the adults that the process is as important as the product. Encourage the adults to intervene only when necessary, being careful not to supply answers.

These city searches do take a fair amount of preparation. Although these are public places, it is necessary to visit every site and talk to the people who will be approached by the students. Usually these folks are very willing to chat with the small groups that come to visit, especially since each class has about six to eight groups going to different places so that each official is dealing with only one small group. It is good practice to check in with them in advance so that they know groups of students will be coming around during the next week or two. If they do not wish to meet with the students, then they can voice that, and the students can go somewhere else.

Once the search is set, it can be reused every year, with only a small amount of follow-up. Every town has its share of history and interesting sites, yet it is surprising how little many of us know about the communities in which we live. Some other searches used in Madison are: state historical museum, the state capitol (including the supreme court, governor's office, and state legislature), public library, civic center, city convention center, senior center, many sites on the university campus (geology museum, student union, athletic facilities, dairy sciences), and the school district administration building.

Preparation with the students is essential. Discussions and role plays about whom to approach for help, and how, are necessary. Help students identify who is safe to approach for directions. Teach young students how to ask for help from someone they do not know. Here is a six-step process:

1. Say "excuse me" to get the person's attention.
2. Tell them what you are doing. Say something like, "We're on a field trip for school."
3. Ask them your question.
4. Wait and listen for the answer.
5. Repeat the answer to make sure you heard correctly.
6. Say "thank you."

I once accompanied a group of 5th-graders on **an urban experience** in Madison. Our task was to visit the South Union at the university, Camp Randall Stadium, and the geology museum on campus. After they found the union, and we explored that for a bit, we stepped outside. In front of us was the tallest building around – the meteorology building. Two of the students had never been in a building that had more than two floors, so they said, "Let's go to the top!"

That's exactly where we went. As we entered the building, they spent some time pushing the buttons on the computer in the lobby and looking at the different satellite pictures. Then we hopped in the elevator. This was the first time these two had ever been in an elevator, and it was wonderful to relive this experience through their eyes.

The doors opened on the top floor, and we stepped out into a hallway with a bunch of offices. They were looking for a door to the roof, and they stopped at an office where someone was working. They knocked politely and asked the man inside if he could show them the way to the roof. Surprisingly, this man dropped everything and took us straight to the roof. He showed us the views and then offered to give us a tour of the building. What a treat. It turned out he was the chair of the meteorology department, and we all learned more about weather in that hour than many learn in a lifetime.

We never did make it to the geology museum. It didn't matter. The exploration by these students turned the day into a great adventure, and the learning was invaluable on many levels. It was a day we would never forget.

Many times young students run up to someone, ask the question, and leave without hearing the response. Much of this is due to anxiety, and role-play practice can be quite helpful.

Community Exploration

This exploration was written for high-school students. The main focus was an extension of the community-building and problem solving that they had done as a class. Give your students instructions like those that follow.

You and your base team are to go into the community. You have a variety of tasks:
1. *Create a challenge* for yourselves. (e.g., Talk to someone for 10 minutes, go to a place you normally wouldn't go and interview people – like a government building or a senior center.)
2. Discover an *unknown resource* – something that will be of use to you.
3. Perform an *act of kindness*.
4. *Interview 20 people* re: What do they think are the biggest problems facing our schools and how do they propose solving them?
5. *Create a skit* depicting your day. Present it to the whole group during the next class session.

What do you want to get out of this experience?
A. Write down a personal goal for each person in the group.
B. Develop a group goal for the community exploration. What do you, as a group, wish to get out of this?
C. What is your challenge?

Debrief. To be done at the end of the experience.
What? Discuss what happened during the experience. What was the hardest thing you did? The scariest? The most rewarding? What did you do together that made the tasks easier/harder? Describe any surprises or anecdotes about the day. Review your goals. Did you accomplish them?

So what? What does this mean? Why might some things have happened the way they did? How did you handle difficult situations as a team (or not handle them)? Why was this? What caused you to accomplish/not accomplish your goals?

Now what? What can we take from this experience? Did you learn anything about yourself and/or your partners? Do you have any new goals that grew from this experience?

Facilitation Notes
A community exploration can take many forms and have many focuses. If the students have been studying government, for example, the search can be geared toward finding resources within the town or city that use town, city, state, or federal funding. How might one register a vehicle? To whom does one report a stolen bike? Students can generate a list of questions, then search for the answers in their own communities.

Public Presentations and Projects

Small groups can be assembled within the class to design projects that are connected to academics or community service.* The object here is to plan and carry out the project so that it has some benefit outside the classroom community. Examples include:
- Fund-raising for a community organization.
- Organizing snow shoveling and raking for elderly neighborhood residents.
- Designing an orientation program for newcomers to the school.

---

* See the *Kid's Guide to Service Projects* by Barbara A. Lewis for over 500 service ideas.

- Testing a nearby water source for pollution and reporting the results to the city council.
- Cleaning up a nearby park.
- Researching and designing new playground equipment for the neighborhood.
- Compiling oral histories from longtime neighborhood residents.
- Mapping the area to include highlights and things for visitors to do.

In Exploring Issues of Diversity, Consider Projects Like:

- Taping and sharing stories from relatives about family traditions.
- Interviewing a variety of people from the neighborhood and compiling these stories into a book.
- Visiting various places of worship.
- Exchanging with others in the school – go to dinner at their houses, invite them to yours.
- E-mailing and becoming pen pals with people further away.
- Researching and arranging for local speakers on topics of interest that have to do with equal opportunities, civil rights, or cultural awareness.

There is a 4th-grade class at Lincoln Elementary School in Madison, Wisconsin that goes on an expedition every year. Since Wisconsin history is part of the curriculum, Dave Spitzer helps the students design a trek through Wisconsin. They research Wisconsin history, make contacts with people, and create their own textbooks. Then they're off for a week on a bus, visiting small towns, historical sites, and other schools. They sleep on gym floors and are welcomed into the homes of gracious hosts. One year, the city kids from Madison visited a veal farm in Brillion, a Menominee tribal school in Keshena, and the Green Bay Packer Hall of Fame as part of their trip.

The list is endless; it is only limited by the imaginations of your students. Resources, of course, also play a role in what can actually be done.

Summary: Where to Go From Here?

This class of individuals has gone from being dependent on you to becoming independent. They understand interdependence and collaboration because they do it. They have ownership in their community because each of them is a vital part of it. If even one of them leaves, the community is changed. They have arrived at this place over a winding path that has included some tears, joy, frustration, laughter, and struggle. No matter where these individuals go, the experience of community stays with them. They carry along a feelings vocabulary and conflict-resolution skills. They have experienced empathy and trust. Because they have experienced it, they can now duplicate it in other parts of their lives. This is one step in a very long journey, but it creates hope and optimism. It is one leg of the *journey toward the caring classroom*.

Your equipment bag now contains a compass and a map. These may get you where you want to go, but not in one piece. Your pack still needs provisions to take care of daily needs. This section addresses how to structure adventure activities to create community.

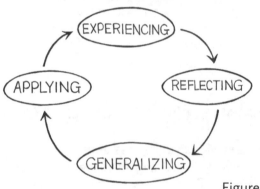 Shaping an Adventure Program

How activities are presented is usually more important than the activity itself. Clifford Knapp shares that "direct experience is not enough. If such experiences are to be meaningful and applied to life situations, teachers must help students learn from carefully planned and guided reflection sessions."[1] A discussion about formulating an adventure program means we must revisit the Experiential Learning Cycle (figure 8.1).

As discussed earlier, the Experiential Learning Cycle is an integral part of experiential education. Kolb created this basic model in the mid-1980s to represent an innate process in which people learn from experience. Without it, learning would consist of one activity after another with nothing to hold the experiences together. People may or may not gain insight from the experiences, and they may or may not find them useful.

Figure 8.1

The cycle begins with an **experience**. This can be one occurring naturally in the environment, or in the case of formal education, it can be a contrived experience chosen to meet certain goals or address certain issues. For example, when a group gets together for the first time, an Ice Breaker activity is chosen because the goals of the group include meeting each other. If left to chance, people may or may not get to know each other (witness many college level classes where, even after months together, it is possible not to know anybody's name in the entire class).

After an experience, people are given an opportunity to **reflect** upon the experience. This can involve quiet time, discussion, writing, drawing, working with clay, etc. People can look back on what they did, thought, saw, and how they behaved. At this point, the process has turned into experiential learning.

The experience, however, is still one in isolation unless people take time to **generalize** how this experience relates to others. They should look at prior experiences and see how this one measures up. For example, are there patterns in their behavior or in how they approached a risk-taking situation? Is there new information on which this experience can connect? This is the search for meaning.

Finally, people are asked to look for insights that **apply** to their real life or make sense when working with this particular group on the next activity. While the other parts of the cycle are concerned with the present and past, this one brings the future into the picture. Participants are asked to consider how learning from this experience, in combination with past experiences and new information, can impact their lives in the future. In this way, learning is incorporated into a whole mural, rather than a painting hanging on an otherwise empty wall.

The group now will put to use the learning of the last experience into a new experience, thus starting the next spiral in the cycle.

The Experiential Learning Cycle in action might look something like this:

Activity
A group of 6th-graders has been working on issues around problem solving. They have just completed the problem-solving initiative Marshmallow River, where they had to get the group across a 20-foot span using only small boards. No one was allowed to touch the ground. The group members argued about strategy; some people talked loudly, while others were silent. After having to start over five times because someone stepped off a board, the group finally started holding hands to steady each other and completed the task.

Reflection
The group members were asked to think of one word or perform one action that described how they felt during the activity. Everyone was given time to think. They held up a thumb to indicate they were ready. When everyone was ready, students went around the group to see or hear what people had come up with. Words were thrown out such as frustrated, confident, left out, stressed, confused. One boy showed what he felt by putting his hands over his face, and a few people passed.

Next, students were asked to share why they chose that word or action. One person shared that she was confused because everyone was talking at once, and she felt that she was not part of the decision. "I wasn't really sure about what to do, which is why I kept messing up. I felt kind of stupid." "Yeah," said another, "I said 'left out' because I couldn't get a word in at all. I just went along so that we could finish the job."

Generalizing
After sharing feelings and thoughts around this activity, the group was asked to look back at other activities to see how they handled this one in comparison. One student noticed that they were still having trouble communicating. "We kept yelling instead of talking, and it seemed like the same people were making all the decisions." Others agreed, even those who had occupied most of the airtime during the activities. They, too, were tired of the inefficiency.

At this point the facilitator introduced a concept called "the rule of loud." She explained that it was common for people in groups to use this rule when trying to work together. The problem, though, was that it allowed only the people with the loudest voices to be heard. Some people were left out of decision making when this rule was being used, and many times group members were confused about what to do because there were many ideas being discussed at the same time. She concluded with a comment that there were more efficient ways to communicate when working together.

Application
Finally, the group members were asked to glean gems of knowledge or insight from what just occurred. One person said, "I think we should take time to plan as a whole group before we start doing something." Another chimed in with, "Let's stand in a circle so we can see everyone." One of the louder group members said, "I'm not going to be the first person to talk next time and let others have a chance."

Experience
Given the previous discussion, the facilitator chose to do the activity Balloon Frantic because it required planning and discussion. She reminded the class about the "rule of loud" and the strategies they discussed after the last activity. The learning from the previous activities was blended into the next in the continuing spiral of the Experiential Learning Cycle.

 Processing

Processing is a process. It refers to an "activity that is structured to encourage individuals to plan, reflect, describe, analyze, and communicate about experiences."[2] Processing can occur at any time before, during, or after the experience. We do not do these activities just so people will know what to do if they are walking around in the woods and happen to find an oversized spider web hanging there. The Experiential Learning Cycle provides for the application, or transfer, of learning to participants' lives. Processing is the vehicle with which to accomplish the transfer.

Michael Gass discusses three theories of transfer in Adventure Education: specific, nonspecific, and metaphoric. Specific transfer is directly related to learning skills, such as climbing on a ropes course in order to help someone learn rock climbing skills, or the connection between learning how to belay and learning how to rappel. Nonspecific transfer is connected more with attitudes or beliefs. An example would be when someone explores leadership skills during a group Problem-Solving initiative, then transfers those leadership skills back to the school setting. Metaphoric transfer is the most abstract; people glean the essential principles from a learning situation, then transfer them to a seemingly unrelated environment – thus using the specific learning situation as a metaphor for more general learning. After working together to get across the cable event called Walk of Life and learning that it cannot be done alone, participants are able to ask for help in other parts of their lives.[3]

All of these types of transfer can occur in Adventure Education. It is processing that helps participants make the connections. Sometimes the participants themselves will share these moments of insight. At other times, the facilitator creates this fertile ground by introducing activities with ready-made metaphors. This is known as *framing*, or frontloading, the metaphors. In the Marshmallow River activity, for example, students are told that their task is to help everyone graduate. The area between the boundaries represents their time in school together, and the boards represent the tools, resources, and support they have to help everyone get to graduation. In this way processing can focus on how they helped each other across the pretend river, and then discussion can turn toward the very real journey they have together in school. What tools, resources, and support can they use, and what can they give to others to help everyone graduate?

One way to structure activities is to use a model called the Adventure Wave (see figure 8.2). The Adventure Wave is the core structure of Adventure-Based Counseling as described in *Islands of Healing*.[4]

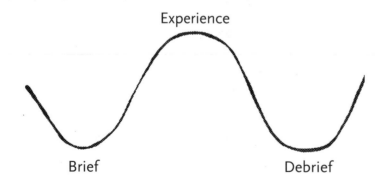

Figure 8.2: The Adventure Wave

 Briefing

- Describe the activity (this is the time to frontload a story or metaphor to go with the activity, if you have one to share).
- State any rules.
- Cover all safety considerations.
- Answer questions.

If you forget something, it will become obvious in a very short time. When this occurs, you have two choices:

1. Stop the activity and clarify.
2. Go with it.

Just remember that if you choose to change the rules in the middle of an activity, you may have a mutiny on your hands. If your omission has made the activity easy for the group, you can let it go. When students have finished, ask them to do the activity again with the additional rules.

Although uncomfortable, this mutinous situation offers grist for the debriefing mill. It may allow both you and the group members to understand more clearly the power structure in the group. It may provoke changes that benefit everyone. Of course, if there is a safety issue, always stop and clarify.

Experience

Where the group is in the sequence dictates your role as facilitator. If you are just starting out, your role may be more assertive and directive. As things progress and students can assume more control of events, your role may be more of an observer, mediator, or clarifier. A guideline is to give the group as much control over their destiny as possible. If they end up in a situation they cannot handle, it is time to process and analyze what is (or what is not) going on. These are the moments of insight that allow people to make choices about their behavior. Once awareness is raised, people are operating from a vantage point of understanding.

Debriefing

After an activity is a natural time to reflect upon or debrief the what, why, and how of things. It is a time for asking questions, and maybe answering some of them. Many times we leave a debriefing session with more questions to ponder. It is the stuff of growth. Here is one model for structuring a debriefing session:

What?
So What?
Now What?

What? So what? Now what? comes from Terry Borton as quoted in Clifford Knapp's book, *The Art and Science of Processing Experience*, pp. 6-7. *Islands of Healing* and its sequel *Exploring Islands of Healing,* both utilize this structure as a method of exploring the debriefing experience. It is utilized for "sequence" debriefing, which gives the debrief structure. As you will see, this structure helps us use the Experiential Learning Cycle to greater advantage.

What?

What happened? Everyone in the class will have a different perspective. Some heard put-downs, others heard only put-ups. Some were left out, while others were too busy to notice. Some were active participants, others observers. Every perspective is valid. The "what" gives everyone a chance to state a perspective. Some people naturally skip this step because they are already generalizing the experience, or even looking at how it transfers. However, it is important to maintain this part of the debrief in order to allow those who need the reflection time the opportunity to have their needs met.

This is the beginning of reflecting on the experience. It is common to see a group of students who have difficulty articulating what they have just experienced. Since the class contains a variety of people with a variety of processing styles, it is important to offer differing strategies with which to reflect. Holding an outright discussion is great for the verbal folks, but what about those who process best through artwork, are kinesthetic by nature, or would rather write? Mix it up. Here are a variety of reflection methods.

Reflection ("What") Strategies

Some of these strategies can take a few seconds, while others might require longer periods of time for reflection. Using a range of times and a variety of reflection approaches will not only keep it interesting but will create opportunities for richer and deeper exploration of experience.

It is common for a group to get into a routine of doing an activity and then settling into a circle for a large group discussion. Some people will be uncomfortable sharing in a large group and appreciate an opportunity to share in a smaller group setting. Consider using a variety of formats:

Whole Group: Discussion and sharing as individuals with the whole group.

Small Group: Discussion and sharing with a small group. Information can then be summarized or shared with the larger group, but this is not always necessary.

Pairs: Students discuss, create, and share with a partner.

Individual: Students write in journals, reflect on goals, or think about a question. This format is especially helpful for those with high intrapersonal skills.

Ratings

Create ways for students to rate activities. How do the students think the group worked together? If you are focusing on caring, for example, how well do you think you, as an individual, showed caring for yourself and others? Notice the ratings of each student. You can then ask them to share why they rated it the way they did. Depending on the age and experience of your students, you can choose from a variety of rating styles:

Thumbs up, thumbs down: Rate how we did with a thumbs up, thumbs down, or thumbs halfway sign. Say why you rated it that way.

Happy face, neutral face, sad face: Draw a happy face, a neutral face, and a sad face on the board. Ask students to choose one that described how they felt they did.

Faces with numbers attached (1–3): Add numbers under the happy, neutral, or sad face. Ask participants to rate according to the number. This is a nice transition for young students to help them connect the faces with numbers. Later you can do away with the faces and simply ask them for numbers.

Choose a number: Choose a number from 1 to 3, 1 to 5, or 1 to 10 to rate how they feel they did.

Ruler: Have a ruler to pass around. Each student can show how they rate the activity by touching a number and sharing why they touched that number. You can do the same with a thermometer.

How's the weather?: Have pictures of a sun, a sun with a cloud over it, and a storm cloud. Pass them around and have each student choose the one closest to how they think they did.

Words and Drawings

Words and drawing can be used in a variety of ways to reflect upon experience. Here are some examples:

Journals: Write or draw about one's experience in a personal or group journal.

Feelings Cards: For younger students, lay out 5 to 10 feelings cards. Have them each choose one to describe their experience and explain why they chose it. For older students, lay out as many cards as you have. Ask them to choose one or more to describe their experience, and then share what they chose. They can be used in a variety of ways. Spread them out on the floor, and have people choose one to three cards describing their emotions during an activity. Do a round-robin or volunteer to give people a chance to show and tell. Another strategy is to pass out three cards to every person. Then give them a few moments to trade cards with others before they share their cards with the group. It's also fun to play emotion charades with these cards. Feelings cards can be homemade or purchased.

QRAI Cards: This is a set of 350 ready-to-use Quality and Role cards created by Al Katz. Quality cards include words like: *overcoming obstacles, understanding others,* and *making fun of others.* Role cards have words such as: *victim, learner,* and *passive.* These cards are a wonderful tool for use with older students to encourage them to think about the roles and styles that people take on within a group.

Think/Pair/Share: Have students partner up and think about a posed question. Discuss the question with their partners and share about their discussion with the larger group.

Historical Mural: Have a large piece of butcher paper available. Give students some time to draw on a part of it to document their experience. They can share what they drew. Roll it up and bring it out periodically to document another experience. In this way, they can compare a series of experiences and see where they have come as a group.

Full Value Contract: Use your Full Value Contract as a processing tool. Use it to reflect upon a given activity, or every now and again check in with the class to see how they think they are doing with the words and ideals that are expressed in their contract. Encourage students to take sticky notes and write a comment about one or more of the parts of the Full Value Contract during class. They can stick it up next to the word it relates to. Later, you can check in to see what was written and talk about it as a class (thanks to Nancy Stratton for this idea).

Poetry: T. A. Loeffler once had a group create haiku poems as a reflection for a workshop. The creations and sharing were stunning. Working in pairs to create a poem encourages deeper discussion about what happened.

Metaphorical

Any time we use pictures, toys, stuffed animals, etc. to represent an experience, thought, or a feeling, it is a metaphorical moment.

Picture Cards/Post Cards: Collect postcards (remember to laminate them!) or buy a set of picture cards. Have students choose one or more cards to represent how they felt, what they thought about, or how they experienced the activity. Of course, you can put out word cards and picture cards at the same time ....

Chiji Cards: Created by the folks at the Institute for Experiential Education, these are a playing card-sized deck of cards with a variety of pictures on them.

Body Parts: Show pictures of a heart, brain, hand, ear, etc., or get the bag of squishy body parts developed by Michelle Cummings. Pull out the brain and ask students to pass it around and say something they thought about during the activity, or pass the ear and eye to find out about what they heard and saw. Pass the hand to learn about how people felt supported or helped others ....

Play Food: Every toy store has play food. Get a cart-full and spread them out. Ask students to choose food to describe their experience. Some may choose the makings of a sandwich to show how people worked well together, others may choose the ice-cream cone because people were "sweet," and another may choose the hot dog because they thought someone was showing off ....

Boxes: Credit goes to Floyd Asonwha for this idea. He noticed that food boxes seem to have an abundance of adjectives and pictures. He cut out the words and pictures to use as reflection tools. Not only are they useful, but easy to replace.

Stuffed Animals: What to do with all those little stuffed toys someone in your household used to collect? They're wonderful reflection tools! Put them out and ask students to choose one or more that represent how they participated in a given activity. You can begin the class with students choosing an animal to represent how they hope the class will go for them. At the end check in to see if they would still choose the same animal, or if things have changed for them.

Art-Related

Some people express themselves well through media such as musical, visual, and dramatic arts. Your more verbal students may be confused about where to begin at first. Of course, this is what your more artistic students experience during the talking circle ....

Drawings: Have students draw their experience and share.

Group Murals: Similar to historical murals, but more group-focused, this strategy entails bringing out large pieces of paper. Small groups work together to depict their version of what happened. Small groups then share with the whole class.

Sculptures: Use clay, pipe cleaners, Legos™, building blocks, etc. to create a sculpture to represent an individual, pair, or small group experience.

Performance: Create a rap, song, chant, or skit related to what happened.

Collages: Create a collage to show feelings and thoughts about an experience, or a series of experiences.

Creation: Provide clay/paper/scissors/pipe cleaners, etc. Give everyone a chance to sculpt/draw/paste together something that represents how they think the group did or how they felt during an activity, etc. Then give them an opportunity to describe it to the group.

Activities

As we have seen above, reflection can be an activity in and of itself.

The Round-Robin/Whip/Go Around: Give everyone a chance to say one thing by "whipping" around the circle. For example: "Say one thing that you saw or did during that activity," or "Give one word about how you felt during that activity." Everyone has a chance to say something or pass. My recent favorite thing to pass is a "Giggle" ball. This is actually a toy you can find at pet stores. When rolled, it makes a random giggle noise. Students of all ages love it and are happy to hold it still while they talk (sometimes with a reminder or two).

The Snapshot: Tell the group that there are a whole stack of photos laid out in front of them that were taken of them during the activity. If they were allowed to take only one picture home with them to put on their wall or refrigerator, what would it be? Do a round robin or volunteers.

Crumpled Paper: Give everyone an identical piece of paper and a pen (no pencils, they smear). Ask them to write how they think the activity went, or how they feel, or how they think things are going. It can also be totally

A Talking Circle * offers everyone an opportunity to share. The group sits in a circle and an item is chosen to designate the speaker. If the item has meaning, all the better. People are asked to speak from the heart and listen from the heart. When a person has the item, s/he can choose to sit silently, speak, or simply pass the item on. Everyone else is silent and listens. The item can go around more than once if there is time.

A talking circle can address specific or open-ended question. It is also invaluable if a group is having difficulty. Maybe there's a white elephant in the room that nobody wants to talk about. Convene a talking circle. Many times, the issues will come out.

Dan Creely, who uses a talking circle extensively in his work, says, "This is the most powerful tool I use. A very, very powerful processing tool." He has some suggestions:

• Use an object that has meaning to you. Tell the story of the object, and it will receive respect from the students.

• After each student is done talking he or she says "thank you," and the group responds with "thank you." It is a chance to honor what has been shared.

• Add a candle to the circle. Students know that when the candle is lit, what we talk about is important (from *Calling the Circle* by Christina Brown).

---

* Thanks to Dorothy Davids for teaching me about talking circles.

open-ended – "Write anything you want about the group." Then crumple them up, throw them in a can/hat/bowl, and mix them up. Everyone takes one and reads it aloud to the group. This is done anonymously. If someone gets their own, they read it anyway.

Make sure to offer this method of reflection at a time when it is possible to address issues that come up. Since it is anonymous, people may feel freer to vent. If you have 5 minutes at the end of the day, and someone puts down another person in the group, it does not give the group members time to deal with it. Another strategy is to structure your questions with the caution about keeping the thoughts free of put-downs, and asking students not to use anyone's name in their writing.

The Bouncing Ball: The group stands in a circle. A ball is used to bounce around the circle at random. It can be bounced to anyone. If they have something to say (either in general or to a specific question) they say it, or they say "pass."

Balloons: Give everyone a balloon and indelible marker. They draw a face on the balloon in regard to how they think things went, how they felt, etc. Paper plates can also be used. They can present it to the group.

The Magic Circle: Everyone gets really close in a circle. Shuffle to the right. Someone says "stop" and says one quick thing about how things went. Then shuffle to the left until someone says "stop" and says something that happened. Keep going until people run out of things to say, or you run out of time.

Anticipation/Result: Before a particularly difficult challenge or task, have the group write down on a card what they anticipate the activity to be like. After they finish have them write on the other side of the card what it was really like. Share, compare, and discuss.

Beach Ball: Write questions on a beach ball, such as: "Something that went well," or "Someone who showed leadership and why." Throw the ball to whoever wants it. Each person answers whichever question is closest to them.

Journals are great tools for processing. It is helpful to have three different journals:

- One that is public, where everyone knows that what they write will be shared with the group
- One that is between student and teacher only, where students can communicate with the teacher in private, and share journal entries with the class only with permission from the author.
- One that is absolutely private. The writing only gets shared if the author chooses to do so.

Have students create their journals. Offer books of quotes so that people can embellish their journals with words of wisdom from those who have gone before them. Whenever there is formal journal writing time, allow students to choose which journal to write in. Store the private journals in a locked cabinet to ensure privacy, but have the public ones out for people to read at their leisure.

Dice: Same as beach ball, but people roll dice to get a question that corresponds with the number.

So What?

Once students have had an opportunity to establish the "what," it is time to search for the patterns. These areas of discussion come from the "what." If someone saw something particularly good, it is time to explore that. For example, if someone said in a round-robin, "We were all included," you might ask, "What caused us to be included?" It may sound like an odd question, but there is a reason for it; it usually means that everyone felt the activity was important and did something to make it happen. Other questions might include, "Do all of you always feel included? Where/how do you feel included or not included?" Explore it, mess with it, bat it around.

Another example of using the "what" to lead the "so what" would be when using the balloons strategy. After observing all of the balloon faces, you might say, "I see that there are quite a few sad faces. What do you think caused so many people to draw sad faces?" The students can come up with reasons, and explore why people may have felt sad. It may be that people were being put down, or one person took over and wouldn't listen to any other ideas. Maybe the task was frustrating. A follow-up question might be: "How could we have done this activity differently so that people could feel better about it?" All of these "so whats" lead to the next stage.

Now What?

After the class has reflected and spent time putting this activity into context with other experiences, it is helpful to bring some sort of closure to a discussion by exploring ways to put the "so what" into action in real life. For example a "now what" response to the balloon situation could be, "What can we do to make people feel included in our group when we're doing something else – like math or recess or physical education?" The students can then brainstorm ways to include people. This moves them much closer to putting these ideas into action. Once articulated, thoughts become real possibilities. In the case of the sad balloons, the "now what" could be, "How can we make sure everyone's ideas are heard from now on?" or "How can we handle frustration without putting ourselves or other people down?" In this way, people can transfer the learning from this experience to the rest of their lives.

It is the act of processing that allows students to learn from their actions – and from each other. It is what differentiates the community-building process from pure recreation. When engaged in recreational activities, individuals have the opportunity to learn from their experiences. When participating in a community-building process, individuals consciously try to learn from their experiences, and then apply their learning to the next activity – hence the wave. When joined together, these waves facilitate the continuation of learning from one activity to another (figure 8.3).

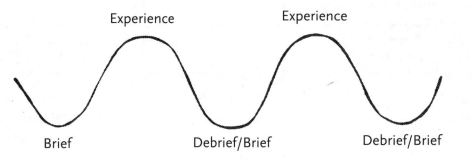

Figure 8.3

The Adventure Wave, then, fits into the experiential learning cycle in this way:

Experiential Learning Cycle and Adventure Wave

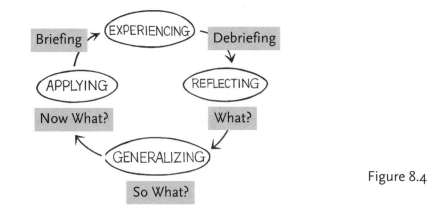

Figure 8.4

Finally, if we put all of the models together (figure 8.5), the Experiential Learning Cycle actually gives the Adventure Wave its energy (thanks to Jim School for this concept).

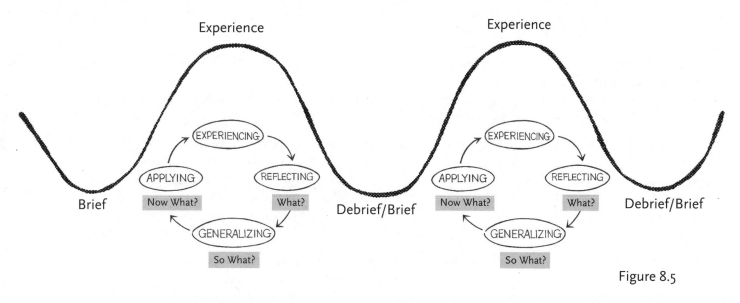

Figure 8.5

In its pure form, people have experiences, process the experiences through reflection ("what"), generalization ("so what"), and application ("now what"). This process then leads to the next experience. As with any model, this snapshot may or may not depict reality at any given time. It does, however, give us a tool with which to structure experiences to intentionally maximize learning.

Debriefing Strategies

Debriefing is a process by which one idea leads to another. There is no one right way to go through a debriefing session. Facilitators must consider their own style, the reason the group was formed, developmental level of the group, time available, and experience level. Given these factors, here are a few guidelines:

If an issue is not dealt with, it will come back: Sometimes there are too many issues to address. Which one should be considered first? Maybe one just jumps right out at you. The others will still be around later. Participants often remind you of these issues later by bringing it to your attention either verbally or through their behavior.

Sometimes an issue is right in front of everyone, but people are choosing to avoid it. This could mean they are not ready to deal with it. Maybe it is too threatening or brings up too many bad memories. Yet the issue will not go away. There will be other opportunities to address it. Maybe working on trust issues will allow the participants to become more comfortable with each other and, therefore, be more willing to open up to each other.

Try to work on one issue at a time: Sometimes the issues are intertwined. If it is possible to sort them out into individual issues, they are easier to resolve. For example, you are told that Robyn hit Chris. On examination, here is what actually happened: Stacy bumped a desk, which hit Robyn. Robyn thought Chris hit her. She hit back. There are a few issues here. First, Stacy bumped a desk. Was it an accident or intentional? This is important because if Stacy meant to set up Chris, then we are dealing with a hidden agenda. If not, then we are dealing with Robyn's quick and erroneous judgment and reaction. Chris ends up being a victim either way. Maybe Chris is regularly scapegoated. Maybe Robyn has trouble controlling her temper. The bottom line is that things can get very complicated very fast. Try to focus on one issue at a time, and then build one on another.

The facilitator's responsibility is to provide opportunity: As facilitators, we can only open doors. The participants choose whether or not to walk through them. A safe environment is the key to these doors.

Engage in active listening: Make eye contact with speakers. Acknowledge the person speaking. Clarify what he or she might be trying to say. It is very disconcerting for a person to say something and get no reaction.

Encourage communication that connects people: Early on, group members will focus on you as the leader. They will talk to you, answer your questions, and speak in generalities. As the process continues, encourage them to talk to each other, especially when trying to make decisions. It may even be necessary to remove yourself physically from the group for this to happen.

Also encourage participants to say how they feel, such as: "I felt angry when the group voted for Anita's idea because I think people were voting for their friend," rather than "People were just voting for their friend." A related communication concern is to encourage students to personalize their statements by saying "we" instead of "they" when talking about the group. For example, when asked about how students felt about group cooperation, a student can say, "We worked hard to get the task done," instead of "They worked hard to get the task done." This simple turn of phrase is a subtle thread that can tie people together in the group.

Have participants refrain from personal attacks: No problem is unique. Certain issues permeate our lives; they are part of the human condition. If someone hears a put-down, or if someone is excluded, encourage participants to avoid "pointing the finger" at specific people, unless the people involved are active in the discussion. Blaming helps no one. Examining the general issue of exclusion and name-calling can be helpful, though, and it is useful to label it as something that everyone has probably done.

Also, talking about people in the third person – as if they were not in the room – is hurtful. Referring to specific students by name causes blame to be cast, and defensiveness is not far behind. The issue then becomes a power struggle, and the real issue gets lost. If this happens, you need to stop the argument and try to return to the original issue. Once this is addressed, the argument is usually moot.

Be prepared to be challenged: There comes a time in the development of every group when issues of influence arise. Sometimes this means that students will challenge your authority as the leader. When this happens it is time to cheer. The message is very clear: "We want to control our own destiny." It is then time to renegotiate the power structure in the group. New limits must be established and new norms incorporated. The facilitator's role is to provide enough structure to allow the students to debate their issues in a safe environment. The Full Value Contract is an invaluable tool at this stage. Use it to reaffirm ground rules and norms. Add new ones that students feel are useful and appropriate. As the students become more interdependent, your role changes to one of active observer, rather than an active participant.

Try to keep your ego in your pocket and not on your sleeve: This is difficult, especially if the class is challenging your authority. Although it may sound and feel personal, it is not. Every individual strives for power and control over his or her own life. Sometimes this means that it is necessary to challenge the closest authority figure. If the goal is for students to have as much control and responsibility as possible, a power struggle is counterproductive. Try to stand back from the personal attacks and address the issue as a participant, not as the authority figure. You have the right to voice your feelings and thoughts. This does not mean that you are a peer with your students, however. You are modeling the egalitarian nature of a true community, yet some things are nonnegotiable (e.g., safety, respect for each other and oneself). Issues of safety require a reassertion of your role as the authority in the classroom.

Listen to what people are saying: Try to keep your agenda in the back of your mind. Hear what the students are saying to you and to each other. It may mesh with your agenda, or it may not. Try to go with the class's agenda except in cases of safety or confusion. For example, I know that gender issues are common to many groups, so I am always on the lookout. If the group I am working with is dealing with something else entirely, and I push my agenda about gender roles, it is at best unproductive. At worst, it can cause conflict where none existed. Tune in.

Debrief with yourself or a colleague: Check up on yourself. Keep a journal. Ask yourself "what, so what, now what" after a session. Share your experiences with colleagues to see how they might have handled different situations, or how they think you handled it. Keep the process of growth going.

Be true to yourself: If a discussion feels superficial and fake, it probably is. Follow your instincts, be sincere, and you will be on the right track. Remember, your facilitation style is unique.

If all else fails – punt: There will be moments when the following will probably float through your head: "What am I doing here?" "I have no idea what's going on!" "What happens next?" Then it might be time to take a deep breath, see where the discussion is going and let it flow. Maybe it's time to finish up and move on to another activity. Maybe you can even share with the group, "I'm confused. Can someone tell me what we're talking about?!" As a last resort, stop everything and bring out a treat to share. Be careful about taking things too seriously. Have fun!

Common Themes

Whether or not you know what's going on, some themes tend to be present in many groups, regardless of age or maturity level. I have seen these in groups of 3rd-graders and in groups of high-functioning adults. The package may be different, but underneath, the issues are the same. Here are the most common themes to look for. (Please remember, however, that many issues are unique to your particular group. Those listed here are not the only ones!)

Doers vs. Reflectors. I can safely say that every group I have ever worked with has had to deal with the issue of balancing time between doing and reflecting. During activities, it is possible to see the same people run to the front, get the equipment, and start the process rolling. Meanwhile, others continually stand back and watch. Are they just shy? Are the others just overbearing? Generally not. Usually the people who are action-oriented make quick decisions and start things going. People who are more reflection-oriented need time to consider options and talk the decisions through. This difference in style is grist for the processing mill, which the reflectors are happy to engage in. The doers, at this point, become antsy and can't wait to get back to the activity.

It is possible to attain a balance if the students recognize what is going on. You will need to make many attempts to find the balance point as the pendulum swings between overprocessing and too much activity.

Gender Issues. As much as I would like to believe that gender is not an issue, it keeps cropping up. Young children show signs of gender distinction, and it continues through adulthood. In general, it shows itself when students begin group challenges together. At a place like the Spider Web, for example, the girls step back when it is time to do the lifting, and the boys step in to lift. This is not a case where the boys barge their way in; it is a two-way street. There may be times when a bigger, stronger person may be chosen to lift because she or he may be one of two people left and is the one better able to take on that task. In general, though, when there is a team of people working together, it is unnecessary to differentiate based on gender.

With some classes, this is a big issue; with others it is a non-issue. Encourage students to make decisions based on their combined attributes rather than on assumed individual strengths or weaknesses. This issue offers an opportunity to discuss how people can get pigeonholed based on stereotypes, reputation, or cultural norms.

Objectification. One of the main goals of community building is to humanize rather than objectify people. This is usually accomplished at the beginning stages of group work. Later, however, objectification can reappear when the class is solving problems together. It can be seen during lifting activities, or if a person has been asked to take on a particular role, such as having their eyes covered during an activity. Early on, group members may begin to refer to certain people by labels such as "the blind guy," or the "small one." You hear things like, "Let's get the big person over first." As you can imagine, this objectification can be harmful to a person's self image. It is worth putting on the table for discussion. It can also lead to a general discussion about stereotyping and labeling.

Body Image: Many activities require decisions based on size. Depending on how cohesive the class is and how much trust has built up, this can be cause for grave embarrassment, with people opting out of activities. If this occurs, it is imperative to be sensitive to what is going on and work with the individual to explore how he or she might choose to be involved in the activity. At the Spider Web (an activity that deals directly with body size), that person may choose to go under the web or walk around and help spot. Bringing this issue up for the group to process is very delicate for the individuals involved. The issue of body size at the Spider Web might be explored at a deeper level back at school through personal journals, where what is written can remain private. Students can choose to share what they have written, and the discussion can lead to the more global topic of body image in our society.

Your Reputation Precedes You: There is a constant dilemma about students who have a history of behavioral problems in school and their participation in community building. On the one hand, we want everything to go smoothly, and their behavior issues make it more challenging. On the other hand, we know that these students can benefit from community building, and we don't want to exclude them. What to do? Consistency demands that we include students as much as possible. Often, behavior turns out to be a non-issue. As a matter of fact, many times these students surprise us and become leaders in the community. At other times, safety concerns are paramount, with students exhibiting behavior that could put themselves or others at risk. In these cases, it might be beneficial to search for adults who can act as mentors. Ask a parent, counselor, social worker, educational assistant, or friend of the family to be present whenever possible. Make sure this person is available for field trips. This adult can discuss problems that arise with the student that are outside the scope of the community. This adult can also intervene, if necessary, when a safety situation occurs. In this way, your focus can be on the community as a whole, while the student can have more individual needs met. Although it may be difficult to find someone who can give the time and energy to one student, it is well worth the effort.

"We Act Different in Here ..." Sometimes students develop situational relationships in which they are trusting and trustworthy in the class, but harass each other outside of the room. If this issue is not addressed in the community, it will not change. Talk about what makes students behave differently outside of the group, and how their outside behavior toward each other affects the relationships in the room. Generally it has more to do with peer groups than with their individual perceptions of each other.

There is a time for doing and a time for reflecting. Deciding when to do an activity and when to process is one of the more difficult tasks for a facilitator. There will be times when you do one activity after another and no issues arise – it is enough to do and have fun. At other times it is impossible to do anything because there are too many unresolved issues floating around – whatever you do has no spark. Then it is time to talk. There are days when all we do is talk, but it provides the space to get back to business when the air is clear. As we all know, it is difficult to go very far with a ton of baggage on one's back.

Please remember that this is a process – it is never completely smooth and rarely easy. Some groups go far; others seem to stay in the same rut day in and day out. You have helped to open the doors, and they have chosen to walk through or stay put. That, more than anything, is what this process is all about: making educated, responsible choices in the context of the whole. As Tom Smith would say, "If you can't see the big picture, you think you are the big picture." *

Sequence and Flow

If the world were a static place, with everything predictable and orderly, a group would proceed from Co-operation to Trust, then into issues of Problem Solving, and finally wind up at Challenge as neatly and tidily as it is described in this book. **If** the world were a static place ...

---

* Tom, a long-time adventure educator from Cazenovia, WI, attributes this quote as a collaborative insight between himself and Keith King, also a weathered experiential educator from Alton Bay, NH.

Thus, we are back to the question of sequence and flow. The **sequence**, again, is the set of concrete activities outlined by the facilitator planning a program according to the theoretical development of a group. The **flow** is how that sequence plays out according to the *real* development of the group. The reality of group work is that the flow is quite tidal – it ebbs and flows depending on individual personalities, backgrounds, age, maturity level, and the like. As soon as you think the group is on firm ground with trust, someone new joins the class and you're back to the beginning. After a long history of problem solving, one student refuses to spot another on an element because she thinks he has spread a rumor about her. Back we go to trust issues.

We must also deal with external pressures such as time and scheduling. Every time a class gets together, it is necessary to back up a bit to help ease back into the group process. This means starting a session with an activity from an earlier step in the sequence. In a 45-minute class three times a week, this is a slower process. It is less conducive to community building than a class that is together every day.

If you have contracted with an outside agency to go to their ropes course on, say, April 14, chances are there are few options when April rolls around and you are wondering if your class is ready for that experience. You can decide to cancel the trip, or head out anyway to help students progress from where they are in the process at that moment. It is important to remember this: **It is not the activity that dictates what is accomplished, but the level at which the group is operating.** If the class is still working with trust issues, and you decide to do a problem solving initiative, they will work together on the initiative like a group that is still dealing with issues of trust.

In an ideal world, flow and sequence blend. In the world in which we live, they sometimes trip over each other. You can help facilitate students' issues rather than push them into places where they are not ready to go. This is the value of understanding the life cycle of a group.

How you handle these situations as a facilitator depends on these factors:
- The purpose for the group
- Your personality and style
- Where the group is in its life cycle

Group Purpose

There are many reasons for groups to undertake an adventure-based community-building process in school. A continuum (shown below in figure 8.6) depicts one way of looking at the different types of groups and their purposes.

Adventure-Based Groups in Schools

Recreation	Classroom	Counseling
(Adventure Programming)	(Adventure in the Classroom)	(Adventure Based Counseling)

Figure 8.6

Each of these three approaches has a different focus (i.e., one is physical, one cognitive, one emotional). Of course, all of these approaches incorporate the other focuses as well. Their one shared focus is social. The social nature of community helps every group achieve its goals.

The chosen approach leads the teacher to choose activities in a sequence to help further the group's goals. A physical education teacher, for example, may choose activities that require the members to be more physical (e.g., running tag games, doing physical trust activities, taking risks in the context of climbing). A classroom teacher, on the other hand, might choose more sedate activities that get group members thinking through problems and might bring academic content into the activities. A counselor could focus activities on emotional trust and taking emotional risks with friends and family.

The Gift

It was a crisp day in October at the SPRITE ropes course near Oregon, Wisconsin. The 6th-graders were in the middle of a full day. After a morning of low ropes, we were preparing to try a high element or two. I was still fairly new at facilitating, having been practicing for a couple of years. I felt good about my skills — maybe too good.

My belaying post was at the Pamper Pole, where students were being asked to go on belay, climb to the top of a 25-foot pole, dive off, and try to hit a bell. One of the smaller girls in the class was suited up in the harness and ready to go. Then she got cold feet. In my great "wisdom," I knew that she would feel wonderful if she could get up there and jump toward that bell. So, I proceeded to talk her into climbing, talk her up the pole, and talk her into jumping. She did it all, and I felt great!

What happened next is what I now consider a great gift. She came down, walked over to me and said, "I wish you hadn't done that. I didn't need to do that."

I came to the quick realization that **I** needed her to climb that pole. It was **my** agenda, not hers. My ego was at stake, and she paid the price for it. Given the power differential between us (me, the facilitator, teacher, and adult) and her (the participant, student, and child), it took courage for her to speak her mind. I am grateful, for with that realization I finally began to walk the path of becoming a true facilitator – and not a manipulator – of experiences.

The depth of processing also reflects the group's mission. A counseling group, for example, might spend more time processing than actually engaging in activities. On the other end of the continuum, the physical education class will spend more time in activity than processing. The classroom group will be somewhere in between.

Although the focus, the selected activities, and discussion time may look different from group to group, the process is the same. There are a profusion of activities to choose from, variations on the activities, and metaphors that can be drawn from each activity to make it useful to a group.

Facilitator Personality and Style

I love to process; I could sit for hours and chew a problem to death. This is how I make sense of the world. There are other people who would rather spit the problem out and get to work on it. They want to yell at people like me, "Quit sitting around and get on with it!" They make sense of their world by testing problems.

As a facilitator you have choices about sequence flow, as well as how to deal with issues as they come up during activities. One of the most difficult hurdles a facilitator must face is balancing the need to sit and process with the need to be active. As a processor by nature, I have had to subdue my need in order to provide space for other styles. I remind myself that, although I learn an enormous amount from the actions and insights of the participants, that is not the main reason I am there. I am there to facilitate the learning of the students in this developing community. Their needs are paramount. As Steve Butler says in *Quicksilver*, facilitating means "helping [group members] learn from each other."[5]

In reflecting on my own facilitation, many times I reach the conclusion that we processed too much. That is the side I err on as a facilitator. There are other times when (in an effort to correct my propensity to overprocess) I don't give the students enough time to process; we run from one activity to another without even taking a breath. As the pendulum swings back and forth, I search for balance. It is a never-ending process. The important thing is to think about it. Be aware of your style, your personality, and your habits. The better you know yourself, the better you can step out of your own head and make decisions based on what is right for your group.

Figure 8.7 is a rubric that can be helpful for assessing your own facilitation skills.

Facilitation Rubric

Criteria	Needs Improvement	Sufficient	Advancing	Bonus
Uses activities in an intentional and purposeful way.	Does an activity for no real reason.	Can state a reason for using the activity (e.g. energizer, fun, teaching a particular life-skill, engagement).	Introduces/frontloads a metaphor or purpose for the activity with participants.	Chooses an activity that highlights, connects, assesses, or applies to content learning.
Sequences activities.	Chooses an activity solely because he or she likes it.	Chooses an activity according to an acknowledged sequence.	Assesses where the group is in their development and chooses an activity to help meet their needs at that particular time.	When an activity is not working, adapts the activity to meet the developmental needs of the group.
Gets the group's attention before starting.	Gives directions without getting people's attention.	Gets people's attention, but gives directions before everyone is ready to listen.	Gets people's attention and waits until everyone is ready.	Has a strategy to get people's attention besides yelling (e.g., "If you can hear me, clap once") or uses a time-out signal.
Gets the group in a place where everyone can see and hear (circle, line, etc.).	Does nothing to situate group so that everyone can see and hear.	Gathers people but allows them to sit or stand in a clump.	Asks for and waits for people to get into a circle or a line so that everyone can see and hear.	When people stand in front of others, reminds them to make space so that everyone is included in the circle.
Activity introduction.	Gives long and rambling directions that are not sequential, and leaves out rules or directions.	Gives sequential directions for the activity that include all the rules.	After giving directions, asks if there are any questions.	Tells directions *and* shows them.
Activity safety.	Does not notice possible safety problems nor cover safety procedures in directions.	Tells participants the safety rules and possible safety issues.	Emphasizes that people have the right to pass or change the way something is done in order to feel physically and emotionally safe.	Suggests to a participant how s/he may do the activity in a different way, or suggests that it is okay to "opt out," when appropriate.
Observes activity.	Talks to a co-facilitator during the activity or ignores the activity.	Watches how people do the activity and watches for safety issues. Stops the action when there is a physical or emotional safety problem.	Takes mental or written notes about things to process after the activity.	Sees connections between what is happening and the metaphor, goals, past issues, and focus of the group.
Processes (reflects on) activity.	Does not process the activity at all.	Asks questions for participants to answer about the activity.	Asks follow-up questions when an issue is brought up by a participant.	In addition to talking, uses a way to process that is visual, physical, or artistic.
Wraps up.	Ends activity abruptly.	Says something after the activity and processing is done to signify that they will move on.	Summarizes what was said in the processing.	Finds a way to flow into the next activity.

Figure 8.7

Chapter 8: Facilitating the Process   249

Group Development Cycle: It Never Goes Away

If a group is struggling with issues of influence, choosing a get-to-know-you name game will seem stale and superficial. People who are ready to get into the meat of an issue need something to sink their teeth into, and playing silly games just doesn't cut it. On the other hand, offering a Trust activity to people who are just getting to know each other can elevate the anxiety level – sometimes to the point of panic. People will be bailing out right and left. Challenge by Choice is more than a concept in this case; it becomes a survival tool.

The closer the activities – and subsequent processing – are aligned with the group cycle, the more likely group members will get their needs met, so the process can forge ahead. As we know, internal and external factors affect this process, so that each group travels as far as it can in the time allotted.

Summary

Facilitating is both a science and an art. It takes some theoretical knowledge about sequencing and flow, the Experiential Learning Cycle, group development, and the Adventure Wave. Processing the experience can be enhanced by an awareness of general themes that crop up, as well as by procedural knowledge about effective facilitation. This chapter has offered some guidelines for facilitation along with strategies to get at the "what," "so what," and "now what" of adventure-based learning.

How one approaches facilitation has much to do with the purpose of the class, one's own personality/style, and where the class is in its life cycle. Overall, though, learning to facilitate is a process in itself. Just as taking the first step off the Zip Line platform is generally the hardest, it requires commitment to take that first step and persevere down the path to facilitation. We must be prepared to make mistakes and learn from those mistakes. Inevitably, the students have much to teach us if we are willing to learn.

---

[1] *Lasting Lessons*, (pp. 2-3)
[2] *Processing the Experience*, (p. 8)
[3] *Theory of Experiential Education*, (pp. 132-135, 1995)
[4] See *Islands of Healing*, by Schoel, Prouty and Radcliffe, 1988.
[5] *Quicksilver*, (p. 8)

9 Starting an Adventure Program

The first step in establishing an adventure program is to review your own perspectives about the nature of education, the roles of student and teacher, and the most important goals for young people as they become adults in our society.

The philosophy of community building views learning as a process that includes the ability to take risks. Risk taking allows students to push their boundaries, make discoveries that may otherwise be out of reach, and be open to new insights and ideas that spring from their own reflections. The consequent opportunities for learning increase exponentially. Learning is transformed from a one-way conduit between teacher and student to a "learning web" where everyone exchanges ideas.

The next step is to review your own situation. If you are a classroom teacher, the place to start is in your classroom. Try a few activities, begin regular class meetings to encourage processing, create a Full Value Contract. Begin to share some decision making with your students. Embark on your own tour through the Experiential Learning Cycle by trying activities, reflecting, looking for patterns, and applying them to your classroom. At first, it might feel painfully slow and arduous. Like any expedition, it takes time to get the muscles toned and attitudes shifted from the regular routine.

Once you have decided to begin the journey, go to a conference on Experiential Education, or get some specific training through workshops offered from an organization like Project Adventure. Look for educational conferences that have people like Alfie Kohn, Howard Gardner, Susan Kovalik, or Daniel Goleman as speakers. Ask your administration or professional organization to sponsor workshops and speakers on these subjects. Much is available if one is willing to do the research.

Another step is to research ropes courses in your area. If you find an appropriate one, take your students. Consider advocating to build such a course in your school or district. Without exception, ropes courses are established in school districts when there is a person – a champion – who sees the project through from beginning to end. Sometimes this is an administrator. More often it is a teacher, social worker, counselor, or psychologist. Sometimes it's a parent. Frequently, this person has worked for almost a decade looking for funding, convincing administrators, and persuading colleagues. The end result has been the same: success through tenacity.

Although community building can be accomplished without a ropes course, it can be a valuable tool to address specific issues around trust, problem solving, and challenge. A pitfall, however, is when the ropes course alone is viewed as community building. Using a ropes course as an end in itself reduces it to the level of a playground, and an expensive one at that. Given this pitfall, it is vital to understand the process of community building so the ropes course can be put into perspective. It is a tool, much as a book is a tool to promote reading.

Modeling the Community-Building Process

A typical educational scenario goes something like this: Politicians dump on school boards, who dump on administrators, who dump on principals, who dump on teachers, who then dump on students. When students dump on each other, we wonder what's wrong with them.

Try this simple activity with your colleagues: Hold your arms straight out in front of you, one arm above the other, and palms facing each other. Clap your hands together. Then say, "When I say 'go,' clap your hands." Get everyone into position, then say, "One, two, three ..." [Clap your hands], "GO!" Most people will clap when you clap your hands, not when you say "go." This is but a small example of how powerful modeling can be. Talk really is cheap. It is what we do, not what we say, that carries the true power.

If we are to advocate community building with our students, we must look at the school as a whole. How do decisions get made? Are there opportunities for collaboration? Do people take time to get to know each other, share ideas, and discuss educational philosophy?

The reality, of course, is that this is easier in some situations than others. For some, especially if a large grant is available, people will commit to taking the time needed to engage in their own community-building process. If the administration is working in partnership with teachers, and if teachers are willing to examine their own philosophies, the goal of aligning the school environment with the classroom is on solid footing. This is the "whole-school" approach that is best for making large-scale changes.

As a recovering control freak, it took me years to let go of my iron grip on the classroom. I began the process by taking off my watch. Since the clock in our room was broken, I had to rely on others for the time of day. Since we were in a self-contained class, the other outcome was that the rigid schedule began to bend. It became unnecessary to stop math at 10:52; we moved on when we were ready. The result was that we actually accomplished more by removing the invented structure – there were fewer distractions and transitions. This new structure made me open up to the idea of integrated curriculum; it just suddenly made sense.

Libby Roderick wrote a song that helps remind me to let go of artificial structures in my classroom, and in my life:

"Lay it all down, when you can't hold it

Let it all fall, set it all free

When the night falls and it grows cold in

The midst of the journey, and you fall to your knees

Sometimes two legs simply can't hold us

Sometimes two arms are simply too weak

Lay it all down when you can't hold it

Let your life carry you like a boat on the sea ..."

(Lay it All Down, 1997)

At other times, this holistic approach is not possible due to lack of resources like time, money, and just plain energy. Then it is necessary to become a grassroots organizer. Examine your sphere of influence. Talk to people who are open to your ideas, and model the process in your own situation. Create partnerships with others who are like-minded. Whether you are an administrator, teacher, or support staff, there are opportunities to promote a sense of community.

Madison Metropolitan School District (MMSD) Stress/ Challenge Program: A Grassroots Effort

The MMSD Stress/Challenge Program began with the vision of Pete Albert. As an Outward Bound instructor, he had witnessed the power of experiential and adventure education. In 1979, as a social worker, he brought these ideas to the Madison School District. It all began with the support of one teacher and a group of at-risk students. Over time, Pete made connections with people in the juvenile justice system and the county. Together, they built the first ropes course in the area that would serve kids from the schools and juvenile corrections.

By 1984, the program had caught the eye of a few administrators and many teachers who were looking for ways to promote community in the classroom. Middle-school principals donated one day per week of one teacher's time for someone to focus on the program. Dee Tull, an administrator for students with learning disabilities, donated another 2.5 days per week of a teacher's time. I had received some training at Project Adventure and became the first formal Stress/Challenge facilitator. Eventually, the position became full-time.

This program operated on "soft money" for a decade, risking the chance of being cut at any moment. It was only through the commitment of a few administrators that the funding continued. Stress/Challenge was finally brought to the level of a department in 1994. During that time, I worked with hundreds of teachers and thousands of students. I only went to a class if invited. At first, that meant a dozen or so. Soon, however, I could not keep up. As with any grassroots organization, ours took the route of water. At first, water flows into areas of least resistance. Eventually, as the areas get full, water begins to defy gravity, and the container begins to fill.

People who were the most skeptical of the program became our biggest advocates. And, in 1994, we needed all the advocates we could get. The program had just achieved departmental status, and it was on the chopping block. I sent out a letter to teachers informing them of this development. The evening that our program was slated for discussion at the school board meeting, over 150 students, teachers, parents, administrators, and other supporters came. People spoke about what the program had to offer, what it meant to them, and how it had even changed their lives. Stress/Challenge was no longer a mere program; it had taken on a life of its own. The school board let the program stand.

Verona, Wisconsin calls itself "Hometown USA." Just outside of Madison, it has one middle school. Ruth Heffron, longtime and well-known Verona resident was one of the physical education teachers there. She had a vision to build a ropes course to enhance her students' learning. She maintained this vision for a long time because there was never the money or the structural will to make it happen.

Joy Pfeffer is a mom and a registered nurse who lives in Verona. Her son Patrick died suddenly when he was a 6th-grader at Verona Middle School. From this tragedy came a great gift. Joy wanted something to come of Patrick's death that could benefit all kids in Verona. When Joy's energy met with Ruth's vision, the money was raised in Patrick's name to build an indoor ropes course at Verona Middle School.

The Patrick Pfeffer annual run-walk event continues to support the program. Joy remains a moving force in raising money, working with students and offering training to keep this ropes course available to all middle-schoolers in Verona.

Today, MMSD has 10 ropes courses. It has provided hundreds of people who have formal training, and has given thousands of students, teachers, and administrators the opportunity to learn about being part of a community.

This is just how the vision of a single person can make a powerful difference.

Summary

Starting your own adventure program can take many forms depending upon resources, interest, and collective will of the school community. Because using adventure to create community requires the belief in a particular philosophy, it may be necessary to start alone, working with other like-minded people in the school and the larger community. As the anecdotes in this chapter demonstrate, one person's commitment can have a large effect over time.

Afterword

> Step by step the longest march
> Can be won, can be won
> Many stones do form an arch
> Singly none, singly none
> And by union what we will
> Can be accomplished still
> Drops of water turn a mill
> Singly none, singly none
> — United Mine Workers preamble

Is our society really going down the tubes? Marian Wright Edelman and the Children's Defense Fund reveal some stark statistics:

> Every 3 hours, a child or teen is a homicide victim; every 18 minutes a baby dies; every day, 8 children or teens are killed from firearms; every day, 1 person under age 25 dies from HIV infection; every day, 4 children or youths commit suicide; 1 in every 3 children is behind a year or more in school; every 40 seconds, a baby is born into poverty; every minute, a baby is born to a teen mother; every 8 minutes, a child is arrested for a violent crime; every 4 minutes, a child is arrested for drug abuse; every day, 388 babies are born to mothers who received late or no prenatal care; and, every 33 seconds, a child is born to a mother who is not a high school graduate.[1]

The above statistics offer a barometer for our society. These statistics are further illuminated by our response to crime in our society – in the past 12 years, the prison population in the United States has more than *doubled*. Even Captain Kangaroo (Bob Keeshen) charged that "... there is a 'mean-spiritedness' in America's failure to commit itself to the upbringing of young children, particularly those from at-risk backgrounds."[2]

Is there no hope?

We seem to be surrounded by both hand-wringing and cynicism. However, neither attitude will change the world. Hand-wringing denotes powerlessness – people who worry, but feel there is nothing to be done. The cynics are *sure* that nothing can be done, and are quick to point blame at everything and everyone for the mess we are in. No, the world cannot change if we adopt these attitudes.

Yet look around. Look at all the kids who, against all odds, have stayed *off* drugs, who have *not* committed suicide, who cooperate with others, who can look toward the future as a better place for themselves and their contemporaries. It is the norm; it points to what is possible for every human being.

Yes, circumstances may dictate a person's attitude. Poverty, racism, classism, violence, homophobia, addiction all play a part in a person's outlook on life. These environmental circumstances can wreak havoc on a person's sense of hope and optimism. A Pollyanna is not born from need. As a society, however, we have control over these environmental influences. We can choose to wring our hands in blighted hope, or we can choose to pursue an optimistic course of change. We can, if we so choose, focus on the positive, while doing everything in our power to transform the negative.

To make these changes, we are compelled to examine our own spheres of influence – to determine what we have control over and work with it, while letting go of those areas that are out of reach. As educators, this means we can create a safe environment in our classrooms and in the school community as a whole. This vision does not represent a place without conflict, but a place where people have the skills to resolve conflict without resorting to violence. It is a place where students can take risks, thus maximizing their growth. Even if one must walk through a metal detector to get inside, a school can be a haven and a place of empowerment. If we can develop a spirit of collaboration, where all students have the opportunity to be leaders, imagine what could eventually happen when they get out into the "real" world as adults. It is one step in a very long process.

Arthur Wellington Conquest III, a longtime Adventure/Experiential educator states: "[Adventure] Education is the key ingredient for developing and nurturing our children so they can live productive lives, adapt to today's rapidly changing society and, more importantly, begin to learn how to control the factors which most profoundly affect their destiny ...."[3]

The change process exists inside each and every one of us. It begins with an attitude that sees the possible rather than the unobtainable, that sees potential in every human being, and that knows it is necessary to work, and to work hard. It is truly a *journey toward the caring classroom*.

––––––––––––––––––

[1] Children's Defense Fund Web site: www.childrensdefense.org, 2004
[2] Associated Press, 1996
[3] Zip Lines, Summer 1996

Activity List

Activity	Type	Grade Levels
1,2,3 Mississippi, p. 54	Deinhibitizer	3 and higher
1001 Questions, p. 79	Challenge by Choice	K–3
60-Second Speeches, p. 110	Trust	6 and higher
Airport, p. 118	Trust	K and higher
All Aboard, p. 166	Problem Solving	K and higher
All Toss, p. 171	Problem Solving	9 and higher
Alphapong, p. 186	Problem Solving	4 and higher
Anonymous Goals, p. 142	Behavioral Goal Setting	5 and higher
Balloon Frantic, p. 163	Problem Solving	8 and higher
Batten Down the Hatches, p. 214	Conflict Resolution	6 and higher
Being, The p. 86	Full Value Contract	K–5
Big Question, The, p. 53	Ice Breaker/Acquaintance	4 and higher
Blue Jellybeans, p. 135	Feelings Literacy	K–1
Books and Quilts, p. 220	Academic Content	
Brainstorming, p. 209	Conflict Resolution	3 and higher
Butter Battle Escalator, p. 206	Conflict Resolution	3 and higher
Catch As Catch Can, p. 188	Problem Solving	6 and higher
Categories and Lineups, p. 47	Ice Breaker/Acquaintance	K and higher
Catwalk, The, p. 226	High Ropes Course	
Centipede, The, p. 225	High Ropes Course	
Channels, p. 182	Problem Solving	2 and higher
Choice and Consequences, p. 215	Conflict Resolution	2–5
Clean and Messy, p. 148	Behavioral Goal Setting	K–2
¿Como Estás?, p. 55	Deinhibitizer	3 and higher
Collaborative Numbers, p. 178	Problem Solving	5 and higher
Compass Walk, The, p. 218	Academic Content	4 and higher
Conflicts – the Real ... the Imagined, p. 210	Conflict Resolution	3 and higher
Crossing the Feelings Line, p. 132	Feelings Literacy	3 and higher
Differences and Commonalties, p. 48	Ice Breaker/Acquaintance	2 and higher
Don't Touch Me, p. 181	Problem Solving	6 and higher
Dream Catcher, p. 106	Trust	1 and higher
Elbow Tag, p. 61	Deinhibitizer	4 and higher
Emotion Motions, p. 134	Feelings Literacy	3 and higher
Everybody Up, p. 105	Trust	K and higher
Everybody's It, p. 73	Challenge by Choice	K and higher

Activity List (cont.)

Activity	Type	Grade Levels
Feelings Baseball, p. 136	Feelings Literacy	K–1
Feelings Cards: Charades, p. 130	Feelings Literacy	K and higher
Feelings Cards: Stories, p. 132	Feelings Literacy	K and higher
Feelings Speed Rabbit, p. 129	Feelings Literacy	K–3
Five Finger Contract, p. 82	Full Value Contract	K–6
Five Ways to Show You Care, p. 128	Trust	K–1
Fusion, p. 198	Problem Solving	5 and higher
Get the Point, p. 58	Deinhibitizer	1 and higher
Giving and Receiving, p. 149	Behavioral Goal Setting	K–2
Goal Challenge, pl. 144	Behavioral Goal Setting	5 and higher
Goal Toss, p. 143	Behavioral Goal Setting	6 and higher
Group Bingo, p. 45	Ice Breaker/Acquaintance	3 and higher
Group Interview, p. 78	Challenge by Choice	4 and higher
Group Cheers, p. 71	Deinhibitizer	5 and higher
Group Juggle and Variations, p. 173	Problem Solving	K and higher
Basic Juggle, p. 173		
You're In or You're Out, p. 173		
Low-Drop Juggle, p. 173		
Juggling for Our Lives, p. 174		
Growth Circles, p. 75	Challenge by Choice	5 and higher
Hands All Around, p. 88	Full Value Contract	4 and higher
Help Tag, p. 126	Trust	3 and higher
Hidden Polygon, p. 177	Problem Solving	K and higher
High Risk, Low Risk, p. 119	Trust	4 and higher
Hog Call, p. 102	Trust	4 and higher
Human Machines, p. 197	Problem Solving	4 and higher
Interactive Video, p. 49	Ice Breaker/Acquaintance	4 and higher
Integrity Ball, p. 123	Trust	5 and higher
Islands, p. 199	Low Challenge Ropes Course: Problem Solving	5 and higher
King/Queen Frog, p. 50	Ice Breaker/Acquaintance	3 and higher
Keypunch, p. 191	Problem Solving	6 and higher
Knots, p. 185	Problem Solving	4 and higher
Laughing Matters, p. 80	Challenge by Choice	K–5
Little Bert, p. 63	Deinhibitizer	3 and higher
Marshmallows, p. 170	Problem Solving	K and higher
Martian/Politician/Tiger/Salmon, p. 68	Deinhibitizer	2 and higher
Memory Circle, p. 37	Ice Breaker/Acquaintance	K and higher

Activity List (cont.)

Activity	Type	Grade Levels
Metaphorical Tableaus, p. 195	Problem Solving	9 and higher
Mixing Game, p. 69	Deinhibitizer	K–2
Moonball, p. 161	Problem Solving	2 and higher
Morpheelings, p. 137	Feelings Literacy	K–5
Morphing, p. 56	Deinhibitizer	K and higher
Name Tag, p. 39	Ice Breaker/Acquaintance	K and higher
Neighbors, p. 72	Challenge by Choice	K and higher
Night at the Improv, p. 65	Deinhibitizer	5 and higher
Nitro Crossing, p. 201	Low Challenge Ropes Course: Problem Solving	3 and higher
Paired Activities, p. 40	Ice Breaker/Acquaintance	K and higher
Last Detail, p. 40		
Tie Your Shoe, p. 42		
Me Switch, p. 42		
Macro Rock/Paper/Scissors, p. 42		
High Fives, p. 43		
1-1 Interview, p. 43		
Celebration, p. 44		
Paired Trust Activities, p. 100	Trust	2 and higher
Trust Walk, p. 100		
Search and Rescue, p. 101		
Drive My Car, p. 101		
Pamper Pole, p. 227	High Ropes Course	
Pathfinder, p. 164	Problem Solving	4 and higher
PEEP, p. 83	Full Value Contract	6 and higher
People to People, p. 67	Deinhibitizer	K and higher
Pendulum Trust Lean, p. 114	Trust	5 and higher
Play Hard, Safe, Fair, Have Fun, p. 85	Full Value Contract	K and higher
Puzzles, p. 176	Problem Solving	8 and higher
Rearrange the Classroom, p. 212	Conflict Resolution	4 and higher
Red/Yellow/Green, p. 66	Deinhibitizer	K–3
River of Life, The, p. 138	Behavioral Goal Setting	6 and higher
Screaming Toes, p. 57	Deinhibitizer	2 and higher
Setting the Table, p. 168	Problem Solving	5 and higher
Shakers, p. 104	Trust	2 and higher
Sherpa Walk, p. 111	Trust	K and higher
Song Tag, p. 77	Challenge by Choice	4 and higher
Speed Rabbit, p. 59	Deinhibitizer	K and higher

Activity List (cont.)

Activity	Type	Grade Levels
Spider Web, p. 202	Low Challenge Ropes Course: Problem Solving	K and higher
Stargate, p. 184	Problem Solving	K–1
Tabletop Puzzle, p. 192	Problem Solving	1–5
Tension Traverse, p. 152	Low Challenge Ropes Course: Trust	3 and higher
Three-Person Trust Walk, p. 140	Behavioral Goal Setting	6 and higher
Toss 10, p. 194	Problem Solving	5 and higher
Trust Lean, p. 112	Trust	5 and higher
Turn Over a New Leaf, p. 167	Problem Solving	5 and higher
Turnstile, p. 98	Trust	4 and higher
Two Line Bridge, p. 226	High Ropes Course	
Venn Diagrams, p. 217	Academic Content	2–5
Village, The, p. 87	Full Value Contract	8 and higher
Walk of Life (Mohawk Walk), p. 151	Low Challenge Ropes Course: Trust	4 and higher
Wall, The, p. 204	Low Challenge Ropes Course: Problem Solving	8 and higher
Warp Speed, p. 160	Problem Solving	5 and higher
Welcome Circle, p. 51	Ice Breaker/Acquaintance	K and higher
What Do I Need, What Can I Give?, p. 89	Full Value Contract	9 and higher
Who's the Leader?, p. 189	Problem Solving	1–6
Wild Woosey, p. 151	Low Challenge Ropes Course: Trust	5 and higher
Willow in the Wind, p. 116	Trust	5 and higher
Winless Zax, The, p. 213	Conflict Resolution	K–3
Yurt Circle, p. 108	Trust	4 and higher
Zip Line, p. 228	High Ropes Course	
Zip, Zap, Pop, p. 125	Trust	2 and higher

Where Do the Activities Come From?

Adventure games and activities are similar to folk songs. Sometimes it is possible to trace their origin, but many times it is not. Every person who uses an activity presents it in her or his own way, adding a flair here and an adaptation there. In this way, the activities continue to evolve.

How one uses an activity has as much to do with sequencing as the activity itself. A simple game of tag can be turned into a Trust activity by making the boundaries closer together, thus causing a greater likelihood of contact between participants. Age and maturity level play a part in where an activity fits in a sequence. Speed Rabbit, an activity in which people are asked to act silly in front of each other, can be used on day one with a class of 1st-graders, but will surely fail with 8th-graders on the first day of school. They need much more time to get to know their classmates before pretending to be an elephant in front of them. Once they know that classmates will not put them down, a rousing game of Speed Rabbit is a winner even in middle school.

Most of the activities in this book have been written about in previous books. Below is a list of these activities and where to find them.* By reading the descriptions in each book, you will find different perspectives on how to use the activity. Please use this only as a guide and remember to trust your judgment about the needs of your students and the issues that are important to your class. Each activity is assigned according to the part of the process where I might begin using the activity. In other words, an activity might require some problem solving, but it can be used as a Cooperation activity (such as Lineups or A What?). Other activities require a higher degree of trust or more complex problem solving, so they are put at the Trust or Problem-Solving level.

Undoubtedly you (and the authors of these books) will find activities on this grid and wonder, "What was she thinking?!" No two people will ever agree on the "correct" sequence. Consider these grids as a starting point, and when you start questioning my motives here, it means that you are well on your way to creating your own sequencing instincts. The activities are organized in alphabetical order according to how they are titled in this book. In each box, then, are the titles for the same activity in other books.

AECC: *Adventure Education for the Classroom Community* (Frank and Panico)

AIP: *Adventures in Peacemaking* (Kreidler and Furlong)

AP: *Affordable Portables* (Cavert)

CTM: *Changing the Message* (Albin)

DIA: *Diversity in Action* (Chappelle and Bigman)

GFC: *Games for Change* (Dodds and Prosser-Dodds)

GFT: *Games (& Other Stuff) for Teachers* (Cavert and Frank)

GFG 1: *Games (& Other Stuff) for Group, Book 1* (Cavert)

GFG 2: *Games (&Other Stuff) for Group, Book 2* (Cavert)

JTCC: *Journey Toward the Caring Classroom* (Frank)

NGFWF: *New Games for the Whole Family* (LeFevre)

QS: *Quicksilver* (Rohnke and Butler)

SB: *Silver Bullets* (Rohnke)

TWTP: *Teamwork and Teamplay* (Cain and Jolliff)

* Please see the Bibliography for a more detailed description of each book.

Cooperative Activities

Activity	JTCC	AECC	AIP	AP	CTM	DIA	GFC	GFT	GFG 1	GFG 2	NGFWF	QS	SB	TWTP
1, 2, 3 Mississippi	**p. 54**													
Bumpity Bump Bump Bump											p. 107	p. 84		
Community, Community, Community		p. 65												
1001 Questions	**p. 79**													
Big Question, The	**p. 53**													
Categories & Line Ups	**p. 47**													
Find Your Place			p. 205											
The Line Forms Here			p. 65											
Chronological Line Up													p. 163	
Where in the Circle Am I?												p. 92		
Name by Name												p. 126		
Line Ups		p. 67												p. 113
Line Up Like This – No, Line Up Like That														
Differences & Commonalities	**p. 48**													
Commonalities			p. 202									p. 76		
Classroom Commonalties		p. 74												
Elbow Tag	**p. 61**													
Cat and Mouse													p. 47	
Three's a Crowd											p. 76			
Everybody's It	**p. 73**		p. 68			p. 340							p. 153	
Hospital Tag													p. 154	
Get the Point	**p. 58**	p. 54												
Gotcha Lines								p. 114						
Group Bingo	**p. 45**													
Human Bingo			p. 214											
Autographs														p. 39
Group Cheers	**p. 71**													
Group Interview	**p. 78**													
Interviewing			p. 210											

Cooperative Activities (cont.)

Activity	JTCC	AECC	AIP	AP	CTM	DIA	GFC	GFT	GFG 1	GFG 2	NGFWF	QS	SB	TWTP
Growth Circles	p. 75	p. 102												
Interactive Video	p. 49													
Captain Video		p. 259									p. 42			
King/Queen Frog	p. 50	p. 196												
King Frog			p. 165			p. 309								
Emotion Motions	p. 134													
Laughing Matters	p. 80													
Mookie			p. 153											
Little Bert	p. 63													
Little Ernie											p. 61			
Martian/Politician/ Tiger/Salmon	p. 68													
Memory Circle	p. 37													
Toss a Name Game									p. 15				p.17	
Name Game Circle		p. 45												
Mixing Game	p. 69													
The Mixing Game								p. 105						
Morphing	p. 56													
Morpheelings	p. 137													
Metamorphosis Tag					p. 25									
Name Tag	p. 39													
MeYouLisa			p. 52											
Hustle Bustle									p. 17				p. 87	
Name Ball				p. 25										
Neighbors	p. 72		p. 188											
Have You Ever?			p. 256	p. 207			p. 67					p. 224		
Switcheroo				p. 209								p. 209		
Pile Up											p. 78			
Fruit Basket					p. 35									
I Want to Know Somebody Who...														

Cooperative Activities (cont.)

Activity	JTCC	AECC	AIP	AP	CTM	DIA	GFC	GFT	GFG 1	GFG 2	NGFWF	QS	SB	TWTP
Night at the Improv	p. 65													
Theater Sports														p. 328
Story Circle		p. 186												
Paired Activities	p. 40													
Last Detail	p. 40											p. 123		
Details, Details			p. 114											
Tie Your Shoe	p. 42	p. 288												
Me Switch	p. 42													
Macro R/P/S	p. 42													
High Fives	p. 43													
One-to-One Interview	p. 43	p. 163								p. 7				
Celebration	p. 44													
People to People	p. 67													
Student to Student		p. 72												
Red/Yellow/Green	p. 66													
Screaming Toes	p. 57													
Making Connections		p. 70												
Song Tag	p. 77													
Speed Rabbit	p. 59													
Speedy Threesome			p. 161											
Elephant, Rabbit, Palm Tree											p. 132			
Feelings Speed Rabbit	p. 129													
Welcome Circle	p. 51													

Trust Activities

Activity	JTCC	AECC	AIP	AP	CTM	DIA	GFC	GFT	GFG 1	GFG 2	NGFWF	QS	SB	TWTP
60-Second Speeches	p. 110	p. 105												
Airport	p. 118													
Anonymous Goals	p. 142													
Blue Jellybeans	p. 135													
Mookie			p. 123											
Clean and Messy	p. 148													
Crossing the Feelings Line	p. 132													
Cross the Line						p. 242								
Dream Catcher	p. 106													
Yurt Rope												p. 258		
Raccoon Circles				p. 20										p. 151
Depending on You							p. 41							
Emotion Motions	p. 134													
Everybody Up	p. 105		p. 89			p. 137							p. 100	
Feelings Baseball	p. 136													
Feelings Cards: Charades	p. 130													
Feelings Cards: Stories	p. 132													
Feelings Speed Rabbit	p. 129													
Five Ways to Show You Care	p. 128													
Giving and Receiving	p. 149													
Goal Challenge	p. 144													
Goal Toss	p. 143													
Toss 10	p. 194													
Help Tag	p. 126													
Help Me Tag		p. 205			p. 30									
Pass the Chicken			p. 157											
Flip Me the Bird Tag													p. 155	
High Risk, Low Risk	p. 119	p. 109												

Activity	JTCC	AECC	AIP	AP	CTM	DIA	GFC	GFT	GFG 1	GFG 2	NGFWF	QS	SB	TWTP
Hog Call	**p. 102**											p. 202	p. 98	
Find Your Partner														
Integrity Ball	**p. 123**	p. 90												
Fireball				p. 35					p. 33					
Morpheelings	**p. 137**													
Morphing	**p. 56**													
Metamorphosis Tag						p. 25								
Paired Trust Activities	**p. 100**													
Trust Walk (Pairs Walk)	**p. 100**					p. 344	p. 116							
Search & Rescue	**p. 101**													
Evidence Rescue		p. 92												
Rabid Nugget Rescue													p. 118	
Car & Driver	**p. 101**													
Bumper Cars			p. 124											
Driving in the Dark								p. 137						
Car Car											p. 57			
Pendulum Trust Lean	**p. 114**													
Three Person Trust Lean						p. 172								
River of Life, The	**p. 138**	p. 123												
Minefield				p. 121		p. 283							p. 24	
Challenge Field								p. 143						
Conflict Field, The			p. 270											
3-D Minefield												p. 148		
Minefield in a Circle												p. 205		
Pitfall												p. 232		
Life's Journey					p. 60									
Passages							p. 68							
Shakers	**p. 104**													
Warning Bells				p. 35					p. 31					
Sherpa Walk	**p. 111**	p. 96												

Trust Activities (cont.)

Activity	JTCC	AECC	AIP	AP	CTM	DIA	GFC	GFT	GFG 1	GFG 2	NGFWF	QS	SB	TWTP
Tension Traverse	p. 152													
Three-Person Trust Walk	p. 140													
Trust Lean	p. 112					p. 106								
Two-Person Trust Lean									p. 31					
Partner Lean					p. 59									
Turnstile, The	p. 98												p. 156	
All Together Now			p. 88											
Community Jump Rope														p. 91
Walk of Life (AKA: Mohawk Walk)	p. 151											p. 205	p. 140	
Rooftops					p. 160									
Wild Woosey	p. 151				p. 59									
Friendship Walk				p. 149										
Field Wild Woosey						p. 347								
Two Woosey Variations												p. 215		
Willow in the Wind	p. 116	p. 114			p. 51									
Circle Pass									p. 28					
Circle of Friends						p. 207								
Yurt Circle	p. 108		p. 58		p. 52									
Hang Together to Hang Extreme		p. 62												
Zip, Zap, Pop	p. 125	p. 80												
Peter, Paul, & Mary										p. 13				

Problem-Solving Activities

Activity	JTCC	AECC	AIP	AP	CTM	DIA	GFC	GFT	GFG 1	GFG 2	NGFWF	QS	SB	TWTP
All Aboard	**p. 166**	p. 136											p. 106	p. 70
Box Top				p. 135										
All Toss	**p. 171**											p. 191		
Up Chuck or Barf Ball														
All Catch		p. 121												
Alphapong	**p. 186**													
Balloon Frantic	**p. 163**												p. 19	
Balloon Bash								p. 85						
Equally Frantic						p. 205								
Basic Group Juggle & Variations	**p. 173**											p. 201		
Messages	**p. 173**								p. 37					
Group Anger Juggle			p. 182											
Group Juggling						p. 169								
Community Juggling														p. 89
Emotional Gifts		p. 100												
Juggling for Our Lives	**p. 174**	p. 128												
Low-Drop Juggle	**p. 173**	p. 182												
The "I" Juggle														
You're In or You're Out	**p. 173**													
Batten Down the Hatches	**p. 214**													
Books & Quilts	**p. 220**													
Brainstorming	**p. 209**		p. 269											
Enumerating			p. 281					p. 59						
Brainstorming Our Brains		p. 233												
Butter Battle Escalator	**p. 206**													
Conflict Escalates			p. 241											
Catch as Catch Can	**p. 188**													
Quail Shooter's Delight													p. 63	

Problem Solving Activities (cont.)

Activity	JTCC	AECC	AIP	AP	CTM	DIA	GFC	GFT	GFG 1	GFG 2	NGFWF	QS	SB	TWTP
Channels	**p. 182**													
Pipeline		p. 88												
Marble Tubes				p. 55										p. 128
Gutterball									p. 63					
Choice & Consequences	**p. 215**													
Collaborative Numbers	**p. 178**													
Number Game, The								p. 29						
Group Number Game								p. 34						
Boundaries							p. 12							
Compass Walk, The	**p. 218**												p. 176	
Conflicts – the Real … the Imagined	**p. 210**													
Don't Touch Me	**p. 181**		p. 274			p. 109						p.156		
Centerpiece								p. 117						
Traffic Circle														p.189
Fusion	**p. 198**													
Lily Pads & Islands				p. 45										
Cliques						p. 178	p. 21							
Jumping Stars			p. 97											
Mergers												p.172		
Hidden Polygon	**p. 177**													
Blind Polygon		p. 165												
Rope Shapes					p. 88									
Human Machines	**p. 197**													
Humachines			p. 64											
Islands	**p. 199**													
Mountain Tops				p. 141										
Keypunch	**p. 191**											p.169		
Numbermania							p. 61							

Activity	JTCC	AECC	AIP	AP	CTM	DIA	GFC	GFT	GFG 1	GFG 2	NGFWF	QS	SB	TWTP
Knots	p. 185												p. 117	
Tangles				p. 65										
All Knotted Up			p. 63											
Marshmallows	p. 170		p. 86											
Stepping Stones						p. 350						p. 186		
Graduation Trail		p. 82												
River Crossing					p. 46									
Metaphorical Tableaus	p.195													
Moonball	p. 161	p. 130		p. 27								p. 206	p. 31	
Islands Moonball												p. 165		
Moonball – Level II & Level III												p. 176		
Nitro Crossing	p. 201					p. 281							p. 139	
Pathfinder	p. 164	p. 230												
Carpet Maze				p. 93										
Gridlock							p. 82							p. 103
Stepping Stones														
Puzzles	p. 176													
Real Estate														p. 153
Rearrange the Classroom	p. 212													
Roomination								p. 55						
Setting the Table	p. 168	p. 309												
Spider Web	p. 202					p. 245						p. 209	p. 114	
Surfing the Web I-V				p. 154										p. 169
Web, The														
Table Top Web					p. 57									
Stargate	p. 184													
Tabletop Puzzle	p. 96													
Table Top Keypunch										p. 61				
The Winless Zax	p. 213													

Problem Solving Activities (cont.)

Activity	JTCC	AECC	AIP	AP	CTM	DIA	GFC	GFT	GFG 1	GFG 2	NGFWF	QS	SB	TWTP
Toss 10	p. 194													
Goal Toss	p. 143													
Turn Over a New Leaf	p. 167						p. 88							
All Aboard Squared AKA Flip Side													p. 106	
Magic Carpet														p. 125
Flipper				p. 14										
Tarp Turn					p. 89									
Venn Diagrams	p. 217													
Wall, The	p. 204													
Climbing the Wall						p. 353								
Warp Speed	p. 160	p. 126	p. 70		p. 47	p. 314								
Eggspeediency												p. 159		
Who's The Leader?	p. 189													
Instigator			p. 277											

Challenge Activities

Activity	JTCC	AECC	AIP	AP	CTM	DIA	GFC	GFT	GFG 1	GFG 2	NGFWF	QS	SB	TWTP
Catwalk	p. 226													
Centipede	p. 225				p. 108									
Community Exploration	p. 231													
Pamper Pole	p. 227				p. 111									
Public Presentations	p. 232													
Two Line Bridge	p. 226													
Urban Experience	p. 230													
Zip Line	p. 228													

Challenge Ropes Course Construction: Some Considerations

Building a ropes or challenge course entails more than getting a contractor to put the physical elements into the ground, up in the trees, or into the rafters. Because we are dealing with a process, it is important to see the whole picture. It is also necessary to look into liability and risk management concerns.

Following is an annotated outline to help you develop not just a course, but a useful and meaningful program:

I. **Preplanning**
    A. Goals
        Your goals will drive the choices of elements for your program. For example, if your main goals center around teamwork, cooperation, collaboration, and problem solving, then you are probably looking to build only low-challenge course elements. If, on the other hand, your goals encompass all of the above *and* an exploration of risk taking, challenge, and personal goal setting, then you may wish to consider adding some high elements.

        Training goals are important here, as well. The addition of a high course means that training is longer, more involved, and specific.

        It is helpful to bring together stakeholders in the project. These are people who will be directly affected either by its use or by the fact that it physically exists. Find out the concerns, level of enthusiasm, hopes, and fears for the project. Make sure you include custodians who will be responsible for cutting the grass around the poles, or might be worried about how they are going to work around the elements when trying to change a light bulb. If possible, bring in potential participants (students, business community) as well.

        Set goals together to make sure people's concerns and agendas are being addressed.

    B. Site Selection – indoor and outdoor
        Some factors to consider:
        • Purpose of course – will it only be used by this school? Will outside groups contract to use the course?
        • Population(s) to be served.
        • Available land that can either handle the inclusion of poles or has mature and healthy trees.
        • Accessibility for participants in wheelchairs or other physical issues.
        • Accessibility when not in use. Can the doors be locked? Is it in a high-traffic area? (These issues can be remedied by making it possible to set up and take down the course elements.)
        • Scheduling – if indoor, is the gym used so much that the course is rarely available?
        • Weather considerations – indoor courses can be used more in extreme climate areas.
        • Aesthetics/Environment – being outside and getting out of the usual environment can have a positive effect on some groups/participants. It can also have a negative effect if people are not used to being in a more rugged environment.

    C. Choose Possible Elements
        Choose according to the goals, populations to be served, money, and available time for training.

D. In-House Risk Management Consultation
   1. Existing policies.
   2. Check with the insurance provider about standards.
      Some school districts have risk-management departments, or at least a risk-management supervisor. It is important to bring these people into the process from the beginning.

      Some insurance providers have installation standards that need to be met when building a course. Also, check with the insurance provider about additional insurance needs if necessary.

E. Choose Builder
   1. ACCT (Association for Challenge Course Technology) guidelines.
   2. Get initial estimates from prospective builders.
   3. Make a decision.
      ACCT is an organization that is setting installation, management, and ethics standards for the ropes course building industry. Although not required, it is highly recommended that a builder be a Professional Vendor Member of ACCT. That way you know they are building to industry standards.

      There are many qualified ropes course builders in every region. Take the time to get bids from at least three builders. This allows you to get ballpark cost estimates based on individual elements, travel, lodging, etc. You can then compare basic costs between builders. Contact ACCT for a list of Professional Vendor Members.

F. Fund-Raising
   1. In-house funding.
   2. Grants.
   3. Foundation support.
   4. Fund-raising events.

G. Site Evaluation from Builder
   1. Revisit elements based on site evaluation.
   2. Get revised estimate based on site evaluation and new element choices.
      Once a builder is chosen based on preliminary bids, they will usually want to visit your site to see what is actually possible to build. Indoor courses, for example, are unique because every building is different (the builder would appreciate blueprints if you can locate them). A tree course can only be built where the trees actually exist. A pole course, though, is more flexible because poles can be set according to the elements that are chosen.

      At this time the revised estimate will more accurately reflect the total cost of the project.

H. Bring Together All Parties to Discuss Next Steps
   1. Maintenance/Custodial staff.
   2. Administrators.
   3. Representatives of possible users.
   4. Purchasing department.
   5. Risk management/insurance representatives.
   6. Others?
      Now that you have the course laid out, costs figured, and fund-raising started, bring together stakeholders again to revisit goals and tasks. Create new goals to address new information.

II. Building of Challenge/Ropes Course
A. Set Dates with Builder

B. Logistics
   1. Arrange for housing and transportation for builders.
   2. Have someone available to take care of logistics for builders while there.

C. Assemble First Aid Kit for the Ropes Course

D. Obtain Rescue Kit if High Ropes

E. Identify Locked Storage Area for Ropes Course Equipment

F. Organize and Store Equipment/Create "Bag of Tricks"

G. Future Facilitators Obtain First Aid and CPR Certification

H. Identify Person to Be Course Manager
   It is essential that someone be designated as course manager. This person makes sure that required maintenance and inspections are performed, equipment is logged and stored properly, and that only people who are trained are actually using the course. She or he will also maintain records for all facilitators to make sure they are current on training and refreshers.

III. Initial Preparation and Staff Training
A. Learn Standard Operating Procedures (SOPs) from a Reputable Vendor
   1. 5-day skills workshop (low/high elements).
   2. 3-day skills workshop (low elements only).
   3. Advanced skills and workshop which includes rescue training (high elements).
      You can generally get training either through your builder or through other organizations that offer ropes course training. When looking for a ropes course facilitation provider, keep in mind that there is more to ropes course facilitation than physically doing the elements. Ask them for a curriculum outline and references. Make sure they are teaching more than technical skills and are addressing the needs of your client population.

      If a high course is built, it is highly recommended that at least one person has been trained in advanced skills, and that a person with advanced skills training be on the course whenever it is in use.

B. Develop Local Operating Procedures (LOPs)
   Every course needs a manual that articulates the protocols of that course. Your builder and training providers can help you establish the standard operating procedures. They can also offer insight into areas that are unique to your course and that must be included in your local operating procedures.

C. Develop Evacuation Plan in Case of Injury at Course/Phone Access

D. Write Initial Ropes Course Manual with Protocols and LOPs

E. Develop Equipment Usage Log
   1. History of equipment usage.
   2. Ropes course log for high elements.

F. Develop Curriculum to Meet Needs of User Groups

IV. Maintenance

A. Yearly Inspections by ACCT Professional Vendor Member Builder
It is important that all ropes courses be inspected by an ACCT Professional Vendor Member builder every year. They will inspect the hardware, ropes, elements, and logs. They will then write a report with suggestions and recommendations about your course so that it can remain in safe operating condition. This can be built into a yearly budget so that it is sure to happen.

B. Yearly Facilitator Refreshers
Some facilitators use the course weekly or even daily. Others use it sporadically at best. There should be a yearly refresher course to update facilitators on both old and new protocols. You can also take the opportunity to answer questions, go over incidents, and offer new techniques.

C. Plan for Training New Facilitators
Some facilitators are there for life. Others move away, retire, have health problems, or simply lose interest. How will you get new people trained? The continued use of an outside vendor for training helps assure that your program stays current with new information. Bringing new people into the mix can also jump-start the cycle of low energy that is bound to come.

D. Usage Plan: Who, Why, How, When?
Who is using your course and how do they get to use it?

E. Equipment Maintenance and Replacement Budget
Make sure to include a yearly inspection in the budget!

NOTE: Every challenge/ropes course is unique, as are the needs of the organization installing a ropes course. Therefore, this is intended only as a guide for planning. Other questions, issues, and considerations may arise according to the needs of the sponsoring agency.

Questions to Ask Ropes/ Challenge Course Providers

There are many providers of ropes/challenge course experiences out there. As more organizations build courses and market to a variety of audiences, the variety of programming grows as well. Can all ropes course providers be all things to all people? How do you know that your group is getting a quality experience?

Most providers are well-trained, with state-of-the-art equipment and up-to-date methods. Staff are enthusiastic and willing to meet your needs. What makes the difference between a good experience and a great one? As with any experience, some providers are a better fit for your group than others. Here are some questions to ask that may help you find a provider who can meet your particular needs and ensure a safe experience, both physically and emotionally.

First, look for an organization that focuses on your population. If, for example, you take your class to a provider that works primarily with corporate groups, the facilitators may have difficulty relating to the developmental level of the students. On the other hand, if you take your class to a YMCA camp where they are used to working with youth, they may be better prepared to deal with the dynamics and needs of your students.

Here are some questions to ask of a ropes/challenge course provider that may help you determine a good fit with your class's needs:

- **Who built your course?**
  These days, the Association for Challenge Course Technology (ACCT) is recognized as a leader in determining standards for ropes/challenge course construction. A course that is built by ACCT Professional Vendor Members means that a certain level of quality and safety standards has been met. Sometimes organizations build their own courses, and then have it inspected by an ACCT Professional Vendor Member to verify that the standards have been met.

- **When was the last time your course was inspected?**
  ACCT recommends a yearly inspection by an ACCT Professional Vendor Member, in addition to periodic inspections by the people who run the course. If the course has not been inspected by an outside source in a while, ask why. Also, if this organization has not had its course inspected, or does not feel it is important, consider taking your group elsewhere. An outside inspection is a small price to pay to ensure the physical safety of your class.

- **What kind of training do you require for your staff?**
  Typically, staff engage in an adventure skills workshop from a reputable vendor that includes facilitation techniques, technical/safety skills, and program philosophy. Some staff have this training when they are hired, while others go through the training after being hired. In addition, initial orientation for course protocols and periodic refreshers are given to staff so they can maintain their skills. More training and staff development is a bonus.

  At least one person with first aid and CPR certification should be working on the course while groups are there. If you are doing high elements, at least one person who is trained in rescue techniques should be on the course.

- **Is your program accredited?**
  Much like AAA for hotels and dining, and American Camping Association (ACA) for camps, the Association for Experiential Education (AEE) offers an accreditation program for ropes and challenge courses. Using industry standards, they have teams visit courses to look over entire programs. When a course is subsequently accredited, it is a sign that certain minimum standards are met. **Accreditation is voluntary and is not required.** There are many ropes/challenge course programs out there that far exceed minimum industry standards yet are not accredited.

- **What is your plan in case of injury?**
  This should be a no-brainer. If they cannot rattle off what to do in case of an emergency, be wary.

- **Describe a typical day at your course.**
  Look for signs that they pay attention to the sequencing of activities, and that they are prepared to alter their plan depending upon the needs of the group.

- **What is your organization's philosophy on Challenge by Choice?**
  Ropes/challenge courses regularly put participants in vulnerable situations. Participants need to be allowed to choose their own level of challenge. This does not mean that facilitators take a hands-off approach because there are times when students need an emotional nudge or encouragement to push themselves. It does mean that staff have thought about this in advance and understand that individuals react differently to anxiety. A one-size-fits-all approach is problematic.

- **Do you have any ideas about how to help us transfer this experience back at school?**
  Although they are not responsible for connecting learning from this short experience back to the classroom, it is nice to know that they are thinking about it. Some organizations have strategies to help with this.

- **How do you deal with conflicts between group members?**
  Conflict is a natural part of the group process. Chances are that your students will experience some level of conflict during the day at a ropes/challenge course. Have they thought about it? You know your students much better than a facilitator who just met them, which can cause some awkward moments during a conflict situation. Are you ready to defer to them, and are they ready to enlist your help if necessary?

Although there are many more questions that could be listed here, these questions will give you the ability to "feel out" the ropes/challenge course provider. If you can find the right provider to meet your needs, your students will have a more powerful experience.

Educational Standards & Adventure Education

There is much debate these days about the efficacy of educational standards and how they are assessed through standardized tests.* The standards do, however, have redeeming value in that they offer a way for us to focus on student learning. Authentic assessment techniques can then be used to inform our teaching to maximize learning potential.†

In determining outcomes and goals for a program, educational standards offer suggestions that are highly useful. These days there is a recognition that students bring more to school than their heads, and standards have been developed to address thinking and reasoning, self-regulation, and working with others, to name a few. In Wisconsin, along with academic standards, there are the "Standards of the Heart," which address safety, relationships, engagement, and more. These can be found on the Wisconsin Department of Public Instruction Web site at: www.dpi.state.wi.us/sig/assessment/sa1.html

The following are examples that, in my opinion, relate to community building in the classroom and have been developed by McRel†† as standards and benchmarks.

Standards that deal directly with Community Building and the tools in this book:

Self-Regulation

Standard 3: Considers Risks / *Grades K–12*
- Weighs risks in making decisions and solving problems
- Uses common knowledge to avoid hazard or injury
- Applies preventative measures prior to a task to minimize security or safety problems
- Selects an appropriate course of action in an emergency
- Identifies emergency and safety procedures before undertaking hazardous procedures
- Thinks clearly under stress

Standard 4: Demonstrates Perseverance / *Grades K–12*
- Demonstrates perseverance relative to personal goals
- Demonstrates a sense of purpose
- Maintains a high level of energy over a prolonged period of time when engaged in tasks
- Persists in the face of difficulty
- Concentrates mental and physical energies

---

* For a comprehensive discussion on these topics, please read *The Schools Our Children Deserve* by Alfie Kohn. This is a must-read for educators and parents alike.

† Beverly Falk, in *The Heart of the Matter*, does a wonderful job of outlining how to go about using standards to inform our teaching and learning, rather than as mechanisms for high-stakes testing that punish students for not "measuring up."

†† Used with permission ©1997 Mid-Continent Research for Education & Learning. You can find the McRel Standards on the Internet at www.mcrel.com, or purchase a copy from them (See Resources in this section under Kendall, J.S., and Marzano, R.J.).

Standard 5: Maintains a Healthy Self-Concept / *Grades K–12*
- Has basic belief in ability to succeed
- Uses techniques to remind self of strengths
- Uses techniques to offset the negative effects of mistakes
- Avoids overreacting to criticism
- Uses affirmations to improve sense of self
- Analyzes self-statements for their positive and negative effects
- Examines "shoulds" to determine their negative and positive effects
- Revises "shoulds" to reflect the reality of personal needs
- Understands that everyone makes mistakes
- Understands that mistakes are a natural consequence of living and of limited resources
- Takes criticism in a dispassionate manner
- Analyzes criticisms to determine their accuracy and identifies useful lessons learned
- Uses high self-esteem body language

Standard 6: Restrains Impulsivity / *Grades K–12*
- Keeps responses open as long as possible
- Remains passive while assessing situations
- Suspends judgment

Working with Others

Standard 1: Contributes to the Overall Effort of a Group / *Grades K–12*
- Challenges practices that are not working in the group
- Demonstrates respect for others in the group
- Identifies and uses the strengths of others
- Takes initiative when needed
- Identifies and deals with causes of conflict in a group
- Helps the group establish goals
- Engages in active listening
- Takes the initiative in interacting with others
- Evaluates the overall progress of a group toward a goal
- Keeps requests simple
- Contributes to the development of a supportive climate in groups

Standard 2: Uses Conflict-Resolution Techniques / *Grades K–12*
- Communicates ideas in a manner that does not irritate others
- Resolves conflicts of interest
- Identifies goals and values important to opponents
- Understands the impact of criticism on psychological state, emotional state, habitual behavior, and beliefs
- Understands that three ineffective responses to criticism are (1) being aggressive, (2) being passive, and (3) being both
- Understands that three effective responses to criticism are (1) acknowledgment, (2) token agreement with a critic, and (3) probing clarifications
- Determines the causes of conflicts
- Does not blame
- Identifies an explicit strategy to deal with conflict
- Determines the seriousness of conflicts
- Identifies mutually agreeable times for important conversations with opponents
- Identifies individual versus group or organizational interests in conflicts
- Establishes guidelines and rules for negotiating
- Determines the mini-max position of those in a conflict

Standard 3: Works Well with Diverse Individuals and in Diverse Situations / *Grades K–12*
- Works well with the opposite gender
- Works well with different ethnic groups
- Works well with those of different religious orientations

Standard 4: Displays Effective Interpersonal Communication Skills / *Grades K–12*
- Displays empathy with others
- Displays friendliness with others
- Displays politeness with others
- Seeks information nondefensively
- Provides feedback in a constructive manner
- Uses nonverbal communication such as eye contact, body position, voice tone effectively
- Does not react to a speaker's inflammatory deliverance
- Identifies with speaker while maintaining objectivity
- Uses emotions appropriately in personal dialogues
- Makes use of confrontation when appropriate
- Makes eye contact when speaking
- Reacts to ideas rather than to the person presenting the ideas
- Adjusts tone and content of information to accommodate the likes of others
- Communicates in a clear manner during conversations
- Acknowledges the strengths of others

Standard 5: Demonstrates Leadership Skills / *Grades K–12*
- Occasionally serves as a leader in groups
- Occasionally serves as a follower in groups
- Enlists others in working toward a shared vision
- Plans small wins
- Celebrates accomplishments
- Recognizes the contributions of others
- Passes on authority when appropriate

These standards and benchmarks can be emphasized while engaged in community-building activities:

Self-Regulation
Standard 1: Sets and Manages Goals / *Grades K–12*
- Sets explicit long-term goals
- Identifies and ranks relevant options in terms of accomplishing a goal
- Prepares and follows a schedule for carrying out options versus needs
- Establishes personal milestones
- Identifies resources necessary to complete a goal
- Displays a sense of personal direction and purpose
- Maintains an awareness of proximity to goal
- Makes a cumulative evaluation of goal
- Understands the differences between various types of goals
- Sets routine goals for improving daily life
- Identifies explicit criteria for evaluating goals
- Makes contingency plans

Standard 2: Performs Self-Appraisal / *Grades K–12*
- Distributes work according to perceived strengths
- Identifies personal styles
- Identifies personal strengths and weaknesses
- Utilizes techniques for overcoming weaknesses
- Identifies basic values
- Performs analysis of employability
- Understands preferred working environments
- Understands career goals
- Identifies a compensating strength for each weakness
- Develops an inventory of wants versus needs
- Determines explicit behaviors that are used and should be adopted to obtain wants and/or needs
- Identifies personal motivational patterns
- Keeps a log documenting personal improvement
- Summarizes personal educational background
- Summarizes personal work experience
- Identifies key accomplishments and successes in life
- Identifies peak experiences and significant life experiences
- Identifies desired future accomplishments
- Identifies preferred lifestyle

Thinking & Reasoning

Standard 5: Applies Basic Troubleshooting and Problem-Solving Techniques /
Grades K–2
- Identifies simple problems and possible solutions (e.g., ways to make something work better)

Grades 3–5
- Identifies issues and problems in the school or community that one might help solve
- Studies problems in the community and how they were solved
- Analyzes the problems that have confronted people in the past in terms of the major goals and obstacles to those goals

Grades 6–8
- Identifies alternative courses of action and predicts likely consequences of each
- Selects the most appropriate strategy or alternative for solving a problem
- Examines different alternatives for resolving local problems and compares the possible consequences of each alternative

Grades 9–12
- Applies troubleshooting strategies to complex real-world situations
- Understands that troubleshooting almost anything may require many-step branching logic
- Engages in problem finding and framing for personal situations and situations in the community
- Represents a problem accurately in terms of resources, constraints, and objectives
- Provides summation of the effectiveness of problem-solving techniques
- Reframes problems when alternative solutions are exhausted
- Evaluates the feasibility of various solutions to problems; recommends and defends a solution

Standard 6: Applies Decision-Making Techniques /
Grades K–2
- Makes and defends decisions about daily activities (e.g., what books to read)

Grades 3–5
- Studies decisions that were made in the community in terms of the alternatives that were considered
- Analyzes important decisions made by people in the past in terms of possible alternatives that were considered

Grades 6–8
- Identifies situations in the community and in one's personal life in which a decision is required
- Secures factual information needed to evaluate alternatives
- Identifies the values underlying the alternatives that are considered and the criteria that will be used to make a selection among the alternatives
- Predicts the consequences of selecting each alternative
- Makes decisions based on the data obtained and the criteria identified
- When appropriate, takes action to implement the decision
- Analyzes personal decisions in terms of the options that were considered

Grades 9–12
- Evaluates major factors that influence personal decisions

Academic content can be presented experientially using the Experiential Learning Cycle,* and it can also be woven into community-building activities. The concepts encompassed in the following standards and benchmarks can easily be addressed during problem-solving activities, and then transferred to academic content:

Life Work

Standard 7: Displays Reliability and a Basic Work Ethic / *Grades 9–12*
- Completes tasks on time
- Chooses ethical courses of action
- Uses appropriate language in work situations
- Requests clarification when needed

Standard 8: Operates Effectively within Organizations / *Grades 9–12*
- Understands the organization's basic goals and values
- Understands the extent to which organizational values are compatible with personal values

Thinking & Reasoning

Standard 1: Understands and Applies the Basic Principles of Presenting an Argument /
Grades K–2
- Understands that people are more likely to believe a person's ideas if that person can give good reasons for them
- Provides coherent (though not necessarily valid or convincing) answers when asked why one believes something to be true or how one knows something
- Asks "How do you know?" in appropriate situations

Grades 3–5
- Understands that reasoning can be distorted by strong feelings
- Raises questions that are based on the assertion that "everybody knows" or "I just know"
- Seeks reasons for believing things other than the assertion that "everybody agrees"
- Recognizes when a comparison is not fair because important characteristics are not the same

Grades 6–8
- Identifies and questions false analogies
- Identifies and questions arguments in which all members of a group are implied to possess nearly identical characteristics that are considered to be different from those of another group
- Compares and contrasts the credibility of differing accounts of the same event

---

* See *Adventure in the Classroom*, by Mary Henton for a comprehensive discussion on this topic. Project Adventure teaches a workshop on this topic as well.

Grades 9–12
- Understands that when people try to prove a point, they may at times select only the information that supports it and ignore the information that contradicts it
- Identifies techniques used to slant information in subtle ways
- Identifies or seeks out the critical assumptions behind a line of reasoning and uses that to judge the validity of an argument
- Understands that to be convincing, an argument must have both true statements and valid connections among them
- Evaluates the overall effectiveness of complex arguments

Standard 2: Understands and Applies Basic Principles of Logic and Reasoning /
Grades 6–8
- Understands that some aspects of reasoning have very rigid rules and others aspects do not
- Understands that when people have rules that always hold for a given situation and good information about the situation, then logic can help them figure out what is true about the situation
- Understands that reasoning by similarities can suggest ideas but cannot be used to prove things
- Understands that a single example can never prove that something is true, but a single example can prove that something is not true
- Understands that some people invent a general rule to explain how something works by summarizing observations
- Understands that people over-generalize by making up rules on the basis of only a few observations
- Understands that personal values influence the types of conclusions people make
- Recognizes situations in which a variety of conclusions can be drawn from the same information

Grade 9–12
- Analyzes the deductive validity of arguments based on implicit or explicit assumptions
- Understands that people sometimes reach false conclusions either by applying faulty logic to true statements or by applying valid logic to false statements
- Understands that a reason may be sufficient to get a result but may not be the only way to get the result (i.e., may not be necessary), or a reason may be necessary to obtain a result but not sufficient (i.e., other things are also required; some reasons may be both necessary and sufficient)

Standard 4: Understands and Applies Basic Principles of Hypothesis Testing and Scientific Inquiry /
Grades K–2
- Asks "How do you know?" in appropriate situations and attempts to provide reasonable answers when others ask the same question
- Understands that changing one thing sometimes causes changes in something else and that changing the same thing in the same way usually has the same result

Grades 3–5
- Distinguishes between actual observations and ideas or conclusions about what others observed

Grades 6–8
- Understands there are a variety of ways people can form hypotheses, including basing them on many observations, basing them on very few observations, and constructing them on only one or two observations
- Verifies results of experiments
- Understands there may be more than one valid way to interpret a set of findings
- Reformulates a new hypothesis for study after an old hypothesis has been eliminated
- Makes and validates conjectures about outcomes of specific alternatives or events regarding an experiment

Grades 9–12
- Presents alternative explanations and conclusions to one's own experiments and those of others
- Critiques procedures, explanations, and conclusions in one's own experiments and those of others

Adventure/Experiential Education Resources

Publications and Teaching Materials

Albin, J. (2004). *Changing the message: A handbook for experiential prevention.* Oklahoma City, OK: Wood 'N' Barnes Publishing.

Archambault, R.D. (1964), editor. *John Dewey on education: Selected writings.* New York, NY: Random House.

Bigelow, B. et al., eds. (1994). *Rethinking our classrooms: Teaching for equity and justice.* Milwaukee, WI: Rethinking Schools.

Bower, N.M. (1998). *Adventure play: Adventure activities for preschool and early elemenatry age children.* Needham Heights, MA: Simon and Schuster Custom Publishing, 1998.

Cain, J., & Jolliff, B. (1998). *Teamwork and teamplay: A guide to cooperative, challenge adventure activities.* Dubuque, IA: Kendall/Hunt Publishing Co.

Cavert, C. & Sikes, S. (1997). *50 ways to use your noodle: Loads of land games with foam noodle toys.* Tulsa, OK: Learning Unlimited Corporation.

Cavert, C. (1999). *Affordable portables: Working-book of initiative activities & problem solving elements – Revised and Expanded.* Oklahoma City, OK: Wood 'N' Barnes Publishing.

Cavert, C. (1999). *Games (& other stuff) for group book. (Revised and Expanded).* Oklahoma City, OK: Wood 'N' Barnes Publishing.

Cavert, C. (1998). *Games (& other stuff) for group book 2.* Oklahoma City, OK: Wood 'N' Barnes Publishing.

Cavert, C. & Frank, L. (1999). *Games (& other stuff) for teachers.* Oklahoma City, OK: Wood 'N'Barnes Publishing.

Cavert, C. & Sikes, S. (2002). *50 more ways to use your noodle: Loads of land games with foam noodle toys.* Tulsa, OK: Learning Unlimited Corporation

Cavert, C. & Hammond, D. (2003). *The empty bag: Non-stop, no-prop adventure-based activities for community building.* Flagstaff, AZ: FUNdoing Publications.

Chappelle, S. & Bigman, L. (1998). *Diversity in action: Using adventure activities to explore issues of diversity with middle school and high school age youth.* Hamilton, MA: Project Adventure, Inc.

Chiji Cards. Institute for Experiential Education (IEE), 115 Fifth Avenue South, Suite 430, La Crosse, WI 54601. 608/784-0789. www.chiji.com

Conquest, Arthur Wellington. What (African American) Children Need. *Ziplines* 29 (Summer 1996), 44-45.

Conzemius, A. & O'Neill, J. (2001). *Building shared responsibility for student learning*. Alexandria, VA: Association for Supervision & Curriculum Development.

Conzemius, A. & O'Neill, J. (2002). *The handbook for SMART school teams*. Bloomington, IN: National Education Service.

Cousins, E. & Melissa R. (1995). *Fieldwork: An expeditionary learning outward bound reader, Volume I*. Dubuque, IA: Kendall/Hunt Publishing Company.

Dewey, J. (1938). *Experience and education*. New York, NY: Touchstone.

Dodds, T. & Porsser-Dodds, L. (2003). *Games for change: Group activities with creative spritual concepts on the side*. Oklahoma City, OK: Wood 'N' Barnes Publishing.

Ellmo, W. & Jill G. (1995). *Adapted adventure activities: A rehabilitation model for adventure programming and group initiatives*. Dubuque, IA: Kendall/Hunt Publishing Company.

Falk, B. (2000). *The heart of the matter: Using standards and assessment to learn*. Portsmouth, NH: Heinemann.

Feelings Marketplace Cards (1995). Medway, MA: Effectiveness Resources International

Frank, L. S. (1988). *Adventure in the classroom: A stress/challenge curriculum*. Madison, WI: Madison Metropolitan School District.

Frank, L. S. & Stanley, J. (1997). *Manito-wish leaders manual: Teacher Edition*. Waukesha, WI: The Manito-wish YMCA.

Frank, L. S. & Panico, A. (2000). *Adventure education for the classroom community*. Bloomington, IL: National Education Service.

Frank, L. S. (2001). *The caring classroom: Creating community in the classroom and beyond*. Beverly, MA: Project Adventure, Inc.

Gaetano, R. J., Grout, J. & Klassen-Landis, M. (1991). *Please talk with me: A guide to teen-adult dialogue*. Dubuque, IA: Kendall/Hunt Publishing Company.

Gardner, H. (1993). *Multiple intelligences: The theory in practice*. New York, NY: Basic Books.

Gardner, H. (2000). *Intelligence reframed: Multiple intelligences for the 21st century*. New York: NY: Basic Books.

Gass, M. A. (1995). *Book of metaphors, Volume II*. Boulder, CO: Association for Experiential Education.

Gillis, L. & Hirsch, J., eds. (1997). *Food for thought: A Workbook for developing metaphorical introductions to group activities*. Dubuque, IA: Kendall Hunt Publishing Company.

Gibbs, J. (2000). *TRIBES: A new way of learning and being together*. Sausalito, CA: CenterSource Systems.

Glasser, W. (2001). *Choice theory in the classroom*. New York, NY: HarperCollins Publishers.

Goleman, D. (1997). *Emotional intelligence: Why it can matter more than IQ.* New York, NY: Bantam Books.

Gregson, B. (1982). *The incredible indoor games book.* Belmont, CA: David S. Lake, Publishers.

Gregson, B. (1984). *The outrageous outdoor games book.* Belmont CA: David S. Lake, Publishers.

Hart, L. A. (1998). *Human brain and human learning.* Kent, WA: Books for Educators, Inc.

Havens, M. D. (1991). *Bridges to accessibility: A primer for including persons with disabilities in adventure curricula.* Hamilton, MA: Project Adventure, Inc.

Henton, M. (1996). *Adventure in the classroom: Using adventure to create a community of life-long learners.* Hamilton, MA: Project Adventure, Inc.

Johnson, D. W. & Johnson, F.P. (2002). *Joining together: Group theory and group skills (8ᵗʰ Edition).* Boston, MA: Allyn & Bacon Publishers.

Kamiya, A. (1985). *Elementary teacher's handbook of indoor and outdoor games.* West Nyack, NY: Parker Publishing Company.

Kocs, Katherine J. (1999). *Sticks and stones: Changing the dynamics of bullying and youth violence.* Madison, WI: Wisconsin Clearinghouse for Prevention Resources.

Kohl, H. (1984). *Growing minds: On becoming a teacher.* New York, NY: Harper and Row, Publishers.

Kohn, A. (1986). *No contest: The case against competition.* Boston, MA: Houghton Mifflin.

Kohn, A. (1990). *The brighter side of human nature.* New York, NY: BasicBooks.

Kohn, A. (1993). *Punished by rewards: The trouble with gold stars, incentive plans, A's, praise, and other bribes.* Boston, MA: Houghton Mifflin.

Kohn, A. (1996). *Beyond discipline: From compliance to community.* Alexandria, VA: ASCD.

Kohn, A. (1999). *The schools our children deserve.* Alexandria, VA: ASCD.

Kohn, A. (2000). *The case against standardized testing: Raising the scores, ruining the schools.* Portsmouth, NH: Heinemann.

Kornblum, Rena (2002). *Disarming the playground: Violence prevention through movement and pro-social skills.* Oklahoma City: Wood 'N' Barnes Publishing Company.

Kovalkic, S. (1994). *ITI: The model: Integrated thematic instruction.* Kent, WA, Susan Kovalic & Associates.

Kozol, J. (1991). *Savage inequalities: Children in America's schools.* New York, NY: Crown Publishers.

Kozol, J. (1995). *Amazing Grace.* New York, NY: Crown Publishers.

Kreidler, W. J. (1984). *Creative conflict resolution.* Glenview, IL: Scott, Foresman and Company.

Kreidler, W. J. & Furlong, L. (1996). *Adventures in peacemaking: A conflict resolution activity guide.* Cambridge, MA: Educators for Social Responsibility and Project Adventure, Inc.

Kreidler, W. J. & Whittall, S. T. (1999). *Adventures in peacemaking: Early childhood. Second Edition.* Cambridge, MA: Educators for Social Responsibility.

Lewis, B. A. (1995). *The kid's guide to service projects.* Minneapolis, MN: Free Spirit Publishing.

Lewis, B. A. (1998). *What do you stand for?: A kid's guide to building character.* Minneapolis, MN: Free Spirit Publishing.

Lewis, B. A. (1998). *The kid's guide to social action.* Minneapolis, MN: Free Spirit Publishing.

Lieber, C. (1998). *Conflict resolution in the high school.* Cambridge, MA: Educators for Social Responsibility.

Lieber, C. (2002). *Partners in learning: From conflict to collaboration in secondary classrooms.* Cambridge, MA: Educators for Social Responsibility.

Lowe, R. & Miner B., eds. (1996). *Selling out our schools.* Milwaukee, WI: Rethinking Schools.

Luckner, J. L. & Nadler, R. S. (1997). *Processing the experience: Strategies to enhance and generalize learning, Second Edition.* Dubuque, IA: Kendall/Hunt Publishing Company.

Miles, J. C. & Priest S., eds (1999). *Adventure programming.* State College, PA: Venture Publishing, Inc.

Olson, K. & Pearson, S (2000). *Character begins at home: Family tools for teaching character and values.* Kent, WA: Susan Kovalik and Associates, Inc., Available from Books For Educators Inc.

Orlick, T. (1978). *The cooperative sports and games book.* New York, NY: Pantheon Books.

Orlick, T. (1982). *The second cooperative sports and games book.* New York, NY: Pantheon Books.

Palmer, L., et al. (1999). *Adventures in architectue: An activity-based science curriculum.* Needham Heights, MA: Simon and Schuster Custom Publishing.

Pearson, Sue (2000). *Tools for citizenship and life: Using the ITI lifelong guidelines and LIFESKILLS in your classroom.* Kent, WA: Susan Kovalik and Associates, Inc.

Purkey, W.W. & Novak, J.M. (1995). *Inviting school success.* Belmont, CA: Wadsworth Publishing Company.

Roehlkepartain, Jolene L. & Leffert, Nancy (2000). *What young children need to succeed: Working together to build assets from birth to age 11.* Minneapolis, MN: Free Spirit Publishing, Inc.

Roehlkepartain, Jolene L. (1997). *Building assets together: 135 group activities for helping youth succeed.* Minneapolis, MN: The Search Institute.

Rohnke, K. (1989). *Cowstails and cobras II.* Dubuque, IA: Kendall/Hunt Publishing Company.

Rohnke, K. (1984). *Silver bullets: A guide to initiative problems, adventure, games and trust activities.* Dubuque, IA: Kendall/Hunt Publishing Company.

Rohnke, K. (1992). *Forget me knots.* Dubuque, IA: Kendall/Hunt Publishing Company.

Rohnke, K. (1993). *The bottomless bag, again!* Dubuque, IA: Kendall/Hunt Publishing Company.

Rohnke, K. (1996). *Funn stuff: Volume I*. Dubuque, IA: Kendall/Hunt Publishing Company.

Rohnke, K. (1996). *Funn stuff: Volume II*. Dubuque, IA: Kendall/Hunt Publishing Company.

Rohnke, K. (1998). *Funn stuff: Volume III*. Dubuque, IA: Kendall/Hunt Publishing Company.

Rohnke, K. (2000). *Funn stuff: Volume IV*. Dubuque, IA: Kendall/Hunt Publishing Company.

Rohnke, K. (1996). *Top tricks*. Dubuque, IA: Kendall/Hunt Publishing Company.

Rohnke, K. & Butler, S. (1995). *Quicksilver*. Dubuque, IA: Kendall/Hunt Publishing Company.

Rohnke, K., Tait, C. & Wall, J. (1997). *The complete ropes course manual, Second Edition*. Dubuque, IA: Kendall/Hunt Publishing Company.

Rohnke, K. & Jim Grout (1998). *Back pocket adventure*. Needham Heights, MA: Simon and Schuster Custom Publishing.

Schoel, J., Prouty, D., & Radcliffe, P. (1988). *Islands of healing: A guide to adventure based counseling*. Hamilton, MA: Project Adventure.

Schoel, J. & Stratton, M. (1990). *Gold nuggets: Readings for experiential education*. Hamilton, MA and Covington, GA: Project Adventure.

Search Institute (1998). *Healthy communities: 40 developmental assets*. Minneapolis, MN: Search Institute.

Starkman, N., Scales, P.C., & Roberts, C. (1999). *Great places to learn: How asset building schools help students succeed*. Minneapolis, MN: Search Institute.

Thomson, B. J. (1993). *Words can hurt you: Beginning a program of anti-bias education*. Menlo Park, CA: Addison-Wesley.

Webster, S. E. (1989). *Project adventure ropes course safety manual*. Dubuque, IA: Kendall/Hunt Publishing Company.

Weinstein, M. & Goodman, J. (1980). *Playfair: Everybody's guide to noncompetitive play*. San Luis Obispo: Impact Publishers.

Organizations

Association for Challenge Course Technology (ACCT).
PO Box 255, Martin, MI 49070-0255
269-685-0670, www.acctinfo.org
Ropes course building and standards.
Yearly Conference. Memberships available.

Association for Experiential Education (AEE).
3775 Iris Avenue, Suite #4, Boulder, CO 80301-2043
866-522-8337, www.aee.org
Yearly international conference and regional conferences.
Educational materials. Memberships available.

Project Adventure, Inc.
701 Cabot Street, Beverly, MA 01915
978/468-7981, www.pa.org
Workshops in adventure education, equipment catalog, and course building.
Educational materials. Memberships available.

Teachers of Experiential and Adventure Methodology (TEAM).
Physical Education Program Northeastern Illinois University, 5500 N. St. Louis, Chicago, IL 60625,
773/442-5569, www.neiu.edu/~team.
Yearly conference. Newsletter sent at no cost.

Safety: 4, 7, 10, 21-22, 27-28, 31, 56, 66, 73, 81-84, 86, 93, 96-97, 114, 118-19, 141, 148, 150, 182, 184, 193, 205, 226, 239, 244, 246, 249, 264

    emotional safety: 7, 10, 19, 28, 31-32, 79, 84, 94-95, 153-54, 249

    equipment: 225

    guidelines: 100

    inspection: 225

    issues: 31, 36, 84, 95, 200, 237, 244

    personal safety: 84, 95, 229

    physical safety: 7, 28, 84, 94-95, 153-54, 262

Scapegoat/Scapegoating: 20, 35, 92, 243

Schoel, Jim: 4n, 7-8, 23, 243

Scholastic Aptitude Test: 9

School Age Parent Program: 229n

Schools Our Children Deserve, The: 264n

Search Institute: 3, 5, 12-13, 15

Sectarianism: 33

Self-Concept: 7, 15, 280

Self Discipline: (life skill link): 54, 61, 79, 81, 83-88, 90, 98, 105, 107, 109, 112-13, 115, 117, 126, 140-42, 144-45, 148, 160, 164-65, 167-68, 170, 172, 175, 177-78, 181, 183, 186-88, 190-91, 193-94, 196, 199-201, 203, 205, 207, 210-12, 214-16

Sense of Humor: (life skill link): 49, 54, 56-58, 60, 64, 129, 196, 207

Sequence/Sequencing: 3, 26, 30, 34, 97, 99, 102, 107, 114, 117, 138, 222, 225, 228, 237, 257, 263

    of activities: 14, 249

    art of sequencing: 24-25

    community building sequence: 26, 34, 159

    and flow: 23-24, 246-48, 250

    and group development: 24

    hypothetically correct sequence: 23-24

    science of sequencing: 23, 25

Service Learning: 2, 8, 127, 168

Shatz, Sarah: 53, 68, 143

Shaw, Cindy: 175

Silver Bullets: 261

Smith, Tom (Raccoon): 23, 106n, 107, 246

Sorting (see *Storming*)

Spiral of Renewal: 21

Spitzer, Dave: 223

Spotting/Spotter: 97, 103-05, 111, 113-17, 150-52, 167, 204-05

Standard Operating Procedures (SOP's): 260

Standards: academic/educational standards: 5, 10

    community standards: 22, 62, 82, 90, 264-69

    industry (ropes course construction) standards: 150, 225, 259, 262-63

    safety standards: 259

Starkman, N.: 13

Stating/Communicating Needs: 27, 34, 92, 97, 151-52, 222-24

Stereotype/Stereotyping: 205, 245

Stewardship: 228

Stimac, Jane: 220n

Storming/Sorting: stage of group development: 19-24, 155

Struggle: 2-4, 11, 18-19, 29, 43, 99, 126, 145, 19, 166, 171, 178, 189, 215, 217, 220, 222, 226-27, 233

    power struggle: 73, 158, 244

    through conflict: 27

About the Author

Laurie Frank is a former public school teacher who has worked in the adventure field for 20 years. She began her career as a special education teacher in emotional disabilities, working with students of all ages. Her path diverged upon the discovery of adventure education and experiential methodologies. The need to develop community within the school setting was apparent, and the adventure philosophy seemed the perfect vehicle to achieve that goal.

Ms. Frank was a leader in designing the nationally recognized Stress/Challenge adventure program for Madison (Wisconsin) Metropolitan School District, and wrote their curriculum, "Adventure in the Classroom," in 1988.

Laurie is the owner/director of GOAL Consulting, working with school districts, camps, and non-profit organizations around the country to create environments where students, faculty, staff, and families are invited into the educational process. She also helps schools develop experiential education curriculum for children and young adults.

Ms. Frank wrote the Camp Manito-wish (Collaborative) Leadership manual in 1997. Her book, *The Caring Classroom: Using Adventure to Create Community in the Classroom and Beyond* was published in 2001, and is the basis for this expanded edition. She also collaborated on two books: one with Chris Cavert, titled *Games (& Other Stuff) for Teachers* (1999), and the other with Ambrose Panico titled, *Adventure Education for the Classroom Community* (2000). At this time, she is working with the Wisconsin Leadership Institute to develop a Collaborative Leadership Curriculum for high-school students.

Laurie has been a Certified Trainer with Project Adventure, and is a recipient of the Michael Stratton Practitioner of the Year award from the Association for Experiential Education.

Laurie S. Frank
GOAL Consulting
1337 Jenifer Street, Madison, WI 53703
608.251.2234 (phone) 608.251.5212 (fax)
lsfrank@tds.net
www.goalconsulting.org